Genealogies of Religion

Genealogies of Religion

ꙅꙮꙅꙮ

DISCIPLINE AND REASONS
OF POWER IN CHRISTIANITY
AND ISLAM

Talal Asad

The Johns Hopkins University Press
Baltimore and London

This book was originally brought to publication with the generous
assistance of the Karl and Edith Pribram Endowment.

The Johns Hopkins University Press
2715 North Charles Street
Baltimore, Maryland 21218-4319
The Johns Hopkins Press Ltd., London

Library of Congress Cataloging-in-Publication Data

Asad, Talal.
   Genealogies of religion : discipline and reasons of power in Christianity
and Islam / Talal Asad.
       p.   cm.
   Includes bibliographical references (p.   ) and index.
   ISBN 0-8018-4631-5 (alk. paper). — ISBN 0-8018-4632-3 (pbk. :
alk. paper)
   1. Religion. 2. Civilization, Christian. 3. Civilization, Islamic.
4. Rushdie, Salman. I. Title.
BL50.A85 1993
306.6—dc20   93-21831

A catalog record for this book is available from the British Library.

Genealogies of Religion

ʕƆʔ CONTENTS

ᘒᘓᘔ   INTRODUCTION

The essays brought together in this volume deal with historical topics that vary in time and place, ranging from the rites of medieval European monks to the sermons of contemporary Arab theologians. What links them all together is the assumption that Western history has had an overriding importance—for good or ill—in the making of the modern world, and that explorations of that history should be a major anthropological concern. It has sometimes been noted that peoples from non-Western countries feel obliged to read the history of the West (but not each other's histories) and that Westerners in turn do not feel the same need to study non-Western histories. The history of modern Western thought, for example, can be (and is) written on its own, but not so the history of contemporary Arab thought. One opposition between the West and the non-West (and so a mode of connection between them) is constructed historically by these asymmetrical desires and indifferences.

My anthropological explorations into Christian and post-Christian history are therefore motivated by the conviction that its conceptual geology has profound implications for the ways in which non-Western traditions are now able to grow and change. More particularly, I hold that anthropologists who would study, say, Muslim beliefs and practices will need some understanding of how "religion" has come to be formed as concept and practice in the modern West. For while religion is integral to modern Western history, there are dangers in employing it as a normalizing concept when translating Islamic traditions.

The genealogy of religion is a central theme in my essays. Thus, chapters 1 and 2 sketch the emergence of religion as a modern historical object. In the next two chapters I approach the problem obliquely, by discussing in turn two elements in medieval Christianity that are no longer generally accepted by modern religion: the productive role of physical pain and the virtue of self-abasement. From the point of view of theological modernism, as well as of secular morality, they are both archaic ("uncivilized") conditions. Chapters 5 and 6 address aspects of the asymmetry between Western and non-Western histories: the former deals with problems of anthropological translation, the latter with the limitations of a non-Christian religious tradition when juxtaposed with the Enlightenment doctrine of critical reason. They deal with translation in a double sense: interpreting from one language into another, and conveying sacred relics from one shrine to another. The two final chapters (7 and 8) were written at the height of the so-called Rushdie affair in response to the angry positions then taken up in the name of liberalism about religious intolerance. All the chapters thus deal with fragments of the West's religious history, because I assume that the West's definition of itself—and therefore its engagement with non-Western cultures—includes that history.

Among anthropologists, "history" is a notion that few would now dare to despise. On the contrary, all of us solemnly acknowledge it. But what kind of history? More often than not, it is history in the active voice: everywhere, local people are "making their own history," "contesting" it, "borrowing" meanings from Western dominators, and "reconstructing" their own cultural existence.[1] This notion of history emphasizes not only the unceasing work of human creators but also the unstable and hybrid character of their creation. In some versions, therefore, the determining character of "world system" and "dependent structure" is rejected; in others, what is repudiated are claims about "authenticity," "a different people," "a unitary culture," "tradition," and so on. Intelligent and influential people writing today are committed to this view of history making. Nevertheless, I

---

1. As J. and J. Comaroff (1991, 18) put it in the introduction to their fascinating account of missionaries and colonialism in nineteenth-century South Africa: "Here, then, was a process in which signifiers were set afloat, fought over, and recaptured on both sides of the colonial encounter. What is more, this encounter led to the objectification of 'the' culture of the colonized in opposition to that of whites. . . . While signs, social relations, and material practices are constantly open to transformation— and while meaning may indeed *become* unfixed, resisted, and reconstructed—history everywhere is actively made in a dialectic of order and disorder, consensus and contest" (emphasis in original).

remain skeptical. So I shall begin by rehearsing briefly what I find to be unconvincing about it, and at the same time sketch—through a process of resistance—alternative conceptions that orient the following chapters, even though most of these conceptions are not treated explicitly in them.

Early in his recent Radcliffe-Brown lecture,[2] Marshall Sahlins (1988, 2-3) declared his intention "to join the anthropological chorus of protest against the idea that the global expansion of Western capitalism, or the World System so-called, has made the colonized and 'peripheral' peoples the passive objects of their own history and not its authors, and through tributary economic relations has turned their cultures likewise into adulterated goods."

Sahlins proceeds to chide Eric Wolf for reducing the histories of non-European peoples to the history of global capitalism, despite Wolf's proclaimed wish to make non-Europeans the authors of their own history. The trouble with Wolf, Sahlins tells us, is his attachment to economistic Marxism. If only we had a more sophisticated Marxist understanding of production as a *cultural* process, we would at once see the falsity of assuming that "the world expansion of capitalism brings all other cultural history to an end" (6).

Sahlins's histories of the British opening up of imperial China, the European commercial penetration into Hawaii, and the Kwakiutl appropriation of European goods are intended to show how each encounter was guided by the cultural logic of the local people concerned. Sahlins's narratives are learned and persuasive—although a rigorous Marxist might want to point out that he draws his examples from the early phases of European expansion, which makes it easier to identify capitalism with exchange and consumption rather than with the transformation of production and the reorganization of power relations.[3]

2. This lecture elaborates an argument presented in Sahlins 1985.

3. Marx himself would say that the buying and selling of commodities is as old as recorded history; that the distinctive feature of modern capitalism, by contrast, was the buying and selling of labor power and the consequent penetration of capital into the production process in the unceasing drive for profit at home and abroad; that at home this process required reform of the law, new factory discipline, and technological innovation, while abroad it fueled trade, colonization, and imperial reconstruction. One might, of course, want to shrug off what Marx said about industrial capitalism, but that would not be consistent with also wanting to invoke his authority—as Sahlins in fact does. Incidentally, a useful discussion from a neo-Marxist perspective of the incorpora-

I have no wish to defend economistic Marxism here—or Wolf, for that matter.[4] What worries me is that the arguments espoused by this "anthropological chorus" (now joined by a chorus of historians) are not as clear as they might be. Thus, when Sahlins protests that local peoples are not "passive objects of their own history," it should be evident that this is not equivalent to claiming that they are its "authors." The sense of author is ambiguous as between the person who produces a narrative and the person who authorizes particular powers, including the right to produce certain kinds of narrative. The two are clearly connected, but there is an obvious sense in which the author of a biography is different from the author of the life that is its object— even if it is true that as an individual (as an "active subject"), that person is not entirely the author of his own life. Indeed, since everyone is in some degree or other an object for other people, as well as an object of others' narratives, no one is ever entirely the author of her life. People are never only active agents and subjects in their own history. The interesting question in each case is: In what degree, and in what way, are they agents or patients?

"Western capitalism," Sahlins observes, "has loosed on the world enormous forces of production, coercion and destruction. Yet precisely because they cannot be resisted, the relations and goods of the larger system also take on meaningful places in local schemes of things" (4). If that is so, then local peoples have to be seen in a crucial sense as "the passive objects of their own history and not its authors." Their authorship consists merely in adjusting consciously to those forces and giving that adjustment a meaning. But in that sense they are no different from local peoples in Western societies for whom the relations and goods of "the larger system" also take on meaningful places in the local scheme of things. To take an extreme example: even the inmates of a concentration camp are able, in this sense, to live by their own cultural logic. But one may be forgiven for doubting that they are *therefore* "making their own history."

---

tion of the Ottoman Empire into the world economy is Islamoglu-Inan's (1987) collec-
tion. In her introduction, she outlines a framework in which the transformation of Ottoman structures can be understood with reference to the changing options available to local actors as a consequence of European economic and cultural penetration. Although she rejects the idea that inhabitants of the Ottoman Empire were the passive objects of their history, she does not find it necessary to resort instead to the idea of "cultural logic."

4. My discussion of Wolf 1982 appeared in Asad 1987.

To the extent that what Sahlins calls the larger system determines the conditions within which things take on meaningful places, all peoples can be said to be the passive objects of their own history and not its authors. And that is precisely what Sahlins sometimes seems to be saying: "Not to suggest, then, that we ignore the modern juggernaut, only that its historical course be viewed as a cultural process" (4). But why essentially as a cultural process? One could put it this way, perhaps: the main story line is authored by the capitalist juggernaut, and local peoples provide their own interpretations in local performances. Yet even here we are offered the thought that world capitalism is the primary agent, local peoples at best the secondary ones.

In a widely read review article on contemporary anthropological theory (which must be included in the anthropological chorus Sahlins alludes to), Sherry Ortner (1984) has written feelingly against this very view: "Whether it be the hidden hand of structure or the juggernaut of capitalism that is seen as the agent of society/history, it is certainly not in any central way real people doing real things" (144). Her suggestion seems to be that "Western capitalism" is an abstraction (a mere fiction, to be signaled by quaint metaphors or ironic quotation marks) which does not, therefore, determine the lives of "real people doing real things." This theoretical objection is not Ortner's only complaint, nor is it always compatible with others she makes.

"Specifically," she says at one point, "I find the capitalism-centered view of the world questionable, to say the least, *especially for anthropology*" (142, emphasis added). We should not assume, she goes on, either that everything anthropologists encounter in the field must already have been affected by the capitalist world system or that everything is best explained as a response to the latter. Now this in itself is an empirical point about the extent of capitalist influence throughout the world. But it is based on the assumption that "world capitalism" exists and that its effects can be confirmed or denied in the places where anthropologists work. It therefore also presupposes the theoretical problem of identifying world capitalism— whether as something prior to, or as inclusive of, its local effects. It suggests, especially for anthropology, that some theoretical idea of world capitalism is necessary if its historical consequences are to be recognized.

There is, however, yet another sense of disquiet that Ortner has about the capitalism-centered world-view, this time related to the special role that a fieldwork-defined anthropology can play in the academy—a site that it shares with other human sciences:

> The attempt to view other systems from ground level is the basis, perhaps the only basis, of anthropology's distinctive contribution to the human sciences. It is our capacity, largely developed in fieldwork, to take the perspective of the folks [among whom we research], that allows us to learn anything at all—even in our own culture—beyond what we already know. . . . It is our location "on the ground" that puts us in a position to see people not simply as passive reactors to and enactors of some "system," but as active agents and subjects in their own history. (143)

The ethnographer may come from another system (say, a major capitalist country), but her task is to observe and describe the practices of people "on the ground," not to intervene in what she sees.

For Ortner, there is, therefore, a sense in which anthropology's viewpoint is complementary to that of the sciences that study world capitalism, since it directs the attention of researchers at a different level of other systems. However, if anthropology's distinctive contribution requires it to take a *ground level* view of things, it is difficult to see how confining oneself to that level is sufficient to determine in what degree and in what way other levels become relevant.

The difficulty with this kind of talk is that it employs two different images simultaneously—one having to do with "real people" (which implies that systems are unreal), and the other with "ground level" (which concedes that there are other levels but claims that the latter are dependent on the former rather than the other way around). The two images are then used to define the theoretical autonomy as well as the distinctive contribution of fieldwork-based anthropology.

The fact is that all the human sciences deal with real people (even psychiatry deals with real people thinking/feeling unreal things). It is an old empiricist prejudice to suppose that things are real only when confirmed by sensory data, and that therefore people are real but structures and systems aren't. There are systematic features of human collectivities that are real enough even though you can't see them directly—for example, life expectancies, crime ratios, voting patterns, and rates of productivity. (You can see them once they are represented as tables, graphs, and maps, on a sheet of paper or a computer screen: here seeing and manipulating are closely connected.) Various kinds of social practice are inconceivable without such representations. Governments, businesses, churches, and other social bodies in the contemporary world cannot do without them—even in places as "peripheral" as Papua New Guinea. But note that the issue here is not whether a local culture is pure or derivative, unitary or contested. Nor is it being proposed that there is a super causality (the historical law of capitalism) that determines how everybody on the ground must live. I am concerned with how systematicity (including the kind that is essential to what is called capitalism) is apprehended, represented, and used in the contemporary world. When quantitative data relating to a local population are aggregated, analyzed, and manipulated, the results can be used to inform particular kinds of systematic practice directed at that population. The representation of the data also becomes essential to a distinctive style of argument by which such practices are justified or criticized.[5] The system with which I am concerned here therefore relates to a mode of human agency ("real people doing real things"), one that conditions other people's lives. The immediate objective of *this* agency, however, is not to cause individual actors to behave in one way rather than another. It is to change aggregate human conditions (distributions, trends, etc.) that are profitable or useful—in, for example, matters of landed property, disease, and literacy. Its systematicity lies, therefore, in probabilities, not causalities (Hacking 1990). But it is a kind of systematicity (and, therefore, of power) that is not easily grasped through what is typified as anthropological fieldwork. For although it represents people and their activities at ground level, it does not mirror them.

In fairness, it should be said that Ortner may not really subscribe to the empiricist prejudice I have adverted to, in spite of the language she uses. Probably all she wants to say, somewhat like Sahlins, is that world capitalism has not homogenized the cultures of local peoples. And that, I repeat, is prima facie a reasonable claim, although it doesn't tell us whether, and if so how, local peoples make their own history.

The term *local peoples*—now increasingly used by ethnographers instead of the older *primitive, tribal, simple, preliterate,* and so on—can

---

5. This is an extension of Ian Hacking's concept of "styles of reasoning" (in turn borrowed and developed from recent historians of science), which create, as he puts it, "the possibility for truth and falsehood." Thus, the emergence of statistical reasoning has brought into being new propositions as candidates for true-or-false judgments. See Hacking 1982.

be misleading in an interesting way and calls for some unpacking. In a literal sense, of course, all people most of the time are "local" in the sense of being locatable. Since anthropologists now generally claim that their distinctiveness rests on a method (fieldwork) rather than an object (non-European cultures), this sense recommends itself to them: fieldwork defines privileged access to the local.[6] Yet not everyone who is local in this sense has the same opportunity for movement, or the same practical *reach:* national politicians in the Sudanese capital and nomads and peasants in the provinces; corporation directors in an Australian metropolis and mineworkers in the New Guinean Highlands; generals in the Pentagon and front-line soldiers in the gulf, and so on. They are all locatable, but not equally so by each other.

To say of people that they are local is to imply that they are attached to a place, rooted, circumscribed, limited. People who are not local are thought of either as displaced, uprooted, disoriented—or more positively as unlimited, cosmopolitan, universal, belonging to the whole world (and the world belonging to them). Thus, Saudi theologians who invoke the authority of medieval Islamic texts are taken to be local; Western writers who invoke the authority of modern secular literature claim they are universal. Yet both are located in universes that have rules of inclusion and exclusion. Immigrants who arrive from South Asia to settle in Britain are described as uprooted; English officials who lived in British India were not. An obvious difference between them is power: the former become subjects of the Crown, the latter its representatives. What are the discursive definitions of authorized space? Everyone can relate themselves (or is allocated) to a multiplicity of spaces—phenomenal and conceptual—whose extensions are variously defined, and whose limits are variously imposed, transgressed, and reset. Modern capitalist enterprises and modernizing nation-states are the two most important powers that organize spaces today, defin-

---

6. In his brief sketch of the history of anthropological fieldwork, Evans-Pritchard (1951, 74) wrote: "We have now reached the final, and natural, stage of development, in which observations and the evaluation of them are made by the same person and the scholar is brought into direct contact with the subject of his study. Formerly the anthropologist, like the historian, regarded documents as the raw material of his study. Now the raw material was social life itself." Most contemporary anthropologists have come to identify fieldwork with direct access to "social life itself," thereby underwriting the eye's epistemological sovereignty. "Documents" are not regarded as part of social life itself but as (unreliable) evidence of it—not as elements that enable or prevent or subvert social events, only as (incomplete) traces that record them.

ing, among other things, what is local and what is not. Being locatable, local peoples are those who can be observed, reached, and manipulated as and when required. Knowledge *about* local peoples is not itself local knowledge, as some anthropologists have thought (Geertz 1983). Nor is it therefore simply universal in the sense of being accessible to everyone.

Anthropologists such as Sahlins and Ortner assume that the thesis of agency and creativity in the non-European world requires that the idea of cultural autonomy be defended. More recently, a very different argument has been advanced for that thesis. Among anthropologists, James Clifford is its most eloquent exponent:

> This century has seen a drastic expansion of mobility, including tourism, migrant labor, immigration, urban sprawl. More and more people "dwell" with the help of mass transit, automobiles, airplanes. In cities on six continents foreign populations have come to stay—mixing in but often in partial, specific fashions. The "exotic" is uncannily close. Conversely, there seem no distant places left on the planet where the presence of "modern" products, media, and power cannot be felt. An older topography and experience of travel is exploded. One no longer leaves home confident of finding something radically new, another time or space. Difference is encountered in the adjoining neighborhood, the familiar turns up at the ends of the earth. . . . "Cultural" difference is no longer a stable, exotic otherness; self-other relations are matters of power and rhetoric rather than of essence. A whole structure of expectations about authenticity in culture and in art is thrown in doubt. (Clifford, 1988, 13–14)

In this vision of a fractured, fluid world, all human beings live in the same cultural predicament.[7] There is no single, privileged narrative of

7. Thomas (1991) has made similar points, although he does not hold to quite the same position as Clifford. He attacks ethnographic discourse for its attachment to "exoticism" and for "suppressing mutual entanglement and the perspectival and political fracturing of the cultures of both observers and observed." Like Clifford, he does not deny the existence of cultural differences but condemns "ethnographic representations of stable and unitary cultures" (309). There is some hesitation in the position Thomas wants to take, however. Thus, he concedes that "anthropology has dealt effectively with implicit meanings that can be situated in the coherence of one culture" but pleads that "contemporary global processes of cultural circulation and reification demand an interest in meanings that are explicit and derivative." This seems to imply that unitary-culture monographs may be successful at representing some things but not others. Yet

the modern world, and therefore the history of global capitalism is rejected. Everyone is *dis*located; no one is rooted. Because there is no such thing as authenticity, borrowing and copying do not signify a lack. On the contrary, they indicate libidinal energies and creative human agency. For everyone, Clifford insists, cultural identity is mixed, relational, inventive.

Not all readers will find such representations of modern history (of which there are many within as well as outside anthropology) acceptable. What is striking, however, is the cheerfulness with which this predicament of culture is proffered. Indeed, in spite of frequent references to unequal power (which is explored only in the context of fieldwork and ethnography), we are invited to celebrate the widening scope of human agency that geographical and psychological mobility now afford.

Hannah Arendt had a very different response to mobility in her famous analysis of European totalitarianism, first published in the 1950s. There she spoke of "uprootedness and superfluousness which have been the curse of modern masses since the beginning of the industrial revolution and have become acute with the rise of imperialism at the end of the last century and the break-down of political institutions and social traditions in our own time" (Arendt 1975, 475).

Arendt's sense of deep pessimism may be put down to someone who had herself experienced the horrors of Nazism, and her analysis of totalitarianism may be criticized for some oversimplifications. She is, nevertheless, aware of a problem that has escaped the serious attention of those who would have us celebrate human agency and the decentered subject: the problem of understanding how dominant power realizes itself through the very discourse of mobility. For Arendt is very clear that mobility is not merely an event in itself, but a moment

---

he also wants to say that they never were valid: "It's not clear that the unitary social system ever was a good model for anthropological theory, but the shortcomings are now more conspicuous than ever." The universal existence of cultural borrowings and accretions demands a different approach, as in the study of creoles: "Derivative lingua franca have always offended those preoccupied with boundaries and authenticity, but they offer a resonant model for the uncontained transpositions and transcultural meanings which cultural enquiry must now deal with" (317). Thomas has put his finger on an area of unclarity that has long disturbed anthropology: how to represent historical differences and connections in a world where social identities change. Leach, it may be recalled, made a famous attempt to resolve this problem by drawing on the neo-Kantian philosopher Vaihinger and speaking of "scientific fictions."

in the subsumption of one act by another. If people are physically and morally uprooted, they are more easily moved, and when they are easy to move, they are more easily rendered physically *and* morally super-fluous.

From the point of view of power, mobility is a convenient feature of the act subsumed, but a necessary one of the subsuming act. For it is by means of geographical and psychological movement that modern power inserts itself into preexisting structures. *That* process is neces-sary to defining existing identities and motives as superfluous, and to constructing others in their place. Meanings are thus not only created, they are also redirected or subverted—as so many novels about indige-nous life in the colonies have poignantly depicted.

The positive connection between mobility and modernity is fairly well established in sociological literature. I take one instructive exam-ple. In 1958, Daniel Lerner published an academic bestseller on mod-ernization in the Middle East entitled *The Passing of Traditional Society*. Its thesis was that modernity in the West had depended principally on "the mobile personality"—that is, on a type of person eager to move, to change, and to invent. Empathy was said to be central to that per-sonality, and Lerner (1958, 50) defined it as "the capacity to see oneself in the other fellow's situation." Only the mobile personality, he con-tended, was able to relate creatively to the modern condition. Many of us in Middle East studies criticized it in the 1960s and 1970s for its inadequate scholarship and careless methodology. However, the most illuminating engagement with that book was undertaken in 1980 by a student of sixteenth-century English literature. In chapter 6 of his *Renaissance Self-Fashioning*, Stephen Greenblatt developed the bril-liant insight that "what Professor Lerner calls 'empathy,' Shakespeare calls 'Iago' " (225). He proposed that the idea shared by Lerner's "em-pathy" and Shakespeare's Iago was *improvisation:* "the ability both to capitalize on the unforeseen and to transform given materials into one's own scenario." I quote in full:

> The spur-of-the-moment quality of improvisation is not as critical here as the opportunistic grasp of that which seems fixed and established. Indeed, as Castiglione and others in the Renaissance well understood, the impromptu character of an improvisation is itself often a calcu-lated mask, the product of careful preparation. Conversely, all plots, literary and behavioral, inevitably have their origin in a moment prior

to formal coherence, a moment of experimental, aleatory impulse in which the available, received materials are curved toward a novel shape. We cannot locate a point of pure premeditation or pure randomness. What is essential is the Europeans' ability again and again to insinuate themselves into the preexisting political, religious, even psychic structures of the natives and to turn those structures to their advantage. . . . Professor Lerner is right to insist that this ability is a characteristically (though not exclusively) Western mode, present to varying degrees in the classical and medieval world and greatly strengthened from the Renaissance onward; he misleads only in insisting further that it is an act of imaginative generosity, a sympathetic appreciation of the situation of the other fellow. For when he speaks confidently of the "spread of empathy around the world," we must understand that he is speaking of the exercise of Western power, power that is creative as well as destructive, but that is scarcely ever wholly disinterested or benign. (227–28)

The point I want to draw out from this perceptive account of Western power relates not to the moral status of its intentions but to its transforming work. In any case, the European wish to make the world in its own image is not necessarily to be disparaged as ungenerous. If one believes oneself to be the source of salvation, the wish to make others reflect oneself is not unbenign, however terrible the practices by which this desire is put into effect. Besides, in a tradition that connects pain with achievement, the inflicting of suffering on others is not in itself reprehensible: it is to be condemned only when it is gratuitous—where the pain as means is out of proportion to an objective end (hence, the subjective enjoyment of pain is regarded as both immoral and pathological).

But the question I want to raise here is this: to the extent that such power seeks to normalize other people's motivations, whose history is being made? Note that my question is not about the authenticity of individual agency but about the structure of normal personhood (normal in both the statistical and the medical sense) and the techniques for securing it. I ask whether improvisation becomes irrelevant when the agents are non-Europeans acting within the context of their own politically independent state to implement a European project: the continuous physical and moral improvement of an entire governable population through flexible strategies. Whose improvised story do these agents construct? Who is its author, and who its subject?

The idea that cultural borrowing must lead to total homogeneity and to loss of authenticity is clearly absurd, but the idea of projects' having translatable historical structures should not be confused with it. When a project is translated from one site to another, from one agent to another, versions of power are produced. As with translations of a text, one does not simply get a reproduction of identity. The acquisition of new forms of language from the modern West—whether by forcible imposition, insidious insertion, or voluntary borrowing— is part of what makes for new possibilities of action in non-Western societies. Yet, although the outcome of these possibilities is never fully predictable, the language in which the possibilities are formulated is increasingly shared by Western and non-Western societies. And so, too, the specific forms of power and subjection.

Choices and desires make actions before actions can make "history." But predefined social relations and language forms, as well as the body's materiality, shape the person to whom "normal" desires and choices can be attributed. That is why questions about what it is possible for agents to do must also address the process by which "normal persons" are constituted. Meanings are never simply generated by a cultural logic; they belong variously to conventional projects, occasional intentions, natural events, and so on (see Grice 1989). For theologians such as Augustine and al-Ghazali, they also relate to all-encompassing divine purposes. The medieval Christian monk who learns to make the abbot's will into his own learns thereby to desire God's purposes. In an important sense, the meaning of his actions is what it is by virtue of their being part of a transcendent project. (And so, too, the actions of all agents are part of transcendent temporal structures. The fact that the further significance of actions becomes apparent only when a certain time has elapsed is one to which working historians are likely to be more sensitive than working ethnographers.)

Even among nonbelievers, few would claim that the human agent is sovereign, although post-Enlightenment moral theory insists that she ought to be autonomous. This theory has long been criticized by conservative as well as socialist writers. Moral considerations apart, it is evident that the increasingly sophisticated division of labor and the consumer culture of modern capitalism renders individual autonomy less and less feasible as a practical possibility. More recently, some radical critics (particularly those concerned with third world studies) have drawn on poststructuralist ideas to attack the Enlightenment idea of autonomy. A thoughtful example is the Indianist Rosalind O'Hanlon, who questions the "liberal humanist notions of subjectivity and agency" in a review of the work of the *Subaltern Studies* group of historians (O'Hanlon 1988). The starting point for the latter was their dissatisfaction with the "elite historiography" of India, which denied subordinate peoples a consciousness of their own, and hence the capacity to make their own history. Orientalist and functionalist anthropologies of India were also condemned for their alleged essentialism.[8] (Note the first assumption of the "history-making" thesis: that history is not made unless significant change occurs. It is not sufficient for events to succeed one another; something substantial must be transformed.)

O'Hanlon sympathizes with the Subaltern historians' wish to recover suppressed histories but points to the theoretical danger such an agenda conceals of slipping into "essentialist humanism." One must reject, she says,

> the myth . . . of the self-constituting subject, that *a consciousness or being* which has an origin outside itself is no being at all. From such a rejection, we can proceed to the idea that though histories and identities are necessarily *constructed and produced from many fragments,* fragments which do not contain the signs of any essential belonging inscribed in them, this does not cause the history of the subaltern to dissolve once more into invisibility. This is firstly because we apply exactly the same decentring strategies to the monolithic subject-agents of elite historiography; and second, because it is the creative practice of the subaltern which now becomes the focus of our attention, his ability to appropriate and mould cultural materials of almost any provenance to his own purposes, and to discard those . . . which no longer serve them. (197; emphases added)

O'Hanlon's criticism reaches its target, although occasionally at the cost of reproducing the ambiguity in the different senses of "authoring" that I touched on earlier. Thus, to decenter "subject-agents"

8. And yet some of the Subaltern historians have invoked structural-functionalist ethnographies (of places other than India) to develop their own comparative ideas. (See, for example, the interesting contributions by Pandey and Chatterjee, in Guha and Spivak 1988.) What this indicates is that no ethnographies are *essentially* essentialist, that like all verbal representations they can be broken up, appropriated, and re-presented in the service of different intentions.

of elite historiography is not at all identical with subverting people in positions of governmental authority. The idea of self-constitution is not merely a historiographical option but a liberal humanist principle that has far-reaching moral, legal, and political implications in modern/modernizing states. That is why we find O'Hanlon—as a progressivist—obliged to reintroduce that principle in order to authenticate the subaltern subject. For how else could the subaltern's *authentic* purposes ("his own purposes") be distinguished from those of his master's if not through the struggle for self-constitution? (Note the second assumption of the history-making thesis: that an agent cannot make his "own" history unless he is autonomous. It is not enough that he acts purposively; his purposes must be in conflict with others'.)

The essence of the principle of self-constitution is "consciousness." That is, a metaphysical concept of consciousness is essential for explaining how the many fragments come to be construed as parts of a single self-identifying subject. Yet if we set aside the Hegelian concept of consciousness (the teleological principle starting from sense-certainty and culminating in Reason) and the Kantian concept of the transcendental subject, which Hegel rewrote as consciousness, it will have to be admitted that consciousness in the everyday psychological sense (awareness, intent, and the giving of meaning to experiences) is inadequate to account for agency. One does not have to subscribe to a full-blown Freudianism to see that instinctive reaction, the docile body, and the unconscious work, in their different ways, more pervasively and continuously than consciousness does. This is part of the reason why an agent's act is more (and less) than her consciousness of it.

Another part has to do with the subsumability of her acts into the projects of other agents: beyond a certain point, an act no longer belongs exclusively to its initiator. It is precisely because this fact is overlooked that the historical importance of consciousness is exaggerated in the literature that takes consent and repression to be the two basic conditions of political domination. For to explain the latter in terms of these conditions, whether singly or in combination, is to resort to explanation exclusively in terms of consciousness. It is, consequently, to ignore the politically more significant condition that has to do with the objective distribution of goods that allows or precludes certain options. The *structures* of possible actions that are included and excluded are therefore logically independent of the consciousness of actors.[9]

Another way of putting this is to say that the systematic knowledge (e.g., statistical information) on which an agent must draw in order to act in ways that "make history" is not subjective in any sense. It does not imply "the self." The subject, on the other hand, is founded on consciousness of self. My argument, in brief, is that contrary to the discourse of many radical historians and anthropologists, *agent* and *subject* (where the former is the principle of effectivity and the latter of consciousness) do not belong to the same theoretical universe and should not, therefore, be coupled.

Gyan Prakash is a talented Subalternist who appears to have read and approved of O'Hanlon's critique. In an invigorating essay on "post-Orientalist" historiography of India (Prakash 1990), he argues for a more radical poststructuralist position intended to supersede conventional ethnography and historiography.[10] Anthropologists drawn to the idea of "real people making their own history" will want to read this provocative piece, because it exposes metaphysical traces in historical narration that, he argues, reproduce the capitalist-centered view of the world.

Prakash is against "foundational" history, by which he means two things: (1) a history whose subject (individual, class, or structure) is taken to be irreducible, and (2) teleological history—for example, a historical narrative of (aborted, delayed, or distorted) capitalism. Foundationalism in these two forms is rejected in order to widen the space for "excluded histories."

While narrative history does not have to be teleological,[11] it does presuppose an identity ("India," say) that is the subject of that narrative. Even when that identity is analyzed into its heterogeneous parts (class, gender, regional divisions, etc.), what is done, surely, is to reveal

9. I have argued this point with reference to ethnographic material in Asad 1970 and 1972, and more generally in Asad 1987.

10. Prakash's name is acknowledged in O'Hanlon's (1988) text, among others. This does not prove anything about influence, of course; it only suggests a measure of agreement, which is confirmed in note 34 of Prakash 1990. That agreement was short-lived, however. In a subsequent polemic, coauthored with D. Washbrook (O'Hanlon and Washbrook 1992) and directed against Prakash, O'Hanlon retreats to a more conventional Marxism, while in his rejoinder Prakash (1992) takes up a more defiant Derridean position.

11. An early criticism of teleological histories is Butterfield 1931.

its constitution, not to dissolve its unity. The unity is maintained by those who speak in its name, and more generally by all who adjust their existence to its (sometimes shifting) requirements. The claim of many radical critics that hegemonic power necessarily suppresses difference in favor of unity is quite mistaken. Just as mistaken is their claim that that power always abhors ambiguity. To secure its unity—to make its own history—dominant power has worked best through differentiating and classifying practices. India's colonial history furnishes ample evidence of this. In this context power is constructive, not repressive. Furthermore, its ability to select (or construct) the differences that serve its purposes has depended on its exploiting the dangers and opportunities contained in ambiguous situations. And ambiguity—as we saw in Greenblatt's example—is precisely one of the things that gives "Western power" its improvisational quality.

By a curious irony, Prakash's rejection of "the modernization narrative" on the grounds that it is teleological indirectly reveals something about the sense of the phrase "making one's own history," which many anthropologists also employ. For while the expression indicates a disapproval of historical narratives of the non-West in which Europe is too prominent (as actor or as norm), it also conceals a concept of history making that is parasitic on those very narratives.

If the modernizing project is more than merely an accumulating narrative of India's past, if we understand it as the project of constructing "India" (an integrated totality defined according to progressive principles), which requires the continuous calculation of India's future, then teleology is precisely what that project must reflect. (A project is, after all, by definition teleological.) The career of the Indian nation-state is itself part of that project. To say this is to say something not merely about those who ruled India in the effort to change it in a particular direction but also about those who struggled against them. The struggle is carried out more often than not in a new language initiated by the European Enlightenment: liberty, equality, reason, progress, human rights, and so forth, and (more important) within new political-legal spaces built up under British colonialism. To recount the career of the Indian nation-state is to try to understand how and why the modernization project succeeds or fails in particular times and places—and how it constructs and redefines itself as a project. One may wish to oppose that project, and hence to redescribe it in terms that its supporters would reject, *but it must be understood as a teleology,* whose desired future, in important respects, is foreshadowed in the present of Western liberal capitalist states. It does not follow that the project is driven by lawlike forces, that its ultimate success is inevitable or that it cannot be reformulated.

However, to those who have been taught to regard essentialism as the gravest of intellectual sins, it is necessary to explain that certain things are *essential* to that project—as indeed there are to "India" as a nation-state. To say this is not equivalent to saying that the project (or "India") can never be changed; it is to say that each historical phenomenon is determined by the way it is constituted, that some of its constitutive elements are essential to its historical identity and some are not. It is like saying that the constitutive rules of a game define its essence—which is by no means to assert that that game can never be subverted or changed; it is merely to point to what determines its essential historical identity, to imply that certain changes (though not others) will mean that the game is no longer the same game.

The project of modernization (Westernization), including its aim of material and moral progress, is certainly a matter of history making. But it is a project whose innumerable agents are neither fully autonomous nor fully conscious of it. Indeed, in a crucial sense it is that project, inaugurated in Europe over two centuries ago, that articulates our concept of human beings making history. For that project was intertwined with a new experience of historical time, and thus with a novel conception of historicity—historical time divided into three great periods (Antiquity, the Middle Ages, and Modernity), accelerating forward into an open future. The West defines itself, in opposition to all non-Western cultures, by its modern historicity. Despite the disjunctions of modernity (its break with tradition), "the West" therefore includes within itself its past as an organic continuity: from "the Greeks and Romans" and "the Hebrews and Early Christians," through "Latin Christendom," "the Renaissance," and "the Reformation," to "the universal civilization" of modern Europeans. Although it is spatially discontinuous and internally diverse, "the West" is not a mere Hegelian myth, not a mere representation ready to be unmasked by a handful of talented critics. For good or ill, it informs innumerable intentions, practices, and discourses in systematic ways. This is not to say that there is an integrated Western culture, or a fixed Western identity, or a single Western way of thinking, but that a singular collective identity defines itself in terms of a unique historicity in contrast to all others, a historicity that shifts from place to place—Greece, Rome, Latin Christendom, the Americas—until it embraces the world.

It was in Europe's eighteenth century that the older, Christian attitudes toward historical time (salvational expectation) were combined with the newer, secular practices (rational prediction) to give us our modern idea of progress (Koselleck 1988, 17). A new philosophy of agency was also developed, allowing individual actions to be related to collective tendencies. From the Enlightenment philosophes, through the Victorian evolutionist thinkers, to the experts on economic and political development in the latter half of the twentieth century, one assumption has been constant: to make history, the agent must create the future, remake herself, and help others to do so, where the criteria of successful remaking are seen to be universal. Old universes must be subverted and a new universe created. To that extent, history can be made only on the back of a universal teleology. Actions seeking to maintain the "local" status quo, or to follow local models of social life, do not qualify as history making. From the Cargo Cults of Melanesia to the Islamic Revolution in Iran, they merely attempt (hopelessly) "to resist the future" or "to turn back the clock of history."

Anthropology is thus inserted into modern history in two ways: first, through the growth in Europe's political, economic, and scientific powers, which has provided anthropologists with their means of professional existence and their intellectual motive; and second, through the Enlightenment schematization of progressive time that has provided anthropology with its conceptual site: modernity. It is not just that anthropology is a modern creation born out of Europe's encounter with non-Europeans. It is that the major ideas it uses to grasp its subjects (nonmodern, local, traditional) are often dependent on its contrastive sense of the modern.[12]

Modern anthropology's theoretical focus on human diversity has its roots in Renaissance Europe's encounter with "the savage." That brutal encounter in Africa and the New World produced disturbing theological problems for reflective Christians: How to explain the variety of human beings, given the Mosaic account of Creation? This was the primary question that animated scholars who read the exotic

12. Two outstanding examples of studies by anthropologists in which such ideas have been critically examined are Steiner 1956 and Schneider 1984.

descriptions by explorers, and the great range of religious belief and practice among other peoples was the primary object of their attention.[13]

It is often said that the Renaissance "discovered man,"[14] but that discovery was in effect a psychological reconstruction of European individuality. The accounts of savages by explorers returning from Africa and the New World produced a very different phenomenon[15]— a man whose kinship to Christian Europeans was highly problematic. Some writers even held that he was not quite human. The eventual solution adopted in the late seventeenth and early eighteenth centuries, according to Margaret Hodgen, was a synthesis of two old ideas: the chain of being and the genetic principle. In this way, "a spatial arrangement of forms [was converted] into an historical, developmental, or evolutionary series" (Hodgen 1964, 389–90). A common human nature was thus accorded to all human beings, but one that was assumed to exist in various stages of maturity and enlightenment. A prehistoric period was added to the historical triad—the time of "primitive" man. And just as some contemporaneous "local peoples" could be assigned to the prehistoric period, others were placeable in the medieval. The early preoccupation with saving the biblical story of man's Creation and Fall gave way to a new concern with narrating the secular story of European world hegemony in developmental terms.[16] As a result of developments in Higher Criticism, a problem of *Chris-*

13. See the absorbing study by Hodgen (1964).

14. Thus, Burckhardt's classic (1950); part 4 is entitled "The Discovery of the World and of Man."

15. It was not only verbal accounts that the explorers brought back: "When Christopher Columbus dropped anchor in the Tagus River at the port of Lisbon on the fateful day of his return to the Old World, he brought with him seven kidnapped Indians of the so-called Taino culture of the Arawack linguistic group. . . . During the years which followed, Indians captured by other explorers were exhibited in other capitals of Europe. . . . The first Indians to appear in France were brought by Thomas Aubert in 1506. Taken to Rouen, they were described in a Paris chronicle as sooty in color, black-haired, possessing speech but no religion. . . . In 1565, during a festival in Bordeaux, 300 men at arms conducted a showing of captives from twelve nations, including Greece, Turkey, Arabia, Egypt, America, Taprobane, the Canaries, and Ethiopia. Outside the city wall, in the midst of an imitation Brazilian landscape, a veritable savage village was erected with several hundred residents, many of whom had been freshly abducted from South America" (Hodgen 1964, 111–12).

16. Not entirely secular, though. See Bowler 1989 for the way the idea of "progressive evolution"—biological as well as social—responded to Christian sensibilities in the latter part of the nineteenth century.

tian theology has virtually evaporated, but some of the ideas generated to address it remain in secular disciplines, formed in pursuit of a new universality.

Of course, significant mutations have occurred in the historical schemata for classifying and explaining human diversity during the eighteenth, nineteenth, and twentieth centuries. But there have been continuities, too, including historical periodization and direction. Another continuity, as George Stocking notes, was the assumption of a single human nature underlying cultural plurality (Stocking 1987, 313). In practice, however, anthropology and orientalism between them dealt conceptually with existing "local peoples" left behind in the progressive evolution of modern (European) "civilization," while a number of specialist disciplines dealt with the latter.[17] In this way, the idea of a single nature for all humans appeared to concede that some are evidently "more mature" than others.

It has become a truism to say that most anthropologists in Britain and the United States were antievolutionist—and therefore relativist— in the first half of the twentieth century. Some historians of the discipline have connected this to the general mood of disillusion with the idea of progress prevailing in the West after World War I.[18]

This view is not entirely accurate, however—at any rate for British social anthropology. Neither Malinowski (1945, 1-2; 1938) nor Radcliffe-Brown (1952) rejected the idea of higher and lower cultures and of the upward development of the latter. Godfrey and Monica Wilson (1945) saw no difficulty in presenting the evolution of relations and ideas in Africa "from primitive to civilized"; nor did Max Gluckman in depicting the adoption of "White culture" by Africans as "progressive."[19] Lucy Mair spoke unapologetically of the effects of Euro-

17. E. B. Tylor (1893, 805) delineated the region to which orientalists and anthropologists primarily applied themselves: "In the large definition adopted by this Congress, the Oriental world reaches its extreme limits. It embraces the continent of Asia, stretching through Egypt over Africa, and into Europe over Turkey and Greece, while extending in the far East from group to group of ocean islands, where Indonesia, Melanesia, Micronesia, and Polynesia lead on to the continent of Australia and its outlier, Tasmania. Immense also is the range of time through which the culture-history of this Oriental region may be, if often but dimly, traced."

18. See, for example, the fine study by Kuklick (1991), though it should be borne in mind that this disenchantment did not significantly affect those responsible for the government of colonial peoples. There the effort at the material and moral improvement of non-European subjects continued in full force.

19. Exemplifying the interdependence of cause and effect in processes of social change,

pean colonial rule in Africa as "the spread of civilization,"[20] and Mary Douglas reaffirmed the importance of an evolutionary perspective.[21] So too, some in ways more explicit and others in ways less so, did the scores of anthropologists who attended to problems of particular social change in the non-Western world. Their lack of interest in tracing the development of Culture as a human universal, and their attachment to the idea of social systems in (temporary) equilibrium, did not mean the rejection of progressive evolution in every form. Indeed, it could be argued that there was less concern with demonstrating the principle of a common human nature, and more with describing "normal" historical developments in various parts of the non-European world.

The major point, at any rate, is that whether they were concerned with customary beliefs and practices or with contemporary social and cultural changes, anthropologists saw themselves—and were seen by others—as dealing typically with nonmodern lives. Certainly, if anthropology was expected to deal with political, economic, religious, legal, medical, poetic, and historical events, it was only when these objects of modern disciplines were situated in a nonmodern social totality. Like other modern writers on the nonmodern world, anthropologists used a dual modality of historical time, which enabled them

---

Gluckman (1958, 75) could observe quite unselfconsciously that "progressive intelligent men tend to find scope for their ability in education and Christianity, and Christians, freed from intellectually clogging beliefs and some suspicion of the Whites, tend to progress in the acceptance of White culture." In respect to whole societies, too, Gluckman was a progressivist: "In this respect a study of Lozi law, as of law in most simple societies, validates Maine's most widely accepted generalization, 'that the movement of progressive societies has hitherto been a movement *from Status to Contract*' i.e. that early law is dominantly the law of status" (Gluckman 1955, 28).

20. "The [European] individuals who put these policies into practice were sustained in the difficulties of their task, and in over-ruling opposition, by the dogma that civilization was a blessing that its possessors ought to spread; just as they civilized their own children by obliging them to do things they did not want to, and sometimes by punishing them severely. And nobody today is saying that they ought not to have spread civilization; today's complaint is that they did not spread enough of it, or the right parts" (Mair 1962, 253).

21. "The right basis for comparison is to insist on the unity of human experience and at the same time to insist on its variety, on the differences that make comparison worth while. The only way to do this is to recognise the nature of historical progress and the nature of primitive and of modern society. Progress means differentiation. Thus primitive means undifferentiated; modern means differentiated. Advance in technology involves differentiation in every sphere, in techniques and materials, in productive and political roles. . . . Differentiation in thought patterns goes along with differentiated social conditions" (Douglas 1966, 77–78).

to represent events as at once contemporaneous and noncontemporaneous (Koselleck 1988, 249)—and thus some conditions as more progressive than others.

It has been said that this focus has made anthropology a marginal discipline in comparison to those that deal with modern civilization itself, "culturally marginal to its own society as well as to the groups that were the subject of ethnographic fieldwork" (Stocking 1987, 289). The rejection of anthropology by Westernizing elites in former colonial countries is well known, and the reasons for it are not hard to understand. But the assumption that anthropology is culturally marginal to modern European society needs to be reexamined. It is true that anthropological theories have contributed very little to the formation of theories in politics, economics, and other social sciences. And yet, paradoxically, aspects of anthropology's discourse on the nonmodern—those addressing "the primitive," "the irrational," "the mythic," "the traditional"—have been of central importance to several disciplines. Thus, psychoanalysis,[22] theological modernism,[23] and modernist literature,[24] among others, have continually turned for support to anthropology in their attempts to probe, accommodate, celebrate, or qualify the essence of modernity.

Anthropology, then, appears to be involved in definitions of the West while Western projects are transforming the (preliterate, precapitalist, premodern) peoples that ethnographers claim to represent. Both processes need to be studied systematically. To understand better the local peoples "entering" (or "resisting") modernity, anthropology must surely try to deepen its understanding of the West as something more than a threadbare ideology. To do that will include at-

---

22. Freud's major interest in the primitive is too well known to be rehearsed here.

23. Theological modernism, strictly speaking, refers to an intellectual trend in late nineteenth- and early twentieth-century Catholicism concerning methods of interpreting Scripture: see Vidler 1961, chap. 16. However, I use it here to indicate the general movement among liberal Christians to apply to the Scriptures approaches in keeping with the findings of anthropology and historical methodology. For a review of biblical scholarship that has drawn on successive theories in anthropology since the nineteenth century, see Rogerson 1978.

24. The importance of Frazer for literary modernism is amply documented. See, for example, T. S. Eliot's references to him, as well as to other anthropological writers, in his notes to "The Waste Land." The attempt by modern aesthetics to recapture the freshness of "childhood perception" and to make new beginnings (de Man 1983, 157) led at once to an appropriation of a concept of the primitive and to a rejection of a concept of tradition.

tempting to grasp its peculiar historicity, the mobile powers that have constructed its structures, projects, and desires. I argue that religion, in its positive and negative senses, is an essential part of that construction.

The following chapters engage with fragments of Western history approached as genealogies, archaisms, translations, and polemics. They are intended as a contribution to a historical anthropology that takes the cultural hegemony of the West as its object of inquiry. More precisely, they explore ways in which Western concepts and practices of religion define forms of history making.

Genealogies

THE CONSTRUCTION
OF RELIGION AS
AN ANTHROPOLOGICAL
CATEGORY

In much nineteenth-century evolutionary thought, religion was considered to be an early human condition from which modern law, science, and politics emerged and became detached.[1] In this century most anthropologists have abandoned Victorian evolutionary ideas, and many have challenged the rationalist notion that religion is simply a primitive and therefore outmoded form of the institutions we now encounter in truer form (law, politics, science) in modern life. For these twentieth-century anthropologists, religion is not an archaic mode of scientific thinking, nor of any other secular endeavor we value today; it is, on the contrary, a distinctive space of human practice and belief which cannot be reduced to any other. From this it seems to follow that the essence of religion is not to be confused with, say, the essence of politics, although in many societies the two may overlap and be intertwined.

In a characteristically subtle passage, Louis Dumont has told us that medieval Christendom was one such composite society:

> I shall take it for granted that a change in relations entails a change in whatever is related. If throughout our history religion has developed (to a large extent, with some other influences at play) a revolution in social values and has given birth by scissiparity, as it were, to an autonomous world of political institutions and speculations, then surely religion itself will have changed in the process. Of some important

1. Thus, Fustel de Coulanges 1873. Originally published in French in 1864, this was an influential work in the history of several overlapping disciplines—anthropology, biblical studies, and classics.

and visible changes we are all aware, but, I submit, we are not aware
of the change in the very nature of religion as lived by any given
individual, say a Catholic. Everyone knows that religion was formerly
a matter of the group and has become a matter of the individual (in
principle, and in practice at least in many environments and situations). But if we go on to assert that this change is correlated with the
birth of the modern State, the proposition is not such a commonplace as the previous one. Let us go a little further: medieval religion
was a great cloak—I am thinking of the Mantle of Our Lady of Mercy.
Once it became an individual affair, it lost its all-embracing capacity
and became one among other apparently equal considerations, of
which the political was the first born. Each individual may, of course,
and perhaps even will, recognise religion (or philosophy), as the same
all-embracing consideration as it used to be *socially.* Yet on the level of
social consensus or ideology, the same person will switch to a different configuration of values in which autonomous values (religious,
political, etc.) are seemingly juxtaposed, much as individuals are juxtaposed in society. (1971, 32; emphasis in original)

According to this view, medieval religion, pervading or encompassing
other categories, is nevertheless *analytically* identifiable. It is this fact
that makes it possible to say that religion has the same essence today as
it had in the Middle Ages, although its social extension and function
were different in the two epochs. Yet the insistence that religion has
an autonomous essence—not to be confused with the essence of science, or of politics, or of common sense—invites us to define religion
(like any essence) as a transhistorical and transcultural phenomenon.
It may be a happy accident that this effort of defining religion con-
verges with the liberal demand in our time that it be kept quite separate from politics, law, and science—spaces in which varieties of power
and reason articulate our distinctively modern life. This definition is
at once part of a strategy (for secular liberals) of the confinement, and
(for liberal Christians) of the defense of religion.

Yet this separation of religion from power is a modern Western
norm, the product of a unique post-Reformation history. The attempt
to understand Muslim traditions by insisting that in them religion and
politics (two essences modern society tries to keep conceptually and
practically apart) are coupled must, in my view, lead to failure. At its
most dubious, such attempts encourage us to take up an a priori posi-

tion in which religious discourse in the political arena is seen as a disguise for political power.

In what follows I want to examine the ways in which the theoretical search for an essence of religion invites us to separate it conceptually from the domain of power. I shall do this by exploring a universalist definition of religion offered by an eminent anthropologist: Clifford Geertz's "Religion as a Cultural System."[2] I stress that this is not primarily a critical review of Geertz's ideas on religion—if that had been my aim I would have addressed myself to the entire corpus of his writings on religion in Indonesia and Morocco. My intention in this chapter is to try to identify some of the historical shifts that have produced our concept of religion as the concept of a transhistorical essence—and Geertz's article is merely my starting point.

It is part of my basic argument that socially identifiable forms, preconditions, and effects of what was regarded as religion in the medieval Christian epoch were quite different from those so considered in modern society. I want to get at this well-known fact while trying to avoid a simple nominalism. What we call religious power was differently distributed and had a different thrust. There were different ways in which it created and worked through legal institutions, different selves that it shaped and responded to, and different categories of knowledge which it authorized and made available. Nevertheless, what the anthropologist is confronted with, as a consequence, is not merely an arbitrary collection of elements and processes that we happen to call "religion." For the entire phenomenon is to be seen in large measure in the context of Christian attempts to achieve a coherence in doctrines and practices, rules and regulations, even if that was a state never fully attained. My argument is that there cannot be a universal definition of religion, not only because its constituent elements and relationships are historically specific, but because that definition is itself the historical product of discursive processes.

A universal (i.e., anthropological) definition is, however, precisely what Geertz aims at: A *religion,* he proposes, is "(1) a system of symbols which act to (2) establish powerful, pervasive, and long-lasting moods and motivations in men by (3) formulating conceptions of a general order of existence and (4) clothing these conceptions with

2. Originally published in 1966, it was reprinted in his widely acclaimed *The Interpretation of Cultures* (1973).

such an aura of factuality that (5) the moods and motivations seem uniquely realistic" (90). In what follows I shall examine this definition, not only in order to test its interlinked assertions, but also to flesh out the counterclaim that a transhistorical definition of religion is not viable.

The Concept of Symbol as a Clue to the Essence of Religion

Geertz sees his first task as the definition of symbol: "any object, act, event, quality, or relation which serves as a vehicle for a conception—the conception is the symbol's 'meaning'" (91). But this simple, clear statement—in which *symbol* (any object, etc.) is differentiated from but linked to *conception* (its meaning)—is later supplemented by others not entirely consistent with it, for it turns out that the symbol is not an object that serves as a vehicle for a conception, *it is itself the conception*. Thus, in the statement "The number 6, written, imagined, laid out as a row of stones, or even punched into the program tapes of a computer, is a symbol" (91), what constitutes all these diverse representations as versions of the same symbol ("the number 6") is of course *a conception*. Furthermore, Geertz sometimes seems to suggest that even as a conception a symbol has an intrinsic connection with empirical events from which it is merely "theoretically" separable: "the symbolic dimension of social events is, like the psychological, itself theoretically abstractable from these events as empirical totalities" (91). At other times, however, he stresses the importance of keeping symbols and empirical objects quite separate: "there is something to be said for not confusing our traffic with symbols with our traffic with objects or human beings, for these latter are not in themselves symbols, however often they may function as such" (92). Thus, "symbol" is sometimes an aspect of reality, sometimes of its representation.[3]

These divergencies are symptoms of the fact that cognitive ques-

---

3. Compare Peirce's more rigorous account of *representations*. "A representation is an object which stands for another so that an experience of the former affords us a knowledge of the latter. There must be three essential conditions to which every representation must conform. It must in the first place like any other object have qualities independent of its meaning. . . . In the 2nd place a representation must have a real causal connection with its object. . . . In the third place, every representation addresses itself to a mind. It is only in so far as it does this that it is a representation" (Peirce 1986, 62).

tions are mixed up in this account with communicative ones, and this makes it difficult to inquire into the ways in which discourse and understanding are connected in social practice. To begin with we might say, as a number of writers have done, that a symbol is not an object or event that serves to carry a meaning but a set of relationships between objects or events uniquely brought together as complexes or as concepts,[4] having at once an intellectual, instrumental, and emotional significance.[5] If we define symbol along these lines,[6] a number of questions can be raised about the conditions that explain how such complexes and concepts come to be formed, and in particular how their formation is related to varieties of practice. Half a century ago, Vygotsky was able to show how the development of children's intellect is dependent on the internalization of social speech.[7] This means that the formation of what we have here called "symbols" (complexes, concepts) is conditioned by the social relations in which the growing child is involved—by the social activities that he or she is permitted or encouraged or obliged to undertake—in which other symbols (speech and significant movements) are crucial. The conditions (discursive and nondiscursive) that explain how symbols come to be constructed, and how some of them are established as natural or authoritative as opposed to others, then become an important object of anthropological inquiry. It must be stressed that this is not a matter of urging the study of the origin and function of symbols in addition to their meaning—such a distinction is not relevant here. What is being argued is that the authoritative status of representations/discourses is dependent on the

4. Vygotsky (1962) makes crucial analytical distinctions in the development of conceptual thought: heaps, complexes, pseudoconcepts, and true concepts. Although, according to Vygotsky, these represent stages in the development of children's use of language, the earlier stages persist into adult life.

5. Cf. Collingwood (1938, bk. 2) for a discussion of the integral connection between thought and emotion, where it is argued that there is no such thing as a universal emotional function accompanying all conceptualization/communication: every distinctive cognitive/communicative activity has its own specific emotional cast. If this view is valid, then the notion of a generalized religious emotion (or mood) may be questioned.

6. The argument that symbols *organize practice,* and consequently the structure of cognition, is central to Vygotsky's genetic psychology—see especially "Tool and Symbol in Child Development," in Vygotsky 1978. A cognitive conception of symbols has recently been revived by Sperber (1975). A similar view was taken much earlier by Lienhardt (1961).

7. "The history of the process of *the internalization of social speech* is also the history of the socialization of children's practical intellect" (Vygotsky 1978, 27). See also Luria and Yudovich 1971.

appropriate production of other representations/discourses; the two are intrinsically and not just temporally connected.

Systems of symbols, says Geertz, are also *culture patterns,* and they constitute "extrinsic sources of information" (92). Extrinsic, because "they lie outside the boundaries of the individual organism as such in that inter-subjective world of common understandings into which all human individuals are born" (92). And sources of information in the sense that "they provide a blueprint or template in terms of which processes external to themselves can be given a definite form" (92). Thus, culture patterns, we are told, may be thought of as "models *for* reality" as well as "models *of* reality."[8]

This part of the discussion does open up possibilities by speaking of modeling: that is, it allows for the possibility of conceptualizing discourses in the process of elaboration, modification, testing, and so forth. Unfortunately, Geertz quickly regresses to his earlier position: "culture patterns have an intrinsic double aspect," he writes; "they give meaning, that is objective conceptual form, to social and psychological reality both by shaping themselves to it and by shaping it to themselves" (1973, 93). This alleged dialectical tendency toward isomorphism, incidentally, makes it difficult to understand how social change can ever occur. The basic problem, however, is not with the idea of mirror images as such but with the assumption that there are two separate levels—the cultural, on the one side (consisting of symbols) and the social and psychological, on the other—which interact. This resort to Parsonian theory creates a logical space for defining the essence of religion. By adopting it, Geertz moves away from a notion of symbols that are intrinsic to signifying and organizing practices, and back to a notion of symbols as meaning-carrying objects external to social conditions and states of the self ("social and psychological reality").

This is not to say that Geertz doesn't think of symbols as "doing" something. In a way that recalls older anthropological approaches to ritual,[9] he states that religious symbols act "by inducing in the wor-

8. Or, as Kroeber and Kluckhohn (1952, 181) put it much earlier, "Culture consists of patterns, explicit and implicit, of and for behaviour acquired and transmitted by symbols."

9. If we set aside Radcliffe-Brown's well-known preoccupation with social cohesion, we may recall that he too was concerned to specify certain kinds of psychological states said to be induced by religious symbols: "Rites can be seen to be the regulated symbolic expressions of certain sentiments (which control the behaviour of the individual in his relation to others). Rites can therefore be shown to have a specific social

shipper a certain distinctive set of dispositions (tendencies, capacities, propensities, skills, habits, liabilities, proneness) which lend a chronic character to the flow of his activity and the quality of his experience" (95). And here again, symbols are set apart from mental states. But how plausible are these propositions? Can we, for example, predict the "distinctive" set of dispositions for a Christian worshiper in modern, industrial society? Alternatively, can we say of someone with a "distinctive" set of dispositions that he is or is not a Christian?[10] The answer to both questions must surely be no. The reason, of course, is that it is not simply worship but social, political, and economic institutions in general,[11] within which individual biographies are lived out, that lend a stable character to the flow of a Christian's activity and to the quality of her experience.

Religious symbols, Geertz elaborates, produce two kinds of dispositions, *moods* and *motivations:* "motivations are 'made meaningful' with reference to the ends towards which they are conceived to conduce, whereas moods are 'made meaningful' with reference to the conditions from which they are conceived to spring" (97). Now, a Christian might say that this is not their essence, because religious symbols, even when failing to produce moods and motivations, are still religious (i.e., true) symbols—that religious symbols possess a truth independent of their effectiveness. Yet surely even a committed Christian cannot be unconcerned at the existence of truthful symbols that appear to be largely powerless in modern society. He will rightly want to ask: What are the conditions in which religious symbols can actually produce religious dispositions? Or, as a nonbeliever would put it: How does (religious) power create (religious) truth?

---

function when, and to the extent that, they have for their effect to regulate, maintain and transmit from one generation to another sentiments on which the constitution of society depends" (1952, 157).

10. Some ways in which symbolization (discourse) can *disguise lack of distinctiveness* are well brought out in MacIntyre's trenchant critique of contemporary Christian writers, where he argues that "Christians behave like everyone else but use a different vocabulary in characterising their behaviour, and also to conceal their lack of distinctiveness" (1971, 24).

11. The phenomenon of declining church attendance in modern industrial society and its progressive marginalization (in Europe, at least) to those sectors of the population not directly involved in the industrial work process illustrates the argument that if we must look for causal explanations in this area, then socioeconomic conditions in general will appear to be the independent variable and formal worship the dependent. See the interesting discussion in Luckman 1967, chap. 2.

The relation between power and truth is an ancient theme, and no one has dealt with it more impressively in Christian thought than St. Augustine. Augustine developed his views on the creative religious function of power after his experience with the Donatist heresy, insisting that coercion was a condition for the realization of truth, and discipline essential to its maintenance.

For a Donatist, Augustine's attitude to coercion was a blatant denial of Christian teaching: God had made men free to choose good or evil; a policy which forced this choice was plainly irreligious. The Donatist writers quoted the same passages from the Bible in favour of free will, as Pelagius would later quote. In his reply, Augustine already gave them the same answer as he would give to the Pelagians: the final, individual act of choice must be spontaneous; but this act of choice could be prepared by a long process, which men did not necessarily choose for themselves, but which was often imposed on them, against their will, by God. This was a corrective process of "teaching," *eruditio,* and warning, *admonitio,* which might even include fear, constraint, and external inconveniences: "Let constraint be found outside; it is inside that the will is born."

Augustine had become convinced that men needed such firm handling. He summed up his attitude in one word: *disciplina.* He thought of this *disciplina,* not as many of his more traditional Roman contemporaries did, as the static preservation of a "Roman way of life." For him it was an essentially active process of corrective punishment, "a softening-up process," a "teaching by inconveniences"—*a per molestias eruditio.* In the Old Testament, God had taught his wayward Chosen People through just such a process of *disciplina,* checking and punishing their evil tendencies by a whole series of divinely-ordained disasters. The persecution of the Donatists was another "controlled catastrophe" imposed by God, mediated, on this occasion, by the laws of the Christian Emperors. . . .

Augustine's view of the Fall of mankind determined his attitude to society. Fallen men had come to need restraint. Even man's greatest achievements had been made possible only by a "straight-jacket" of unremitting harshness. Augustine was a great intellect, with a healthy respect for the achievements of human reason. Yet he was obsessed by the difficulties of thought, and by the long, coercive processes, reaching back into the horrors of his own schooldays, that had made this intellectual activity possible; so "ready to lie down" was the fallen human mind. He said he would rather die than become a child again. Nonetheless, the terrors of that time had been strictly necessary; for they were part of the awesome discipline of God, "from the schoolmasters' canes to the agonies of the martyrs," by which human beings were recalled, by suffering, from their own disastrous inclinations. (Brown 1967, 236–38)

Isn't Geertz's formula too simple to accommodate the force of this religious symbolism? Note that here it is not mere symbols that implant true Christian dispositions, but power—ranging all the way from laws (imperial and ecclesiastical) and other sanctions (hellfire, death, salvation, good repute, peace) to the disciplinary activities of social institutions (family, school, city, church) and of human bodies (fasting, prayer, obedience, penance). Augustine was quite clear that power, the effect of an entire network of motivated practices, assumes a religious form because of the end to which it is directed, for human events are the instruments of God. It was not the mind that moved spontaneously to religious truth, but power that created the conditions for experiencing that truth.[12] Particular discourses and practices were to be systematically excluded, forbidden, denounced—made as much as possible unthinkable; others were to be included, allowed, praised, and drawn into the narrative of sacred truth. The configurations of power in this sense have, of course, varied profoundly in Christendom from one epoch to another—from Augustine's time, through the Middle Ages, to the industrial capitalist West of today. The patterns of religious moods and motivations, the possibilities for religious knowledge and truth, have all varied with them and been conditioned by them. Even Augustine held that although religious truth was eternal, the means for securing human access to it were not.

From Reading Symbols to Analyzing Practices

One consequence of assuming a symbolic system separate from practices is that important distinctions are sometimes obscured, or even explicitly denied. "That the symbols or symbol systems which

12. This was why Augustine eventually came around to the view that insincere conversion was not a problem (Chadwick 1967, 222–24).

induce and define dispositions we set off as religious and those which place these dispositions in a cosmic framework are the same symbols ought to occasion no surprise" (Geertz, 98). But it does surprise! Let us grant that religious dispositions are crucially dependent on certain religious symbols, that such symbols operate in a way integral to religious motivation and religious mood. Even so, the symbolic process by which the concepts of religious motivation and mood are placed within "a cosmic framework" is surely quite a different operation, and therefore the signs involved are quite different. Put another way, theological discourse is not identical with either moral attitudes or liturgical discourses—of which, among other things, theology speaks.[13] Thoughtful Christians will concede that, although theology has an essential function, theological discourse does not necessarily induce religious dispositions, and that, conversely, having religious dispositions does not necessarily depend on a clear-cut conception of the cosmic framework on the part of a religious actor. Discourse involved in practice is not the same as that involved in speaking about practice. It is a modern idea that a practitioner cannot know how to live religiously without being able to articulate that knowledge.

Geertz's reason for merging the two kinds of discursive process seems to spring from a wish to distinguish in general between religious and secular dispositions. The statement quoted above is elaborated as follows: "For what else do we mean by saying that a particular mood of awe is religious and not secular, except that it springs from entertaining a conception of all-pervading vitality like mana and not from a visit to the Grand Canyon? Or that a particular case of asceticism is an example of a religious motivation except that it is directed toward the achievement of an unconditioned end like nirvana and not a conditioned one like weight-reduction? If sacred symbols did not at one and the same time induce dispositions in human beings and formulate . . . general ideas of order, then the empirical differentia of religious activity or religious experience would not exist" (98). The argument that a particular disposition is religious partly because it occupies a concep-

13. A modern theologian puts it: "The difference between the professing, proclaiming and orienting way of speaking on the one hand, and descriptive speech on the other, is sometimes formulated as the difference between 'speaking about' and 'speaking to.' As soon as these two ways of speaking are confused, the original and unique character of religious speech, so it is said, is corrupted so that reality-for-the-believer can no longer 'appear' to him as it appears in professing speech" (Luijpen 1973, 90–91).

tual place within a cosmic framework appears plausible, but only because it presupposes a question that must be made explicit: how do
authorizing processes represent practices, utterances, or dispositions
so that they can be discursively related to general (cosmic) ideas of
order? In short, the question pertains to the authorizing process by
which "religion" is created.

The ways in which authorizing discourses, presupposing and ex-
pounding a cosmology, systematically redefined religious spaces have
been of profound importance in the history of Western society. In the
Middle Ages, such discourses ranged over an enormous domain, defining and creating religion: rejecting "pagan" practices or accepting
them;[14] authenticating particular miracles and relics (the two confirmed each other);[15] authorizing shrines;[16] compiling saints' lives,

14. The series of booklets known as Penitential manuals, with the aid of which Christian discipline was imposed on Western Europe from roughly the fifth to the tenth
centuries, contains much material on pagan practices penalized as un-Christian. So, for
example, "The taking of vows or releasing from them by springs or trees or lattices,
anywhere except in a church, and partaking of food or drink in these places sacred to the
folk-deities, are offenses condemned" (quoted in McNeill 1933, 456). (For further details, see McNeill and Gamer 1938.) At the same time, Pope Gregory the Great (A.D.
540-604) "urged that the Church should take over old pagan temples and festivals and
give them a Christian meaning" (Chadwick 1967, 254). The apparent inconsistency of
these two attitudes (rejection or incorporation of pagan practices) is less important
than the systematic exercise of Church authority by which meaning was assigned.

15. "On the one hand, then, bishops complained of crude and too-avid beliefs in
unauthorized and unexamined wonders and miracles, while on the other theologians
(possibly also these same bishops) tried to come to terms with the matter. Although
they attempted to define miracle by appeals to universal natural law, such definitions
were not entirely successful, and in specific, individual cases, common sense was a better guide than medieval cosmology. When papal commissioners sat down to hear testi-
mony about Thomas Cantilupe's miracles at London and Hereford in 1307 they had in
front of them a schedule of things to ask about such wondrous events: they wanted to
know, for example, how the witness came to learn of the miracle, what words were used
by those who prayed for the miracle, whether any herbs, stones, other natural or medicinal preparations or incantations had accompanied the miracle; the witness was expected
to say something about the age and social situation of the person experiencing the miracle, where he came from and of what family; whether the witness knew the subject
before as well as after the miracle, what illness was involved, how many days he had seen
the ill person before the cure; whether the cure was complete and how long it took for
completion. Of course witnesses were also asked what year, month, day, place and in
whose presence the wonderful event itself occurred" (Finucane 1977, 53).

16. By being authorized, shrines in turn served to confirm ecclesiastical authority:
"The bishops of Western Europe came to orchestrate the cult of the saints in such a way
as to base their power within the old Roman cities on these new 'towns outside the
town.' Yet it was through a studiously articulated relationship with great shrines that

both as a model of and as a model for the Truth;[17] requiring the regular telling of sinful thoughts, words, and deeds to a priestly confessor and giving absolution to a penitent;[18] regularizing popular social movements into Rule-following Orders (for example, the Franciscans), or denouncing them for heresy or for verging on the heretical (for example, the Beguines).[19] The medieval Church did not attempt to establish absolute uniformity of practice; on the contrary, its authoritative discourse was always concerned to specify differences, gradations, exceptions. What it sought was the subjection of all practice to a unified authority, to a single authentic source that could tell truth from falsehood. It was the early Christian Fathers who established the principle that only a single Church could become the source of authenticating discourse.[20] They knew that the "symbols" embodied in the

---

lay at some distance from the city—St. Peter's, on the Vatican Hill outside Rome, Saint Martin's, a little beyond the walls of Tours—that the bishops of the former cities of the Roman Empire rose to prominence in early medieval Europe" (Brown 1981, 8).

17. The life of St. Antony by Athanasius was the model for medieval hagiographies, and the Antonine sequence of early life, crisis and conversion, probation and temptation, privation and renunciation, miraculous power, together with knowledge and authority, was reproduced again and again in that literature (Baker 1972, 41).

18. The Lateran Council of 1215 declared that annual private confession should be mandatory for all Christians: "Every *fidelis* of either sex shall after the attainment of years of discretion separately confess his sins with all fidelity to his priest at least once in the year: and shall endeavour to fulfil the penance imposed upon him to the best of his ability, reverently receiving the sacrament of the Eucharist at least at Easter: unless it happens that by the counsel of his own priest for some reasonable cause, he hold that he should abstain for a time from the reception of the sacrament: otherwise let him during life be repelled from entering the church, and when dead let him lack Christian burial. Wherefore let this salutary statute be frequently published in churches, lest any assume a veil of excuse in the blindness of ignorance" (quoted in Watkins 1920, 748–49).

19. For a brief introduction to the varying reaction of ecclesiastical authority to the Franciscans and the Beguines, see Southern 1970, chaps. 6, 7. "Beguines" was the name given to groups of celibate women dedicated to the religious life but not owing obedience to ecclesiastical authority. They flourished in the towns of western Germany and the Low Countries but were criticized, denounced, and finally suppressed in the early fifteenth century.

20. Thus, Cyprian: "If a man does not hold this unity of the Church, does he believe himself to hold the faith? If a man withstands and resists the Church, is he confident that he is in the Church? For the blessed Apostle Paul has the same teaching, and sets forth the sacrament of unity, when he says, 'There is one body, one Spirit, one hope of our calling, one Lord, one faith, one baptism, one God.' This unity we ought firmly to hold and defend, especially we who preside in the Church as bishops that we may prove the episcopate also to be itself one and undivided. Let no one deceive the brethren by falsehood; let no one corrupt the truth of our faith by faithless transgression" (quoted in Bettenson 1956, 264).

practice of self-confessed Christians are not always identical with the theory of the "one true Church," that religion requires authorized practice and authorizing doctrine, and that there is always a tension between them—sometimes breaking into heresy, the subversion of Truth—which underlines the creative role of institutional power.[21]

The medieval Church was always clear about why there was a continuous need to distinguish knowledge from falsehood (religion from what sought to subvert it), as well as the sacred from the profane (religion from what was outside it), distinctions for which the authoritative discourses, the teachings and practices of the Church, not the convictions of the practitioner, were the final test.[22] Several times before the Reformation, the boundary between the religious and the secular was redrawn, but always the formal authority of the Church remained preeminent. In later centuries, with the triumphant rise of modern science, modern production, and the modern state, the churches would also be clear about the need to distinguish the religious from the secular, shifting, as they did so, the weight of religion more and more onto the moods and motivations of the individual believer. Discipline (intellectual and social) would, in this period, gradually abandon religious space, letting "belief," "conscience," and "sensibility" take its place.[23] *But theory would still be needed to define religion.*

21. The Church always exercised the authority to read Christian *practice* for its religious truth. In this context, it is interesting that the word *heresy* at first designated all kinds of errors, including errors "unconsciously" involved in some activity *(simoniaca haersis)*, and it acquired its specific modern meaning (the verbal formulation of denial or doubt of any defined doctrine of the Catholic church) only in the course of the methodological controversies of the sixteenth century (Chenu 1968, 276).

22. In the early Middle Ages, monastic discipline was the principal basis of religiosity. Knowles (1963, 3) observes that from roughly the sixth to the twelfth centuries, "monastic life based on the Rule of St. Benedict was everywhere the norm and exercised from time to time a paramount influence on the spiritual, intellectual, liturgical and apostolic life of the Western Church. . . . the only type of religious life available in the countries concerned was monastic, and the only monastic code was the Rule of St. Benedict." During the period the very term *religious* was therefore reserved for those living in monastic communities; with the later emergence of nonmonastic orders, the term came to be used for all who had taken lifelong vows by which they were set apart from the ordinary members of the Church (Southern 1970, 214). The extension and simultaneous transformation of the religious disciplines to lay sections of society from the twelfth century onward (Chenu 1968) contributed to the Church's authority becoming more pervasive, more complex, and more contradictory than before—and so too the articulation of the concept and practice of lay religion.

23. Thus enabling the Victorian anthropologist and biblical scholar Robertson Smith to say that in the age of scientific historiography, "it will no longer be the results of

The Construction of Religion in Early Modern Europe

It was in the seventeenth century, following the fragmentation of the unity and authority of the Roman church and the consequent wars of religion, which tore European principalities apart, that the earliest systematic attempts at producing a universal definition of religion were made. Herbert's *De veritate* was a significant step in this definitional history. "Lord Herbert," writes Willey,

> differs from such men as Baxter, Cromwell, or Jeremy Taylor mainly in that, not content with reducing the creed to the minimum number possible of fundamentals, he goes behind Christianity itself, and tries to formulate a belief which shall command the universal assent of all men as men. It must be remembered that the old simple situation, in which Christendom pictured itself as the world, with only the foul paynim outside and the semi-tolerated Jews within the gates, had passed away for ever. Exploration and commerce had widened the horizon, and in many writers of the century one can see that the religions of the East, however imperfectly known, were beginning to press upon the European consciousness. It was a pioneer-interest in these religions, together with the customary preoccupation of Renaissance scholars with the mythologies of classical antiquity, which led Lord Herbert to seek a common denominator for all religions, and thus to provide, as he hoped, the much-needed eirenicon for seventeenth-century disputes. (1934, 114)

Thus, Herbert produced a substantive definition of what later came to be formulated as Natural Religion—in terms of beliefs (about a supreme power), practices (its ordered worship), and ethics (a code of conduct based on rewards and punishments after this life)—said to exist in all societies.[24] This emphasis on belief meant that henceforth

---

theology that we are required to defend, but something prior to theology. What we shall have to defend is not our Christian knowledge, but our Christian belief" (1912, 110). Christian belief is no longer expected to fasten on the Bible as divine revelation but as "the record of divine revelation—the record of those historical facts in which God has revealed himself to man" (1912, 123). Therefore, the principles of historical interpretation were no longer strictly Christian, only the beliefs which that interpretation served.

24. When Christian missionaries found themselves in culturally unfamiliar territory, the problem of identifying "religion" became a matter of considerable theoretical difficulty and practical importance. For example, "The Jesuits in China contended that the reverence for ancestors was a social, not a religious, act, or that if religious, it was

religion could be conceived as a set of propositions to which believers gave assent, and which could therefore be judged and compared as between different religions and as against natural science (Harrison 1990).

The idea of scripture (a divinely produced/interpreted text) was not essential to this "common denominator" of religions partly because Christians had become more familiar, through trade and colonization, with societies that lacked writing. But a more important reason lies in the shift in attention that occurred in the seventeenth century from God's words to God's works. "Nature" became the real space of divine writing, and eventually the indisputable authority for the truth of all sacred texts written in merely human language (the Old Testament and the New). Thus:

> Locke's *The Reasonableness of Christianity* popularized a new version of Christianity by reducing its doctrine to the lowest common denominator of belief in Jesus as the Messiah, whose advent had been foretold in the prophecies of the Old Testament. Even this reduced creed was to be measured against the background of Natural Religion and of the Religion of Natural Science, so that Revelation in addition to being required to justify itself by Locke's standard, had to present itself as a republication of Natural Religion. For a time indeed the Word of God assumed a secondary position to his works as set forth in the created universe. For whereas the testimony of the latter was universal and ubiquitous, the evidence of Revelation was confined to sacred books written in dead languages, whose interpretation was not agreed even amongst professed Christians, and which related moreover to distant events which had occurred in remote times and in places far removed from the centres of learning and civilization. (Sykes 1975, 195–96)

---

hardly different from Catholic prayers for the dead. They wished the Chinese to regard Christianity, not as a replacement, not as a new religion, but as the highest fulfillment of their finest aspirations. But to their opponents the Jesuits appeared to be merely lax. In 1631 a Franciscan and a Dominican from the Spanish zone of Manila travelled (illegally, from the Portuguese viewpoint) to Peking and found that to translate the word *mass*, the Jesuit catechism used the character *tsi*, which was the Chinese description of the ceremonies of ancestor-worship. One night they went in disguise to such a ceremony, observed Chinese Christians participating and were scandalized at what they saw. So began the quarrel of 'the rites,' which plagued the eastern missions for a century and more" (Chadwick 1964, 338).

In this way, Natural Religion not only became a universal phenomenon but began to be demarcated from, and was also supportive of, a newly emerging domain of natural science. I want to emphasize that the idea of Natural Religion was a crucial step in the formation of the modern concept of religious belief, experience, and practice, and that it was an idea developed in response to problems specific to Christian theology at a particular historical juncture.

By 1795, Kant was able to produce a fully essentialized idea of religion which could be counterposed to its phenomenal forms: "There may certainly be different historical *confessions*," he wrote,

> although these have nothing to do with religion itself but only with changes in the means used to further religion, and are thus the province of historical research. And there may be just as many religious *books* (the Zend-Avesta, the Vedas, the Koran, etc.). But there can only be *one religion* which is valid for all men and at all times. Thus the different confessions can scarcely be more than the vehicles of religion; these are fortuitous, and may vary with differences in time or place. (Kant 1991, 114)

From here, the classification of historical confessions into lower and higher religions became an increasingly popular option for philosophers, theologians, missionaries, and anthropologists in the nineteenth and twentieth centuries. As to whether any particular tribe has existed without any form of religion whatever was often raised as a question,[25] but this was recognized as an empirical matter not affecting the essence of religion itself.

Thus, what appears to anthropologists today to be self-evident, namely that religion is essentially a matter of symbolic meanings linked to ideas of general order (expressed through either or both rite and doctrine), that it has generic functions/features, and that it must not be confused with any of its particular historical or cultural forms, is in fact a view that has a specific Christian history. From being a concrete set of practical rules attached to specific processes of power and knowledge, religion has come to be abstracted and universalized.[26] In this movement we have not merely an increase in religious toleration, cer-

---

25. For example, by Tylor in the chapter "Animism" in part 2 of *Primitive Culture*.
26. Phases in the gradual evacuation of specificity from public religious discourse in the eighteenth century are described in some detail in Gay 1973.

tainly not merely a new scientific discovery, but the mutation of a concept and a range of social practices which is itself part of a wider change in the modern landscape of power and knowledge. That change included a new kind of state, a new kind of science, a new kind of legal and moral subject. To understand this mutation it is essential to keep clearly distinct that which theology tends to obscure: the occurrence of events (utterances, practices, dispositions) and the authorizing processes that give those events meaning and embody that meaning in concrete institutions.

Religion as Meaning and Religious Meanings

The equation between two levels of discourse (symbols that induce dispositions and those that place the idea of those dispositions discursively in a cosmic framework) is not the only problematic thing in this part of Geertz's discussion. He also appears, inadvertently, to be taking up the standpoint of theology. This happens when he insists on the primacy of meaning without regard to the processes by which meanings are constructed. "What any particular religion affirms about the fundamental nature of reality may be obscure, shallow, or, all too often, perverse," he writes, "but it must, if it is not to consist of the mere collection of received practices and conventional sentiments we usually refer to as moralism, affirm something" (98–99).

The requirement of affirmation is apparently innocent and logical, but through it the entire field of evangelism was historically opened up, in particular the work of European missionaries in Asia, Africa, and Latin America. The demand that the received practices must *affirm something about the fundamental nature of reality,* that it should therefore always be possible to state meanings for them which are not plain nonsense, is the first condition for determining whether they belong to "religion." The unevangelized come to be seen typically either as those who have practices but affirm nothing, in which case meaning can be attributed to their practices (thus making them vulnerable), or as those who do affirm something (probably "obscure, shallow, or perverse"), an affirmation that can therefore be dismissed. In the one case, religious theory becomes necessary for a correct reading of the mute ritual hieroglyphics of others, for reducing their practices to texts; in the other, it is essential for judging the validity of their cosmological utterances. But always, there must be something that exists beyond the observed practices, the heard utterances, the written words, and it is the function of religious theory to reach into, and to bring out, that background by giving them meaning.[27]

Geertz is thus right to make a connection between religious theory and practice, but wrong to see it as essentially cognitive, as a means by which a disembodied mind can identify religion from an Archimedean point. The connection between religious theory and practice is fundamentally a matter of intervention—of constructing religion in the world (not in the mind) through definitional discourses, interpreting true meanings, excluding some utterances and practices and including others. Hence my repeated question: how does theoretical discourse actually define religion? What are the historical conditions in which it can act effectively as a demand for the imitation, or the

27. The way in which representations of occurrences were transformed into meanings by Christian theology is analyzed by Auerbach in his classic study of representations of reality in Western literature and briefly summed up in this passage: "The total content of the sacred writings was placed in an exegetic context which often removed the thing told very far away from its sensory base, in that the reader or listener was forced to turn his attention away from the sensory occurrence and toward its meaning. This implied the danger that the visual element of the occurrences might succumb under the dense texture of meanings. Let one example stand for many: It is a visually dramatic occurrence that God made Eve, the first woman, from Adam's rib while Adam lay asleep; so too is it that a soldier pierced Jesus' side, as he hung dead on the cross, so that blood and water flowed out. But when these two occurrences are exegetically interrelated in the doctrine that Adam's sleep is a figure of Christ's death-sleep; that, as from the wound in Adam's side mankind's primordial mother after the flesh, Eve, was born, so from the wound in Christ's side was born the mother of all men after the spirit, the Church (blood and water are sacramental symbols)—then the sensory occurrence pales before the power of the figural meaning. What is perceived by the hearer or reader . . . is weak as a sensory impression, and all one's interest is directed toward the context of meanings. In comparison, the Greco-Roman specimens of realistic presentation are, though less serious and fraught with problems and far more limited in their conception of historical movement, nevertheless perfectly integrated in their sensory substance. They do not know the antagonism between sensory appearance and meaning, an antagonism which permeates the early, and indeed the whole, Christian view of reality" (1953, 48–49). As Auerbach goes on to demonstrate, Christian theory in the later Middle Ages invested representations of everyday life with characteristic figural meanings, and so with the possibilities for distinctive kinds of religious experience. Figural interpretation, in Auerbach's usage, is not synonymous with symbolism. The latter is close to allegory, in which the symbol is substituted for the object symbolized. In figural interpretation the representation of an event (Adam's sleep) is made explicit by the representation of another event (Christ's death) that is its meaning. The latter representation fulfills the former (the technical term, Auerbach tells us, was *figuram implire*)—it is *implicit* in it.

prohibition, or the authentication of truthful utterances and practices? How does power create religion?

What kinds of affirmation, of meaning, must be identified with
practice in order for it to qualify as religion? According to Geertz, it is
because all human beings have a profound need for a general order of
existence that religious symbols function to fulfill that need. It follows that human beings have a deep dread of disorder. "There are at
least three points where chaos—a tumult of events which lack not just
interpretations but *interpretability*—threatens to break in upon man: at
the limits of his analytic capabilities, at the limits of his powers of
endurance, and at the limits of his moral insight" (100). It is the function of religious symbols to meet perceived threats to order at each of
these points (intellectual, physical, and moral): "The Problem of Meaning in each of its intergrading aspects . . . is a matter of affirming, or at
least recognizing, the inescapability of ignorance, pain, and injustice
on the human plane while simultaneously denying that these irration-
alities are characteristic of the world as a whole. And it is in terms of
religious symbolism, a symbolism relating man's sphere of existence to
a wider sphere within which it is conceived to rest, that both the
affirmation and the denial are made" (108).

Notice how the reasoning seems now to have shifted its ground
from the claim that religion must affirm something specific about the
nature of reality (however obscure, shallow, or perverse) to the bland
suggestion that religion is ultimately a matter of having a positive attitude toward the problem of disorder, of affirming simply that in some
sense or other the world as a whole is explicable, justifiable, bear-
able.[28] This modest view of religion (which would have horrified the
early Christian Fathers or medieval churchmen)[29] is a product of the
only legitimate space allowed to Christianity by post-Enlightenment
society, the right to individual *belief*: the human condition is full of

28. Cf. Douglas (1975, 76): "The person without religion would be the person content to do without explanations of certain kinds, or content to behave in society without a single unifying principle validating the social order."

29. When the fifth-century bishop of Javols spread Christianity into the Auvergne,
he found the peasants "celebrating a three-day festival with offerings on the edge of a
marsh. . . . 'Nulla est religio in stagno,' he said: There can be no religion in a swamp"
(Brown 1981, 125). For medieval Christians, religion was not a universal phenomenon:
religion was a site on which universal truth was produced, and it was clear to them that
truth was not produced universally.

ignorance, pain, and injustice, and religious symbols are a means of coming positively to terms with that condition. One consequence is that this view would in principle render any philosophy that performs such a function into religion (to the annoyance of the nineteenth-century rationalist), or alternatively, make it possible to think of religion as a more primitive, a less adult mode of coming to terms with the human condition (to the annoyance of the modern Christian). In either case, the suggestion that religion has a universal function in belief is one indication of how marginal religion has become in modern industrial society as the site for producing disciplined knowledge and personal discipline. As such it comes to resemble the conception Marx had of religion as ideology—that is, as a mode of consciousness which is other than consciousness of reality, external to the relations of production, producing no knowledge, but expressing at once the anguish of the oppressed and a spurious consolation.

Geertz has much more to say, however, on the elusive question of religious meaning: not only do religious symbols formulate conceptions of a general order of existence, they also clothe those conceptions with an aura of factuality. This, we are told, is "the problem of belief." *Religious belief* always involves "the prior acceptance of authority," which transforms experience: "The existence of bafflement, pain, and moral paradox—of the Problem of Meaning—is one of the things that drives men toward belief in gods, devils, spirits, totemic principles, or the spiritual efficacy of cannibalism, . . . but it is not the basis upon which those beliefs rest, but rather their most important field of application" (109). This seems to imply that religious belief stands independently of the worldly conditions that produce bafflement, pain, and moral paradox, although that belief is primarily a way of coming to terms with them. But surely this is mistaken, on logical grounds as well as historical, for changes in the object of belief change that belief; and as the world changes, so do the objects of belief and the specific forms of bafflement and moral paradox that are a part of that world. What the Christian believes today about God, life after death, the universe, is not what he believed a millennium ago—nor is the way he responds to ignorance, pain, and injustice the same now as it was then. The medieval valorization of pain as the mode of participating in Christ's suffering contrasts sharply with the modern Catholic perception of pain as an evil to be fought against and overcome as Christ the Healer did. That difference is clearly related to the post-Enlightenment secularization of Western society and to the moral language which that society now authorizes.[30]

Geertz's treatment of religious belief, which lies at the core of his conception of religion, is a modern, privatized Christian one because and to the extent that it emphasizes the priority of belief as a state of mind rather than as constituting activity in the world: "The basic axiom underlying what we may perhaps call 'the religious perspective' is everywhere the same: he who would know must first believe" (110). In modern society, where knowledge is rooted either in an a-Christian everyday life or in an a-religious science, the Christian apologist tends not to regard belief as the conclusion to a knowledge process but as its precondition. However, the knowledge that he promises will not pass (nor, in fairness, does he claim that it will pass) for knowledge of social life, still less for the systematic knowledge of objects that natural science provides. Her claim is to a particular state of mind, a sense of conviction, not to a corpus of practical knowledge. But the reversal of belief and knowledge she demands was not a basic axiom to, say, pious learned Christians of the twelfth century, for whom knowledge and belief were not so clearly at odds. On the contrary, Christian belief would then have been built on knowledge—knowledge of theological doctrine, of canon law and Church courts, of the details of clerical liberties, of the powers of ecclesiastical office (over souls, bodies, properties), of the preconditions and effects of confession, of the rules of religious orders, of the locations and virtues of shrines, of the lives of the saints, and so forth. Familiarity with all such (religious) knowledge was a precondition for normal social life, and belief (embodied in practice and discourse) an orientation for effective activity in it—whether on the part of the religious clergy, the secular clergy, or the laity. Because of this, the form and texture and function of their beliefs would have been different from the form and texture and function of contemporary belief—and so too of their doubts and their disbelief.

30. As a contemporary Catholic theologian puts it: "The secularistic challenge, even though separating many aspects of life from the religious field, brings with it a more sound, interpretative equilibrium: the natural phenomena, even though sometimes difficult to understand, have their cause and roots in processes that can and must be recognized. It is man's job, therefore, to enter into this cognitive analysis of the meaning of suffering, in order to be able to affront and conquer it. The contemporary condition of man, of the believer on the threshold of the third millennium, is undoubtedly more adult and more mature and allows a new approach to the problem of human suffering" (Autiero 1987, 124).

The assumption that belief is a distinctive mental state characteristic of all religions has been the subject of discussion by contemporary scholars. Thus, Needham (1972) has interestingly argued that belief
is nowhere a distinct mode of consciousness, nor a necessary institution for the conduct of social life. Southwold (1979) takes an almost
diametrically opposed view, asserting that questions of belief do relate
to distinctive mental states and that they are relevant in any and every
society, since "to believe" always designates a relation between a believer and a proposition and through it to reality. Harré (1981, 82), in a
criticism of Needham, makes the more persuasive case that "belief is a
mental state, a grounded disposition, but it is confined to people who
have certain social institutions and practices."

At any rate, I think it is not too unreasonable to maintain that
"the basic axiom" underlying what Geertz calls "the religious perspective" is *not* everywhere the same. It is preeminently the Christian
church that has occupied itself with identifying, cultivating, and testing belief as a verbalizable inner condition of true religion.[31]

Religion as a Perspective

The phenomenological vocabulary that Geertz employs raises two
interesting questions, one regarding its coherence and the other concerning its adequacy to a modern cognitivist notion of religion. I want
to suggest that although this vocabulary is theoretically incoherent, it
is socially quite compatible with the privatized idea of religion in modern society.

Thus, "the religious perspective," we are told, is one among several—common-sense, scientific, aesthetic—and it differs from these as
follows. It differs from the *common-sense* perspective, because it "moves
beyond the realities of everyday life to wider ones which correct and
complete them, and [because] its defining concern is not action upon
those wider realities but acceptance of them, faith in them." It is
unlike the *scientific* perspective, because "it questions the realities of
everyday life not out of an institutionalized scepticism which dissolves
the world's givenness into a swirl of probabilistic hypotheses, but in
terms of what it takes to be wider, nonhypothetical truths." And it is
distinguished from the *aesthetic* perspective, because "instead of ef-

31. I have attempted a description of one aspect of this process in Asad 1986b.

fecting a disengagement from the whole question of factuality, deliberately manufacturing an air of semblance and illusion, it deepens the concern with fact and seeks to create an aura of utter actuality" (112). In other words, although the religious perspective is not exactly rational, it is not irrational either.

It would not be difficult to state one's disagreement with this summary of what common sense, science, and aesthetics are about.[32] But my point is that the optional flavor conveyed by the term *perspective* is surely misleading when it is applied equally to science and to religion in modern society: religion is indeed now optional in a way that science is not. Scientific practices, techniques, knowledges, permeate and create the very fibers of social life in ways that religion no longer does.[33] In that sense, religion today *is* a perspective (or an "attitude," as Geertz sometimes calls it), but science is not. In that sense, too, science is not to be found in every society, past and present. We shall see in a moment the difficulties that Geertz's perspectivism gets him into, but before that I need to examine his analysis of the mechanics of reality maintenance at work in religion.

Consistent with previous arguments about the functions of reli-

32. Philosophical attempts to define science have not reached a firm consensus. In the Anglo-Saxon world, recent arguments have been formulated in and around the works of Popper, Kuhn, Lakatos, Feyerabend, Hacking, and others; in France, those of Bachelard and Canguilhem. One important tendency has been to abandon the attempt at solving what is known in the literature as the demarcation problem, which is based on the assumption that there must be a single, essential, scientific method. The idea that the scientist "dissolves the world's givenness into a swirl of probabilistic hypotheses" is as questionable as the complementary suggestion that in religion there is no scope for experimentation. On this latter point, there is massive evidence of experiment, even if we went no farther than the history of Christian asceticism. Equally, the suggestion that art is a matter of "effecting a disengagement from the whole question of factuality, deliberately manufacturing an air of semblance and illusion" would not be taken as self-evident by all writers and artists. For example, when the art critic John Berger argues, in his brilliant essay "The Moment of Cubism," that cubism "changed the nature of the relationship between the painted image and reality, and by so doing expressed a new relationship between man and reality" (1972, 145), we learn something about cubism's concern to redefine visual factuality.

33. In case some readers are tempted to think that what I am talking about is not science (theory) but technology (practical application), whereas Geertz is concerned only with the former, I would stress that any attempt to make a sharp distinction between the two is based on an oversimplified view of the historical practice of both (cf. Musson and Robinson 1969). My point is that science and technology *together* are basic to the structure of modern lives, individual and collective, and that religion, in any but the most vacuous sense, is not.

gious symbols is Geertz's remark that "it is in ritual—that is, consecrated behavior—that this conviction that religious conceptions are
veridical and that religious directives are sound is somehow generated"
(112). The long passage from which this is taken swings back and forth
between arbitrary speculations about what goes on in the consciousness of officiants and unfounded assertions about ritual as imprinting.
At first sight, this seems a curious combination of introspectionist
psychology with a behaviorist one—but as Vygotsky (1978, 58–59) argued long ago, the two are by no means inconsistent, insofar as both
assume that psychological phenomena consist essentially in the consequence of various stimulating environments.

Geertz postulates the function of rituals in generating religious
conviction ("In these plastic dramas men attain their faith as they
portray it" [114]), but how or why this happens is nowhere explained.
Indeed, he concedes that such a religious state is not always achieved in
religious ritual: "Of course, all cultural performances are not religious
performances, and the line between those that are, and artistic, or
even political, ones is often not so easy to draw in practice, for, like
social forms, symbolic forms can serve multiple purposes" (113). But
the question remains: What is it that ensures the participant's taking
the symbolic forms in the way that leads to faith if the line between
religious and nonreligious perspectives is not so easy to draw? Mustn't
the ability and the will to adopt a religious standpoint be present prior
to the ritual performance? That is precisely why a simple stimulus-
response model of how ritual works will not do. And if that is the case,
then ritual in the sense of a sacred performance cannot be the place
where religious faith is attained, but the manner in which it is (literally) played out. If we are to understand how this happens, we must
examine not only the sacred performance itself but also the entire
range of available disciplinary activities, of institutional forms of knowledge and practice, within which dispositions are formed and sustained
and through which the possibilities of attaining the truth are marked
out—as Augustine clearly saw.

I have noted more than once Geertz's concern to define religious
symbols according to universal, cognitive criteria, to distinguish the
religious perspective clearly from nonreligious ones. The separation of
religion from science, common sense, aesthetics, politics, and so on,
allows him to defend it against charges of irrationality. If religion has a
distinctive perspective (its own truth, as Durkheim would have said)

and performs an indispensable function, it does not in essence compete with others and cannot, therefore, be accused of generating false consciousness. Yet in a way this defense is equivocal. Religious symbols create dispositions, Geertz observes, which seem uniquely realistic. Is this the point of view of a reasonably confident agent (who must always operate within the denseness of historically given probabilities) or that of a skeptical observer (who can see through the representations of reality to the reality itself)? It is never clear. And it is never clear because this kind of phenomenological approach doesn't make it easy to examine whether, and if so to what extent and in what ways, religious experience relates to something in the real world that believers inhabit. This is partly because religious symbols are treated, in circular fashion, as the precondition for religious experience (which, like any experience, must, by definition, be genuine), rather than as one condition for engaging with life.

Toward the end of his essay, Geertz attempts to connect, instead of separating, the religious perspective and the common-sense one—and the result reveals an ambiguity basic to his entire approach. First, invoking Schutz, Geertz states that the everyday world of common-sense objects and practical acts is common to all human beings because their survival depends on it: "A man, even large groups of men, may be aesthetically insensitive, religiously unconcerned, and unequipped to pursue formal scientific analysis, but he cannot be completely lacking in common sense and survive" (119). Next, he informs us that individuals move "back and forth between the religious perspective and the common-sense perspective" (119). These perspectives are so utterly different, he declares, that only "Kierkegaardian leaps" (120) can cover the cultural gaps that separate them. Then, the phenomenological conclusion: "Having ritually 'leapt' . . . into the framework of meaning which religious conceptions define, and the ritual ended, returned again to the common-sense world, a man is—unless, as sometimes happens, the experience fails to register—changed. *And as he is changed, so also is the common-sense world,* for it is now seen as but the partial form of a wider reality which corrects and completes it" (122; emphasis added).

This curious account of shifting perspectives and changing worlds is puzzling—as indeed it is in Schutz himself. It is not clear, for example, whether the religious framework and the common-sense world, between which the individual moves, are independent of him or not.

Most of what Geertz has said at the beginning of his essay would imply that they are independent (cf. 92), and his remark about common sense being vital to every man's survival also enforces this reading. Yet it is also suggested that as the believer changes his perspective, so he himself changes; and that as he changes, so too is his common-sense world changed and corrected. So the latter, at any rate, is not independent of his moves. But it would appear from the account that the religious world *is* independent, since it is the source of distinctive experience for the believer, and through that experience, a source of change in the common-sense world: there is no suggestion anywhere that the religious world (or perspective) is ever affected by experience in the common-sense world.

This last point is consistent with the phenomenological approach in which religious symbols are sui generis, marking out an independent religious domain. But in the present context it presents the reader with a paradox: the world of common sense is always common to all human beings, and quite distinct from the religious world, which in turn differs from one group to another, as one culture differs from another; but experience of the religious world affects the common-sense world, and so the distinctiveness of the two kinds of world is modified, and the common-sense world comes to differ, from one group to another, as one culture differs from another. The paradox results from an ambiguous phenomenology in which reality is at once the distance of an agent's social perspective from the truth, measurable only by the privileged observer, and also the substantive knowledge of a socially constructed world available to both agent and observer, but to the latter only through the former.[34]

34. In the introduction to his 1983 collection of essays, Geertz seems to want to abandon this perspectival approach: "The debate over whether [art] is an applicable category in 'non-Western' or 'pre-Modern' contexts has, even when compared to similar debates concerning 'religion,' 'science,' 'ideology,' or 'law,' been peculiarly unrelenting. It has also been peculiarly unproductive. Whatever you want to call a cave wall crowded with overlapping images of transfixed animals, a temple tower shaped to a phallus, a feathered shield, a calligraphic scroll, or a tattooed face, you still have *the phenomenon* to deal with, as well as perhaps the sense that to add kula exchange or the Doomsday Book would be to spoil the series. The question is not whether art (or anything else) is universal; it is whether one can talk about West African carving, New Guinea palm-leaf painting, quattrocento picture making, and Moroccan versifying in such a way as to cause them to shed some sort of light on one another" (1983, 11; emphasis added). The answer to this question must surely be: yes, of course one should try to talk about disparate things in relation to one another, but what exactly is the purpose of

Conclusion

Perhaps we can learn something from this paradox which will help us evaluate Geertz's confident conclusion: "The anthropological study of religion is therefore a two-stage operation: first, an analysis of the system of meanings embodied in the symbols which make up *the religion proper,* and, second, the relating of these systems to social-structural and psychological processes" (125; emphasis added). How sensible this sounds, yet how mistaken, surely, it is. If religious symbols are understood, on the analogy with words, as vehicles for meaning, can such meanings be established independently of the form of life in which they are used? If religious symbols are to be taken as the signatures of a sacred text, can we know what they mean without regard to the social disciplines by which their correct reading is secured? If religious symbols are to be thought of as the concepts by which experiences are organized, can we say much about them without considering how they come to be authorized? Even if it be claimed that what is experienced through religious symbols is not, in essence, the social world but the spiritual,[35] is it possible to assert that conditions in the social world have nothing to do with making that kind of experience accessible? Is the concept of religious training entirely vacuous?

The two stages that Geertz proposes are, I would suggest, one. Religious symbols—whether one thinks of them in terms of communication or of cognition, of guiding action or of expressing emotion— cannot be understood independently of their historical relations with nonreligious symbols or of their articulations in and of social life, in which work and power are always crucial. My argument, I must stress, is not just that religious symbols are intimately linked to social life (and so change with it), or that they usually support dominant political power (and occasionally oppose it). It is that different kinds of practice and discourse are intrinsic to the field in which religious representations (like any representation) acquire their identity and their truth-

---

constructing a series whose items can all easily be recognized by cultivated Westerners as instances of *the phenomenon* of art? Of course, any one thing may shed light on another. But is it not precisely when one abandons conventional perspectives, or preestablished series, for opportunistic comparison that illumination (as opposed to recognition) *may* be achieved? Think of Hofstadter's splendid *Gödel, Escher, Bach* (1979), for instance.

35. Cf. the final chapter in Evans-Pritchard 1956, and also the conclusion to Evans-Pritchard 1965.

fulness. From this it does not follow that the meanings of religious practices and utterances are to be sought in social phenomena, but only that their possibility and their authoritative status are to be explained as products of historically distinctive disciplines and forces. The anthropological student of *particular* religions should therefore begin from this point, in a sense unpacking the comprehensive concept which he or she translates as "religion" into heterogeneous elements according to its historical character.

A final word of caution. Hasty readers might conclude that my discussion of the Christian religion is skewed towards an authoritarian, centralized, elite perspective, and that consequently it fails to take into account the religions of heterodox believers, of resistant peasantries, of all those who cannot be completely controlled by the orthodox church. Or, worse still, that my discussion has no bearing on nondisciplinarian, voluntaristic, localized cults of noncentralized religions such as Hinduism. But that conclusion would be a misunderstanding of this chapter, seeing in it an attempt to advocate a better anthropological definition of religion than Geertz has done. Nothing could be farther from my intention. If my effort reads in large part like a brief sketch of transmutations in Christianity from the Middle Ages until today, then that is not because I have arbitrarily confined my ethnographic examples to one religion. My aim has been to problematize the idea of an anthropological definition of religion by assigning that endeavor to a particular history of knowledge and power (including a particular understanding of our legitimate past and future) out of which the modern world has been constructed.[36]

---

36. Such endeavors are unceasing. As a recent, engaging study by Tambiah (1990, 6) puts it in the first chapter: "In our discussion hereafter I shall try to argue that from a general anthropological standpoint the distinctive feature of religion as a generic concept lies not in the domain of belief and its 'rational accounting' of the workings of the universe, but in a special awareness of the transcendent, and the acts of symbolic communication that attempt to realize that awareness and live by its promptings."

2 ⟨⟨⟨   TOWARD A GENEALOGY
OF THE CONCEPT OF
RITUAL

What the symbolic action is intended to
control is primarily a set of mental and moral
dispositions.
> —Godfrey Lienhardt, *Divinity and Experience*

Every ethnographer will probably recognize a ritual when he or she sees one, because ritual is (is it not?) symbolic activity as opposed to the instrumental behavior of everyday life. There may be some uncertainty and disagreement over matters of explanation, but not in identifying the phenomenon as such (Skorupski 1976). But was this always the case? When did we, as anthropologists, begin to speak of "ritual"? And why did we decide to speak of it in the way we do now? In this chapter, I try to answer these questions in an exploratory way in the hope that this will help identify some conceptual preconditions for our contemporary analyses of religion. I must stress that my primary concern here is not to criticize anthropological theories of ritual, still less to propose or endorse alternatives. It is to try and discover what historical shifts might have made our contemporary concept of ritual plausible.

I begin by examining some general statements on the subject which can be found in old encyclopedias, because they provide us with clues to the shifts that are worth investigating. I then enlarge, tentatively, on points that emerge from this examination by discussing medieval and early modern developments. Finally, I comment briefly on modern anthropological writings. My general suggestion is that changes in institutional structures and in organizations of the self make possible, for better or worse, the concept of ritual as a universal category.

I emphasize again that the following notes are no more than preliminary explorations across a large terrain. They are intended as first steps in a historical inquiry into the conditions that made ritual in its contemporary sense visible to and theorizable by modern anthropology.

Changing Definitions

In the first edition of the *Encyclopaedia Britannica,* published in Edinburgh in 1771, there is a brief entry under "ritual": a "book directing the order and manner to be observed in celebrating religious ceremonies, and performing divine service in a particular church, diocese, order, or the like." In the third edition (1797), this entry is expanded to include, by analogy, a reference to religious observances in the classical world:

> RITUAL, a book directing the order and manner to be observed in performing divine service in a particular church, diocese, or the like. The ancient heathens had also their rituals, which contained their rites and ceremonies to be observed in building a city, consecrating a temple or altar, in sacrificing, and deifying, in dividing the curiae, tribes, centuries, and in general, in all their religious ceremonies. There are several passages in Cato's books *De Re Rustica,* which may give us some idea of the rituals of the ancients.

The first edition also contains an entry under "rite': "RITE, among divines," it reads, "denotes the particular manner of celebrating divine service, in this or that country." Thus, although the two terms are distinguished, they are complementary.

Both entries are repeated in successive editions up to the seventh (1852). After that, there is no entry at all for "rite" or "ritual" until the eleventh edition (1910), when a completely new entry appears under the latter for the first time. It is now five columns long and divided, after an introductory passage, into named subsections: "The Magical Element in Ritual," "The Interpretation of Ritual," "Changes in Ritual," "The Classification of Rites," "Negative Rites." This article is also supplemented by a substantial bibliography, which contains references to general works by Tylor, Lang, Frazer, Robertson Smith, Hubert, and Mauss, as well as ethnographic items by Spencer and Gillen and by Cushing.

The length of the 1910 entry seems to indicate that far more was now known about "ritual" as a cultural phenomenon than was the case in the eighteenth century, but in fact what we are given here is an account of something quite new, something that the first entries did not attempt to deal with. Although many of the exemplifications are related to concerns that flow from evolutionist assumptions, the central questions which were to occupy later anthropologists are already evident. Ritual, we learn, is found not only in Christianity or in the religions that Christianity superseded.

A crucial part of every religion, ritual is now regarded as a type of routine behavior that symbolizes or expresses something and, as such, relates differentially to individual consciousness and social organization. That is to say, it is no longer a *script* for regulating practice but a type of practice that is interpretable as standing for some further *verbally definable,* but tacit, event.

The routine, repetitive character of ritual is firmly linked in the 1910 entry to psychological and sociological functions:

> Ritual is to religion what habit is to life, and its *rationale* is similar, namely that by bringing subordinate functions under an effortless rule it permits undivided attention in regard to vital issues. . . . Just as the main business of habit is to secure bodily equilibrium . . . so the chief task of routine in religion is to organize the activities necessary to its stability and continuance as a social institution.

But given its essentially symbolic character, ritual is not confined to religion. The concept presented in 1910 allows that symbolic action is an integral part of ordinary life because it is essential to any system of interlocking social roles, and therefore also to the social structure as a whole:

> In order that inter-subjective relations should be maintained between fellow-worshippers, the use of one or another set of conventional symbols is absolutely required; for example, an intelligible vocabulary of meet expressions, or (since this is, perhaps not indispensable) at any rate sounds, sights, actions, and so on, that have come by prescription to signify the common purpose of the religious society, and the means taken in common for the realization of that purpose. In this sense, the term "ritual," as meaning the prescribed ceremonial routine, is also extended to observances not strictly religious in character.

This emphasis on ritual as symbolic behavior that is not necessarily religious is entirely modern, although some other notions are not. Perhaps the most important difference between the concept of ritual presented here and that found in later anthropological writings hinges on the fact that more sophisticated theories of interpretation are employed in some of the latter. But both share the idea that ritual is to be conceived essentially in terms of signifying behavior—a type of activity to be classified separately from practical, that is, technically effective, behavior. And it is this idea that the earliest entry in the *Encyclopaedia Britannica* lacks—or at any rate does not make explicit. There is, however, another idea, which is central to the 1771 entry and which becomes marginalized in the 1910 version. This is the conception of ritual as a manual.

The conception of ritual as a book directing the way rites should be performed is very much older than the eighteenth century. Rituals appeared as early as the ninth century, though only in monasteries (Sigler 1967). However, according to the *Oxford English Dictionary*, it was not until the middle of the seventeenth century that the word *ritual* entered English as a substantive conveying the sense either of the prescribed order of performing religious services or of the book containing such prescriptions. Significantly, in 1614 the Catholic church had just produced the first authorized version of the Roman Ritual (Cross 1974, 1189). And, of course, the term *ritual* continues to be used in certain circles to denote prayer manuals even today. But now this sense has been displaced, in the normal vocabulary of most nonreligious people, by the modern conception of ritual as enacted symbols. As such, *ritual* becomes virtually synonymous with *rite*, which may help to explain why the later editions of the *Encyclopaedia Britannica* do not have separate entries for "rite" and "ritual" as the earliest ones do.[1]

The shift in the usage of "ritual" from what is literally a script (including texts to be uttered and instructions on how and by whom, as well as on the accompanying actions, etc.) to behavior, which is itself *likened* to a text, is connected with other historical changes. Among these is the nineteenth-century view that ritual is more primitive than myth—a view that neatly historicizes and secularizes the Reformation doctrine that correct belief must be more highly valued than correct practice.[2] Thus, the 1910 entry states:

A valuable truth insisted on by the late W. Robertson Smith . . . is that in primitive religion it is ritual that generates and sustains myth,

---

1. And why anthropologists commonly employ the words *rite* and *ritual* interchangeably. For a recent example, see J. S. La Fontaine 1985.

2. It was Robertson Smith's interest in biblical exegesis that gave modern anthropology its first comprehensive theory of ritual, as Franz Steiner points out (1956).

and not the other way about. Sacred lore of course cannot be dispensed with; even Australian society, which has hardly reached the stage of having priests, needs its *Oknirabata* or "great instructor." . . . The function of such an expert, however, is chiefly to hand on mere rules for the performance of religious acts. If his lore include sacred histories, it is largely, we may suspect, because the description and dramatization of the doings of divine persons enter into ritual as a means of magical control. Similarly, the sacred books of the religions of middle grade teem with minute prescriptions as to ritual, but are almost destitute of doctrine. Even in the highest religions, where orthodoxy is a main requirement, and ritual is held merely to symbolize dogma, there is a remarkable rigidity about the dogma that is doubtless in large part due to its association with ritual forms many of them bearing the most primeval stamp. As regards the symbolic interpretation of ritual, this is usually held not to be primitive; and it is doubtless true that an unreflective age is hardly aware of the differences between "outward sign" and "inward meaning," and thinks as it were by means of its eyes.

The semantic distinction between "outward sign" and "inward meaning" is in fact an ancient one and has been drawn on by Christian reformers throughout the ages.[3] As the logical precondition of the claim to have penetrated through some formal appearance to the essential reality within, this distinction has been central to theological discourse. But not only to theological discourse, for the claim that the unsophisticated who employ "outward signs" in formal behavior and speech do not understand the entire meaning being signified or expressed has served as an important principle of anthropological interpretation from Tylor onward,[4] although few anthropologists today would endorse the derogatory judgment contained in the final sentence of the extract quoted above.

The 1910 article does include a reference to indigenous experts, who specify procedures for the proper conduct of rites, but this matter is brushed aside as being of little interest: "The function of such an expert, however, is chiefly to hand on mere rules for the performance

3. It is sometimes mistakenly supposed by modern students of the Middle East that this distinction is a special feature of Islamic thought.
4. I refer here to Tylor's decoding of the "real meaning" of "superstitious" beliefs and practices as *survivals*.

of religious acts." What now preoccupies the writer of the entry under "ritual" is its symbolic character, the meanings attached to it, and the fact that it is a universal phenomenon. Some later anthropologists were to trace these meanings to magical attempts at dealing with the natural environment (e.g., Malinowski) or to effects that maintained the continuity of social structures (e.g., Radcliffe-Brown); yet others to cultural categories by which messages are communicated (e.g., Leach) or to religious experiences that transcend cultural categories and social structures (e.g., Turner). But all of them regard ritual as essentially a species of representational behavior, present in every culture—typically as part of its "magic" or its "religion"—and identifiable by the ethnographer prior to its meaning and effect being determined.[5]

The idea that symbols need to be decoded is not, of course, new, but I think it plays a new role in the restructured concept of ritual that anthropology has appropriated and developed from the history of Christian exegesis.[6] Anthropologists have, I would suggest, incorporated a theological preoccupation into an avowedly secular intellectual task—that is, the preoccupation with establishing as authoritatively as possible the meanings of representations where the explanations offered by indigenous discourses are considered ethnographically inadequate or incomplete.

Of course, in the case of Christianity, it is the Church that embodies

5. In a recent survey of anthropological studies on ritual in Melanesia, R. Wagner (1984, 143-55, at 143) writes: "If ritual is, in its usual definition, what Mary Douglas calls a 'restricted code' . . . then the anthropologist's job is to decipher it. But *what* is encoded and why? And what is the nature of the code and why is it formulated in that way? These questions bear upon the relational role of ritual within the subject-culture, what it *does* as communication, regulation, or whatever." In this way, the notion of ritual aims to unify an enormous variety of culturally constituted events. But because "elaborated" and "restricted" codes are mutually dependent in every communicative event, and because each type of communicative event presupposes a distinctive arrangement of meaning, feeling-tone, mode, and effectivity, and presupposes too a historically constituted self that speaks, hears, and *does* things with signs, the notion of ritual as coded action is at once too narrow and too undiscriminating.

6. Thus, for medieval Christians, Scripture could be interpreted in four different ways. This was popularly illustrated by reference to the four kinds of sense indicated by the sign *Jerusalem* in the Old Testament: "These four meanings can, if it is desired, combine with each other and the same Jerusalem can be understood in four different ways: historically as the city of the Jews, allegorically as the Church of Christ, anagogically as God's heavenly city, a mother for all of us, and tropologically as the soul of each individual, which is often reproached or praised in the Scriptures under this appellation" (Piltz 1981, 30).

the authority to interpret the meanings of scriptural representations, although that authority is variously exercised according to whether the Church is more elitist or more populist. In societies that lack the notion of authoritative exegesis, however, the problem of interpreting "symbolic actions" is quite different. The most important difference relates not to greater uncertainty in the interpretation of symbols in such societies but to the fact that things have first to be construed as symbolic before they become candidates for interpretation, and in fieldwork situations it is the ethnographer who identifies and classifies symbols,[7] even where he or she then draws on the help of indigenous exegetes to interpret them.[8]

In this anthropological concept of ritual, an idea belonging to

7. A. Gell, in his analysis of the *ida* ritual among the Umedas of New Guinea (1975, 211), states: "Among my Umeda informants I found none willing to discuss the meaning of their symbols—to discuss their symbols *as* symbols 'standing for' some other thing or idea, rather than as concrete things-in-themselves. In fact I found it impossible to even pose the question of meaning in Umeda, since I could not discover any corresponding Umeda word for English 'mean,' 'stand for,' etc. Questions about symbols were taken by Umedas as questions about the *identity* rather than the *meaning* of a symbol: 'what is it?' not 'what does it mean?'" For Gell, this situation is no bar to carrying out a symbolic analysis based on the mirror theory of meaning, because he can claim to present an "observer's construct" whose validity is "external" rather than internal. But his discreet allusions to psychoanalytic method provoke the following doubt: what can the validation of "meanings" be in a situation where the ethnographer takes the part both of *analysand*, by putting visual images in words, and of *analyst*, by organizing these descriptive words into a coherent "symbolic" narrative in which *certain things stand for others?* For an illuminating discussion of the difficulties of securing symbolic interpretations in psychoanalysis, see D. P. Spence 1982.

8. D. Sperber (1975, 112) attempts to overcome the difference I refer to by arguing that symbolism should be defined in cognitive rather than communicative terms: "Symbolicity is therefore not a property either of objects, or of acts or of utterances, but of conceptual representations that describe or interpret them. Theoretical approaches that would look in objects, acts, or utterances for the properties constitutive of symbolism must be bound to fail. By contrast, an adequate theory of symbolism will describe the properties which a conceptual representation must possess to be the object of a putting in quotes and of a symbolic treatment." His overall argument employs a distinction between types of knowledge—for example, "semantic" as against "encyclopedic" knowledge—which recalls the old distinction between analytic and synthetic statements (subverted in W. O. Quine 1961 [1953]). "Symbolic knowledge," we are told, has to do with the way "encyclopedic knowledge" is organized, so that some statements (e.g., about mime) will be interpreted in a metaphorical sense, and others (e.g., about sacrifice) in a metaphysical one. It should be noted that, like other modern theorists, Sperber's preoccupation is with *propositional* knowledge (knowing that), not with *practical* knowledge (knowing how). And *propositional* knowledge (e.g., in theology, science, or law) invariably raises questions of authoritative interpretation. I return to the importance of this distinction below in my reading of Mauss's "Techniques of the Body."

premodern Christian traditions (especially monasticism) is now absent. This idea has to do with the shift in sense from a script (a text to be read and performed) to an action (a social fact to be observed and inscribed), and it can be described as follows. If there are prescribed ways of performing liturgical services, then we can assume that there exists a requirement to master the proper performance of these services. Ritual is therefore directed at the apt performance of what is prescribed, something that depends on intellectual and practical disciplines but does not itself require decoding. In other words, apt performance involves not symbols to be interpreted but abilities to be acquired according to rules that are sanctioned by those in authority: it presupposes no obscure meanings, but rather the formation of physical and linguistic skills.[9]

Rites as apt performances presuppose codes—in the regulative sense as opposed to the semantic—and people who evaluate and teach them.

The Medieval Christian Concept of Moral Discipline

In the early Middle Ages, the *Rule* of Saint Benedict became established as virtually the sole program for the proper government of a monastic community and the Christian formation of its members (Lawrence 1984). "We are about to open," states a famous sentence in the prologue to the *Rule*, "a school for God's service, in which we hope nothing harsh or oppressive will be directed." Although most Christians in feudal society lived outside monastic organizations, the disciplined formation of the Christian self was possible only within such communities. The ordered life of the monks was defined by various tasks, from working to praying, the most important being the singing of divine services *(Opus Dei)*. Because the monk's day was intended to be organized around the routine performance of the liturgy (Knowles 1963, 448–71), the *Rule* is often as specific about the content and timing of the service to be sung as it is about other matters. It is striking that in the *Rule*, the proper performance of the liturgy is regarded not only as integral to the ascetic life but also as one of the "instruments"

9. It is worth noting that Steiner (*Taboo*, 79) was clear that "meanings" of rites are a property of what he called "texts" (verbal accounts) and not of acts or things in themselves.

of the monk's "spiritual craft," which he must acquire by practice (see chap. 4, "The Instruments of Good Works"). The liturgy is not a species of enacted symbolism to be classified separately from activities defined as technical but is a practice among others essential to the acquisition of Christian virtues. In other words, the liturgy can be isolated only conceptually, for pedagogic reasons, not in practice, from the entire monastic program.

While it is true to say that the monastic program was conceived in terms of distinctive images—a school for the Lord's service *(domini schola servitii)*, a second baptism *(paenitentia secunda)*—it was practices that were to be organized by such figures. The figures were intrinsic to an inscribed program, to the language of prescription, exhortation, exegesis, and demonstration, not to the meaning of individual gestures in themselves.[10] In the *Rule* all prescribed practices, whether they had to do with the proper ways of eating, sleeping, working, and praying or with proper moral dispositions and spiritual aptitudes, are aimed at developing virtues that are put "to the service of God."

The learning of virtues according to the medieval monastic program (which, though based on the *Rule,* included other textual and oral traditions) took place primarily by means of imitation. The idea of following a model seems to have become especially important in the many religious organizations that proliferated during the High Middle Ages (Bynum 1980, 1–17), but from the start it was central to the Benedictine program, which aimed at the development of Christian virtues.

The virtues were thus formed by developing the ability to behave in accordance with saintly exemplars. Acquiring this ability was a teleological process. Each thing to be done was not only to be done aptly in itself, but done in order to make the self approximate more and more to a predefined model of excellence. The things prescribed, including liturgical services, had a place in the overall scheme of training the Christian self. In this conception, there could be no radical disjunction between outer behavior and inner motive, between social rituals and individual sentiments, between activities that are expressive and those that are technical.

10. My comments on images here should not be confused with M. Jackson's arguments for the experiential priority of bodily movements in relation to words and symbols (1983, 327–45). I want to draw attention to the teleological character of *learning to be capable.* The logical irrelevance of mental representations to the concept of skilled performance (whether physical or verbal) is argued out in J. Searle 1985.

For example, the copying of manuscripts, which occupied generations of monks, was a formally recognized type of asceticism.

> Deciphering from an often poorly preserved manuscript [writes an ecclesiastical historian] a text which was often long and badly written and *reproducing it correctly* constituted a task which, however noble it was, was also hard and therefore meritorious, and medieval scribes have taken pains to inform us of this fact: the whole body is concentrated on the work of the fingers, and constant and precise attention must be exercised.

Monks described this labor of transcribing manuscripts as being "like prayer and fasting, a means of correcting one's unruly passions" (Leclercq 1977, 153–54; emphasis added). In this sense the technical art of calligraphy was, like the liturgy, one part of a monastic program and therefore expressive, like divine service; a rite, like any act of penance.

It is precisely through the concept of a disciplinary program that "outer behavior" and "inner motive" were connected. This can be seen most clearly in the case of the sacrament of confession, so central to monastic life and developed by monks in the form that was later extended to Christians at large. But that connection was sought in everything that the program prescribed. A remarkable example, much written about in monastic literature, was the cultivation of "tears of desire for Heaven" (Leclercq 1977, 72–73): because the compunction for one's sins had to accompany the desire for virtue, the ability to weep became at once the sign of the genuineness of that compunction and of the progress attained by that desire.[11] In this way, emotions, which are often recognized by anthropologists as inner, contingent events, could be progressively organized by increasingly apt performance of conventional behavior.

Of course, medieval monks knew, as everyone knows, that signs of a particular virtue could be displayed or read when that virtue was lacking. But that did not mean that they regarded "external" behavior as detachable from an "essential" self. On the contrary, the presence of hypocrisy, like self-deception, indicated that the learning process was incomplete—or, more drastically, that it had failed. However, the converse, *not* displaying signs of virtue even when one possessed it,

11. A comparable phenomenon has been described for sixteenth-century Spain—see W. A. Christian 1982.

was itself recommended as a means of acquiring the highest virtue of all: humility.

The monastic community was far from being the whole of medieval life, but I am not aiming at a social history of manners. My interest is in trying to draw out some concepts of apt utterance and behavior in relation to moral structures of the self, when "ritual" has not yet become a separate category of behavior—repetitive, nonrational, expressive. Given this perspective, I want to move a step beyond Lienhardt's statement in the epigraph to this chapter and ask, by what systematic practices are particular moral dispositions and capacities created and controlled?

The Self and Its Representations: Some Renaissance Concerns

When the display of "proper" behavior is disconnected from the formation of a virtuous self and acquires the status of a tactic, it becomes the object of a different kind of theorizing—a meditation not on virtue but on power. But in this case behavioral signs need to be seen as representations conceptually detachable from what they represent; only then can they invite readings in a game of power, a game in which the "true" self is masked by its representations, and where this masking is aptly done.

A fascinating early modern attempt to conceptualize the role of representational behavior in the field of power is Bacon's "Of Simulation and Dissimulation." Bacon's world is, of course, more fluid and individualistic in comparison not only with the medieval monastic community but with society outside it. It is a world that encourages a double fragmentation—in individual roles and social arenas—which was to emerge more clearly in later centuries with the development of bourgeois society.

Bacon's essay is interesting because it takes for granted the possibility of analyzing individuated acts of representation. It does this first in distinguishing three degrees of masking: secrecy, dissimulation, and simulation. "Therefore set it downe: *That an Habit of Secrecy, is both Politick, and Morall.* And this Part, it is good, that a mans Face, give his Tongue, leaue to speak. For the Discouery, of a Mans Selfe, by the Tracts of his Countenance, is a great Weaknesse, and Betraying; By how much, it is many times more marked and beleeued, then a Mans words."

But secrecy cannot be maintained without a form of behavior which protects the truth by misrepresenting it. "It followeth many times vpon *Secrecy*, by a necessity; So that, he that will be *Secret*, must be a *Dissembler*, in some degree." Now, while dissimulation is the "negative" form of misrepresentation, that is, pretending not to be what one is (feigning innocence), simulation is the "affirmative" form—appearing to be what one is not (impersonating). Both involve playing a part in a drama of power, but the former is viewed as defensive and the latter as offensive. The text therefore cautions against excessive resorting to simulation on prudential grounds: "But for the third Degree, which is *Simulation*, and false Profession; That I hold more culpable, and lesse politicke; except that it be in great and rare Matters" (Bacon 1937 [1597], 24–25). Representational behavior is theorized for a self confronting potential opponents and allies. Bacon's text enumerates the uses and dangers of these tactics and balances the demands of traditional morality with those of an uncertain world. To the extent that precise calculation is impossible in the courtly world for which Bacon writes, the political effectiveness of conventional behavior requires the devising of strategies, not the imitation of models or the following of rules. It is only here, in the hidden exercise of strategic power, that symbolic behavior becomes what I think one may now call ideological.

The emerging modern distinction underlying Bacon's comments is, of course, between mind and body. In *The Advancement of Learning*, it is employed explicitly to classify knowledge about connections between the two: "how the one discloseth the other, and how the one worketh upon the other" (Bacon 1973 [1605], 106). Knowledge of the former is useful in decoding social behavior. (In the eighteenth century it would also become useful for depicting—in painting, in words, and in theatrical performance—the subject's "character" as revealed in "attitudes," in bodily configurations.) As for knowledge of the latter, it includes the effects on the mind of bodily manipulations in medicine and in "religion or superstition":

The physician prescribeth cures of the mind in phrensies and melancholy passions; and pretendeth also to exhibit medicines to exhilerate the mind, to confirm the courage, to clarify the wits, to corroborate the memory, and the like: but the scruples and superstitions of diet and other regimen of the body in the sect of the Pythagoreans, in the heresy of the Manicheans, and in the law of Mohomet, do exceed. So likewise the ordinances in the ceremonial law, interdicting the eating of the blood and the fat, distinguishing between beasts clean and unclean for meat, are many and strict. Nay the faith itself being clear and serene from all clouds of ceremony, yet retaineth the use of fastings, abstinences, and other macerations and humiliations of the body, as things real and not figurative. (107-8)

The rites and disciplines of medieval monasticism can now be seen as figurative and representational, not real or practical. Of course, medieval monasticism, too, made a distinction between appearance and reality.[12] But it linked "visible sign" indissolubly to "invisible virtue" through a program of Christian discipline. Bacon's distinction, by contrast, is between the real and the figurative. Unlike real things, the latter made statements whose essential meanings must be translated, but precisely because they are conventional statements, they may also need correction and reformulation. For figurative things (again, unlike real things) can lie—most seriously, when they seduce us into taking them to be real. Hence, Bacon is closer to the modern anthropological view, which is expressed in the sentence from the 1910 *Encyclopaedia Britannica* I quoted earlier: "As regards the symbolic interpretation of ritual, this is usually held not to be primitive; and it is doubtless true that an unreflective age is hardly aware of the difference between 'outward sign' and 'inward meaning,' and thinks as it were by means of its eyes."

In this early modern world, the moral economy of the self in a court circle was constructed very differently from the ways prescribed in the medieval monastic program. Created and re-created through dramas of manipulative power, at once personal and political, the self depended now on the maintenance of moral distance between public forms of behavior and private thoughts and feelings.[13] The dramas of power described by historians of the Renaissance were made possible by a sharp tension between the inner self and the outer person. But they were the product, too, of a radical reconceptualization of appro-

12. As in this observation by Hugh of St. Victor: "The eyes of infidels who see only visible things despise venerating the sacraments of salvation, because beholding in this only what is contemptible without invisible species they do not recognise the invisible virtue within and the fruit of obedience" (1951, 156).

13. S. Greenblatt (1980, 163) notes that "dissimulation and feigning are an important part of the instruction given by almost every [Renaissance] court manual."

priate behavior into representations and of skill in manipulating representations, increasingly divorced from the idea of a disciplinary program for forming the self. What kind of effects did these changes eventually have on the concept and practice of Christian rites in an increasingly de-Christianized world?

It is no accident, incidentally, that Bacon's world was one in which the words *policy* and *politic* acquired a strong Machiavellian sense. In late sixteenth- and seventeenth-century plays, it is well known that the politic man was one given to deception and machination. Less well known is the fact that the term *practice* (and its derivatives) had a similar sinister meaning:

> The word became rather widely used in the Elizabethan age, though it never approached the popularity of *policy*. Bacon used the word, for instance, in Essay III, "Of unity in religion," when he repudiates the use of force against religious movements, "except it be in cases of overt scandal, blasphemy or intermixture of practice against the state."
> . . . The corresponding verb is *to practise*, also used by Bacon in a sinister sense: in the Overbury trial he spoke of ciphers as "seldom used but either by princes and their ambassadors and ministers, or by such as work or practice against, or, at least, upon, princes." (Orsini 1946, 131)

Is it necessary to insist that deception and intrigue were not invented in the Renaissance? All one is saying is that practices of representation (and misrepresentation) were now becoming the object of systematic knowledge in the service of power.

I am not suggesting, of course, that representational behavior was involved only in political strategies. In the Renaissance the masque, for example, was regarded as representational and morally educative at one and the same time. Thus, Sir Thomas Elyot, in *The Book Named the Governour* (1531), writes of dancing in general:

> Now because there is no pastime to be compared to that, wherein may be found both recreation and meditation of virtue; I have among all honest pastimes, wherein is exercise of the body, noted dancing to be of an excellent utility, comprehending in it wonderful figures (which the Greeks do call Idea) of virtues and noble qualities, and especially of the commodious virtue called prudence, which Tulley

defineth to be the knowledge of things, which ought to be followed; and also of them which ought to be fled from and eschewed. (Meagher 1962, 273)

Such a conception of the formal dance, by which edifying images are allegorically presented and moral dispositions cultivated, is close to the older conception of the liturgy as part of the communal program for developing Christian virtues—even if the highest virtue envisaged now is prudence, not humility, and even if the cultivation of virtues is increasingly pushed to the margins of serious life (pastime) or at most into a preparatory segment of it (education). It is no accident that these and other comments by Elyot on formal dancing appear in a book devoted to the education of gentlemen (a process that Victorians would call "building character"). But my point here is simply that when conventional behavior is seen as being essentially representational and essentially independent of the self, the possibility is opened up of deploying it in games of power. The Renaissance masque, for all its concern with power, was a calculated display of royal authority in which the king and all his courtiers participated (Cooper 1984). But that display was in the nature of a self-assertion, not a simulation.[14] Unlike the representations discussed by Bacon, the masque presents no more than itself: in it power may be celebrated but is not thereby secured.

Private Essences and Public Representations

In his study of drama in the English Renaissance, Edward Burns (1990) notes that "character" has always had a dual sense. On the one hand it means reputation, how one is known and understood in the world; on the other, mental or moral constitution, that hidden essence by which one's being in the world is determined. "Character," he observes,

14. S. Orgel 1975, 59–60. On the symbolism of the masques, Orgel points out that "then as now, a symbol had meaning only after it was explained. Symbols function as summations and confirmations; they tell us only what we already know, and it is a mistake to assume that the Renaissance audience, unlike a modern one, knew with-out being told. Even emblems that seem perfectly obvious, or those that derive from standard handbooks of symbolic imagery, were relentlessly explicated" (24). This process of explication did not simply provide authoritative meanings, it defined things as symbols.

has in fact a rather unusual history, in that its use in classical, mediaeval and renaissance writing is tied very closely to a sense of its derivation; the word is often written in its original Greek letters, and its meaning explained in terms of metaphor. In its original Greek, a character is a figure (letter or symbol) stamped onto a wax tablet. It can also be the object that stamps that figure. It thus comes to mean a readable sign in a very general sense—the mark by which something is known as what it is. It may extend to aspects of the human—marks of face and body, for example—but it always implies the reading of signs, whether those signs are purposive or not. The metaphor then tends to return us to the production and interpretation of signs in writing and reading, an emphasis which Latin writers reiterate by carefully maintaining a sense of the term's origins. (5)

In postclassical rhetoric, "character" came to refer to the use of language aimed at representing types of person or humor. Right up to and including the Renaissance, the rhetoric required the orator to study and reproduce—according to his own style—the signs that made various human types recognizable in and through discourse. "If," says Burns, "we return to the opposition I made earlier—between character as a process of knowing, and character as individual moral essence—we have a broad definition of a shift in usage. The first gives the term as the rhetoricians understood it, the second isolates that concept of human being to which the term now refers" (6).

Developing from this second sense of character is the notion of essential identity, something unique and private to each individual, an essence separating him or her from other individuals as well as from the visible significations they share. According to this later notion, a human being's moral identity must not be equated with its formal appearance. An important consequence of that is that endless interpretations of essential character—and skill in "judgment of character" —now become possible.

Thus, in a piece entitled "An Essay on the Knowledge of the Characters of Men," Henry Fielding (1967) urges upon his "honest and unexperienced" readers the value of learning how to read the real character of men from their faces and habitual manner:

Thus while the crafty and designing part of mankind, consulting only their own separate advantage, endeavour to maintain one constant imposition on others, the whole world becomes a vast masquerade, where the greatest part appear disguised under false vizors and habits; a very few only showing their own faces, who become, by so doing, the astonishment and ridicule of all the rest.

But however cunning the disguise be which a masquerader wears; however foreign to his age, degree, or circumstance, yet if closely attended to, he very rarely escapes the discovery of an accurate observer; for Nature, which unwillingly submits to the imposture, is ever endeavouring to peep forth and show herself; nor can the cardinal, the friar, or the judge, long conceal the sot, the gamester, or the rake. (283)

Social critics like Fielding believed that it was possible to penetrate beyond the pretense of hypocrites (who appear in Fielding as "types": cardinal, friar, judge, etc.) into their essential moral nature precisely because "the passions of men do commonly imprint sufficient marks on the countenance" (284).

In the later eighteenth century, "passions" were distinguished from "emotions" by their greater force—and their consequent significance for social relations. Although they now became part of a mechanistic psychology, passions occupied a place comparable to medieval virtues and vices.

An internal motion or agitation of the mind, when it passeth away without desire is denominated *an emotion;* when desire follows, the motion or agitation is denominated *a passion.* A fine face, for example, raiseth in me a pleasant feeling: if that feeling vanish without producing any effect, it is in proper language an *emotion;* but if the feeling, by reiterated views of the object, becomes sufficiently strong to occasion desire, it loses its name of emotion, and acquires that of *passion.* The same holds in all the other passions.[15]

Unlike emotion, passion could therefore determine behavior—though only as an uncontrollable force quite unlike the teachable desires of medieval monasticism. For painters, this tendency of the passions (movements of the soul) to become externally visible made physiognomy a valuable professional aid. And they could now aspire not only

15. *Encyclopaedia Britannica,* 1797, 3d ed., s.v. "emotion."

to depict in detail each of the typical passions by reference to recognizable characteristics[16] but also to penetrate, by means of readable signs, into the essential moral character of their subjects.

"Emotion" versus "Ritual" in Anthropology

How did the idea of teaching the body to develop "virtues" through material means come to be displaced by the idea of separating internal feelings and thoughts called "emotions" from social forms/formulas/formalities? A more modest version of that question would be: How did modern anthropology arrive at the distinction between "feelings" as private and ineffable and "ritual" as public and legible? That the two are to be opposed has long been the dominant assumption in the study of ritual in modern anthropology, although there are some indications that this may be changing.[17]

Several decades ago, A. M. Hocart spelled out at length the idea that ritual and emotion are mutually antipathetic, that ritual is an "intellectual construction that is liable to be broken up by emotion" (Hocart 1952, 61). In his case, this idea fitted neatly into the Gibbonian attitude toward "enthusiastic religion," the emotional Christianity of classes who might be difficult to govern, as opposed to the polite, orderly, ceremonial Christianity favored by Enlightenment rulers. "We have seen," wrote Hocart, "that it is chiefly in the lower classes that emotion lets itself go, and breaks up the [ritual] structure. We have also had reason to believe that these popular movements can spread through a society and simplify the whole religion."[18]

Some time later, Evans-Pritchard expressed the orthodox position of British social anthropologists at the time as follows: "Only chaos would result were anthropologists to classify social phenomena by emotions which are supposed to accompany them, for such emotional

16. Thus, the first edition of *The Encyclopaedia Britannica* (1771) contains a separate entry under "passions, in painting," which identifies them as visual representations. Later editions contain plates displaying line drawings of a large number of passions, including "Admiration," "Scorn & Hatred," "Humility," "Desire," and so on. They are now literally *types*—whose etymology, incidentally, overlaps with that of "character."

17. For example, S. Heald 1986. This change is connected with a growing recognition that the language of emotions is intrinsic to their formation: see R. Harré 1986.

18. Hocart 1952, 65. It is interesting that in this article Hocart should cite Islam (Egyptian sufi exercises) as an example of emotion destroying ritual, and Brahmanism as the epitome of ritual constructing hierarchy.

states, if present at all, must vary not only from individual to individual, but also in the same individual on different occasions and even at different points in the same rite" (Evans-Pritchard 1965, 44).

In this and other such formulations, the distinction is apparent between the contingency of individual experience and the systematic character of language. The conception of ritual as a language by which private things become publicly accessible because they can be represented is a familiar enough notion. Here is another, more recent anthropologist:

> Now, if for the purposes of exposition we draw a crude distinction between "ordinary" communicational behaviour and "ritual" behaviour (accepting of course that both kinds are equally subject to cultural conventions), then we could say (forgetting the problem of insincerity and lying) that ordinary acts "express" attitudes and feelings directly (e.g. crying denotes distress in our society) and "communicate" that information to interacting persons (e.g. the person crying wishes to convey to another his feeling of distress). But ritualized, conventionalized, stereotyped behaviour is constructed in order to express and communicate, and is publicly construed as expressing and communicating, certain attitudes congenial to an ongoing institutionalized intercourse. Stereotyped conventions in this sense act at a second or further remove; they code not intentions but "simulations" of intentions. . . . Thus *distancing* is the other side of the coin of conventionality; distancing separates the private emotions of the actors from their commitment to a public morality. (Tambiah 1979, 113–69, at 124)

There are, of course, cultural repertoires that can be brought into play only where a conceptual disjunction exists between the essential self and the means by which that self represents its feelings, intentions, and responses to others. But perhaps in such cases the distinction between "ordinary" communicational activity (including speech) and "ritual" may be less momentous than we suppose, since the guiding principle in both situations may well be prudence—including the prudence of committing oneself to a public morality.

Yet, the meaning given in the preceding quotations to the word *emotion* is evidently something like *sensations,* that is, feelings that are not only spontaneous and ephemeral but essentially internal and unique to each body. In this view, it is indeed difficult to envisage sensations becoming the objects of (ritual) concepts and thereby changing their essentially unique and ephemeral quality.[19]

Durkheim's *Elementary Forms of the Religious Life* (1915) has a more complicated account of the separation between the sensations and desires of the (individual) body, on the one hand, and the concepts and duties of the (collective) soul, on the other.

> It is quite true that the elements which serve to form the idea of the soul and those that enter into the representation of the body come from two different sources that are independent of one another. One sort are made up of the images and impressions coming from all parts of the organism; the others consist in the ideas and sentiments which come from and express society. So the former are not derived from the latter. There really is a part of ourselves which is not placed in immediate dependence upon the organic factor: this is all that which represents society in us. . . . The world of representations in which social life passes is superimposed upon its material substratum; the determinism which reigns there is much more supple than the one whose roots are in the constitution of our tissues and it leaves with the actor the justified impression of the greatest liberty. . . . Passion individualizes, yet it also enslaves. Our sensations are essentially individual; yet we are more personal the more we are freed from our senses and able to think and act with concepts. (271–72)

Durkheim's view of the contradictory relation between the individual and the social *within each human being* provided a basis for his theory of ritual. For it was "the function of public festivals, ceremonies, and rites of all kinds" to "perpetually give back to the great ideals a little of the strength that the egoistic passions and daily personal preoccupations tend to take away from them." For Durkheim, the disjunctions within human beings were irreducible but not absolute. They could be mediated by ritual only because it, too, had a double character:

> Collective representations originate only when they are embodied in material objects, things, or beings of every sort—figures, movements,

---

19. Evans-Pritchard's empiricist psychology may be contrasted with Collingwood's argument (1938) that when sensations are captured in thought (i.e., language), they cease to be fleeting, private, and nondirectional. Collingwood's writings were admired and occasionally cited by Evans-Pritchard, so it is surprising to find that neither he nor his followers at Oxford ever engaged Collingwood's views on emotions and thought.

sounds, words, and so on—that symbolize and delineate them in some outward appearance. For it is only by expressing their feelings, by translating them into signs, by symbolizing them externally, that the individual consciousnesses, which are, by nature, closed to each other, can feel that they are communicating and are in unison. (Wolff 1960, 335–36)

The place of Durkheim's concept of *homo duplex* in his sociology of ritual has been the subject of much comment. But I am not aware that anyone has pointed out how Mauss, who is usually coupled with Durkheim, attempted to move away from this concept in "Techniques of the Body." In this famous essay, Mauss insisted that "the body is man's first and most natural instrument. Or more accurately, not to speak of instruments, man's first and most natural technical object, and at the same time technical means, is his body" (1979, 104). By talking about "body techniques," Mauss sought to focus attention on the fact that if we were to conceptualize human behavior in terms of learned capabilities, we might see the need for investigating how these are linked to authoritative standards and regular practice:

> Hence I have had this notion of the social nature of the *"habitus"* for many years. Please note that I use the Latin word . . . *habitus*. The word translates infinitely better than *"habitude"* [habit or custom], the *"exis,"* the "acquired ability" and "faculty" of Aristotle (who was a psychologist). . . . These "habits" do not vary just with individuals and their imitations; they vary especially between societies, educations, proprieties and fashions, prestiges. In them we should see the techniques and work of collective and individual practical reason rather than, in the ordinary way, merely the soul and its repetitive faculties. (1979, 101)

The concept of *habitus*[20] invites us to analyze the body as an assemblage of embodied aptitudes, not as a medium of symbolic meanings. Hence, Mauss's wish to talk about "those people with a sense of the adaptation of all their well-co-ordinated movements to a goal, who are practised, who 'know what they are up to' " (1979, 108). This concern to identify and analyze bodily competence *at* something led him to

20. Bourdieu (1977) was later to popularize the word *habitus*, but it is strange that he gave Mauss no credit for having originated the concept.

refer to it by the Latin term *habilis* because the French *habile* did not quite convey what he was getting at. I think that Mauss wanted to talk, as it were, about the way a professional pianist's practiced hands remember and play the music being performed, not about how the symbolizing mind "clothes a natural bodily tendency" with cultural meaning.

One might say that Mauss was attempting to define an anthropology of practical reason—not in the Kantian sense of universalizable ethical rules, but in that of historically constituted practical knowledge, which articulates an individual's learned capacities. According to Mauss, the human body was not to be viewed simply as the passive recipient of "cultural imprints," still less as the active source of "natural expressions" that are "clothed in local history and culture,"[21] as though it were a matter of an inner character expressed in a readable sign, so that the latter could be used as a means of deciphering the former. It was to be viewed as the developable means for achieving a range of human objectives, from styles of physical movement (e.g., walking), through modes of emotional being (e.g., composure), to kinds of spiritual experience (e.g., mystical states). This way of talking seems to avoid the Cartesian dualism of the mind and objects of the mind's perception.[22]

It is the final paragraph of Mauss's essay that carries what are perhaps the most far-reaching claims for an anthropological understanding of ritual. Beginning with a reference to Granet's remarkable studies of Taoist body techniques, he goes on: "I believe precisely that at the bottom of all our mystical states there are body techniques which we have not studied, but which were studied fully in China and India, even in very remote periods. This socio-psycho-biological study should be made. I think that there are necessarily biological means of entering into 'communion with God' " (1979, 122). Thus, the possibility is opened up of inquiring into the ways in which embodied practices (including language in use) form a precondition for varieties of religious experi-

21. All these phrases come from Mary Douglas's well-known interpretation of Mauss's essay in Douglas 1970.

22. Starobinski (1982, 23) notes that "in his treatise *The Passions of the Soul*, Descartes put forward a clear distinction between three different categories of perception: 'that which relates to objects external to us' (art. 23), 'that which refers to our body' (art. 24), and 'that which refers to our soul' (art. 25)." It is the second of these that constitutes the object of psychiatric speculations in the nineteenth and early twentieth centuries and is the theme of Starobinski's intriguing historical sketch.

ence. The inability to enter into communion with God becomes a function of untaught bodies. "Consciousness" becomes a dependent concept.

Whatever may be the intellectual appeal of a phenomenology of the body, it seems to me that Mauss's approach also runs counter to the assumption of primordial bodily experiences. It encourages us to think of such experience not as an autogenetic impulse but as a mutually constituting relationship between body sense and body learning. His position fits well with what we know even of something as basic and universal as physical pain, for anthropological as well as psychological research reveals that the perception of pain threshold varies considerably according to traditions of body training—and also according to the pain history of individual bodies (Melzack and Wall 1982; Brihaye, Loew, and Pia 1987). Thus, from Mauss's perspective, an experience of the body becomes a moment in an experienced (taught) body. As in the case of medieval monastic programs, discourse and gesture are viewed as part of the social process of learning to develop aptitudes, not as orderly symbols that stand in an objective world in contrast to contingent feelings and experiences that inhabit a separate subjective one.

Why was "Techniques of the Body" not read in this way but usually as a founding text of symbolic anthropology?[23] Was it because "ritual" was already powerfully in place as symbolic action—that is, as visible behavioral form requiring decoding?

Conclusion

Perhaps at least some of the differences may now be a little clearer between the conception of rites prescribed in the communal Christian program of the Middle Ages for developing virtues and the conception of symbolic behavior in societies where *discipline* is no longer considered indispensable to the formation of moral structures, but *formal manners* are regarded as essential for communicating a prudential "commitment to a public morality." For it is in the latter context, when some particular piece of observed behavior calls for some account of what it might signify, when it invites the observer to discover what truth lies hidden behind the signifying act, apart from an apparent

23. It is cited in that way in, for example, Blacking 1977 and Polhemus 1978.

commitment, that we can call it representational. Clearly, there is a fundamental disparity between a "ritual" that organizes practices aimed at the full development of the monastic self and a "ritual" that offers a *reading* of a social institution. We may speculate on the ways in which the increasing marginality of religious discipline in industrial capitalist society may have reinforced the latter concept.

At any rate, it seems that some contemporary Christian circles regard this symbolic conception of ritual with favor. Thus, a recent book by a theologian entitled *From Magic to Metaphor: A Validation of the Christian Sacraments* draws heavily on modern anthropological work. Christian ritual, it insists, is essentially not instrumental but symbolic:

> Any rebuttal to our theological contentions must also critique the findings of psychology, sociology, and anthropology which support our theological convictions. The lines of convergence between a behavioral and a theological understanding of ritual's operation and meaning are too strong to dismiss one without the other. . . .
>
> Ritual is a medium or vehicle for communicating or sustaining a particular culture's root metaphor, which is the focal point and permeating undercurrent for its worldview. Through ritual's operation, life's binary oppositions are contextualized within a culture's metaphor and "resolved" into positive meaning for a culture's individual members and the social unit as a whole. . . . A people's ritual is a code for understanding their interpretation of life.
>
> Christian sacraments exhibit all the characteristics of ritual in general. They are normal and necessary for Christian culture. They are the medium or vehicle through which the Christian root metaphor of Christ's death-resurrection is expressed and mobilized to "positively" resolve the binary oppositions of life. (Worgul 1980, 224)

This idea of the sacraments as metaphorical representations inhabits an entirely different world from the one that gives sense to Hugh of St. Victor's theology: "Sacraments," he stated, "are known to have been instituted for three reasons: on account of humiliation, on account of instruction, on account of exercise." According to this latter conception, the sacraments are not the representation of cultural metaphors; they are parts of a Christian program for creating in its performers, by means of regulated practice, the "mental and moral dispositions" appropriate to Christians. In modern society, where Christians adopt a wide range of moral positions and live lives that are not clearly differentiated from those of non-Christians, where discipline becomes a matter of strategic interventions and statistical calculations, it is perhaps understandable that rites should have become symbolic occasions.

And so, too, in the world beyond, which post-Enlightenment Europeans sought to penetrate and understand. "Ritual," writes an intelligent student of contemporary Islam, "is for the participant a reenactment of a profound truth. As Geertz has put it, it is realizing that religion is at the same time a model *of* and a model *for* the world. Does one need to be a Muslim in order to capture the essence of Islamic ritual?" (Denny 1985, 66). The answer to this rhetorical question is, the writer observes, no. All that is required is the attempt to understand, with "sympathy and respect as well as openness to the sources," what Islamic rituals "portray and symbolize."

Symbols, as I said, call for interpretation, and even as interpretative criteria are extended, so interpretations can be multiplied. Disciplinary practices, on the other hand, cannot be varied so easily, because learning to develop moral capabilities is not the same thing as learning to invent representations. This leads me to venture a final question: is it possible that the transformation of rites from discipline to symbol, from practicing distinctive virtues (passions) to representing by means of practices, has been one of the preconditions for the larger conceptual transformation of heterogeneous life (acting and being acted upon) into readable text?

Archaisms

ထော်ထော်

3 ❧❧❧   PAIN AND TRUTH IN MEDIEVAL CHRISTIAN RITUAL

Most social anthropologists analyzing religion have tended to look either for symbolic meanings or for social functions, or (occasionally) for both together. Here, however, I am concerned neither with symbolic meanings nor with social functions but with the ways in which particular rituals in the Christian Middle Ages depended on the inflicting of physical pain, and with how their transformation enabled discipline to take effect in different ways. Today, most moderns, whether they are religious or not, regard such practices with suspicious disapproval.

I begin with a sketch of the practice of judicial torture, which in the twelfth century began to replace very different forms of legal procedure in Western Europe. Judicial torture is especially interesting because its appearance in the central Middle Ages seems to have been connected with the formation of a particular kind of politics, a particular kind of religious ritual, a particular kind of knowledge production, and a particular kind of subjectivity. Above all, it was a practice authorized and employed by the Church.

The latter part of this chapter is devoted to developments in the main form of Christian discipline in the Middle Ages (the ritual of sacramental penance) for which the twelfth century was also a crucial period. Their implications for knowledge production and subjectivity will be touched upon but not systematically dealt with here.

In both judicial torture and religious pain, we can detect ways in which power—the most direct, physical effect of power—works to produce truthful discourses and makes subjects respond to authority. This investigation of pain in medieval Latin Christianity is therefore an attempt to explore the ways in which historical forms of power became

not merely the means of coercion and subjection but (more interestingly) the conditions for creating particular potentialities—individual, social, and cultural. What interests me is not so much Christian
ritual *and* power, but the power *of* Christian ritual.

Judicial Torture and the Progress of Rationality

In histories of Western criminal law, judicial torture (i.e., the application of pain to the body of the accused or of a witness, in order to
extract a confession) is invariably treated as an aspect of early *inquisitorial procedure* and is contrasted with the duel, ordeal, and sacred oath
(compurgation), which are elements in primitive forms of *accusatorial
procedure*. Legal historians distinguish several aspects of these two types
of procedure—for example, the part played by "individual citizens" or
by "society" in initiating and conducting the trial, in determining
culpability, in prescribing and carrying out the penalty. But perhaps
the most striking difference lies in the respective modes of determining guilt. According to Esmein, in the early medieval accusatorial
system,

> the chief effort of the prosecution is directed towards the establish-
> ment of the very act. In primitive procedures capture in the act ap-
> pears, indeed, to be the normal hypothesis of repression; the senti-
> ment of vengeance which inspires the penal system is, in this case,
> stronger; the culpability, which it is necessary to establish, is then less
> doubtful. Except in the case of capture in the act, if the accused does
> not confess, it is for him, by an inversion of the proof, to show his
> innocence by taking the exculpatory oath and sustaining it by the
> number of oath-helpers which custom demands. This is the normal
> method of proof. It constitutes a right for the accused. But it may be
> set aside in certain cases and then ordeals are brought into play, by
> which appeal is made to the judgement of the deity. These ordeals are
> of two kinds. In some, only one of the parties takes an active part,
> usually the accused. To instance the most widespread, there is the
> ordeal of branding, that of boiling water, and that of cold water. In
> the others, both parties play an active part, as in the judicial duel and
> the ordeal of the cross. This system is by no means peculiar to the
> Germanic customs; it is characteristic, not of one definite race, but of
> a certain stage of civilization. In the mythological stage of the human

mind the deity was invoked upon the question of guilt or innocence just as it was invoked as to the fate of a battle. In this respect there was a connection between beliefs and legal institutions. The same attitude of mind which allows of divination by auguries and sorcerers leads to the practice and the diffusion of the criminal examination by ordeals and the judicial combat. (1914, 6–7)

In the inquisitorial system, on the other hand, culpability is established by an investigating judge without recourse to the supernatural:

A new method of examination, more cruel perhaps, but more logical, than the ordeals, i.e. that of torture, enters the higher courts of justice and filters through these to the lower tribunals. The confession of the accused having acquired a preponderating influence, the method "par excellence" of extracting this proof is now seen to be torture, e.g. by the wooden horse, the boot, or the water. Torture is an institution of Roman origin. Under the Republic, no doubt, and at the beginning of the Empire, Roman citizens escaped it. The only persons exposed to it then were the slave when he was accused (or simply called to court) and the provincial. But in the early days of the Empire the custom was begun of subjecting to this process of examination the Roman citizen accused of treason. Then torture comes to be of such general application that the handbooks recommend judges not to begin the examination by that, but first to collect the evidence. It is, therefore, not surprising that the diffusion of torture coincides, in modern history, with the revival of the half-forgotten Roman law by the criminalists of the Belogna [sic] school. The transformation of the procedure by the substitution of torture for ordeals really begins to manifest itself from the end of the 1100s. Since that time, no country of Europe has escaped the contagion. At the end of the 1300s torture had become a general custom. It was, to some extent, one of the fundamental institutions of the old criminal procedure. (Ibid., 9)

In the history of medieval Europe, the great shift in legal procedures from trial by ordeal (appropriate to "mythological mentality") to one that was more "logical" has been seen by scholars as part of a wider and more profound movement in which the search for truth changed direction. In place of divine judgment, we are told, men began to value purely human proof. Thus, the medievalist R. W. Southern observes:

At the beginning of the period, the appeal to the supernatural was the most common of all the expedients of government. From the ninth century onwards we have a large number of liturgical forms designed to elicit a divine judgement in all kinds of doubtful cases, whether of crime or disputed ownership. Churches were repositories for the instruments by which the divine judgement was conveyed—the cauldron for the hot water, the brazier for heating the iron, and so on—and one of the commonest functions of the priest must have been the blessing of these instruments for their purpose. . . .

During the twelfth century this habit of mind underwent a rapid change. The change took place at the same time as the change in the attitude to secular government, and some of the causes were operating in both cases. The study of Roman law opened men's eyes to the existence of an elaborate system of purely human proof; and the growth of a uniform Canon Law, which applied the methods of Roman Law, carried the lessons of the lawyers far and wide. . . . Above all men came more and more to doubt the efficiency of judgement by ordeal. . . . When the Lateran Council of 1215 forbade priests to take part in the administration of the ordeal, it was here, as in so much else that it did, expressing a change of attitude which had been developing for a long time. The effect, so far as the regular administration of justice was concerned, was immediate. Men were forced to prefer the probability arrived at by human agencies to the certainties of divine judgement. (1959, 101–2)

Since torture as a technique belonging to inquisitorial procedure was directed at securing the truth with the help of human agents only, its systematic use in the Middle Ages can be construed as a progressive step in the rational development of European law. The reorientation signified by its use was to be retained, but its cruelty and excess eventually eliminated. The nineteenth-century American anthropologist James C. Welling expressed this point succinctly:

From this formal species of proof [duel, ordeal, and compurgation] men pass to a matter-of-fact species of proof according as their reasoning powers grow stronger and their appliances for the rational discovery of truth become more and more available in the domain of justice. In this passage of the human race from a ceremonial and formal species of negative proof to a rationalistic and substantive species of positive proof, the method of proof by the intervention of torture occupies a place which may be described as a sort of "half-way house" situate [*sic*] between these two typical and distinctive forms of judicial procedure. (Quoted in Peters 1973, viii)

Most historians who have dealt with this theme have praised medieval critics of the ordeal for their rationalism. These critics, we are given to understand, noted the obvious failures of ordeals to identify the real culprit; thus, they recognized that reliance on ordeals was mere superstition, and they demanded an approach to the truth which was sounder, more rational.[1] Yet why were the incidents that now came to be represented as failures of the system of the ordeal no longer seen simply as mistakes in the application of the rules, as they must have been in the past? Historians such as Southern have spoken of the influence of a rational Roman law, but clearly this is an inadequate explanation, because the ability and the will to identify aspects of Roman law as "rational" must exist prior to the encounter with that law. Instead, were medievalists familiar with relevant anthropological analysis, they might recognize a historical problem where they see only a triumph. For ever since Evans-Pritchard's *Witchcraft, Oracles, and Magic among the Azande* (1937) it has been clear that obviously wrong judgments reached through oracles, ordeals, etc. can be accommodated within the system without undermining it.[2] Many historians apparently fail to see that it is changes in the practices defining the truth which lead to the apparent recognition of superstition, not the other way round.[3] In other words, the reforming Church did not rediscover rationality, it redefined it. The new rules of rational practice entailed a re-cognition of previous practices as superstition—that is, as practices that had survived beyond their proper time.[4]

   1. One of these twelfth-century critics was Peter the Chanter, whose views have been fully documented in Baldwin 1970.
   2. Mauss's comments on this subject are much older but less well known than Evans-Pritchard's. Thus: "Magic has such authority that a contrary experience does not, on the whole, destroy a person's belief. In fact, it escapes all control. Even the most unfavourable facts can be turned to magic's advantage, since they can always be held to be the work of counter-magic or to result from an error in performance of the ritual. In general, they are seen to stem from the fact that the necessary conditions for the rite were not fulfilled" (1972, 92–93).
   3. An excellent paper by the legal historian Paul Hyams (1981) gives what is, to my knowledge, the only convincing account of the decline of trial by ordeal in medieval Europe.
   4. See the interesting etymology of *superstition* as reconstructed by Benveniste (1973, 516–28).

In recent years, the writer who has done more than most to raise doubts about such triumphalist versions of rationality has been Foucault. In his seminal book *Discipline and Punish,* a horrendous account of the public torture and execution of a regicide in the Classical Age initiates a discussion about the shifting strategies of power in relation to the body, and thus about changing conceptions and practices of punishment. The extravagant demonstration of sovereign power by which the offender's body is tortured, marked, and displayed gives place to an economy of training in which body and soul are molded carefully, almost solicitously, by power. Punishment is transformed from a ritual of political communication to something that may be described as a ritual of social production: where truth was once a spectacle, the public demonstration of power and justice, it has now become a process with an end product—the reformed, socially useful, soundly reasoning ex-criminal.

Of course, torture was not only a demonstration of justice, it was also itself productive of truth. On judicial torture, as opposed to torture that merely serves as punishment, Foucault has written briefly but suggestively in the second chapter of book 1:

> One may see the functioning of judicial torture, or interrogations under torture, as a torture of truth. To begin with, judicial torture was not a way of obtaining the truth at all costs; it was not the unrestrained torture of modern interrogations; it was certainly cruel, but it was not savage. It was a regulated practice, obeying a well-defined procedure; the various stages, their duration, the instruments used, the length of ropes and the heaviness of weights used, the number of interventions made by the interrogating magistrate, all this was, according to the different local practices, carefully codified. . . . Torture was a strict judicial game. And, as such, it was linked to the old tests or trials—ordeals, judicial duels, judgements of God—that were practised in accusatory procedures long before the techniques of the Inquisition. Something of the joust survived, between the judge who ordered the judicial torture and the suspect who was tortured; the "patient"—this is the term used to designate the victim—was subjected to a series of trials graduated in severity, in which he succeeded if he "held out," or failed if he confessed. . . .

Beneath an apparently determined, impatient search for truth, one finds in classical torture the regulated mechanism of an ordeal: a physical challenge that must define the truth; if the patient is guilty, the pains that it imposes are not unjust; but it is also a mark of exculpation if he is innocent. In the practice of torture, pain, confrontation and truth were bound together; they worked together on the patient's body. The search for truth through judicial torture was certainly a way of obtaining evidence, the most serious of all—the confession of the guilty person; but it was also the battle, and this victory of one adversary over the other, that produced "truth" according to ritual. In torture employed to extract a confession, there was an element of the investigation; there was also an element of the duel. (40-41)

This identification of torture (together with ordeal) as ritual is an insight that should help us see that judicial torture is something other than a half-way house in the growth of the human mind from myth to logic, from the ceremonial to the rational. As ritual, torture has its own conditions, its own rules, its own effects, which are different from and not simply better than, those of the ordeal. This is of course precisely the kind of argument that underlies the thesis of *Discipline and Punish*. Yet, at the same time in this passage, Foucault's assimilation of judicial torture to the duel and the ordeal is fraught with some difficulty, and it is liable to obscure his insights. The main problem, as we shall see, is that the truth produced by the one is not quite the same as that which the other produces. It is not enough, after all, to identify a practice as ritual—as Foucault, that consummate ethnographer of Western culture, knows full well. It is only when the differences between the rituals are described that we can begin to understand what each kind of ritual enables, and how it does so. Thus, not only is our understanding of judicial torture enlarged by seeing it as a kind of ritual, but our understanding of ritual, too, is extended by analyzing it as a kind of torture—a practice by which aspects of truth and subjectivity are painfully constructed.

Toward the end of his book, Foucault does explicitly contrast the ordeal with the inquisitorial system: "The investigation as an authoritarian search for a truth observed or attested was thus opposed to the old procedures of the oath, the ordeal, the judicial duel, the judgement of God or even of the transaction between private individuals. The investigation was the sovereign power arrogating to itself the right to establish the truth by a number of regulated techniques" (225). This difference in authority between the ordeal and the inquisitorial system was, as we shall see, indeed crucial. But the concept of applying pain in the interests of truth remains to be explored, and it is this connection that makes judicial torture part of the same story as that which deals with religious asceticism.

The Ordeal Opposed to Judicial Torture

The shift from ordeal to torture in the Middle Ages was not simply a change in the direction of looking for the truth about transgression. It signified a different practice of reaching that truth, in which physical pain played a very different role.

Ordeals and judicial combat were essentially rituals for regulating conflicts between social equals. It is in this sense that Esmein writes, "Torture is out of place in a purely accusatory procedure and in a free country; the accuser and the accused are two combatants who fight in broad daylight and with equal weapons" (107). Anthropologists who have analyzed the principles of feuding in so-called stateless societies have discussed this point thoroughly, although they have not always understood that the equality was ideological and not material—that is, that it concerned the absence of a formal duty to submit to the other side and not the existence of equal resources on both sides. Nevertheless, the point to be stressed is that what anthropologists call feuds, as well as judicial combat and ordeal, are in the first place modes of regulating conflict in which the principal parts are played by the accuser and the accused, according to recognized rules, and not by a judicial authority. As such, it has essentially nothing to do with resolving doubt—neither accuser nor accused is in a state of doubt about the offense at issue, and the outcome of an ordeal or combat cannot therefore be said to resolve it for them. What it does is to provide rules for producing an unequivocal outcome on which a clear decision about social relations can be made.

For example, consider the case of Stephen of Tournai, which took place in a period of mounting criticism by the Church of the old feudal practice of trial by combat and by ordeal:

In 1179, when a dispute arose between himself, as abbot of Sainte Geneviève of Paris, and his tenants of Rosny-sous-Vincennes over the nature of their personal services, Stephen took the case before the court of King Louis VII. In the absence of authentic charters the

King ordered a judicial duel "according to the custom of the Franks." When the champions of the men from Rosny, frightened by those of Sainte Geneviève, retired from the field, the King confirmed the servile services owed by the losers of the ordeal. The affair was witnessed by an imposing array of the Parisian clergy, including the abbots of Saint-Germain-des-Prés and Saint-Denis and the dean and archdeacon of Notre Dame, and the decision was re-confirmed in charters from Pope Lucius III and Clement III. In the twelfth and thirteenth centuries such an affair was not at all unusual in Paris. (Baldwin 1961, 621)

What such an event produced was not evidence for reaching a legal judgment but the definition of a judgment itself—or, more properly speaking, the redefinition of an uncertain social relationship. There were, of course, many differences in the various ordeals employed, although most of them put the body at risk in one way or another (cf. Lea 1866, pts. 1–3). And although a vocabulary of seeking the truth was normally used in connection with them, they were all similar in that they generated a "truth" that was inseparable from the decision. In practice, there might be a judge present, as in the dispute between the abbot of Sainte Geneviève and his tenants. But the judge's role was, strictly, superfluous. In ordeals there was nothing to judge. The judge merely pronounced the truth that was already marked on the bodies of the accuser and/or accused and was apparent for all to see. The facts were either known or insignificant—it was only guilt or innocence that had to be determined.[5]

According to this system, the truth about guilt was nothing other than the first step in the public inscription of justice—and justice in turn was constituted by a proper application of the rules of the ordeal or the duel being employed. It was the outcome that mattered, and for

---

5. On this question, far too much attention has been paid to what medieval Christians are said to have believed ("supernatural forces in the world," "judgments of God," etc.). My argument is that what the people involved believed (in this sense) is less important for the way the ordeal worked than is the power structure by which certain truths about transgression were determined. Thus, we don't know what were the real thoughts and feelings of individuals who could at one time resort to the ordeal and who were later obliged to submit to the inquisitorial courts. But we do know that they were processed through very different political-legal-moral structures, subject to very different powers. Their options, their behavior, their relationship to the personnel necessary for determining guilt or innocence were all very different.

this the bodies of substitutes might do just as well as those of the accuser and the accused.[6] Anthropologists who have analyzed the institution of the feud have shown that there is no reason why, so long as the proper rules are followed, the inscription of justice may not in principle continue indefinitely. In a conflict between two feuding kin groups, the successful wounding or killing of an opponent defines at once the satisfaction of justice and the need for redress. The feud is a permanent process, not an event.[7] This can be rephrased by saying that the determination of guilt by the strict accusatorial system resides not in the victory of truth but in a truce between equal powers.

Torture, as part of the inquisitorial system, produced the truth in a very different way.[8] First, it produced information, facts about things done and said, where, what, and to whom, facts quite distinct from the conclusion to be drawn from them. It was a strategy of inquiry, involving a range of factual questions and answers. (Judicial torture itself came to be known as *quaestio,* and the expression "putting to the question" was used to mean putting to torture.) This process depended on a very different way of articulating the truth in relation to physical pain. In trial by ordeal the defeated body showed its guilt directly by its position or by its marks. (The determination of guilt or innocence by oracle or by oath stands opposed to the ordeal proper precisely in not directly involving the bodies of the contestants or of the accused.) The pain, or at least its immediate cause, was in the past. In the system of judicial torture, it was the voice that had to speak the truth for fear of pain—pain that therefore always lay in the future.

Of course, in the ordeal system, too, the accused might, in fear,

6. This was especially appropriate in cases where women, the sick, or clerics were involved. See Gaudemet 1965, 118.

7. The most famous anthropological account of this institution is to be found in Evans-Pritchard's (1940) monograph on the Nuer. Thus, among the Nuer, he observes, arbitration and payment of compensation by "the guilty party" might settle matters for a time, but the two sides maintained their feud, and overt hostility could and often did break out again—especially if the parties concerned were more distant agnates.

8. "Once the trial was opened, the judge had complete liberty to decide which witnesses should be summoned, which documents produced, and what other evidence was necessary to establish the guilt of the accused. The judge was considered an impartial seeker after truth and therefore no legalistic or procedural impediments were to prevent him from discovering the truth" (Ullmann 1947, 22). This way of putting it is, of course, an exaggeration, for as Ullmann himself describes medieval legal theory, it is clear that judges were bound by rules and limitations. For a more systematic statement of judicial rules in the Middle Ages, see Godding 1973, 17–23.

refuse to undergo trial and thereby concede his guilt. Indeed, the priest who conducted the religious ceremony preceding the ordeal might even invite him to confess. But confession was, strictly speaking, unnecessary, although it might, in particular instances, be forthcoming. In the inquisitorial system employing torture, confession was essential when there was no other way of determining guilt—that is, when the appropriate kind and number of witnesses were not available (see Langbein 1977). Verbal discourse was the indispensable medium of the truth. Secret thoughts had to be made available in the form of utterances—words as inner signs brought out as meaningful sounds. The words were not identical with the truth, in the way that the bodily marks of someone who had submitted to the ordeal were identical with it. For so long as the rules of the ordeal were properly followed, the marks it produced could not lie.[9] Indeed, strictly speaking the notion of a lie in this context did not arise until the system as a whole came under attack—especially in the twelfth century, when ordeals were vigorously denounced as superstitions.

This leads us to the second important difference between the way in which the inquisitorial system employing torture produced the truth and the way in which ordeals did so. The application of physical pain in the inquisitorial system facilitated the pursuit of truth by which guilt was determined. There was nothing automatic about the process, for although guilt might be established by confession, the refusal to confess could never of itself quell all doubt. As in any chase, there was always the possibility of escape, and success was never assured until the quarry was captured. Besides, the hunter must be sure that it was his quarry he was pursuing and not some chance stray.[10] (That is the crucial difference between huntsman and fisherman.) So it was that medieval theorists insisted that the accused should not know the

9. Gaudemet (1965, 105) notes that in the course of the ninth century, the judicial duel began to be preferred to the sacred oath ("which too often led to perjury") and thus became the normal form of trial for free men. Since words can lie, a false oath was an occasion not merely for injustice but also for blasphemy—that is, contempt for God. The outcome of a duel—or, for that matter, of a unilateral ordeal—clearly did not run that risk.

10. Is it entirely without significance that a distinctive type of literature, the hunting manual, began to appear first in the middle of the thirteenth century? Of these books, Thiébaux (1974, 26) observes that "they describe types of equipment, set down correct terms and procedures for judging, pursuing, capturing, and breaking different types of quarry, give the various seasons, and advise in the care of hounds and falcons."

charge; otherwise, he might easily confess to what he had not done for fear of more pain. It was not a matter of finding a victim for revenge (as in the feud) but of finding the truth. Thus, secrecy became an essential element in the strategy for determining the truth about guilt—something quite foreign to the ordeal. The judicious hiding of information is itself a device for decoying the quarry, for making it betray its presence. (In the Anglo-Saxon system, which retained accusatorial procedures within an inquisitorial framework, the device of secrecy became a right granted to the accused: the hunter must not find the chase too easy!)

Confession was therefore intended to confirm and to elaborate what was independently known to the court—or rather, to transform its suspicion into knowledge. In order for the court to effect this transformation from subjective states into objective facts, it was necessary to acquire more information than it had to begin with, and not just any information but only what was relevant. And so, too, it was necessary to develop and establish rules of relevance, rules for hunting the truth, for finally arriving at the correct judgment. The final judgment was to be the authorization of a public knowledge. Of course, ordeals also had their rules, whose infringements (whether deliberate or inadvertent) could be referred to in order to explain why a particular outcome was vitiated. But such rules constituted the truth about guilt or innocence (like losing or winning in a game of dice); they did not aim at its regulation and capture (as in hunting strategy).

Third, confession made in the torture chamber could not in itself serve as the basis for conviction. It had to be repeated willingly in court; if the accused refused to do this, he was led away to be tortured again. Hence, the doctrine that truth cannot be the product of violence—that it must be the free confession of a conscious and sincere subject. Violence done to the body was held to be a condition facilitating the emergence and capture of the truth—not, as in the ordeal and the duel, the condition defining its very being. In very different ways, the body was in both cases an arena for the truth. (For long centuries, as we shall see, this doctrine had been systematically developed and put into practice by Christian monasticism, and now, in the High Middle Ages, its disciplines were beginning to be extended to and remolded for the secular, urban world.)

In sum, the main ways in which torture differed from the ordeal were the following: it facilitated the production of information, it was part of the hunt for the truth, and its violence to the body was a condition for arriving at a judgment and not the form in which judgment was inscribed or read. As such, the use of torture required expertise and experts to connect correctly the body's pain, and its utterances, with the pursuit of verbal truth. A considerable learned literature was gradually produced that defined the forms, advantages, and limits of torture, and thus of its correct use. It is important to stress this last point, for the entire truth about the offense in question was not necessarily known even to the tortured body—especially (but not only) when a confession was being extracted from a witness. Strictly speaking, the truth came out finally only in the words of the judgment.

Since the inquisitorial system shifts the authority of the truth from the bodily marks of the accused to the utterance of a judgment, it enhances the importance of the judge. But such a shift also facilitates the construction of a hierarchy of authority in which one judgment may be superseded by another that can have no precise parallel for bodily marks. And it does so on the basis of a principle that is far more metaphysical, as well as being more ambiguous, than any that the ordeal depends on: that the truth is both the author of the word and the word authorized. This is a principle that today we would call religious.

Not all criminal inquiry involved torture, of course. In fact, the rules on this matter were quite unequivocal: it could only be used in cases where the punishment for the crime was death or mutilation. And even here, torture could not be prescribed unless there was clear evidence that a crime had been committed.

However, there was to be one important medieval exception—heresy. Since the crime of holding heretical views could not be confirmed independently of a confession by the accused, it had to be tried, and torture could be prescribed for it if necessary, *before* the existence of the crime could be established. Since the crime itself was deliberately hidden, the hunt for the truth had to employ its own game of deadly secrets and of salutary fears.

The Sociopolitical Context of Judicial Torture

The Fourth Lateran Council of 1215, which proscribed ordeals, also prescribed mandatory annual private confession for all Christians. It was this council, too, that issued decrees expressing the Church's concern to combat heresy and defining the duty of secular authorities to exterminate it. Since (sacramental) confession had now emerged as the universal discipline for creating the truthful conscience, it is not surprising that (judicial) confession should be recognized as the specific technique for proving heresy. The Church knew full well that confession was not an isolated act, that in its creative aspects, as in its incriminating ones, it was a special modality of dialogue informed by power, a unique process that linked the idea of bodily pain (here, or in the hereafter) with the exchange of question and answer in the pursuit of truth.

Although judicial torture was known to Roman law as a method of extracting confession from certain classes of person (typically, slaves) or in certain categories of crime (especially treason), it never entirely disappeared from Europe, even during the so-called Dark Ages, when Germanic tribal practice replaced most of the Roman legal structure. However, its prevalence and extension in criminal procedure from the thirteenth century onward is clearly connected with the renewed importance of Roman law, as well as with the decline of ordeals as a method of judicial proof. In contributing to both these latter trends, the Church, of course, sought to hierarchize and centralize legal authorities and institutions (as the successful monarchies also did) in the face of opposition from localized, custom-based, feudal interests— both ecclesiastical and secular. The Lateran Council of 1215, which decreed such a remarkable array of disciplinary measures (see Schroeder 1937), represents a massive sign of these trends.

At this point, one could ask about the ways in which the inquisitorial system of judicial procedure came to be established, given that it was so well suited to the developing political-legal institutions and socioeconomic conditions of the High Middle Ages. The growing commercial classes required a rational, standardized, universal form of law, a need that was compatible with the political ambitions of popes and monarchs. Why? (see Tigar and Levy 1977). The answer is because duels were anarchic, ordeals were unpredictable, and the inquisitorial system allowed, in a way that the older procedures could never do, a more persistent, more pervasive exercise of centralized control. Thus, torture may be seen as a ruthless extension and intensification of this dominating, rationalizing power. (Such a view might fit with the claim that the widespread and unrestrained use of torture for extracting confessions is more characteristic of modern states which have greater political ambitions—totalitarian, colonial, and postcolonial—than it is of medieval.) In this vein, one might examine the political and ideological conditions that facilitated or inhibited the employment of judicial torture in medieval criminal procedure. (Thus, torture was notably absent from English Common Law [see Heath 1981]. Why was this so?) Such an investigation would, no doubt, be interesting and valuable.

But one can also follow a very different line of inquiry: one can trace the main stages in the religious history of penance in which the concern for truth, physical pain, and confession (the very elements that are so central to the practice of judicial torture) was played out. Doing this shifts the focus from the familiar story of the growth of the state's coercive apparatuses to something more difficult to trace: the changing forms of disciplinary practices in Latin Christian culture by which characteristic modes of potentiality (moral, political, intellectual) came to be articulated. It is this latter route I want to take for the remainder of this chapter.

Penance and the Early Church

It might seem at first sight that sacramental confession, which is voluntary and spiritual, is totally different from the confession extracted forcibly from a subject under judicial torture. There is, of course, a very great difference between the two kinds of confession, especially to our modern eyes. But perhaps the notion that the one is voluntary and the other forced is not the best way to secure that difference. After all, both kinds of confession, as modes of establishing the truth and as techniques for dealing with the dangers of transgression, are set in motion and regulated by authority.

In the Christian institution of penance, bodily pain and the pursuit of truth have been connected since the earliest centuries, although not always in the same way. In what follows, I shall attempt to trace these connections in three stages: first, the way the body of the Church excluded and then readmitted those who had transgressed, imposing on them a range of physical discomforts and deprivations and requiring from them a confession of the truth about themselves for fear of pain in the life after death; second, and parallel with this exercise of power within the secular community, the practices of ascetic discipline distinctive to the religious community (the monastery), in which processes of observing and testing the body's inclinations were systematically developed by the subjection of the self to the divine authority vested in the community's rule and in the abbot; third, a confluence and adjustment of these two traditions in the twelfth and thirteenth centuries, in which verbal discourse gradually became the preeminent modality of power and the medium through which the collaboration between dominators and dominated could be effected.

From the beginning of Christian history, communities of the faithful were confronted with the problem of religious discipline—that is, of dealing with those of their fellows who had transgressed "the Truth." The offending person was required to confess his sin before the assembled congregation and to beg humbly for their prayers and intercession to help reconcile him to the truth. For minor faults committed in everyday life (and who was without them?), this public confession ended the matter. For more serious sins, including those that caused public scandal, a period of exclusion from the fellowship (and so from participation in sacramental communion) was prescribed. The sinner was readmitted only after she had performed the severe rites of penance which ended with her formal reconciliation. The American medievalist H. C. Lea describes in detail the condition of penitents in the early Church:

> During the lengthened periods prescribed for penance, the head was kept shaven, or in the case of women it was veiled, the vestments were of sackcloth sprinkled with ashes, baths were forbidden and abstinence from wine and meat was strictly enjoined—as St Jerome tells us, the filthier a penitent is the more beautiful is he. The time was passed in maceration, fasting, vigils, prayers and weeping—the penitent, as St Ambrose tells us, must be as one dead, with no care for things of this life. In fact he was forbidden to engage in secular pursuits; if he threw off his penitential garments and returned to the world, he was cut off from all association with the faithful and was segregated with such strictness that anyone eating with him was deprived of communion. Whenever the faithful were gathered together in church, the penitents were grouped apart in their hideous squalor, and either left the church before the sacred mysteries, or, if they were allowed to remain, they were not admitted to the Eucharist, but were brought forward to be prayed for and receive the imposition of hands—in short their humiliation was utilized to the utmost as a spectacle and a warning for the benefit of the congregation. In view of the fragility of

youth, it was recommended that penance should not be imposed on those of immature age; and, as complete separation between husband and wife was enforced, the consent of the innocent spouse was necessary before the sinful one could be admitted to penitence. Trade, if not absolutely forbidden to the penitent, was at most grudgingly allowed; he was prohibited from litigation, but if the matter was of urgent necessity, he might seek justice in an ecclesiastical court. In some respects, indeed, the effects of penance were indelible; no one who had undergone it was allowed to resume the profession of arms or to partake of wine and meat if fish and vegetables were accessible; Pope Siricius forbade absolutely marriage to reconciled penitents and the Council of Arles in 443, in case of infractions of this rule, expelled not only the offender but the newly-wedded spouse. Leo I however, in case the penitent was young and found continence perilous, was willing to admit that marriage was a venial sin, not to be forgiven as a rule, but to be tolerated as the least of two evils, for after performing penance life-long chastity was proper. It was not till the ninth century was well advanced that permission to marry was freely given by Nicholas I. The life of the penitent was truly hard, and we can readily believe the assertion of a council of Toledo in 693 that despairing escape from it was sometimes sought in suicide. (1896, 1:28–30)

Whether the sin had been committed openly or in private, confession of guilt and penance and reconciliation were required to be publicly performed, and indeed each was part of a single sequence of rites known in the earliest period by the Greek word *exomologesis*. The rites of reconciliation marked the progressive reintegration of the sinner with the Church, his reconciliation to the truth. They were similar to those imposed on converts seeking baptism and comprised several formal stages:

The first was *fletus* or weeping, in which he stood outside the church, lamenting his sins and begging the prayers of the faithful as they entered: the second was *auditio* or hearing, when he was admitted to the porch among the catechumens and heard the sermon, but went out before the prayers: the third was *substratio*, lying down or kneeling during the prayers uttered for his benefit: the fourth was *consistentia* or *congregatio*, in which he remained with the faithful during the mysteries, but was not allowed to partake; and after this stage had been duly performed he was finally admitted to the Eucharist after

the ceremony of reconciliation by the episcopal imposition of hands.
(Ibid., 24)

Like baptism, the rite of reconciliation was available only once in every sinner's lifetime.

There has been some argument among historians as to whether these early rites of reconciliation amounted to an "absolution of sins" or merely to a readmission of the penitent to the body of the Church, outside of which there could be no salvation. For reasons not too difficult to understand, Catholic and Protestant historians tend to take opposed views on the question. But on this there is no disagreement: that however the rites of reconciliation (culminating in the laying on of hands by the bishop) are to be interpreted in historical retrospect, they were *not* performed prior to the sinner's undertaking penance. In other words, bodily pain and discomfort required by penance preceded, or at any rate accompanied, reconciliation (i.e., the restoration of truth and justice). This stands in marked contrast to the modern practice, which was established in the later Middle Ages, according to which penance (in which bodily pain was no longer an essential element) follows absolution.

Historians commonly speak of a decline of public penance in the early centuries and attribute this to its severity and nonrepeatability, which allegedly made sinners want to postpone confession and reconciliation until their deathbed. But whatever the reason for the decline of public penance in the older centers of European Christianity, among the recently converted Celtic and Germanic tribes in the northwest things were different. There, a new system of private confession based on the Penitentials gradually established itself from about the end of the sixth century. The Penitentials were manuals, having their origins in Celtic monasteries, which classified sins and specified, often in considerable detail, the penance to be applied in each case. (There was, incidentally, something very mechanical about the determination of penance in a way that is reminiscent of the ordeal.)[11] These sins included transgressions that in later centuries would be called civil crimes and dealt with in lay courts. The Penitentials have therefore been described by historians as having had the social function of "civilizing an

---

11. As in the case of certain ordeals, it was possible for the penitent who could not undergo pain or privation for a legitimate reason to hire a (righteous) substitute. See Oakley 1937, 496.

unruly barbarian population" (see Oakley 1923 and 1932). However, apart from noting the teleological form of this crude sociological thesis, we should remember that the Church was concerned above all to make Christians, not to govern barbarians (see Frantzen 1983). And yet, it is not enough even to say that this meant educating converts in the principles of Christian morals. For the way in which Christians were educated, in which the Penitentials played so important a part, required the making of subjects whose morality was to be constructed around the legal notion of duty (cf. Anscombe 1958, 78).

The fixed tables of prescribed penances—which historians of the Penitentials have referred to as "tariffs"—are a central feature of this system. (This formal feature contrasts, as we shall see, with the strategic character of confession and absolution in the modern system.) For example, in the manual known as the *Penitential of Cummean,* the list of penances for the sin of fornication includes the following:

> 6. He who sins with a beast shall do penance for a year; if by himself, for three forty-day periods, if he has clerical rank, a year; a boy of fifteen years, forty days.
>
> 7. He who defiles his mother shall do penance for three years, with perpetual exile.
>
> 8. Those who befoul their lips shall do penance for four years; if they are accustomed to the habit they shall do penance for seven years.
>
> 9. So shall those who commit sodomy do penance for seven years.
>
> 10. For femoral intercourse, two years.
>
> 11. He who merely desires in his mind to commit fornication, but is not able, shall do penance for one year, especially in the three forty-day periods. 12. He who is polluted by an evil word or glance, yet did not wish to commit bodily fornication, shall do penance for twenty or forty days according to the nature of his sin. 13. But if he is polluted by the violent assault of a thought he shall do penance for seven days. 14. He who for a long time is lured by a thought to commit fornication, and resists the thought too half-heartedly, shall do penance for one or two or more days, according to the duration of the thought.
>
> 15. He who is willingly polluted during sleep, shall arise and sing nine psalms in order, kneeling; on the following day he shall live on bread and water; or he shall sing thirty psalms, bending his knees at the end of each. 16. He who desires to sin during sleep, or is uninten-

tionally polluted, fifteen psalms; he who sins but is not polluted, twenty-four. (Bieler 1963, 115)

In effect, the use of these manuals marks the institutionalization of a new method of penitential discipline, and also of a new means of guiding confessors. First of all, it was now the local priest and not merely the bishop who could administer penance. Confession was told privately to the priest, and the penance he imposed (which included fasting on bread and water, flagellation, and painful vigils) was usually somewhat less harsh than that of the older public penance. And finally, the rite of reconciliation (or "absolution") was repeatable—that is, as often as the sinner confessed his sins and submitted to the prescribed penance, he was reconciled.

(By the early part of the ninth century, when these manuals came to be extensively used among the lay population, ecclesiastical bodies began to denounce them. Some historians say this was because "possession of a penitential rendered a priest comparatively independent of his bishop in the administration of penance," while others maintain that "what the bishops wanted was not the disappearance of these manuals, but their orthodoxy" [McNeill and Gamer 1938, 27]. However that may be, when these Penitentials were gradually abandoned, the autonomy of the parish priest as confessor did not disappear but was retained and even strengthened within the system of private annual confession authorized in 1215 by the centralizing Church.)

It will be noticed that the list of sins quoted above from the *Penitential of Cummean* contains references to thoughts as well as to deeds. The thoughts are sometimes treated as deeds, in which case they are penalized like them for predefined periods (so many days or years); sometimes they are treated as conditions, as signs of an inchoate self, a self whose sensual desire, or *libido*, confuses his Christian duty—in which case they are penalized for as long as the condition lasts.

We have here an important contrast between a sinful *act* (an offense that, like the ordeal, required that the pain of penance directly inscribe the truth about guilt on the body), and a sinful *condition* (calling for a more complex relationship between the enduring of pain and discomfort, the articulation of internal truth, and the development of a will confronting the body's desires). I shall take up this latter point again in a discussion of Foucault's essay "Le combat de la Chasteté," but here I want only to stress that the distinction between sinful act and sinful condition found in the Penitentials is not to be confused with that between "sinful behavior" and "sinful thoughts." The difference is more like one between an *event* (whether physical or mental) and a *potentiality* (whether temporary or endless). An event that constitutes transgression calls for something to counteract its damaging effects; a potentiality for transgression requires that the self's power to act be classified and subdivided in order that it be recognized as dangerous. As a religious condition, such potentiality is therefore at once historically defined and culturally constructed.

A major justification for undertaking penance was that by so doing the sinner avoided the greater pain due in purgatory. Thus, according to the *Penitential of Bartholomew Iscanus,* the priest was required to say to the penitent: "Brother, it is necessary for thee to be punished in this life or in purgatory: but incomparably more severe will be the penalty of purgatory than any in this life. Behold, thy soul is in thy hands. Choose therefore for thyself whether to be sufficiently punished in this life according to canonical or authentic penances or to await purgatory" (McNeill and Gamer 1938, 354). It must be stressed that penance was not a simple matter of punishment automatically imposed, of repressing a disorderly individual. After all, in most cases penance was imposed as a consequence of voluntary and private confession. Penance was, therefore, the effect of a choice about the condition of one's soul which presupposed that in one way or another one would have to face up to the truth. If the pain of purgatory was the greater, that was only because one had already rejected the opportunity of restoring one's sinful soul to the truth in this world through penance, and so denied oneself the spiritual benefits of the Eucharist, without which, as all knew, the soul might perish utterly. The important point was not the threat by the priest of bodily pain in the imagined hereafter but the subject's will in admitting guilt, on which depended his submission to pain in this world as something positive. The admission of guilt by the penitent to the confessor was the recognition of the truth about oneself, and at the same time the presentation of oneself as a sick soul in need of help. It was this collaborative activity that sustained the authority relationship between priest and penitent.

The concept of penance as medicine for the soul was no fanciful metaphor, but a mode of organizing the practice of penance in which bodily pain (or extreme discomfort) was linked to the pursuit of truth —at once literal and metaphysical. For it required that the penitent report the truth about his relevant condition to the physician, information that was essential for the latter to diagnose the sickness properly and to prescribe for it the appropriate cure. A sixth-century treatise on penitence entitled *Liber de Penitentia* explains the logic of the argument nicely in the following passage:

> He desires, therefore, that thou shouldst know better what passes in thyself, that when thou layest bare thy disorder to the physician, he may prescribe for thee the necessary antidote; for then wilt thou be able to attain the full benefit of his treatment *(medicinae)*, if thou conceal not from the physician the wounds of thy conscience. Otherwise how art thou to be cured, if thou do not lay bare what things are hidden within thee? For I am of opinion that unless the physician is called in the sick man is not cured. He waits therefore long for thy trouble to be shown to him, so that when thou art cured thou mayest appreciate the healing of his treatment: for what is due to the physician thou mayest fairly estimate, if thou hast first known in thyself thy disorder. And that I may not keep thee with many words, thy penitent confession is thy medicine, which cures thee and gives thee life; and which suffers not thy wound to retain its corruption, but when thou hast groaned awhile, replaces this by a knotty scar. (Quoted in Watkins 1920, 2: 565)

Thus, in order that the sickness be treated, the sufferer must admit to himself, as well as to the physician, the truth whose denial is in part the very condition of that sickness. But what this passage from the *Liber de Penitentia* does not make explicit is that for the Christian, man's condition is a permanent sickness precisely because he cannot admit the whole truth; therefore, there can never be a full cure in this world, merely a continuous process of curing symptoms. This need for an unending struggle against the permanent potentiality for transgression defines the basic character of Christian asceticism.

The medicinal metaphor is to be found articulating the discourse and practice of penance throughout Christian history, although not always in the same way. Thus, bodily pain in the ancient public system of penance occupies a different place from the one it has in the system of private confession regulated by the Penitentials. But in contrast to both, in the "modern system," which was established in the later Middle Ages, bodily pain gradually disappears altogether from the practice of penance. However, the medicinal metaphor, in which the notions of health and truth were jointly opposed to those of sickness and error, is itself in need of some explanation. For the question still remains: What is the role of bodily pain in spiritual sickness? Why was the body to be *tormented* in the process of achieving the truth?

At least two notions seem to be employed in the discipline of penance. First, in relation to purgatory, there is the concept of physical pain as a punishment which is the measure of transgression, whose application therefore preempts greater chastisement in the afterlife and restores the sinner to divine justice. Second, in relation to the medicinal metaphor, pain is conceived of as a purging, as the salutary effect of treatment to restore the sinner (who is in a dangerous condition) to spiritual health. The two notions may be connected through the notion of purgation, but it is in the latter context that the need for verbalizing the truth about oneself can be seen most clearly. And it is this latter process, therefore, that makes possible the accumulation of specific types of information, the putting into practice of certain kinds of knowledge-based expertise, the exercise of distinctive forms of authority (of the judge, the physician, the priest), and the characteristic justifications for applying—or threatening—pain in the confrontation of guilt, sickness, error.

But before attempting an answer to the question posed above about the role of pain in spiritual sickness, I shall look more closely at the Christian tradition, which was embodied in the disciplined life of monastic communities.

Monastic Asceticism

Historians of the Western Church refer to the period from about the end of the sixth century up to the beginning of the twelfth as the Benedictine centuries, during which "the only type of religious life available in the countries concerned was monastic, and the only monastic code was the Rule of St. Benedict" (Knowles 1963, 3). That religious life was based on ascetic discipline whose basic principles had been laid down by the early Church Fathers. A historian of the patristic period sums these up as follows:

> The Christian life is a combat against oneself, and the weapons are those which give pain to the body and force it to exhibit the practices of virtue. Origen, "the forerunner of Christian monasticism," as

Strathmann calls him, was one of the first, so far as our literary sources go, to practice this external austerity. . . . Origen chastised himself; removing all the material of the passions, he filled his days with austere toil, devoting much of the night to the study of the Scriptures, often going without food and finally taking a short sleep upon the bare floor. (Musurillo 1956, 51)

Origen may have been one of the earliest of the Church Fathers to practice such chastisement of the body,[12] but my only point here is that self-punishment constituted a crucial feature of monastic discipline in the Middle Ages and that its program was provided in the writings of the early Greek and Latin Fathers, which were regularly studied in monastic communities. The body is to be chastised, we are told, because it is an obstacle to the attainment of perfect truth.

Once the conception of the "weakening of the flesh" was established, we find it occurring as a frequent commonplace in the later patristic writers. The sophistic author of *De poenitentia* . . . enumerates the motives for penance and for fasting in particular: to atone for our personal faults and to break the habit of sin. When we commit sin we inscribe, as it were, marks upon a wax-tablet and those marks become deeper by repetition; the only way to erase such marks is to practice penance. The soul's "weapon" against sin is fasting; for it is food that feeds the fires of concupiscence, brings fuel for the passions. Hence fasting is the "bridle for the monk"; it is one of the fundamental pillars on which the ascetical life is to be built. (Ibid., 54)

The marks of sin are made on the soul *and* on the body. It is these marks that penance effaces, inscribing in their place the signs of truth in a steady ritual repetition. This, according to the theory, is one meaning of ascetic practices.

But it is important to go beyond deciphering symbolic meanings and examine, as far as possible, the complex process of subjection achieved by Christian asceticism and the collaboration on which it depended.

Undoubtedly, one of the most impressive analyses of monastic asceticism is Foucault's (1982) discussion of the texts of Cassian (ca.

---

12. For pre-Christian forms of self-mortification, see Olphe-Galliard 1957, 941–60; and, for early Christian forms, Viller and Olphe-Galliard 1957, 960–77.

360–435). Cassian's major works—*The Institutes,* which formed a basis of the more famous *Rule* of St. Benedict, and the *Conferences*—were required reading in medieval monasteries. However, the importance of Cassian's texts, according to Foucault, consists in their articulation of a technology of the self, which plays a crucial part in a distinctive production of truth. In this matter, as Foucault himself is careful to note, Cassian is to be regarded not as an innovator but as a witness.

Cassian's categorization of the eight vices was taken up and adapted to the religious discourse of the Middle Ages (where the vices eventually became the Seven Deadly Sins), as was also the idea of the distinctive connection among them.[13] Thus, Cassian taught that of the eight vices, the first six constituted a causal chain by which the one led on to the other: gluttony provoked lust (fornication), which in turn produced greed and anger, which finally caused sadness and sloth. The last two (vainglory and pride) were also linked in a similar way to each other, but together their relation to the first six was very different: they were engendered not merely by the existence but by the elimination of the others. The only power that could save us from pride—that most dangerous of all sins—was divine grace.

Foucault points out that of all the vices, fornication (lust) is distinguished by being based on an urge at once natural, physical, and innate (like gluttony), and yet it must be completely eliminated (in this unlike gluttony, because the need for food must never be totally denied). This is why it is so difficult to conquer. But the victory over fornication is important precisely because it allows the Christian to live in his body while freeing him from the inclinations of the flesh in a unique way. It lies, therefore, at the heart of ascetic practice.

The essence of Cassian's combat for chastity, Foucault insists, has nothing to do with the sexual act, still less with sexual relations between two people. Referring to Cassian's account of the six stages marking the progress of chastity, he writes:

> In this description of the different features of the spirit of fornication, each being effaced in the degree to which chastity progresses, there is thus no relation whatever with another, no act, and not even the intention of committing one. No fornication in the strict sense of the

13. The standard study on this subject is Bloomfield 1952, but unfortunately, it deliberately omits any consideration of scholastic analyses of the scheme. An interesting preliminary sketch that begins to remedy this deficiency is Wenzel 1968.

term. From this microcosm of solitude are absent the two main elements around which revolved the sexual ethics not only of the ancient
philosophers, but of a Christian like Clement of Alexandria—at least
in letter II of *Pedagogue:* the joining together of two individuals *(sun-
ousia)* and the pleasures of the act *(aphrodisia)*. Instead, the elements
concerned are the movements of the body and of the soul, the images, perceptions, memories, dream-figures, the spontaneous flow of
thought, consent of the will, wakefulness and sleep. And two poles
are depicted here, which do not, be it noted, coincide with the body
and the soul: the involuntary pole, whether of physical movements or
perceptions, which are inspired by memories and images that survive,
and which, being reproduced in the mind, invest, call forth and attract the will; and the pole of the will itself which accepts or repels,
turns away or allows itself to be captured, lingers, or consents. On
the one hand, therefore, there is a mechanism of the body and of
thought which, in circumventing the soul, is charged with impurity
and may lead as far as pollution; on the other, a play of thought with
itself. (1982, 19–20)

Foucault notes that, as Cassian sees it, the basic problem in the
struggle against the spirit of fornication is that of pollution—including
and especially nocturnal pollution—whose complete absence is represented as the ultimate stage of chastity. The reason for this concern
with pollution is not, Foucault argues, simply the traditional one of
ritual purity; pollution for Cassian is not merely something forbidden. It is important because it provides the monk with crucial evidence concerning the progress he makes in his battle for chastity. For it
is vital always carefully to examine precisely how pollution takes place.
Thus, in the penultimate stage, when the will has become completely
disengaged from even the least movement of fleshly desire, and the
pollution that occurs does so without the slightest trace of complicity,
without even the faintest dream-image, it then becomes nothing but a
natural phenomenon, a residue, like blood flowing from a wound.
And as a natural phenomenon, pollution can be eliminated only by a
power greater than nature: divine grace. That is why, says Foucault,
the complete absence of nocturnal pollution is regarded by Cassian as
a mark of sanctity, as the sign of total chastity, of a divine gift of grace.
Such a state is not one that man can hope to achieve by himself. All he
can do is to maintain a state of constant watchfulness over himself.

Foucault concludes that the combat of chastity in Cassian, with its constituent practices, evaluations, and goals, has really nothing to do with the internalization of prohibitions relating to particular actions and intentions. Rather,

It is a matter of opening up a domain (whose importance is already emphasized in texts like those of Gregory of Nyssa and especially Basil of Ancyra)—a domain of thought, with its irregular and spontaneous course, with its images, its memories, its perceptions, with the movements and impressions which are communicated from the body to the soul and from the soul to the body. What is in play is not a code of actions allowed or forbidden, it is an entire technique for analysing and diagnosing thought, its origins, its qualities, its dangers, its powers of seduction, and all the obscure forces which may be hidden under the aspect which it presents. And although the eventual objective is, of course, to expel all that is impure or leads to impurity, this can only be achieved by a vigilance which is never to be relaxed, a suspicion that one must always direct against oneself everywhere and always. The questioning should be posed always in such a way that it flushes out all secret "fornication" which may be hidden in the deepest folds of the soul.

In this asceticism of chastity one may recognise a process of "subjectivation" which does not involve a sexual ethic based on an economy of actions. But one must also emphasize two things. This subjectivation is inseparable from a process of understanding which makes the obligation to search and to tell the truth regarding oneself into a permanent and indispensable condition of that ethic. If there is a subjectivation, then it involves an indefinite objectivation of the self by the self—indefinite in the sense that as it is never acquired once for all, it is endless; and in the sense that one must always push the examination of the movements of thought as far as possible, however tenuous and innocent they may appear. Besides, this subjectivation in the form of a quest for the truth about oneself is brought about across complex relations with others. And in many ways: because it is a matter of flushing out from within the self the power of the Other, of the Enemy, who is hidden there under the appearance of oneself; because it is a matter of conducting an incessant fight against the Other whom one can't conquer without the help of the Almighty, Who is more powerful than him; because, finally, confession to others, submission to their advice, permanent obedience to directors, is indispensable to this combat. (Ibid., 23)

If Foucault's analysis is correct, then pain inflicted on the body may be seen as a crucial part of a monastic technology of the self—not simply because the body was to be despised, and certainly *not* because it had to be killed (although the imitation of Christ's Passion has been historically a powerful symbol in the Christian's search for meaning in self-mortification).[14] Pain was necessary because the involuntary connection of the self with sensations, feelings, and desires required a constant labor of inspection and of testing of the body lest the soul be betrayed. Although Foucault is not dealing directly in his article with pain, his analysis makes it possible to see more clearly how inflicting pain in an ascetic context becomes part of the discipline for confronting the body's desires with the desire for truth on the part of a suspicious will.

In answer to my earlier question about the role of bodily pain in spiritual sickness, I now venture that the body was not merely an obstacle to the truth, as recorded by Musurillo, but was primarily a medium by which the truth about the self's essential potentiality for transgression could be brought into the light, so that it could be illuminated by a metaphysical truth, a process in which pain and discomfort were inescapable elements. Foucault in effect makes us aware that it is not the traditional symbolism attributed to ascetic pain to which we must finally look (chastising or mortifying the body) but the place occupied by bodily pain in an economy of truth. In order to determine this place we must, of course, take the monastic program seriously, but searching for symbolic meanings is not the name of *my* game.

14. Of St. Peter Damian, one of the leaders of ecclesiastical reform in the eleventh century, a Catholic biographer writes: "Love of God was evidently the inspiration that motivated Damian's insistence on a life of mortification. The conviction that Christ's suffering and death were meant to serve as models for our lives led him to advocate the closest imitation of Christ as our exemplar. 'That which He did for us, He would also have us do.' For our redemption he did not offer gold or silver or count out the price of our ransom; He offered Himself by shedding His own precious Blood. Damian therefore counseled his disciples to follow in the footsteps of the Master in this life, if they would wish to be in his company at the journey's end. 'For we cannot rejoice with the world and reign with Christ.' In keeping with this idea, Damian further developed the concept of penance by stressing its value in rendering one a partaker in the passion of Christ. *They communicate in truth in the suffering of the Redeemer who do violence to themselves by bodily fasting,* and in so doing, assure for themselves a portion in the glory of His Resurrection. For, as Christ hung on the cross, they also crucify themselves through the practice of self-denial" (Blum 1947, 106; emphasis added).

Foucault's analysis of the combat of chastity, of which I have given a mere outline, is remarkably rich and suggestive.[15] Yet there is one crucially important fact that appears to be left out—or at least not adequately emphasized—in his analysis. For the Christian monk, humility (the virtue opposed to the sin of pride) was a basic means of spiritual progress. As the *Rule* of St. Benedict puts it, in the famous chapter on humility, "We may think of the sides of the ladder [to the Lord] as our body and soul, the rungs as the steps of humility and discipline we must climb in our religious vocation." The will that the monk's vocation requires him to cultivate is not his own but the Lord's. The Lord is not simply the source of a power without whose help he cannot defeat the enemy within, he is also the authority from whom man, in his Fallen state, has become estranged.

> The first step of humility is taken when a man obeys all of God's commandments—never ignoring them, and fearing God in his heart. . . . The second step of humility is reached when a man, not loving his own will, does not bother to please himself, but follows the injunction of the Lord. . . . The third step of humility is attained when a man, from love of God, obediently submits to a superior in imitation of the Lord. . . . The fourth step of humility is reached when a man, in obedience, patiently and quietly puts up with everything inflicted on him. . . . The fifth step of humility is achieved when a monk, by humble confession, discloses to his abbot all the evil thoughts in his heart and evil acts he has carried out. . . . The sixth step of humility is reached when a monk contentedly accepts all that is crude and harsh and thinks himself a poor and worthless workman in his appointed tasks. . . . The seventh step of humility is attained when a man not only confesses that he is an inferior and common wretch but believes it in the depths of his heart. . . . The eighth step of humility is reached when a monk only does that which the common rule of his monastery or the example of his elders demands. . . . The ninth step of humility is achieved when a monk practicing silence, only speaks

15. The standard English translation of Cassian's works was done by Bishop Gibson and published in 1900. The following portions are omitted in that translation: from *The Institutes*, book 6 ("On the Spirit of Fornication"); from *The Conferences*, section 12 ("On Chastity") and section 22 ("On Nocturnal Illusions"). Bishop Gibson clearly felt, in opposition to Cassian himself, that it was neither seemly nor necessary for Christians to reflect on such matters, but unfortunately these are precisely the passages on which Foucault bases his analyses.

when asked a question. . . . The tenth step of humility is reached
when a man restrains himself from laughter and frivolity. . . . The
eleventh step of humility is arrived at when a monk speaks gently,
without jests, simply, seriously, tersely, rationally and softly. . . . The
twelfth step of humility is reached when a monk shows humility in
his heart and in his appearance and actions. . . . When a monk has
climbed all twelve steps, he will find that perfect love of God which
casts out fear, by means of which every thing he had observed anx-
iously before will now appear simple and natural. (Meisel and Del
Mastro 1975, 57–61)

It will be evident that most of these stages in the progress of humility
are characterized by success identifiable only in and through relations
with others. My point is, therefore, that while Foucault seems to
concentrate his attention entirely on a "microcosm of solitude," these
famous "steps of humility" are precisely enmeshed in social relationships, relationships that are not simply a setting but a means. In the
dominant form of medieval monasticism (cenobitic, as opposed to
eremitic), the technology of the self, which lies at the heart of the
combat of chastity, is itself dependent on the institutional resources of
organized community life. The inspection and disengagement of the
will, which Foucault describes, takes place within the stuff of monastic life guided by the abbot. It is true that Foucault himself does
finally mention "the form of a quest for the truth about oneself [which]
is brought about across complex relations with others," but he does
not explain clearly whether, in his view, this is a necessary fact or one
that is merely contingent, and if it is necessary, why.

Although the battle for chastity, at whose heart lies the technology of the self, has a unique place in Christian ascetic ritual, it is not
unconnected with the other struggles for virtue, and especially for
obedience. (The three great renunciations of the "Evangelical Coun-
sels," the three vows that monks took, it should be remembered, were
those of poverty, *obedience,* and chastity. See Butler 1924, 39.) It was
through obedience that the ascetic could be schooled in humility, and
so hope to keep at bay that most dangerous of all sins, pride. It was
through humility that he could learn to love God—and thereby replace
desires of the flesh with the desire for God.[16] But obedience could be

16. The medievalist Jean Leclercq (1979, 35) takes issue with an idea basic to Freudian

learned only in an organized community subject to the authority and discipline of an abbot—the *Rule* of St. Benedict speaks of the monastic community as "a school for God's service"—in which the neophyte could learn to practice the technology of the self for his own spiritual perfection and the greater glory of God. Of course, there were always ascetics who lived alone. But it is significant that the Rule identifies only one kind of whom it approves, hermits "who have spent time *in the monastery testing themselves and learning* to fight against the devil. They have prepared themselves *in the fraternal line* of battle for the single combat of the hermit. They have *laid the foundation* to fight, with the aid of God, against their own bodily and spiritual vices" (Meisel and Del Mastro 1975, 47; emphasis added).

Relations between the monks which define the duties of each, as well as the manner of their performance, are therefore intrinsic to the development of the ascetic technology of the self, and so to its accuracy and effectiveness. From this condition follows another of very great importance: the body, which Foucault identified as the arena for that continuous labor of inspecting and testing, may now be seen as the monastic body as a whole. In this area there is no longer a single point of surveillance from which the self examines itself, but an entire network of functions through which watching, testing, learning, teaching, can take place—the ordered sequence of activities (mundane tasks, church services) and the formal ranks and roles (abbot, prior, full monks, novices, etc.; choir monks and obedientiaries; the individual rank of each brother; etc.).

Although mutual observation was the duty of all, it was too im-

---

psychology: that, as he puts it, "the most important is that about which we do not speak—the unsaid—because it is repressed, but obsessional. Stretching this to extremes, such medieval literature is chaste because its authors were not." This idea Leclercq firmly rejects: "Any such reaction ignores the difference between the 'double meanings' and the 'hidden meanings.' A 'hyper-eroticized society,' which has been made such by all sorts of ways—publicity and so forth—and has frequently been exploited for economic and commercial purposes—a consumer society, thus a producer society, favours double meanings; but the hidden meanings are those conveyed by symbols which must be interpreted, and which actually are so by a whole cultural make-up, of which symbolism—including and especially biblical symbolism—is such an important part and parcel." Leclercq's thesis is that the verbal elaboration of such symbolism was part of a discourse that helped monks transform and recharge their fleshly desires into the desire for God. Thus, together with the problem of the ascetic's redirection of the will (from the will of the self to the will of God), which I indicated earlier, we have here another problem not treated by Foucault—the reconstruction of (and not merely the detachment from) desires.

portant to be left in the form of a general injunction. Those on whom the primary responsibility for observing was placed were also picked out to be especially observed and to be imitated, as this passage from an eleventh-century customary makes plain:

> The roundsmen of the monastery, who are called the *circas,* shall according to the command of St. Benedict go at certain times the rounds of the monastery's offices, noting the carelessness and negligence of the brethren, and the breaches of regular discipline. They shall be chosen from the worthiest and most prudent of the whole monastery, such as will never denounce any from malice or personal dislike, nor pass over any negligences for friendship's sake. Their number shall vary with the size and needs of the community. On their rounds they shall behave most religiously and orderly, giving an example of religious observance to all beholders; they shall make no sign, and speak no word to any person on any pretext, but they shall straitly regard negligences and faults and nothing else, and, passing by in silence, shall denounce them afterwards in chapter. (Knowles 1951, 78)

Thus, the monastic body observed and tested itself, and its members learned, painfully, the obedience that formed the disciplined will of each as the will not of the self but of the Lord. It was not that the religious community repressed the self—on the contrary, it provided the discipline necessary for the construction of a certain kind of personality: the sinful self living within "the community of those who stand with him as sinners before God" (Dörries 1962, 292). The practice of articulating one's guilt to someone more skilled in the treatment of transgression than oneself was a major part of that construction. There was a formal occasion in the daily assembly known as the Chapter at which, after a recitation from the *Rule* of St. Benedict or from the Gospel, the monks learned to confess the truth with due humility and to undergo penance (flogging). A tenth-century Monastic Agreement from England prescribed how this was to be done:

> Then, all being seated again, the Rule or, on feast days, the Gospel of the day, shall be read and the prior shall explain what has been read according as the Lord shall inspire him. After this, any brother who is conscious of having committed some fault shall humbly ask forgiveness and indulgence. But a brother that is accused, no matter for what reason, by the abbot or by one of the senior officials, shall prostrate

himself before speaking. And when asked by the prior the reason for this, he shall answer by admitting his fault, saying *Mea culpa domine.* Then, when bidden, let him rise. If he acts in any other wise, he shall be deemed guilty. Thus whoever, when rebuked by a superior for any fault or for anything done amiss in the workshops, does not immediately prostrate himself as the Rule ordains, must undergo the greater punishment [i.e., whipping]. Indeed, the more a monk humbles himself and accepts blame, the more mercifully and gently shall he be dealt with by the prior. For it is meet that in all our negligences, whether of thought, word or deed, we should be judged in this present life by sincere confession and humble penance lest, when this life is over, our sins declare us guilty before the judgement-seat of Christ. When this duty of spiritual purgation has been gone through, the five psalms set forth below shall be said for the departed brethren. . . . Nor shall the *schola* even, on the score of their tender age, ever omit this duty but, although they are as yet untroubled by temptations, let them make their confession in the customary way that the elder brethren do. If, moreover, a brother, urged by some temptation of soul or body, needs to confess at any time, let him by no means delay to have recourse to the healing remedy of confession. (Symons 1953, 17–18)

Foucault's "microcosm of solitude" was, as we can now see, from its inception a microcosm of social subjection; the lonely quest for oneself was yet to be launched in a future age. The individual body into which were locked its own sensations and desires was not yet the measure of truth. Nor was the "real truth" about the self drawn from the agony of bodily desire, as was to be the case much later. The Benedictine monk's truthful self was the continuous work of a structured community.

Modern Penance as Inquisitorial Method

Confession and penance were basic to monastic discipline as they had never been outside it in the early Middle Ages. The Penitentials did disseminate the practice of private penance among the lay population, but it was never a compulsory requirement, still less a regular one, until the Lateran Council of 1215 decreed it so. Previously, the lay penitent confessed his secret sins only when he felt the need to do so.

A recent history of medieval confession describes the emergence of the modern system of private penance as follows:

> Between the ninth and the thirteenth centuries four changes occurred in the theology and practice of this sacrament: (1) penances were lightened and made arbitrary; (2) contrition became the essential element for the penitent and pushed penitential exercises into a subservient position; (3) private confession, already accepted as a necessary part of the forgiveness of sins, was declared universally obligatory by the Fourth Lateran Council of 1215; and (4) the meaning of the priest's role was more carefully defined and its importance in the process of forgiveness radically enhanced. (Tentler 1977, 16)

Contemporaries such as Gratian, Alain de Lile, and Robert of Flamborough noted the decline in the severity of penance in the twelfth century and attributed it to the new unwillingness on the part of people to countenance the painful penances of the past—and the historian just quoted seems to agree. However, it is not at all clear that the willingness to endure pain in the cause of truth was generally diminishing: from the eleventh century right through the Middle Ages, there were several waves of ascetic renewal involving self-torture.[17] Still less was there a marked decline in the willingness to inflict pain on others for the sake of truth: this was, after all, precisely the period when judicial torture became established in ecclesiastical courts as well

17. "From the eleventh to the thirteenth century, when the practice of devotional discipline [i.e., flagellation] spread, two modes of infliction were employed. The first, by which the discipline was self-administered, and the second which necessitated recourse to the help of another person. The first was practised from preference, though not exclusively, at Fonte-Avellana. It was well-known to St. Peter Damian, to Poppo of Stavelot, to St. Anthelm . . . (+1178), and to Mary of Oignies (+1213). It was also made use of by the Dominicans at the time of Jordan of Saxony (1222–1237) and in certain Dominican convents in the following century. On the contrary, St. Pardulphus of Gueret, the Blessed Stephen of Aubazine, preferred that the discipline should be administered by another hand. St. Elizabeth of Hungary had recourse to her servants for the purpose. St. Hedwig, Duchess of Silesia, later a Cistercian nun, and the Dominican sister Christina Ebner, made use of the services of their sisters in religion" (Gougaud 1927, 191). The author goes on to describe in detail instances of this practice among religious and lay populations but concludes the chapter with a dismissive comment about the flagellants ("the morbid fanaticism of the Flagellants"), those groups of uncontrollable religious enthusiasts who paraded through the late medieval Italian cities beating themselves. The historical significance of this ascetic movement is treated more seriously in a paper by Henderson (1978).

as lay.[18] The problem is quite different—that of understanding the maturation of a new ritual of truth in which interrogation plays the central part, in which truth about guilt is no longer inscribed on the body but extracted from it and invested in it—in the form of disciplined words and gestures.

In effect, the new regime of penance extends the technology of the self that Foucault describes from its monastic locus (with its captive bodies) to the population as a whole, and especially to the expanding, mobile population of the towns in which irreligion and heresy both seemed to thrive. Writing of these centuries of growth, a historian of the medieval Church notes:

> Indeed the organized church of the Middle Ages had so far scarcely considered the problem of urban society. Despite all the natural disasters and disruptions which afflicted the countryside, it was possible to treat the rural community as a stable and inert mass amenable to organization and control. But what was to be made of the towns— anarchic, engaged in pursuits doubtfully permissible in canon law, embracing extremes of wealth and destitution, subject to over-employment and unemployment, quite different from anything known in the rural community? (Southern 1970, 274–75)

It was to be the newly established mendicant orders, the Franciscans and the Dominicans (both directly subject to central papal authority), who were to help extend the Church's discipline to these urban populations. Preaching and disputing were the skills they needed most in this task, and that was exactly what they developed, through the study of theology and logic, in the new universities.[19]

> Until the friars came the universities had served mainly as a training ground for administrators. They produced the men who developed the legal systems, the law courts, and the organization of government. This was a necessary, but increasingly unsatisfying aim. By contrast the friars in their studies aimed at the conversion of the world.

18. The spread of judicial torture in the countries of western and central Europe during the thirteenth and fourteenth centuries is traced in Caenegem 1965, 735–40.

19. The most important form of teaching in the medieval universities, in theology as in other subjects, was conducted in terms of "questions," with the master in the role of a presiding judge, as in a court of law. See Gilson 1955, 247.

They wanted to convert heretics, to confute the Saracens, to win over the Greeks, to form preachers and confessors, and to instruct those people in western Europe who had been largely left out of the calculations of earlier religious innovators. Theological study was the foundation for this widely diversified activity: in becoming intellectually more refined and difficult, it also became practically more significant. (Southern 1970, 298)

In the new system of confession (in which friars were to play by far the most important role, administering its practice and developing its theory), laymen and laywomen are required to learn not only to speak the truth within themselves, especially when the truth is most difficult to articulate, most painful to admit into the light. They have to learn at the same time to question, to hear, and to identify the truth, something very hard to do by oneself in relation to oneself if one has not spent a lifetime in discipline. (The devil so easily hides the truth.) The interrogator must therefore be another, someone who is trained to press on, whether he happens to know the penitent or not. He must learn to say, in the words of an anonymous twelfth-century treatise:

Confess therefore what thou hast done, as thou hast done it, and when thou hast done it, and in what measure thou hast done it, and who thou art that hast done it, and who and what manner of person it is, with whom thou hast done it: or if it be impersonal, what it is. If thou wilt be safe confess all these circumstances with the number of the occasions, and the measure of the gratification, and the statement of thine age. (Quoted in Watkins 1920, 2: 746)

Mental pain (anguish) accompanying the inquiry is normally a sign that the penitent has admitted the whole truth about his sin and is properly contrite. (In the early thirteenth century, the Dominican St. Raymund of Pennafort described effective confession as bitter [*amara*], speedy, complete, and frequent. See Lea 1896, 1: 347.) And contrition was the essential precondition for absolution.[20] On the

20. Poschmann (1964, 157–58) puts it this way: "An unsolved problem which had been bequeathed by the Fathers and the Carolingian theologians to the scholastics was that concerning the relation of the subjective or personal factor in penance to the objective or ecclesiastical one. This was now approached from a new angle, inasmuch as among the personal factors the emphasis was no longer laid on works of penance *(paenitentia, satisfactio)* but on sorrow *(contritio)*. . . . Before this time such sorrow had been taken for granted as present in all sincere penance, and had hardly received any special treat-

other hand, stubborn resistance in admitting guilt that is consciously hidden within oneself may sometimes (as in heresy) call for the application of *physical* pain.[21] It may be said that physical pain is an effective strategy for securing the truth only when the body subjected to it is at once captive and resistant. If an entire population (and not merely captive bodies) were now to be trained in the regular confession of transgressions, physical torture was neither practicable nor necessary. The form and the means of this painful discipline would have to be essentially verbal.

A vast literature grew up in the later Middle Ages to instruct the confessor in his difficult and dangerous task—how to interrogate, how to listen, and how to identify the guilt that was indicated (or literally created) by the words of the penitent. The Decree of 1215, together with the various local customs and regulations that had preceded it, demanded from the Christian the performance of a precisely defined act. To render such an act possible, it was necessary for the priest to have a number of practical and theoretical skills which were independent of his personal moral dispositions: he must know how to receive the penitent and establish a solid relationship with him quite different from the superficial contact of a chance encounter; he must know how to help the penitent examine his conscience in order to determine the faults he had committed and their degree of gravity, which depended partly on the culpable act in itself but also on the penitent's temperament and other mitigating or aggravating circumstances. Apart from all these skills required for appreciating the precise situation, the confessor must know how to suggest ways of avoiding faults in the future and how to impose the appropriate penance, given their number and gravity (see Michaud-Quantin 1962, 8). Clearly the skills required here were different from those needed to administer the Penitential "tariffs"—if indeed it can be said that the latter needed any skills at all other than literacy. The new system thus depended on specialized forms of training for confessors and on a body of specialized knowledge culti-

---

ment independently of satisfaction *(paenitentia)*. From the start, therefore, the problem as now presented was the question of the relation between sorrow and absolution; or between sorrow and confession, since in ordinary speech absolution and confession stood for the same thing. From this time onwards [i.e. the twelfth century] sorrow is at the centre of the doctrine of penance."

21. The standard authority on this subject is still Lea (1896), who describes the use of judicial torture by the medieval inquisition in volume 1, chapter 9, entitled "The Inquisitorial Process."

vated by theologians, logicians, and grammarians. The characteristic literature that was produced in this connection during the Middle Ages was thus crucial to the system of confession and to the exercise of power it enabled.

In a memorable passage, Lea observes that

> all possible lapses from rectitude in every sphere of human activity were investigated and estimated and catalogued and defined with the minuteness that had never before been attempted by moralists, and huge books were compiled to afford the priest the necessary aid in pushing his enquiries. The Ten Commandments, the seven deadly sins, the five senses, the twelve articles of faith, the seven sacraments, the seven works of temporal mercy and the seven spiritual, were ransacked to find objects of enquiry, and then all classes and callings of men were successively reviewed and lists of questions were drawn up fitted for their several temptations and habitual transgressions. . . . Bartholommeo de Chaimis [end of fifteenth century], after exhausting all the generalities of sins, gives instructions for the examination of children and married folk, princes and magistrates, lawyers, physicians, surgeons, courtiers, citizens, merchants, traders, bankers, partners, brokers, artisans, druggists, goldsmiths, tavern-keepers, butchers, tailors, shoemakers, lenders and borrowers, bakers, actors, musicians, farmers, peasants, tax- and toll-gatherers, rectors and administrators of hospitals and religious houses, clerics, simple priests, canons and incumbents of benefices, bishops and secular prelates, abbots and regular prelates and finally monks and friars. These are only types of a class of works whose multiplication shows the demand existing for them. (1896, 1: 371)

This discourse of sins served to probe, and in so doing, also helped to define and form, specific types of Christian consciousness. Sins were not simply vices in general (pride, fornication, etc.) but types of thought, speech, and action anchored in particular social statuses and indicating by their negativity the virtues of others: "Sins typical of men of the penitent's station must be inquired about. A knight must not be questioned about the sins of the monk, or vice versa. . . . To gain a better understanding of whom you must question about what, observe that princes are to be questioned about justice, knights about plunder, merchants, officials, craftsmen, and workers about perjury, fraud, lying, theft, etc." (*Summa Astesana,* ca. 1317, quoted in Le Goff 1980,

119). The formation of disciplined religious consciousnesses thus came to be rooted in the privileges and responsibilities, the rights and obligations, of the different social classes.

In his work, the confessor had to be alert and vigilant—not only in relation to the truths being objectified in the penitent's confession, but also in relation to himself lest the effect of those guilty words, which he was obliged to elicit, provoke in him feelings of pleasure. This detachment from sensations was crucial not so much for his own spiritual benefit—as in the case analyzed by Foucault—but for his role as inquisitor and judge. (After all, he would in turn confess *his* own sins later to *his* own confessor, including in them such impure thoughts as he had had while listening to his penitents—of course, in a way that would not break thereby the seal of confession.) The primary reason for the state of detachment that the confessor must cultivate had therefore nothing to do with his own spiritual perfection; the primary reason was that he should be as efficient as possible in the pursuit, identification, and capture of the truth that lay hidden so deep within the sinner's soul. And with this we reach a remarkable concern, not merely with spiritual perfection (the goal of traditional asceticism), but also with the perfection of discourse as investigative and educative power. This socially constructed instrument was to become an essential condition, later, for the exploration and cultivation of the "real truth" about the subject—psychological and political.

The history of the ritual of confession shows one of the paths by which all Christians—priest and layman, husband and wife, teacher and pupil, confessor and penitent, judge and accused, even torturer and tortured—came to be subjectified in determinate ways. As the aspirants to distinctive virtues, whose exercise binds the one to the other by reciprocal duties and desires, all become subjects (at once active and passive) of power—but not all, of course, in the same manner.

Conclusion

As my primary aim has been exploratory, all I can offer are some points for further consideration.

I began with a critical look at the triumphalist thesis of certain historians, according to which the formal establishment of judicial torture in the Middle Ages marks a progressive step in the direction of rationality and away from myth and religion. I then examined more closely the procedure of determining guilt by the application of physical pain in the ordeal and contrasted it with the system of which judicial torture was a part. It was not, we saw, simply a question of a worse method of reaching the truth being replaced by a better one. To begin with, both must be recognized as distinctive ways of determining the truth about guilt (itself a socially determined condition)—the one directly through violence done to the body, and the other through the use of violence as a persuasive element in extracting confession. If the latter can be said to be "more rational," it is only in the sense that spoken words are the essential medium as opposed to bodies-as-signs. It was only through the process of question and answer that signs could be evaluated, doubts dispelled, and conviction secured. Where pain applied to the body could be used to facilitate this process—so medieval jurists argued—it was justified.

Contrary to the triumphalist thesis, the rationality of torture in the inquisitorial system did *not* consist in a retreat from the dependence on religious forces. The remarkable spread of the inquisitorial system in the central Middle Ages (to which judicial torture belongs) was deeply embedded in ecclesiastical institutions and practices. Torture was first theorized by medieval canon lawyers, authorized by medieval popes, and used in the medieval inquisitions to extort confessions of heresy. But more important than this institutional association of judicial torture with the Church (with "religion") is the fact that the flowering of the inquisitorial system in the Middle Ages coincides precisely (and is intimately connected with) the massive extension of sacramental penance to the entire Christian population. Is this fact to be seen as a retreat from religious forces?

There can surely be no doubt that the practice of sacramental penance in the later Middle Ages was thoroughly rational, for it involved the critical evaluation of verbal evidence, the working out of significant conceptual distinctions, the drawing of universal conclusions. And it was at the center of a network of disciplines—intellectual, moral, and political. The infliction of physical pain was no longer an essential element in *that* practice as far as the general population was concerned. But it was, nevertheless, retained as a strategic element in heresy trials conducted by episcopal and papal inquisitors, and also in the cultivation of spiritual truth by religious ascetics.

In modern times, inflicting pain has come to be regarded as antithetical to morally acceptable religion. Indeed, pain is now regarded as an evil that "the religious attitude" can help overcome. Yet it continues to be deployed and theorized as rationally justifiable in warfare,[22] criminology, and medical experimentation on animals. The character of rationality in this context is reflected in the fact that inflicted pain and suffering must be justified in terms of their instrumental adequacy to given ends. Indeed, one of the modern definitions of violence is the notion of a mismeasure in inflicting pain and suffering (see Cotta 1985, 49–67).

In medieval Christianity, it was the full development of the "rational" practices at the heart of sacramental penance (with its distinctive economy of pain and truth) which formed an ideological precondition for rejecting the ordeal system as superstition and for rationalizing judicial torture.[23] I have not discussed the political-economic conditions that provided the historical impetus for the increasing institutionalization of the new system, because that is part of another story.

The connection of pain with the objectification of truth has had intriguing forms and effects in Christian history. Always, it seems, pain (at first bodily, and more latterly also mental) has been associated with guilt, error, sickness—with the condition itself, its determination, or its treatment. But the association has mutated several times, producing profound—and profoundly different—social and psychological effects. Since the Enlightenment, the most remarkable of these mutations has appeared in the domain of secular history. For as history became substantialized and singularized, it assumed the form of a universal force that pushes mankind along the path of progress, punishing error and inadequacy—very much as the God of the Old Testament did.[24]

22. But within technically feasible means, a legal distinction is made between weapons that inflict unacceptable forms of suffering (e.g., chemical missiles) and others that are acceptable (napalm, cluster bombs, etc.)—distinctions that are obviously rooted in the European experience of warfare since 1914.

23. In his brilliant study, Langbein (1977) argues that the abandonment of judicial torture in the eighteenth century was due not to the triumph of rational, humanist criticism (as progressivist histories claim) but to the subversion of the Roman-canon law of proof. Whereas the medieval law required full proof (through confession) or release, in early modern states the courts were content with circumstantial evidence. The ease and speed with which the new legal practices could secure criminal conviction was important for disciplining the subjects of absolutist princes. It was thus the inefficiency of the old law to which judicial torture was integral that led to its abandonment.

24. Thus, in 1840, the German statesman von Schön: "If one does not take time as it comes, seizing the good within it and promoting it in its development, then time

Power and rationality were clearly intrinsic to medieval religion. To object that this claim applies only to an illegitimate extension of real religion, that religion in its essence can do without the legal, medical, and political practices I have described is, surely, to resort to anachronistic reasoning. In my opinion, the story I have tried to tell here produces grounds for understanding partly what "religion" was, not for identifying what part of it is "true religion."

punishes" (cited in Koselleck 1985, 296). And, in 1908, Lord Cromer, the British administrator of Egypt, wrote—elaborating on that thought—that "civilisation [as a historical process] must, unfortunately, have its victims" (1913, 44).

4 ✂ ON DISCIPLINE AND HUMILITY IN MEDIEVAL CHRISTIAN MONASTICISM

Rather than attempt an account in terms of the familiar duality of ideology and social structure, I want to examine *disciplinary practices,* including the multiple ways in which religious discourses regulate, inform, and construct religious selves. Such an approach seems to me to require an examination of two kinds of power process: formations of the self and manipulations of (or resistances to) others. Weber's famous definition of power as "the probability that one actor within a social relationship will be in a position to carry out his own will despite resistance" (1947, 152) helps us to focus on repressive or manipulative processes of power, but it obscures something I wish to examine in this chapter: the conditions within which obedient wills are created. A remarkable feature of monastic discipline is that it explicitly aims to create, through a program of communal living, the will to obey. The Christian monk who learns to will obedience is not merely someone who submits to another's will by force of argument or by the threat of force—or simply by way of habitual, unthinking response. He is not someone who has "lost his own will," as though a man's will could be truly his only when it remained opposed to another's. The obedient monk is a person for whom obedience is *his* virtue—in the sense of being his ability, potentiality, power—a Christian virtue developed through discipline. This is certainly one important difference between the medieval Christian monastery[1] and other "total institu-

1. By "medieval Christianity" I refer primarily to Latin Christendom (broadly: northern and central Italy, northern Spain, France, Rhineland, the Low Countries, England) in the central Middle Ages, a period of crucial change in the economic, political, and ideological formations of western Europe.

tions," such as prisons and hospitals, with which the monastery has sometimes been classified (Goffman 1961). The point is not that force has no necessary place in monasteries; of course it has. It is that force is a crucial element in a particular transformation of dispositions, not merely in the keeping of order among inmates.

Monastic rites governed the economy of desire. Force (punishment), together with Christian rhetoric, guided the exercise of virtuous desires. The central principle on which these rites were based assumed that virtuous desire had first to be created before a virtuous choice could be made. It stands, therefore, in contrast to our modern assumption that choices are *sui generis* and self-justifying.

My approach to the analysis of monastic rites differs in certain respects from the dominant concepts of ritual in anthropology. It may therefore be helpful if I deal with this matter briefly before I proceed with my substantive discussion.

Some Recent Approaches to the Analysis of Ritual

Modern anthropologists writing on ritual have tended to see it as the domain of the symbolic in contrast to the instrumental. In British social anthropology it was Radcliffe-Brown who helped to popularize this distinction, as in this typical passage:

> The very common tendency to look for the explanation of ritual actions in their purpose is the result of a false assimilation of them to what may be called technical acts. In any technical activity an adequate statement of the purpose of any particular act or series of acts constitutes by itself a sufficient explanation. But ritual acts differ from technical acts in having in all instances some expressive or symbolic element in them. (1939, 143)

In other words, some actions require an explanation in terms of meaning, others in terms of cause. But this sharp distinction between "expressive or symbolic" activity, on the one hand, and "technical" activity, on the other (which overlapped the older "sacred/profane" dichotomy) was rephrased by Leach in terms of a continuum:

> Ritual, I assert, "serves to express the individual's status as a social person in the structural system in which he finds himself for the time being." . . . For my part I find Durkheim's emphasis on the absolute

dichotomy between the sacred and the profane to be untenable. Rather it is that actions fall into place on a continuous scale. At one extreme we have actions which are entirely profane, entirely functional, technique pure and simple; at the other we have actions which are entirely sacred, strictly aesthetic, technically non-functional. Between these two extremes we have the great majority of social actions which partake partly of the one sphere and partly of the other.

From this point of view technique and ritual, profane and sacred, do not denote *types* of action but *aspects* of almost any kind of action. (1954, 10–11, 12–13)

Leach combined the idea that ritual as an aspect of action signified social status with the older notion that ritual as a structured event served to evoke something in the minds of participants—the ideal social structure:

If anarchy is to be avoided, the individuals who make up a society must from time to time be reminded, at least in symbol, of the underlying order that is supposed to guide their social activities. Ritual performances have this function for the participating group as a whole; they momentarily make explicit what is otherwise a fiction. (16)

What was common to both ideas (ritual as a structured event and ritual as an aspect of action) was, of course, the assumption that ritual is essentially a symbolic form, signifying something to participants, and therefore in need of interpretation.

When Douglas produced her own distinctive analyses of symbolic behavior (1966, 1970, 1978), she emphasized that "ritual is pre-eminently a form of communication" (1970, 20), a form that employs a "restricted code" as opposed to an "elaborated" one. Somewhat like Bernstein, who was the acknowledged source of this distinction, Douglas attempted to correlate forms of communication with social functions and types of person: ritualism (restricted code) maintained a common experience and social solidarity, and secularism (elaborated code) made explicit and helped to bridge unique individual perceptions. The distinction between restricted and elaborated codes figured prominently in the work of many symbolic interactionists (see, e.g., the contributions to Kapferer 1976), who stressed that symbolic meanings were the product of negotiation between interacting agents rather than of a given normative order.

Turner's voluminous writings on the subject are primarily concerned with providing exegeses of the semantics of ritual. Drawing on depth psychology, Turner stressed that ritual symbols should also be interpreted as "a set of evocative devices for rousing, channelling and domesticating powerful emotions" (1969, 42–43). Such an interpretation would show how, for example, certain ritual symbols

> unite the organic with the sociomoral order, proclaiming their ulti-
> mate religious unity, over and above conflicts between and within
> these orders. Powerful drives and emotions associated with human
> physiology, especially the physiology of reproduction, are divested
> in the ritual process of their antisocial quality and attached to compo-
> nents of the normative order, energizing the latter with a borrowed
> vitality, and thus making the Durkheimian "obligatory" desirable.
> Symbols are both the resultants and the instigators of this process,
> and encapsulate its properties. (1969, 52–53)

Jungian rather than Freudian in his religious optimism, Turner was by no means the first to attempt a synthesis of ideas from depth psychology and anthropology. But more important here is the fact that he sought, like other anthropologists, to identify ritual in terms of its symbolic features, as "prescribed formal behaviour not given over to technological routine" (1976, 504), a conception that seems to lead to the preoccupation with deciphering "symbolic codes."

The idea that the ritual process is essentially symbolic and there-fore essentially a matter of the communication of messages has become a central doctrine of anthropology, both British and American. As Wagner put it:

> If ritual is, in its usual definition, what Mary Douglas calls a "restricted
> code" . . . , then the anthropologist's job is to decipher it. But *what*
> is encoded and why? And what is the nature of the code and why is it
> formulated in that way? These questions bear upon the relational role
> of ritual within the subject-culture, and what it *does* as communica-
> tion, regulation, or whatever. (1984, 143)

There are echoes here of Austin's (1962) analysis of discourse into "lo-cutionary," "illocutionary," and "perlocutionary" dimensions, al-though that author is not cited by Wagner. And as with Austin's treat-ment of the meanings and functions of conventional utterances, such approaches carefully separate the (public) meanings of ritual from the (private) feelings and intentions of its performers. Thus:

> Rituals as conventionalized behaviour are not designed or meant to express the intentions, emotions, and states of mind of individuals in a direct, spontaneous, and "natural" way. Cultural elaboration of codes consists in the *distancing* from such spontaneous and intentional expressions because spontaneity and intentionality are, or can be, contingent, labile, circumstantial, even incoherent and disordered. (Tambiah 1979, 124)

It might appear at first sight that such anthropological statements are in opposition to Turner's, but they are not. They do not deny that ritual may affect the individual intentions and emotions of participants; they do imply, however, that the cultural meanings of ritual are not affected by the latter.[2] As Evans-Pritchard earlier argued: "Only chaos would result were anthropologists to classify social phenomena by emotions which are supposed to accompany them, for such emotional states, if present at all, must vary not only from individual to individual, but also in the same individual on different occasions and even at different points in the same rite" (1965, 44).

In views of this kind, ritual becomes principally the object of a reading, like a text with true meanings that can be deciphered only by initiates—practitioners and anthropologists alike. For Geertz, all cultural and social products, not merely ritual events, are symbols to be read: "Arguments, melodies, formulas, maps, and pictures are not idealities to be stared at but texts to be read; so are rituals, palaces, technologies, and social formations" (1980, 135). This reduction of a heterogeneous world to textuality transforms *motive* into a literary figure.

Many French anthropologists too have been concerned with ritual as a distinctive mode of communication, although structuralists have typically been more interested in how ritual communicates than in what is communicated. For example, Lévi-Strauss writes: "How, then, are we to define ritual? We can say it consists of words uttered, gestures performed and objects manipulated, independently of any gloss or commentary that might be authorised or prompted by these three forms of activity" (1981, 671). When ritual is defined thus, it emerges as the mode of communication that "makes constant use of

---

2. Cf. Leach: "For the individual, participation in a ritual may also have other functions—e.g. a cathartic psychological one—but this, in my view, is outside the purview of the social anthropologist" (1954, 16, n. 27).

two procedures: parcelling out and repetition" (672).[3] Smith (1982) builds on Lévi-Strauss to elaborate further characteristics of rites, such as the use of elements to create an illusion that can be believed in (as in the Western theater of the last few centuries), and the marking of periods and occasions having a cosmological significance.[4] Sperber (1975, 1980) has been less preoccupied with rite as symbolic practice, and more with symbolism as a mode of thought.[5]

These references to anthropological writers are not offered as a comprehensive account of anthropological theories of ritual. Rather, I cite them in order to indicate some of the ways that my approach to rites differs from them. Perhaps the most important difference is that I am skeptical of ritual as the object of a general theory. While I take it for granted that communicative discourse is involved in learning, performing, and commenting upon rites, I reject the idea that ritual itself encodes and communicates some special meaning. In what follows I present a specific historical analysis of monastic rites as disciplinary practices. Monastic rites are analyzed in relation to programs for forming or reforming moral dispositions (that is, for organizing the physical and verbal practices that constitute the virtuous Christian self), in particular, the disposition to true obedience. In these programs, as we shall see, the meanings of conventional performances and the feelings and intentions of performers are not sharply separated—on the contrary, in such programs it is precisely their interrelation that is central.[6] For anthropologists who regard ritual as morally formative, this

3. Procedures that are, incidentally, to be found in statistical reasoning also.

4. In this, Smith seems to revert to two old anthropological doctrines—one associated with Tylor and Frazer (rites express and reproduce religio-magical beliefs), and the other with Van Gennep (rites signify times, places, and roles, and regulate transitions between them). Several anthropologists have argued effectively against the definition of rites in terms of "magical beliefs"—for a sensitive discussion of this point in the context of a particular culture, see Lienhardt 1961. Equally problematic is Smith's neo-Tylorian conception of ritual as a special situation designed to create an illusion, which makes apparent what otherwise remains invisible and hides what makes the illusion possible, yet demands of viewers, "Take the rite seriously, but not too seriously" (106). Is this not uncomfortably close to a description of modern Western theater?

5. Toren (1983) offers a critique of Sperber.

6. Collingwood (1938) discusses this interrelation with reference to his idea of language: language in its widest sense, he maintains, was simply "bodily expression of emotion, dominated by thought in its [logically] primitive form as consciousness" (235). Verbal language was not the only, nor yet "the most developed," kind of language; there were several (aural, visual, gestural—and within each, again different kinds), each appropriate to its conceptual object: "The expression of emotion is not, as it were, a

interrelation has often been taken as unproblematic.[7] The problem that has, in my view, received inadequate attention may be stated as follows: although the formation of moral sentiments is dependent on a signifying medium, we cannot read off the formation from the system of significations that may be authoritatively identified and isolated as a distinctive semiotic phenomenon. The reading is a product of social discipline, and the text, the symbol, the rite, is the product of varying disciplined performers who discourse with one another in historically determinate ways.[8]

The monastic program that prescribes the performance of rites is directed at forming and reforming Christian dispositions. The most important of these is the will to obey what is seen as the truth, and therefore the guardians of that truth. The achievement of that disposition is the Christian virtue of humility. Thus, I discuss ritual in rela-

---

dress made to fit an emotion already existing, but is an activity without which the experience of that emotion cannot exist. Take away the language, and you take away what is expressed" (244). The expression need not be verbal, of course. According to Collingwood, there can be feelings (sensations) without language, but no language without feelings (emotions). It is the fact that thought-in-language organizes and objectifies feelings, that it "modifies" and "dominates" them, which makes it possible to "perpetuate" them "at will" (206–11). Thus, he argued in effect that the existence of specific vocabularies of emotion was a precondition for the existence of specific emotions, and that emotions could be learnt and cultivated through discourse.

7. In a thoughtful article, Leavitt argues that anthropologists have produced excessively narrow and one-sided models for understanding expressions of emotion in other cultures. "All the major theories," he claims, "seem to presuppose a dichotomy between a level of culture, understood as distinctive patterns located in a human collectivity, and a level of biology, understood as a universal located in the individual human body. One set of positions defines emotions as essentially individual, bodily, biological, and so both private and universal; the other sees them as essentially cultural, and so as shared, public, and varying from culture to culture" (1986, 4). Neither view involves a systematic examination of how the production of apt behavior and speech depends on varying organizations of emotions within the self.

8. Making a distinction between text and work, Barthes (1977) writes that "the Text is experienced only in an activity of production" (157), and that "the Text requires that one try to abolish (or at the very least try to diminish) the distance between writing and reading, in no way to intensify the projection of the reader into the work but by joining them in a single signifying practice" (162). Such observations on signifying performance make the process of construction clear, but what they may obscure is the degree to which the process is guided by social discipline. Performers learn to read-and-inscribe the rites prescribed in the monastic program, and what they learn is continuously assessed with reference to an authoritative model of excellence. It is an empirical question as to how far that reading-and-writing remains at the level of simulation for the benefit of observers, and how far it serves to organize the thoughts-and-feelings of performers themselves.

tion to processes of power, but again unlike most anthropologists who have addressed the problem of power directly.

For example, in Gluckman's famous (1954) essay, "rituals of rebellion" were seen as a form of catharsis, a ceremonial means of releasing tensions through the evocation and expression of emotions dangerous to hierarchical political order.[9]

Two decades later, Bloch (1974, 1975) described rituals as restricted communication, a form of rhetoric which locked participants into superordinate/subordinate positions:[10] "In the case of political oratory," he wrote, "we saw that the sign and tool of traditional authority was formalised communication and that in the case of religious rituals this formalisation is pushed even further" (1974, 77). In 1981, Paine put forward a more nuanced thesis:

> Politics itself is generally thought of as propositional [because of its strong bargaining aspect]. At a general theoretical level . . . there is complementarity between symbolic and pragmatic action in any undertaking, and *performatory speech is to propositional speech as symbolic action is to pragmatic action*. Rhetoric, then, belongs to the symbolic side of politics, and symbolic systems of action, it is known, reduce people's perception of available choices. However, by attending to the constraints in the "speaking" relationship between politicians and their public, it should be possible to give a grounded explanation that shows how the dominance of the performatory mode actually comes about. (9-10; emphasis added)

The politician must persuade his public, says Paine; he cannot take his power for granted. This persuasion may be achieved by symbolic speak-

9. Criticisms of Gluckman's notion of "rituals of rebellion" include Norbeck (1963), Beidelman (1966), Rigby (1968), and Smith (1982), all of whom take issue with Gluckman's interpretation of the symbolic meanings of the rituals he analyzed.

10. Critics of Bloch's argument, such as Burling (1977), Werbner (1977), and Irvine (1979), question the rigidity attributed by him to traditional oratory. At one level, it is of course an empirical matter as to whether a given performance is "formal" or "informal," "creative" or "imitative," whether it "imposes meanings" on the audience or "negotiates meanings" with them. To my knowledge, no critic has questioned the theoretical advisability of placing different "forms" (of music, dance, rite, oratory) along a single continuum of "articulation," as though they were all interchangeable ways of communicating something. The temptation to collapse different social practices into an essential category, to try to measure them by the same yardstick, is constant in anthropology—and many succumb to it. It is as though Bloch, grounded in political economy, and Geertz, in symbolic anthropology, were engaged in the same enterprise.

ing or by symbolic doing (as opposed to plain speaking and honest doing), which is what accounts for the affinity between rhetoric and ritual and for the role of rhetoric in what Paine regards as the "ritualization of politics." It is on the special political occasions when values are already shared that "we recognize ritual as, at once, symbolic action and a justification for what we have done or have to do" (21–22). Thus, whereas Bloch presents an authoritarian conception of power through discourse, Paine is evidently wedded to a populist one.[11]

Geertz (1980) has been concerned less with symbol as the medium of persuasion and more with symbol as the form of spectacle. Balinese royal rituals, he claims, constituted "metaphysical theatre: theatre designed to express a view of the ultimate nature of reality and, at the same time, to shape the existing conditions of life to be consonant with that reality; that is, theatre to present an ontology and, by presenting it, to make it happen—make it actual" (104). In Geertz's conception, the ceremonial representation of hierarchical power is made equivalent to its social realization:[12]

11. The reference to "performatory speech" and "propositional speech" corresponds to what Austin (who is cited in one of Paine's footnotes) called performatives and constatives—a distinction that he himself eventually undermined in a long and careful argument (see the summary in Austin 1962, 91). The whole of Austin's later work is based on a rejection of the assumption that there are two basic kinds of speech. Paine expresses what he describes as a profound disagreement with Bloch (who also regards political rhetoric as performatory, in Paine's sense), which "reaches even to the epistemological standing of the social world: something 'given' or something negotiated? The principal difficulty arises over the way Bloch associates formalization with an absence of negotiation between speaker and audience. Bloch sees coercion . . . where we see persuasion; whereas he sees formalisation as a 'given,' which constrains the speaker, we see it as the outcome of rhetorical artistry and political acumen by which an audience is constrained; that is to say, the politician strives to have his audience see the world through his interpretation of it in his speeches" (Paine 1981, 2–3). This is not, of course, an epistemological disagreement (epistemology has to do with the foundations of knowledge, not with whether constraint or negotiation is the basis of our political world), nor is it even a profound one. Whether the speaker (as in Bloch) or the audience (as in Paine) is "constrained" is, in one sense, an empirical question. But what is to be understood by constraint? Is the speaker's insinuation of threats that persuade his audience to "see the world through his interpretation of it" to be classed as different from constraint? Is it incompatible with negotiation? Such conceptual questions are not examined in Paine.

12. One is reminded here of Renaissance political theater. A historian of the court masque (Orgel 1975) notes that Renaissance acting was not mere representation but a form of oratory. Masquers were not actors, not impersonators, but ladies and gentlemen at play, idealizing and affirming an aristocratic view of the world. "The masque," Orgel writes, "presents the triumph of an aristocratic community; at its center is a belief in the hierarchy and a faith in the power of idealization. Philosophically, it is both

The exemplary center within the exemplary center, the icon king depicted outwardly for his subjects what he depicted inwardly to himself: the equanimous beauty of divinity. Put that way, the whole thing sounds like so much legerdemain, a Steinberg hand drawing itself. But as imagination for the Balinese was not a mode of fantasy, of notional make-believe, but a mode of perception, representation, and actualization, it did not seem so to them. To visualize was to see, to see to imitate, and to imitate to embody. (130)

In my analysis of monastic rites, I try to show that observation and imitation, although important, were not sufficient for the effective operations of power. The formation/transformation of moral dispositions (Christian virtues) depended on more than the capacity to imagine, to perceive, to imitate—which, after all, are abilities everyone possesses in varying degree. It required a particular program of disciplinary practices. The rites that were prescribed by that program did not simply evoke or release universal emotions, they aimed to construct and reorganize distinctive emotions—desire *(cupiditas/caritas)*, humility *(humilitas)*, remorse *(contritio)*—on which the central Christian virtue of obedience to God depended. This point must be stressed, because the emotions mentioned here are not universal human feelings, not "powerful drives and emotions associated with human physiology," such as those referred to in the quotation from Turner. They are historically specific emotions that are structured internally and related to each other in historically determined ways. And they are the product not of mere readings of symbols but of processes of power.

Formalized speech and behavior were by definition aspects of such rites, as Bloch, in common with most anthropologists, has said of ritual. But in the monastic program it was clearly recognized that the learning of appropriate forms was important because it was essential

---

Platonic and Machiavellian; Platonic because it presents images of the good to which the participants aspire and may ascend; Machiavellian because its idealizations are designed to justify the power they celebrate. As a genre, it is the opposite of satire; it educates by praising, by creating heroic roles for the leader of society to fill. The democratic imagination sees only flattery in this sort of thing, but the charge is misguided, and blinds us to much that is crucial in all the arts of the Renaissance. The age believed in the *power* of art—to persuade, transform, preserve—and masques can no more be dismissed as flattery than portraits can" (40). But Orgel is quite clear that what the masque presented was not equivalent to what the monarchy secured—as the tragedy of Charles I confirms.

to the disciplined development of the self. Increasing formalization did not signify increasing subordination: on the contrary, those less adept in the performance of prescribed forms were placed under the authority of the more adept. Indeed, as we shall see, in medieval Christian society it was precisely those who were virtually excluded from ritual discipline who were subjected to sustained material exploitation—peasants or lay brothers.

And finally, the abbot neither coerced nor negotiated with the monks he addressed in sermons. His ritual discourse played a complex role in the *self*-restructuring of contradictory religious subjectivities. The primary object of that transformation was the development of the Christian virtue of willing obedience, a process that did not "reduce peoples' perception of available choices" (Paine) but ideally reorganized the basis on which choices were to be made.

In spite of these reservations, it remains the case that anthropological work on what is usually called "ritual" in specific cultures has provided many insights. No historian who seeks to understand Christian rites can afford to be ignorant of it. The analysis I present here is tentative and partial, but it is motivated by the conviction that a fuller understanding of connections between religious ideology and political power needs the continuous testing of anthropological texts and historical texts against each other.

The Medieval Concept of Discipline

I begin with a brief historical sketch of the medieval concept of *disciplina* which will help to mark out the basic dimensions of power exercised in the monastery. The medieval Christian concept of discipline was complex, containing a variety of ideas inherited from the ancient world, pre-Christian and Christian (Leclercq 1957). Monks had access to this heritage through the writings of the early Church Fathers, which were read daily in the cloistered community.

In the classical Latin, *disciplina* was applied to the domains of war, politics, and domestic life. In the first, it referred to all the rules and measures necessary to the art of war, and therefore to elements of strategies for defeating an enemy. In the second, it implied order in public life, and hence good government, which was ensured by the censor under the republic, and later by the emperor. In the third domain, it covered all the virtues and obligations that were expected from every member of the family for its collective good: this included absolute obedience to the father as empowered by the law of *patria potestas,* but also modesty, fidelity, the practice of sound economy, and so on, which defined the role of each family member.

In the Bible, *disciplina* is the normal Latin translation of the Greek word *paideia.* In the Hellenic world, *paideia* meant the physical, intellectual, and moral cultivation of the person. In the Old Testament context it was used to convey a very different notion of education—divine education directed not at an individual but at an entire people and achieved through submission to God's law, to the trials imposed by him, and to the exhortations of his prophets. Hence *paideia*—or *disciplina*—acquired a strong sense of chastisement, correction, and the penalty inflicted for a fault. In liturgical and patristic texts, the word was often employed in the plural to mean the process of teaching someone as well as the substance of what is taught, which comes ultimately from God through those who represent him. The military usage of the classical word is also evident in texts that speak of the Christian's combat against the devil. But this is a combat very different from any known to the world of classical antiquity, because in principle its outcome is always certain: victory invariably goes to virtue, virtue that is attained by the grace of God. The notion of discipline in this Christian context has, therefore, no close connection with the idea of strategy. For strategy has to do not with the certain rewards of moral virtue but with the calculation of probable outcomes. In a general sense, *disciplina* covers all that which the bishops do in order to govern the faithful in the name of God (see Brown 1967, 233–43).

In the early Middle Ages, the *Rule* of St. Benedict became established as the sole authoritative text for the government of a monastic community and the formation of its members. Although most Christians lived outside the cloister walls, the disciplined formation of the Christian self was attainable only within such communities. Even hermits were divided by the *Rule* into those who had graduated from monastic life (approved) and those who had never known that discipline (disapproved). The ordered existence of the monks was defined by various tasks, the most important of which was the singing of divine services *(Opus Dei)*. Because the monk's life was organized around the routine performance of the liturgy, the *Rule* is often at least as specific about the content and timing of the services as it is about other matters. A notable feature of the *Rule* is that the proper performance of the liturgy is regarded as something more than the major end of monastic activity: it is also listed as one of the "instruments" of the monk's "spiritual craft" and is thus integral to the idea of discipline.

The *Rule* employs the word *disciplina* in several senses: in the sense of good order, which the *Rule* should create in the monastery, of the *Rule* itself, and of the form of proper conduct, including internal and external attitudes. But most often, the word refers to all the penalties and corrections specified (see Fry 1981). In the *Rule,* discipline therefore connotes (a) divinely derived and divinely oriented knowledge, which is embodied in (b) physical and spiritual practice within (c) an organized community and under (d) the absolute authority of an abbot, whose duty is to apply (e) measures necessary for the attainment of Christian virtues (divine knowledge embodied in human practice).

These different but closely connected senses are reproduced in medieval monastic writing. Thus, in the twelfth century, Peter of Celle wrote a treatise called *De disciplina claustrali* describing the enclosed Christian life, which was common to monks and regular canons. According to this text, *apostolica disciplina* is what the Apostles have taught the religious by their example, and *observantiae disciplinae claustralis* consists of imitating the way of life taught by Christ. For Cistercians, discipline had the senses it possessed in monastic writings generally, but they also applied it to their particular Benedictine program. Thus, Bernard of Clairvaux uses the word sometimes to refer to the doctrine that Christ personally propounded to men, and sometimes to the conduct of the obedient monk. But *disciplina* also signified all the prescriptions that ensure his good behavior, especially the rules defined in the Cistercian program *(ordo cisterciensis)*, and including the decrees issued by the annual general chapter, the supreme legislative and executive body of the order (see Knowles 1963, 654–61). This entire range of meanings is found again in the writings of Hugh of St. Victor, but with an explicit emphasis on the doctrinal senses of discipline. Thus, in the *Eruditio didascalica,* Hugh writes of discipline as "the practical science of good living [whose] principle is humility" (Leclercq 1957, 1300).

More interesting for present purposes is the treatise Hugh wrote for the instruction of novices, in which he propounded the first coherent theory of gesture closely related to the concept of discipline. According to Hugh:

The novitiate is the road to beatitude: virtue leads to the latter, but it is discipline imposed on the body which forms virtue. Body and spirit are but one: disordered movements of the former betray outwardly *(foris)* the disarranged interior *(intus)* of the soul. But inversely, "discipline" can act on the soul through the body—in ways of dressing *(in habitu)*, in posture and movement *(in gestu)*, in speech *(in locutione)*, and in table manners *(in mensa)*.

Gesture is the movement and configuration of the body appropriate to all action and attitude. . . . *Gestus* designates not so much a unique gesture as the animation of the body in all its parts. It describes outwardly a *figure* presented to the gaze of others . . . even as the soul inside is under the gaze of God. (Schmitt 1978, 9–10)

Although gesture in this sense has its own end, maintains Hugh, it should conform to the measure that discipline imposes on it. Disciplined gesture is thus not merely a technique of the body varying from one culture or historical period to another, it is also the proper organization of the soul—of understanding and feeling, desire and will. This concept of discipline, which is the measure as well as the sign of virtue, enables Hugh to make an equivalence between the human body and the community—an equivalence proposed not simply for the collective life of the cloister but, as in other medieval writers, notably John of Salisbury (see Ullman 1975, 121–24; and Struve 1984), for political order too.

The Christian notion of monastic discipline as the force necessary for coordinating an organic whole belongs to the vocabulary of duty. It presupposes a program of learning to lead a virtuous life under the authority of a law, in which everyone has his or her proper place. The program determines for disciples what is to be done, how, in what order, and by whom. The older, pre-Christian notion of discipline as one element in a military strategy is different, in that its overall aim is the disabling—if not the permanent defeat—of an opponent in conditions of uncertainty where precise calculation is impossible.[13] The

---

13. The word *strategy* has become popular in recent anthropology, but it does not always have the military sense in which I use it here. Thus, even one of the most sophisticated exponents of the term, Bourdieu, uses it merely to contrast "practical aims" with "theoretical aims," usage with rules, as when he observes that it was "the gap between the theoretical aims of theoretical understanding and the directly concerned, practical aims of practical understanding, which led me to speak of matrimonial *strategies* or *social uses* of kinship rather than rules of kinship. . . . it is a matter of not grounding the practice of social agents in theory that one has to construct in order to explain

idea of virtue has a place in both settings, but in medieval Christian thought and practice it is subordinated to the discipline required by God's law. [14] That is one reason why a central Christian virtue is humility—a virtue that is not a simple behavioral feature of subordinate social status but an inward condition to be cultivated progressively by ascetic discipline (see the famous chapter on "Humility" in the *Rule*).

Reorganizing the Soul

Hugh of St. Victor's conception of ritual gesture and speech as the discipline of the body that is aimed at the proper ordering of the soul expresses very well the central purpose of the monastic program.

According to medieval Christian doctrine and practice, sin is a constant danger to the soul, and so calls for perpetual combat. The entire life of the Christian should be devoted to dealing with the corrupting effects of Original Sin, to restoring with God's grace the soul made impure and disordered by an original transgression. The Christian's concern is not merely with Original Sin but with "actual sin"— that is, with the attempt to fulfill the inordinate desire for temporal ends which is rooted in the flesh, and which medieval theologians called concupiscence. In his sinful state, man is in mortal danger; yet, God in his infinite mercy has provided for the possibility of man's salvation. It is for this that the monastic program was instituted, for

---

that practice" (Lamaison 1986, 111). This is not the military sense, whose most famous exponent is Clausewitz (1968). For Clausewitz, "strategy" does not merely presuppose a practical aim (my sense of "program" presupposes that too) but a special kind of practical aim; of antagonistic wills struggling for supremacy over a terrain that may not always be delimited, with forces that are not always constant, in conditions whose changing significance cannot always be anticipated. Such an aim *does* require some theoretical understanding and knowledge of rules, although of course that is not all it requires.

14. With reference to the Aristotelian concept of virtue, Anscombe notes: "It is worth remarking that the concepts of 'duty' and 'obligation,' and what is now called the 'moral' sense of 'ought,' are survivals from a law conception of ethics. The modern sense of 'moral' is itself a late derivative from these survivals. None of these notions occur in Aristotle. The idea that actions which are necessary if one is to conform to justice and the other virtues are requirements of divine law was found among the Stoics, and became generally current through Christianity, whose ethical notions come from the Torah" (1957, 78). In his brilliant history of Western ethics, MacIntyre (1981) has described transformations of the concept of virtue from pre-Christian through to Christian times.

the performance of practices specified in that program are in effect attempts at reforming the soul.

The work of reformation involves the elimination of sinful desire, but this is not necessarily to be seen as a mechanical action of denial. The program always calls for the disciplined construction of virtuous desire, but what this means for unlawful desire—how it is to be dealt with—depends on the precise personal condition of the disciples. In one of his Weberian phases shortly before his death, Foucault wrote of Christian asceticism in conventional terms as a sacrifice of the self: "In Christianity asceticism always refers to a certain renunciation of the self and of reality because most of the time your self is part of that reality you have to renounce in order to get access to another level of reality. This move to attain the renunciation of the self distinguishes Christian asceticism" (1988, 35). In the account that follows, I argue for a different conception. I try to show that the rhetoric of renunciation is part of the construction of a self-policing function and that it should not, therefore, be seen as the rejection of a presocialized (real) self.

At the core of the monastic program are a number of texts, differing in content and authority: the *Rule* of St. Benedict, custumals supplementing the *Rule,* the Bible, writings of the Church Fathers, breviaries, and so on. These texts between them contain general statements about the nature and purpose of Christian life, as well as the most precise stipulations regarding what is to be done, how, when, where, and by whom. Thus, programmatic texts relate to performances in a variety of ways—inspiring, recommending, prescribing, authorizing, justifying. Strictly speaking, however, program and performance do not stand alone in relation to each other. Essential to both are the mediating practices concerned with interpreting programmatic texts, applying their principles and regulations to the running of the monastic community, judging and assessing performances, and in general teaching novices to carry out the program. Furthermore, the programmatic texts do not simply regulate performances, standing as it were prior to and outside the latter. They are also literally part of the performance: written words to be variously chanted, recited, read, attended to, meditated on by the monks. From these brief observations, two things follow. First, the distinction between program and performance is in practice not a clear-cut duality; second, the phenomenon I wish to describe is not a theatrical one, in the sense to which we are now accustomed with all its implications of artful impersonation. The program is performed primarily not for the sake of an audience but for the sake of the performers, who are learning to exercise and to develop the Christian virtues, to replace unlawful desires with virtuous ones, not to appreciate an aesthetic representation.

The monastic attempt at forming virtuous desire can perhaps be seen most clearly in the ritual techniques developed by Bernard of Clairvaux. These have been described in detail recently by Leclercq (1979), and it is mainly his account I draw on in this section for my discussion of the creative aspect of disciplinary power.

The starting point of Leclercq's study is the changing pattern of recruitment into the new monastic orders emerging in the twelfth century. In this period the majority of the new recruits were adults, and usually from the noble or knightly classes.[15] They had therefore participated actively in secular society—unlike most recruits to the older monasteries (including the famous monastery of Cluny) who had lived virtually all their lives in the cloister and been raised in it since childhood.[16] This meant that the new monks had had direct, pleasurable experience of sexual love and knightly violence prior to their having taken up the religious life. Such experiences, Leclercq points out, posed a special problem for religious training, distinct from the one encountered in the education of infants for the monastic life. Evidence of how Bernard dealt with this problem is available from a careful analysis of his minor writings, which shows that he sought to exploit rather than to repress these dangerous secular experiences. This argument may be illustrated first by reference to Leclercq's discussion of sexual desire.

For traditional Christians, sensual desire *(cupiditas)* should be replaced by *caritas* (love of God)—but how was this to be accomplished?

> What strikes one as remarkable [Leclercq writes] is that Bernard never says or assumes that the love which tends to union with God excludes

---

15. A major criterion for accepting candidates into monastic life in the Middle Ages was *utilitas*—usefulness, or suitability. This was usually understood to exclude people of low social status—serfs, slaves, peasants—and also candidates who were too young or too weak. The latter consideration, adopted as a matter of principle by the Cistercians and other new orders, became a papal requirement for all monasteries from the thirteenth century on (Lynch 1975, 428-31). The class origins of monastic recruits are reflected also in the study on medieval sanctity by Weinstein and Bell (1982, chap. 7).

16. On child-rearing practices in non-Cistercian medieval monasteries, see Riché 1975 and McLaughlin 1975.

an accompanying love tending to union between human persons, which remains within what he calls the order of charity, or "charity in order." Monastic love and other forms of Christian love have a different quality, but the latter can and ought to be integrated into this love for God. And monastic love for God can and must be expressed in terms of human love; it can assume, retrieve, and integrate images, representations of human love, and even memories of its accomplishment, as seems to have been the case with some young men who had become monks. (23)

Leclercq stresses the compatibility of "love for God" and "human love," which underlies Bernard's program, but in this assertion of compatibility some important differences are obscured.

The Latin word *libido* had the original sense of "pleasure, desire, longing" from which the early Christians derived, through the Stoic tradition, the sense both of "unlawful desire" and of "eagerness for eloquence and glory"—that is, for excellence (Tertullian). (It was in the latter sense that Cicero had spoken of *libido* as the desire for a future good, in contrast to *laetitia*, or joy in a present good.) In this way, one sense of *libido* was linked to a normative concept of divine law, the other to an older, teleological notion of virtue. The former now defines desire as the power deriving from concupiscence, which impels the Christian to transgress, and which must be restrained in order that the law be upheld. In the other sense, desire appears not as something to be repressed but as the essential means for the achievement of excellence, as a precondition for training the virtuous self. The critical distinction is therefore not simply between "love for God" and "human love" but between desire measured by an authoritative law and desire as the motive for exercising virtue. The former is, of course, central to every Christian orientation, and I shall deal with it below in the final section. But here it is particularly the latter notion as employed in Bernard's disciplinary program for his young monks on which I want to focus. As the previous monastic traditions had done, Bernard set before his novices an authoritative model of virtue toward which they were led to aspire, but he also sought to use concupiscence itself as the material for exercising virtue—what medieval theologians called *materia exercendae virtutis*.

It is clear that this work of transformation required a skillful deployment of biblical language so that it might resonate with, and reintegrate, the pleasurable memories and desires that had been fashioned in a previous secular life. This, in turn, was dependent on the allegorical mode of narrating, interpreting, and being motivated by biblical images, a mode characteristic of medieval Christianity.[17] The principal access to this verbal imagery, its authorized reception, was intrinsically connected to the regular performance of the liturgy, to the private reading of the Scriptures, and to the sermons whose style was developed by Bernard.[18]

Thus, the daily performance of liturgy, the reading aloud and the hearing and memorizing of sacred texts—indeed, the entire sequence of monastic practices—were among the material preconditions and the material means for the transforming work of Bernard's sermons. Monastic sermons were themselves, as Leclercq has elsewhere shown (1977, 206–20), rites.

Monastic rites in the program of Clairvaux are thus not to be seen as ways of repressing a socially dangerous psychic force, as some modern historians have maintained with reference to the rites of the earlier Benedictines (e.g., Rosenwein 1971). But neither are they simply to be understood as inculcating new values into participants—a point made innumerable times in anthropological writings about initiation rites (most recently in La Fontaine 1985). Leclercq's account of monastic rites does not lend itself easily to an explanation in terms of inculcation, a process in which passive subjects are filled with new content. Since monastic rites were either spoken or spoken-and-gestured (in

17. John Cassian, whose texts were always required monastic reading, distinguished four senses in biblical discourse—historical, allegorical, anagogical, and tropological: "He gave an example," Smalley writes, "which caught the fancy of the middle ages and became classical: Jerusalem, according to history, is a city of the Jews; according to allegory it is the Church of Christ; according to anagoge it is that heavenly city of God *which is the mother of us all* (Gal. iv. 26); according to tropology it is the soul of man, which under this name the Lord often threatens or praises" (1964, 28). Smalley is critical of the "confused" medieval usage by which history, allegory, and tropology "refer both to the subject-matter of scripture and to the method of its exposition" (88). This is not necessarily a confusion, however, but a commitment to the principle that the meaning of a text is continuous with the discourse by which that meaning is secured. So when Bernard expounds the *Song of Songs* in his sermons, his monks hear its scriptural senses, not Bernard's representation of those senses: the distinction between "real" subject matter and "allegorical" method of exposition is the product of a particular theory of meaning, not a feature of a priori reality.

18. Evans (1983) deals at length with Bernard's preaching, and especially with his sermons on the *Song of Songs* (107–37). For a more general account of the art of preaching as a medieval rhetorical genre, see Murphy 1974, 269–355.

Hugh of St. Victor's sense), the role of language was obviously integral to their performance. In this context, speech is not simply a mode of communication or of conventional representation. It is not an instrument of "social control." Speech in this context is a dialogical process by which the self makes (or fails to make) itself in a disciplined way. Where rites are at the center of the transformation of preexisting ideas,· feelings, and memories, explanations of that process in terms of conditioning are not adequate—as Vygotsky ([1934] 1962) pointed out more than half a century ago.

It should be noted that, in theory, Bernard is not manipulating desires (in the sense that his monks do not know what is happening to them) but instead is creating a new moral space for the operation of a distinctive motivation. In order to do this, he develops a discursive practice—ritual dialogue—for facilitating and regulating a new way of living. The sermons that give authoritative exegesis of biblical texts provide a new vocabulary by which the monks themselves can redescribe, and therefore in effect construct, their memories in relation to the demands of a new way of life.[19] This redescription of memories depends on a long and complex process. In it, (1) the authoritative preacher and the monk addressed, (2) the monk interacting with fellow monks, (3) the confessor and the monk in confession, and (4) the remembering religious self and the secular self remembered, all contribute in the production of a moral description by which the monk's desires and feelings are reconstructed.

Thus the learning of the religious life, no less than the shaping of their own memories, has to be done by the monks themselves in their interchange with those in authority. The desire that motivates this constructive process is not something that can be "internalized" in any rite (as though the self were an empty container). For this reason, one might say that the pedagogic relationship between Bernard and his monks was in principle one of authority, not of domination.

However, the relationship between teacher and pupil, which is described here in terms of authority rather than of domination, is a

19. For relevant discussion of the way memories are formed in the analytic relationship, see Spence 1982. I am *not* equating the medieval monk's condition with that of the modern patient, in the way Freud (1907) first suggested when he equated religious practices with obsessive actions. Nevertheless, any attempt to understand the dynamic relationship between language, memory, and desire must examine critically how the process has been discussed in psychoanalytical literature—and Spence does this impressively.

different matter from what it is that the pupil learns when he tries to transform himself according to an authoritative model. For the program that aims to transform sensual desire (the desire of one human being for another) into the desire for God requires at the same time a change in the status of the monks as lovers. From being masters or equals of human lovers (male or female), they must now learn to become humble subjects of a heavenly Lover. The transformation thus culminates in an unconditional subjection to the law, in desire becoming the will to obey God—the supreme Christian virtue. And it was a transformation that sought to bridge a fundamental contradiction by actively playing on it.

The possibility of failure in such a program is explicitly recognized by medieval writers, as we shall see when we examine what Hugh of St. Victor has to say. Even Leclercq allows for things not going according to plan, though in a somewhat modern way: "It must be admitted, however, that the use of such methods, with the frank expression of the language of aggression and sexual love, has its peculiar risks. We may wonder whether Bernard's pedagogy was always free from such risks and from all ambiguity" (105). But he does not appear to have noticed that the ambiguity and risk derive from Bernard's deliberate decision to court danger in order to overcome it. The novice is thrust into ambiguity and contradiction, and his fragmented self made the precondition of a virtuous reformation. Such a decision was connected to the fact that with adult recruitment the danger of sensual desire could not be dealt with directly by simple rejection: an authoritative redescription of pleasurable memory was necessary.

Summing up the findings of experimental research, the psychoanalyst Donald Spence notes that "the way in which we talk about a memory and the kind of questions we ask of it can easily become part of the original memory" (1982, 89). Bernard's technique appears to have involved precisely this process. His way of talking and questioning took the form of a particular genre (authoritative preaching) with a distinctive content (figurative biblical discourse), through which a collaborative attempt was made to fit memories of the past to programmatic demands of the present.

It was not the case, as Leclercq implies, that only adult entrants had "definite knowledge of secular love" (1979, 14). Children brought up in the early Benedictine monasteries had that knowledge too, but in their case the dangers of sexual love could be managed by trying to control the conditions of experience with the aid of avoidance rules backed by severe penalties. Thus, in the eleventh century, "the punishment recommended for the seduction of a child or youth by a cleric or monk was public beating, loss of the tonsure, imprisonment in chains and irons for six months, and fasting three days a week until vespers; after this another six months of isolation in a cell under strict custody. In earlier medieval penitentials youthful sexual acts were much more lightly punished" (McLaughlin 1975, 171; see also Payer 1984). Such attempts to control the conditions of experience are to be contrasted with Bernard's attempt to transform the structures of memory.

What was defined as primitive observance of avoidance rules in the face of culturally defined dangers (including the dangers of sexual transgression) has been the object of much theorizing since the nineteenth century. In an important but neglected study published posthumously, Steiner (1956) critically examined, first, the eighteenth-century European discovery of "tabu" (ritual avoidance based on fears of supernatural danger), then, the explanations offered of it by Victorian anthropologists and psychologists. His argument was that tabu did not constitute a single institution nor pose a single kind of problem. But out of this critical effort emerged a positive conclusion: Steiner's proposal for developing what he called the sociology of danger, which would inquire into the way all situations of danger (not merely those created by tabu-breaking) were culturally defined and dealt with. In principle, this allowed for the possibility of transformation.

Douglas (1966) took over the idea of a sociology of danger from Steiner but rehabilitated the notion of tabu, which the latter had tried to discredit. Douglas's more widely read book rendered the idea of a sociology of danger narrower than Steiner had intended it to be. Ritual danger was now essentially the danger of pollution ("matter out of place"), and the ritual treatment of danger invariably reinforced existing social, psychological, and cosmological boundaries.[20] It is evident that the monastic treatment of the spiritual danger of sexual love had inquisitive, productive implications, and for this reason it does not fit easily into conventional analyses of so-called ritual avoidance, where

20. The specifically Christian origin of this theoretical concept is worth noting. In 1921, E. Bevan discussed the moral theology of dirt and its significance as "matter in the wrong place"—a phrase said to be first used by the poet Southey, or perhaps by Lord Palmerston. (See Bevan 1921.) Douglas does not cite this work, although Bevan's treatment is not identical with hers.

the emphasis tends to be on the fear of danger and on the reinforcement of categorical boundaries.

The ritual program of the older Benedictine monasteries (notably Cluny) was different from the one at Clairvaux—and the process of relearning described by Leclercq was precisely one of the things that distinguished the latter from the former. All monastic communities had programs for the formation of dispositions. For all of them, the liturgy was an indispensable element in that formation, and sacramental confession the principal means by which the formation was tested and regulated. It is well known that the Cistercians curtailed very considerably the time allotted to liturgical activity *(Opus Dei)* and put much greater emphasis on prescribed manual labor. But by that act of reorganization the Cistercian program reconstituted various kinds of work as devotional and disciplinary, thus making it akin to the liturgy. Work—including economically productive work—became a rite, an appropriate part of the morally transformative program. The rich Cluniac liturgy came to be described by Cistercians as inappropriate to the formation of Christian virtues (see Knowles 1955), especially the virtue of humility.

Such historical reforms indicate that texts comprising the program were capable of variant readings. But it is important to note that alternative readings were not made at random, that they depended on institutional conditions. Indeed, it can be argued that it was the establishment of new disciplines that defined new readings as authoritative rather than the other way around.

Manual Labor and the Virtue of Humility

The "monastic revival" of the twelfth century, out of which the Cistercian Order emerged, has been much written about by historians. A striking feature of this movement for reorganizing monastic discipline was the prominence given to ideas of poverty and manual labor. Many scholars have seen in the new ideas about manual labor an ideological shift of great importance for the development of rational organizations familiar to us in the modern world. One historian has claimed that "by proclaiming the obligation of work on all men, even the rich; by rehabilitating manual labor and by demonstrating, through monastic example, the benefits of charity, of disinterestedness, and of the variety and alternation of work, St. Bernard outlined a plan for an ideal organization, a program for a rational way of life" (Vigne 1928, 585). More recently, in his study of decaying feudal ideology, Duby has written that unlike the older Benedictines, such as the Cluniacs, "the Cistercians chose not to live by the labor of other men, and so took a stance outside the seigniorial mode of production" (1980, 222). What precisely was the place of labor in the Cistercian program? In this section I want to address myself briefly to this question, with special reference to discipline.

Both the older Benedictine and the Cistercian programs were organized around the *Rule* of St. Benedict for cloistered communities subject to the absolute authority of the abbot. Chapter 48 of the *Rule,* which deals with "Daily Manual Labour," begins as follows: "Idleness is an enemy of the soul. Therefore, the brothers should be occupied according to schedule in either manual labour or holy reading." And it proceeds to allocate times to both in between Hours devoted to the *Opus Dei* ("work of God"). It is clear that the *Rule* regards manual labor from the spiritual point of view as a means of avoiding the danger of idleness—this is why it is classed with holy reading. The Cluniacs had tackled this danger by increased effort devoted to the liturgy *(Opus Dei)*. The liturgical splendor at Cluny, which Cistercian reformers denounced in the name of poverty and humility, depended on a productive system that was essentially feudal in character.[21]

Agricultural land acquired by Cluny—whether directly by donation or by exchange—was usually already occupied by serfs who therefore became the absolute property of the monastery. Unworked land was sometimes handed to peasants to settle on and cultivate within a stipulated period on the understanding that when this was done it would be divided between abbey and tenant (Evans 1931, 14–15). Like other feudal properties, Cluny's therefore consisted partly of demesnes (cultivated by servile labor) and partly of rents (paid on agricultural land, but also on churches, etc.). This arrangement provided the monks directly with food for themselves and their servants, and fodder for their horses, as well as money for a variety of commodities (vestments, condiments, books, etc.) and for building.

The Cistercian emphasis on poverty and separation from the world

21. Heath (1976, 87–111) discusses the connection between the elaborate, lengthy liturgy at Cluny and the recurrent donations made to the abbey for the performance of masses for the dead. Cluny's heavy investment in the performance of liturgy was thus an outcome of its modes of property acquisition.

stands in well-known contrast to the opulent, ceremonial life of the Cluniac Order. And it also goes with a different form of productive property. Cistercian estates were made up of farming units called "granges," each grange being managed in effect as a demesne but with the important difference that the agricultural labor was provided from within the order itself. Unlike the older Benedictine abbeys, and unlike the typical secular manors, Cistercians did not exploit the labor of tenants or receive income from rents, at least in the earlier generations (Postan 1975, 102).

The founders of Cîteaux were concerned to reestablish what they saw as the purity of the *Rule*, but it was their explicit commitment to poverty and to separation from the world that produced a distinctive form of agrarian property and conception of manual work. A simplified and abbreviated liturgy followed from the intention to reduce consumption and to renounce the legal privileges of clerics, all for the sake of poverty and humility. "Tithes and other fees belonging to the priestly ministry, the rights and privileges of clerics, the revenue obtained from the work of men belonging to a [servile] class" were all regarded by the Cistercian founders as "a usurpation contrary to the law established by the canonical tradition of the Church. . . . From this point of view, even ecclesiastical property constitutes 'riches of this world' and, like it, must be renounced" (Leclercq 1966, 27).

But this renunciation of tithes, rents, and services[22] entailed the problem of organizing productive work to secure subsistence, a problem that was solved by recruiting laymen into the order. It is certainly not correct to say that in this arrangement the monks were "helped by lay brothers" who, although not themselves monks, "were treated as if they were" (Leclercq 1966, 27). Lay brothers did not live in the enclosure but on cultivated land at a distance from it. They did not follow the same schedule as the monks and were not subject to the same discipline. And it was they who performed the basic agricultural work, assisted at seasonal times by the cloistered monks (Lekai 1977, 367). As Roehl (1972, 87) notes, lay brothers were required to observe fewer

22. Southern (1970, 255) points out that by the twelfth century these sources of endowment were largely in the hands of the older monasteries: "in rejecting these revenues the Cistercians thought that they were renouncing the world; in fact they renounced only its shadow. Their principles forced them to go to the edge of the settled lands of Europe; but the most far-sighted economic prudence would have pointed in the same direction. In an expanding society this was where the future lay."

days of rest and fewer fast days but were entitled to larger rations of food than the monks. Once their monasteries were built, the quantity of time spent on cultivation by Cistercian monks was not adequate even for their own subsistence—let alone for the impressive amounts of wealth they accumulated in later years.

Nevertheless, it is not merely the proportion of productive work done by Cistercian monks (which was not very much) but the change in the monastic concept of work itself that is of interest. As we saw above, historians have typically dealt with this question in terms of the new value accorded to manual labor in the twelfth century. Here is another writer on the same subject in some detail:

> The confrontation between active and contemplative lives was revived in the debate between canons and monks, fed by a number of burning issues of the day. On the theoretical plane, there was a rehabilitation of Martha [the biblical figure representing active as against contemplative life], and in practice, manual labor was restored to a place of honor with the Carthusians and particularly the Cistercians and the Premonstratensians. Of course, the influence of tradition continued, and strong resistance to change appeared. Still, the founding of new orders makes clear that something had changed, that a mutation had occurred in the Benedictine spirit, for why else would such new rules be necessary? It is, of course, possible to point to a Rupert of Deutz, who was irritated by the vogue for manual labor, or to a Peter the Venerable somewhat stunned by the attacks of Saint Bernard, both of whom point out that, according to Saint Benedict, manual labor, advisable but not obligatory, was merely a means and not an end of spiritual life. But there is abundant evidence from every quarter that the new spiritual attitude toward labor was undergoing a crucial development through practice. . . . The concept of penitential labor was supplanted by the idea of labor as a positive means of salvation. (Le Goff 1980, 114–15)

A precursor of the "Puritan ethic"? The origin of a "rationality" distinctive of modern capitalism? However that may be (and some historians have already answered these questions in the affirmative),[23] it is

---

23. In *The Protestant Ethic* (1930, 118–19), Weber postulated a clear line of growing rationality connecting Western monasticism ("in the rule of St. Benedict, still more with the monks of Cluny, again with the Cistercians") to the "practical ideal of Puritan-

not the ideological value given to manual labor but its role in the economy of monastic discipline that I want to identify. If labor was once conceived of as penance, it would be a mistake to think that this meant that penance was not a means to salvation. It had always been that. What seems to have changed is that the concept of manual labor became an important part of the Cistercian program for developing Christian virtues—and especially the virtue of humility. It does not follow from this that *manual* labor in any general sense came to be more highly valued than other kinds of activity. At Cluny, the mending and washing of clothes, the baking of bread, the cooking of food, and the copying of manuscripts all counted as manual work. However, because it was considered particularly demeaning, the first of these was generally done by paid servants (Evans 1931, 87). For Cistercians, it was precisely *humiliation* that constituted the point of manual labor, not its economic instrumentality.

Thus, in the *Dialogus duorum monachorum,* written by a Cistercian monk late in the twelfth century, an argument is represented between a Cluniac and a Cistercian on the subject of manual work. When the former insists that the monks of Cluny did work with their hands—implying among other things the labor of copying manuscripts—his Cistercian opponent responds contemptuously: "What is grinding gold into dust and illuminating huge capital letters with golddust, if it isn't useless and idle work? Even those works of yours which are necessary are contrary to the precepts of the Rule because you pay no attention to the time assigned to them in the Rule" (Idung 1977, 93). Clearly, there was manual labor and manual labor, and what mattered to the Cistercian program was not that work with one's hands was in itself to be exalted over work with one's mind, but that the object of monastic practice was the realization of humility through the discipline prescribed by the *Rule.* The making of gorgeous manuscripts could not, by this measure, have any place in such a program. The fact that it was useful and lucrative work (manuscripts were bought and sold), as well

---

ism" and contrasted this with the "planless otherworldliness and irrational self-torture" of oriental asceticism. Stock (1975), in his exposition of Bernard's views on work, planning, and experience, seeks to provide supporting evidence for Weber's presentation. Holdsworth, focusing on the Cistercian understanding of the value of manual labor, concludes: "Looked at in the broader light that understanding seems to have a part to play in the emergence of attitudes and feelings which have been connected in the past, at least since Weber, with urban communities of a later period" (1973, 76).

as work done with one's hands, was not in itself reason for valuing it highly.

In every society different types of work are, of course, variously esteemed. But in all class societies, whether ancient, medieval, or modern, those who control the basic means of production have always regarded it as more estimable to direct the work of others than to work with their own hands. As ecclesiastical landlords having powers to draw on the labor of laymen, this applies to Cistercians no less than to Cluniacs. Both orders commanded the work of dependent laborers, and if the Cistercian founders rejected the rents of laboring villagers, this was certainly not because they valued manual *laborers* highly. On the contrary, as in the case of colonial settlers in modern times, preexisting cultivators were considered to be an obstacle:

> Because they had no use for tenants, whether servile or free, they sometimes destroyed existing villages to make way for granges, and evicted peasant occupiers, who were settled elsewhere. Investigation of the Cistercian settlement in the north of England has verified the charge of the twelfth-century satirist Walter Map: "they raze villages and churches, and drive poor people from the land." Their preference for estates they could work [i.e. manage] themselves brought them many gifts of virgin land; but where it did not, they showed no scruple in creating the kind of estate they wanted by means of depopulation. The claims of peasants could not be allowed to obstruct the search for the desert. (Lawrence 1984, 162)

The spiritual distance between monks (who were mostly of upperclass origin) and peasants remained as sharp as ever among the Cistercians. Outside the order, peasants were to be excluded—even driven out where necessary; inside it, they acquired the status of lay brothers *(conversi)* and performed the labor necessary for the physical existence of the entire monastery. Because the monastery was conceived of as an organic entity, the law, in the form of the *Rule,* applied to the organism as a whole. The prescription of manual labor was a rule that could, apparently, be satisfied if it was followed by the community as a whole.

But the difficulty is that humility is essentially a virtue, and as such it is an ability of the individual soul, not of the community. If manual labor was to be a discipline for developing and exercising the virtue of humility, that virtue was not equally available to all Cistercians.[24] Those who did manual labor the most ought to have cultivated the greatest measure of humility. But paradoxically, those who did most of the humble work (the *conversi*) were those who rebelled most often (Southern 1970, 259). One reason is perhaps that those who are known to be of servile origin cannot be rendered humble by servile work, for that is what virtually defines them from the start; but they can be further exploited through such work.

Clearly, it is not enough that manual labor be valued highly for it to achieve its desired effects. For this, an entire program of discipline is required by which the virtue of humility can be learnt and exercised by each member of the community. Lay brothers, immersed in the daily demands of agricultural work, were not subject to such a program.

Rites and the Discipline of Obedience

What were the systematic requirements of a program of discipline within a cloistered community? To answer this question, let us first look at two programmatic statements. One of them, by Hugh of St. Victor, expounds a doctrine of the sacraments according to which these rites are to be regarded as the basic practice of Christians for learning the virtue of humility. The other, by Bernard of Clairvaux, explains the law in the *Rule* according to which continuous obedience is owed by monks to their Superior. It is important to bear in mind that these writings are not mere ideological statements opposed to "real life," but discursive interventions by practicing religious people which seek to define and reform ways of performing the monastic program.[25] It was only through such discursive work that a program's intention was integrated, and thus a measure of (temporary) coherence achieved. The coherent program had no existence independent of such authoritative interpretations.

Hugh was not merely a cloistered canon[26] but the most influen-

---

24. The spirituality of the *conversi* during the twelfth and thirteenth centuries is discussed in Mikkers 1962, and in van Dijk 1964. The latter argues against the received view that the *conversi* regarded agricultural labor as a means of attaining virtue.

25. Hugh's text is relevant to a wider community, of course.

26. According to Pope Urban II (d. 1099), "The primitive church had had two forms of religious life: monastic and canonical. In the monastic life men abandoned earthly things and gave themselves up to contemplation. In the canonical life they made use of earthly things and redeemed with tears and almsgiving the daily sins inseparable from the world. The monks therefore played the part of Mary, the canons that of Martha in

tial theologian of the twelfth century, who drew on the doctrines of his contemporaries, including Bernard of Clairvaux. I propose next to examine some aspects of his major text known as *De sacramentis christianae fidei* in a little detail, particularly as laid out in book 1, part 9.

What is a sacrament? Hugh begins his answer to this question by considering the traditional definition: "A sacrament is the sign of a sacred thing" (154) and argues that this is not quite precise enough, because words of Scripture and statues or pictures are all signs of sacred things without being sacraments. So he proposes a more adequate definition: "A sacrament is a corporeal or material element [a word, a gesture, an instrument] set before the senses without, representing by similitude and signifying by institution and containing by sanctification some invisible and spiritual grace" (155). For example, the water of baptism *represents* the washing of sins from the soul by analogy with the washing of impurities from the body, *signifies* it for the believer because of Christ's inaugurating practice, and *is sanctified* by the words of the officiating priest who performs the baptism. The three functions, especially that of representation, are not self-evident but must be identified and expounded by the guardians of true meaning.[27]

Thus, according to Hugh, a sacrament, from its moment of authoritative foundation, is a complex network of signifiers and signifieds which acts, like an icon, commemoratively. What this icon signifies is already present in the minds of participants. It points backward to their memory and forward to their expectation as properly disciplined Christians.[28] "This is why," he writes elsewhere, "the eyes of

---

the church" (Southern 1970, 243-44). But the anonymous author of the twelfth-century *Libellus de diversus ordinibus* proposes a different division: he arranges "the orders of hermits, monks and canons according to whether they live close to towns and villages or at a distance, and he discusses the value of, for instance, the Victorine Canons' attempt to set an example by living near to men, the work of the Premonstratensian Canons who live far from men. Among the monks, the Cistercians remove themselves far from men; the Benedictines of the Cluniac Order live close to men" (Evans 1983, 7). Although canons followed the Rule of St. Augustine, the life of cloistered canons such as those at St. Victor was as austere as that of many monks. In a recent review of the historical debate on this subject, Brooke (1985) comes down firmly against any sharp division between monks and canons in the twelfth century.

27. In its structure and content, the mass made elaborate use of allegory, which medieval Christians learnt about through commentaries such as the *Liber officialis* by Amalarius (see Hardison 1965, 36-79).

28. Hugh is here drawing on Augustine's theory of signs, as expounded in *De doc-*

infidels who see only visible things despise venerating the sacraments of salvation, because beholding in this only what is contemptible without invisible species [i.e., what is accessible to the uninstructed senses] they do not recognize the invisible virtue within and the fruit of obedience" (156). The sacrament presupposes a certain frame of mind in which the work accomplished by it is primarily one of evocation and *recognition*. But that in turn depends on the prior existence of cognitive patterns and patterns of desire, of feelings structured by concepts, that have been built up over time through Christian discipline.[29]

For Hugh there is thus no direct correspondence between what the rite represents and the participant's experience. It is clear that he does not regard the rite as an expression or representation of inner states, but neither does he regard it simply as a "restricted code" bearing cultural meanings. We shall see in a moment that he conceives of rites as the dynamic relation between sign (pointing at once backward and forward in time) and disposition, a structure that has to be regulated and shaped by authoritative discourse in order to secure its authentic meaning.

Having defined sacramental rites, Hugh moves to the next part of his exposition. "Sacraments are known to have been instituted for three reasons: on account of humiliation, on account of instruction, on account of exercise" (156). Hugh's account makes it clear that these are not three separate functions, but aspects of a single practical process. Let us take them in order.

Why *humiliation?* Because, having disobeyed God through pride,

---

trina christiana, which was very influential throughout the Middle Ages. (St. Augustine is cited in *De sacramentis* more frequently than any other nonscriptural authority.) According to Augustine, signs are things that give knowledge of other things, and they can be classified as follows: (1) natural signs *(signa naturalia)* and (2) intentional signs *(signa data)*, the latter being produced by *(a)* animals, or *(b)* humans, or *(c)* God through the medium of humans—that is, authority (see Chydenius 1960, 5-8). It is only to the extent that signs are or can become intentional signs—that is, controlled by human will—that they form the material of Christian discipline.

29. The idea of controlling the conditions for the production of an appropriate memory is an important part of Augustine's sign theory, as it is of Hugh's theory of the sacraments and of Bernard's pedagogy. In her study of Augustine's epistemology, Colish (1968) stresses that the notion of learning to see and to recognize the truth through speech is central to all of his work. For the Christian, this meant "redeemed," or authoritative, speech: prayer, preaching, reading of Scripture, are all varieties of redeemed speech. This notion continued to be central to the medieval monastic program (see Leclercq 1977).

man is now obliged to subject himself to inanimate things, to material elements of the sacrament, which are by nature below him in the scheme of Creation: "there is no one, indeed, who does not know that rational man exists superior by foundation to the mute and insensible elements, and yet when this same man is ordered to seek his salvation in these, to try the virtue of his obedience, what else is this than that a superior is subject to an inferior?" (156).

To try the virtue of his obedience: thus, according to Hugh, there is something to be learnt, and being learnt, to be demonstrated. So in what does the *instruction* consist? By connecting the evidence of his senses to the way this evidence should be understood, man learns to recognize the value of what he handles and sees from those in authority: "And on this account while the invisible good which he lost is returned to him the signification of the same is furnished without through visible species, that he may be stimulated without and restored within; so in that which he handles and sees he may recognise of what nature that is which he received and does not see" (157).

Why *exercise?* Because, explains Hugh, man's erring flesh, which is the very principle of blind desire, cannot grasp the virtues that lie in perceptible things in a single moment, or even in a single continuous activity. It is therefore necessary that the entirety of human life be differentiated, and that events within it be divided, so that through the training of discrimination and disciplined practical work man gradually forms the correct disposition to recognize truth and realize virtue. A structured world of differences is providentially available since Creation:

> Times were divided and places distinguished, corporeal species proposed, pursuits and works to be practised enjoined, that the exterior man might prepare a medicine for the interior man and might learn to be under him and benefit him. For when human life had first run through two kinds of exercises, in the one unto use, in the other unto vice, unto use for nature, unto vice for guilt; the one unto sustenance, the other unto subversion, it was fitting that a third kind of exercise also be added, so that thereby one of the two first might be put aside, since it was harmful, and the other might be perfected, since it was not sufficient. Accordingly works of virtue were proposed to man without for exercising interior edification, so that preoccupied by them he might never be free for works of iniquity nor always so for works of necessity. (158)

Note that his world of differences is not an abstract structure of signs or an endless play of signifiers. It is a collection of abilities—and not human abilities in general, but specific Christian abilities—to be developed by practical exercise. The most important of these is the ability to will obedience.

Hugh is quite explicit that humiliation, instruction, and exercise are all essential to the definition of the sacraments: "This, therefore, is the threefold cause of the institution of all sacraments: humiliation, instruction, and exercise of man. If there were not these causes, [material] elements of themselves could not be sacraments at all, that is signs of instruments of sacred things" (159). Again, note the way Hugh stresses the constructive role of sacramental signs by which the processes of humiliation, instruction, and exercise are to be effected.

Hugh's view on this matter may be summarized as follows: Humiliation ensures that obedience as an act of will is at once a precondition, a continuous accompaniment, and the ultimate objective of Christian rites for restoring purity. Instruction ensures that learning to organize sensory evidence, to see what the untutored eye does not see, and to form desire, takes place by subjecting oneself to authority so that virtue (and truth) can be distinguished from vice (and error). And exercise ensures that the practice of differentiating is necessary to the formation of the Christian's will—that is, by learning what to follow and what to shun in accordance with God's law as conveyed by those who represent him. In the cloister, that representative is the Superior.

This learning always encounters an element of resistance issuing from concupiscence. The process is therefore never mechanically assured, and that is what makes the developing self at once social and nonunitary. The self is irreconcilably divided, so the learning process depends on a permanent separation from what remains an essential part of oneself. Thus, for the Christian the virtue of obedience is built not on a simple identification with an authority figure but on a precarious distancing within a fragmented self—which is one reason why the notion of socialization as a transitive process does not adequately describe how the virtue is achieved.

In this learning process, the sacraments do not stand alone: "There were three indeed which from the beginning, whether before the coming of Christ or after, were necessary for obtaining salvation, namely, faith, sacraments of faith, and good works. And these three so cling together that they cannot have the effect of salvation if they are not simultaneous" (164–65). For Hugh, rites were aspects of the program for constructing obedient wills. Central to this program is—as we shall see in the next section—the sacrament of confession by which the Christian's will is tested and his works are judged and justified.

Hugh's observations on the sacraments are not intended to apply only to the cloistered life, of course, but they do have a special relevance to it. For this program, which aimed at constructing obedient wills, was organized through and around the performance of sacramental rites and was most effective within the enclosed space of the cloister and under the absolute authority of an abbot.

Although the general conception of discipline as a process is clear enough in these writings of Hugh's, a tension is apparent in them, as in all monastic programs: a tension between the idea of learning and exercising a virtue and the idea of respecting and obeying the law—both ideas contained within the medieval Christian concept of discipline. For in relation to virtues, defects can be described in intrinsic terms as inabilities: thus, an ungenerous act is the behavior of an agent who has failed to exercise the moral virtue of generosity appropriate to his social role. In the context of the law, however, faults are identified by reference to an external (i.e., transcendental) rule; a transgression is what it is essentially because it disobeys the law, which commands or forbids something. The requirements of the law and those of the conditions for exercising the virtues are not always easy to reconcile. Yet Bernard of Clairvaux, in a programmatic text composed in 1142, attempted just that.

Bernard's treatise on monastic obedience entitled *De praecepto et dispensatione* soon became an authoritative statement on the subject (Leclercq and Gärtner 1965). In it he builds on the traditional conception of St. Benedict as the special mediator between monks and Christ. St. Benedict is the paternal model for monks, and his *Rule* the master program for their communal life *(regulae . . . magistra vitae)*. For the monks to follow St. Benedict is to obey the *Rule* faithfully, but to the abbot there falls the additional role of guarding the *Rule's* integrity and of conducting his monks in its proper observance. In this role, the abbot is also entitled to absolute obedience from his monks, because in the monastery he is Christ's representative. The *Rule* is thus at once the central text of a program of life in which virtues are to be exercised, and the basic constitution of a corporate legal body to which every monk must submit unconditionally, and the abbot is both a scrupulous teacher and the strict upholder of the law. Bernard attempts to resolve this inconsistency by emphasizing that the *Rule* sets the norm of obedience, and that it is only from the *Rule* that the abbot derives his right to demand obedience. The abbot cannot command what the *Rule* forbids nor forbid what the *Rule* commands. In following a prescription, the monk is therefore expressing the same will as the abbot's in issuing it—the will to obey God's law. Virtuous obedience thus presupposes and results in "a common will" (Leclercq and Gärtner 1965, 51).

This at any rate is one formulation, but according to another the abbot retains a distinct initiative, that of interpreting the *Rule* where it remains inexplicit about requirements and prohibitions. The *Rule* itself is quite explicit that any tendency on the part of the monk to dispute with his abbot must be met by punishment (chapter 3). If there is a disagreement over the interpretation, the monk's *duty* to obey does not construct "a common will": it suppresses a discordant will. This judgment of Bernard's on the nature of monastic obedience (the treatise was, as it happens, a response to troubled questions sent to him discreetly by monks from another monastery) does not set out the conditions for creating willing obedience but for justifying it. Yet, strictly speaking, the practitioner of willing obedience does not seek justification; it is the upholder of the Law who seeks it when it is put in question. And when it is questioned by acts of disobedience, he must seek satisfaction for the transgression in order to vindicate the power of the law.

As it happens, it is in the sacrament of penance that punishment for disobedience and the creation of willing obedience are jointly managed. I shall now look at the structure of this rite in detail.

The Structure of Monastic Obedience and the Rites of Penance

Discipline is a process at once transitive (the maintenance of proper order by the authorities inside and outside the monastery) and intransitive (the learning of proper conduct and the exercise of virtues by the monk). Each aspect of this disciplinary process depends on two functions: (a) continuous observations and (b) periodic correction. We saw above that all the rites of convent life were the means by which the virtuous transformation of Christians was effected. Among these rites the sacrament of penance, which was developed in the Middle Ages within the monastic setting, is unique because it belongs at once to both the disciplinary functions—the supervisory and the correctional. From the point of view of monastic life, the sacrament of penance (confession) is therefore the most important rite; from the point of view of monastic obedience, it is the main technique.

I noted above that one outstanding difference between the Cluniac and the Cistercian orders was the latter's restriction of entry to youths and adults. One result of this rule was to give the novitiate a much greater importance than it had had among previous Benedictines (Knowles 1963, 634–35). It was only after a probationary year, in which the novice's behavior and dispositions were carefully disciplined, that he was admitted to the status of full monk. The fact of being confined to a restricted area (and within it to particular places at specific times) optimized the conditions for discipline. In an obvious way, confinement facilitated the functions of supervision and correction. Confinement to the monastery was therefore a precondition of obedience, a voluntary condition for practicing the religious life.

The closely connected words *carcer*, *claustrum*, and *clausura*, which had conveyed ideas of compulsory confinement since the time of classical antiquity, were used in medieval literature to refer to the religious life of the cloister (Leclercq 1971). Thus, in the polemics of the twelfth century on the respective merits of monastic and clerical life, a "prison vocabulary" is explicitly used. But the idea of the cloister as a prison was invoked not only in controversial writing. In a sermon delivered to his religious, Bernard of Clairvaux declares enthusiastically:

> What a great miracle to see so many young ones, so many adolescents, so many nobles, in short all those who are present here as in a prison with open doors: they are not held back by any tie, they are fixed here only by the fear of God, and here they persevere in a penance so austere that it is beyond the nature and virtue of man, and contrary to his habit. . . . What are these if not manifest proofs that the Holy Ghost lives in you? (Quoted in Leclercq 1971, 413–14)

To incarcerate oneself for the sake of imitating Christ—who was himself "imprisoned in a human body"—and to commence this enclosed life with the vow of obedience to one's abbot did not guarantee that the precise limits of willing obedience would always be clear. Dissatisfied monks sometimes fled from one monastery to another. Conflicts between monks and their abbot, occasionally even leading to violence and homicide, were by no means unknown (see Dimier 1972). But even where disagreements did not issue in open rebellion, the definition of "true obedience" remained a delicate and important matter. The major concern, as always, was not simply one of observing legal duties, but of knowing how to avoid falling into sin. For this it was not enough to do what one was told by the abbot, but to *want* to do so because obedience was a virtue, and disobedience a sin. It was a matter, as Bernard knew, of constructing the desire to become a subject.

One essential condition for this creative work was continuous observation within the "prison with open doors." Although all monks were under the authority of the abbot—as Christ's representative and the representative of the law—there was no single point of surveillance. Within the monastery there existed an entire network of functions through which watching, testing, learning, teaching, could take place. Mutual observation was urged on all, but the matter was too important to be left in the form of a general injunction. Because observation and imitation were defined as interlinked functions, the elevation of particular roles became necessary.

The function of observation and imitation entailed another: the identification and correction of faults, which is the second essential condition for the construction of an obedient will. In this process punishment played a central part, and this is reflected even in the use of the word *discipline* as the common term for legally prescribed flogging. But punishment, or the necessary suffering of pain, was directed at once at vindicating the law and at correcting the path to virtue. Both orientations are present in the sacrament of penance as practiced in the medieval monastery.

The open announcement of faults, the formal humiliation of the transgressor, and his public chastisement all took place in the daily chapter, the general assembly of monks which was held after morning mass.[30] It might seem self-evident that in such a dramatic playing out of conviction and punishment, both culprit and onlookers were subjected to fear and shame, and it might be assumed that in general these emotions ensured obedience among most monks. But in fact the situation is more complicated than that, and it would be misleading to assert a simple causal connection between the emotions of fear and

30. Evans (1931, 85–87) has a dramatic and detailed account of punishment procedures in the Cluny Chapter.

shame supposedly produced by public punishment and monastic obedience allegedly maintained by fear and shame. It must be stressed that
monks were living an enclosed life in order to exercise virtues, not in
order to be beaten into submission. At any rate, cases in which the
latter occurred do not explain the former.

Our modern vocabulary for talking about emotions is notoriously
heterogeneous, a consequence of the fact that we inherit it from various historical layers of discourse about the structure of the self. Thus,
emotions are typically things that happen to the self (passions), but
also ways in which the self expresses its purposes (dispositions); they
are independent of cognition (feelings) and may interfere with it, but
also integral to kinds of understanding (moods); they are universal
instinctual elements, but also culturally variable *gestalts*.[31] However
that may be, what we would call emotions (e.g., fear, anger, pride,
humiliation, guilt) were always of central concern to monastic discipline because and to the extent that they were integral to the monk's
dispositions. Dispositions governed by virtuous feelings were contrasted with those that were rooted in vicious passions.[32] Something
of the way emotions were dealt with is reflected in the structure of
penance, the rite in which dispositions were monitored, perpetuated,
or transmuted.

In this context, a critical emotion was remorse, known in penance
literature as contrition. Remorse is at once a feeling and a cognitive
process of the kind in which the latter structures the former: the emotion's distinctive cast is determined by the conception that one has
sinned. This emotion is therefore not the cause of a changed disposition but its condition: remorse by the transgressor was often regarded
as sufficient reason for reconciling him to the monastic community. It
was exactly when the monk saw that he had sinned, at the point when
he verbalized his feeling into a perception of sin, that remorse was
formed, and consequently the desire for self-correction could begin.
The function of penance was intended to help bring about the feeling
of remorse and the decision not to repeat the sin. But remorse could
sometimes precede penance, as when it motivated the sinner to con-

31. Aylwin (1985, 130–33) enumerates several often contradictory conceptions of emotion found in the writings of professional psychologists, and suggests that they may
reflect different aspects of a multifaceted phenomenon.

32. See Michaud-Quantin's (1949) study of the powers of the soul in twelfth-century
monastic writing.

fess any secret fault of thought, word, or deed, privately to the abbot. Unlike open accusations of public sins, confession (i.e., self-accusation) did not take place at the chapter but at other times set aside for it. Here, penance would of course have a different function, one independent of the transgressor's determination to avoid the sorrow causing sin in the future. The contrasting structures of ritual penance may be seen more clearly in the following table:

1. Fault	1. Fault
2. Public accusation	2. Remorse
3. Penance	3. Self-accusation (private confession)
4. Remorse	4. Penance
5. Reconciliation	5. Reconciliation

In each sequence, fault is the initial element, and reconciliation the concluding one. But in the second, the penance that follows self-accusation appears essentially as a matter of satisfying the law after having offended it. Paradoxically, in the case where penance belongs to the setting most clearly like a punitive court of law, it has a closer connection with the notion of "spiritual therapy"—that is, of creating the appropriate psychological conditions for rectifying dispositions, because a correct disposition is assumed to be necessary both for the learning of individual virtues and for orderly community life. This contrast between the demands of the law and the formation of a virtuous will was, as we know from the history of sacramental penance, the source of a profound theological debate in the twelfth century.

What the table does not show is that when the fault is a sin, it is in the first place an offense against divine law. Reconciliation must therefore be made with the law before the sinner—whom the law has set apart for his transgression—can be brought back into the monastic community. Where the performance of penance precedes (and thus helps create) a rectified disposition, reconciliation can be assumed to take place at the same time for both. Where it remains to be carried out *after* remorse, as in the case of self-accusation, the dual function of reconciliation splits apart: the construction of virtuous dispositions may be seen to be quite a different matter from the power of divine law to forgive an offense. The latter is first and foremost a matter of legal right, which is how divinity comes to have the privilege of forgiving an offense. As the legal representative of God on earth, the confessor has the power to forgive (absolve) the penitent when satisfaction has been duly rendered. The confessor's power derives from the Church's traditional claim to the two keys *(claves ecclesiae)*—the power to bind and to loose, to impose the duty of penance and to remove it, to absolve the penitent from the divine punishment in the hereafter or to deny him that clearance.

St. Bernard's contemporary Peter Abelard was rash enough to attribute forgiveness to the sequence of (1) the state of being contrite, (2) the will to confess and to give satisfaction, and (3) the act of confession followed by the performance of the penalty that was due. When merciful God is satisfied with the sincerity of the penitent's will, forgiveness—so Abelard argued—follows as a matter of course. The production of a humble self thus became central to Abelard's teaching on penance, although it was still set within a legalistic framework. But his doctrine entailed a rejection of the Church's role of forgiveness based on "the power of the keys." The confessor, he argued, was merely an adviser who indicated the proper measure of penance (satisfaction) to be observed (Luscombe 1971). For this view, among others, Abelard was condemned for heresy at the instigation of Bernard of Clairvaux.

Nevertheless, apart from the question of "the power of the keys," Abelard's teachings had a far-reaching effect on medieval theories of penance. Among these was the theory of Hugh of St. Victor, as put forward in book 2, part 14 of *De sacramentis*. Hugh was the first to distinguish a double constraint brought about by the act of sinning: an interior one consisting of stubbornness (a state of will) and an exterior one consisting of liability to future damnation (a legal condition). Remorse (contrition) automatically released the former, by changing a vicious will into virtuous desire, but the latter was loosed only by the confessor's absolution (Poschmann 1964, 161).

What do these theories have to do with the practice of penance? They are the writings of people who practiced the rite of penance, as confessors and penitents. The writings are therefore to be read as successive responses to problems in that practice, which in turn helped to shape it. They constitute what we would today describe as discursive interventions in the practice of a social psychology that aimed at reforming its categories to make them coherent and effective. What became defined as the orthodox practice of penance implied looking for and dealing with "true repentance"—at once a concept, an emotion, and a mental state—which is an intrinsic part of the will to obedience, and therefore of structures of self built around it.

The outstanding feature of penance is not merely its corrective function but its techniques of *self*-correction. It is therefore perhaps not entirely accurate to describe this rite, as some scholars have done (e.g., Tentler 1974), in terms of "social control"—at least if the expression is taken in the manipulative sense. In the context of the medieval monastic program, it was a disciplinary technique for the self to create a desire for obedience to the law—but that was intrinsic to what the self was, not an instrument to be used by authority to keep an already-constituted self in order. There was no guarantee, of course, that the rite of penance always achieved its aim. This rite, like others in the monastery, never stood alone (as Hugh insists in *De sacramentis*) but was part of an entire disciplinary program whose effective performance depended on many contingent factors. But at least the possibilities of failure were fewer here than they were in secular society taken as a whole, because outside the cloister the conditions of discipline were less predictable than within it.

Conclusion

In this exploration of religious discipline in medieval Latin Christianity, I have focused on the formation of willing obedience to authority within the framework of the monastic community. It may be useful, before I conclude, to review the basic points I have tried to make.

In the sketch of the concept of *disciplina,* I introduced a distinction between two forms of power—one involved in the formation of virtues, the other in the exercise of law—which monastic practices attempted to reconcile. I then discussed the pedagogical techniques of Bernard of Clairvaux, and suggested that monastic rites might be analyzed in terms of a program for learning Christian virtues subject to God's law. I pointed to a remarkable feature of these techniques: the appropriation (as opposed to the suppression) of dangerous desires in the cause of Christian virtue. The overall aim of this monastic project was not to repress secular experiences of freedom but to form religious desires out of them.

It is well known that the Cistercians belonged to a monastic movement that emphasized poverty and humility, so I examined the way their conception of manual work helped to organize the virtue of humility as the prerequisite for Christian obedience. My discussion in this part of the chapter dealt with the disciplinary implications of labor in relation to the monastic program, not with the economic implications of Cistercian estate ownership and management—still less with the civilizational origins of Western economic rationality, on which so much has been written. My conclusion to this section was that if manual labor was to secure humility, something other than a mental revaluation was called for: a disciplinary program in which the laborer could be truly humiliated by that work. This was followed, therefore, by a detailed consideration of two programmatic statements in which humility and obedience are theorized by authoritative figures in the life of twelfth-century cloistered communities. I stressed again the tension between the demands of virtue formation and those of subjection to the law. Finally, I analyzed the process of observation, correction, and punishment—in particular as they were structured by the rites of penance. I suggested that in these rites one may detect again the sometimes conflicting pulls of forming virtues and upholding the law.

I have not assumed that power is always interpersonal as opposed to being institutional. I have merely concentrated my attention on aspects of volitional power which were constructed by the Christian monastic project. I have directed my attention at monastic life because it was considered the highest form of religion in the Middle Ages, but it does not follow that I take monastic obedience to be *the* model of all religious authority.

Monastic rites belonged to a particular type of disciplinary regimen, some of whose elements were appropriated and transformed by secular projects in later centuries. Changes in the patterns of discipline within medieval and modern societies made Christian rites different at different times and places. The changes have meant that Christian rites governed different areas of social life, engaged with differently structured selves, and were integrated into different kinds of authorized knowledge.[33] Thus, humility in the form of self-abasement is no longer

33. In a fascinating paper, Sylla (1975) has discussed the contrasting approaches in explaining the Eucharist taken by Aquinas (d. 1274) and Ockham (d. 1349): "In almost every important case," she notes, "Aquinas modifies or 'sublimates' natural philosophy to explain the Eucharist whereas Ockham allows natural philosophy its own autonomy—where natural philosophy is not applicable Ockham refers to God's direct intervention rather than assuming a modified physics. Thus in Ockham, but not in Aquinas, natural philosophy has its proper autonomy even within a theological context" (363).

admired in "normal" Christianity, and modern secular thought and practice classify and treat it as one of the standard personality disorders. Rituals of humiliation and abasement are now symptoms of patients, not the discipline of agents.

In brief, it does not seem to me to make good sense to say that ritual behavior stands universally in opposition to behavior that is ordinary or pragmatic, any more than religion stands in contrast to reason or to (social) science. In various epochs and societies, the domains of life are variously articulated, and each of them articulates endeavors that are appropriate to it. How these articulations are constructed and policed, and what happens when they are changed (forcibly or otherwise), are all questions for anthropological inquiry. But unless we try to reconstruct in detail the historical conditions in which different projects and motivations are formed, we shall not make much headway in understanding agency.

Sylla argues that the implications of Ockham's position (condemned in the fourteenth century by the Church) were compatible with the growth of scientific ideas in the seventeenth century.

Translations

✢✢✢✢

5 ⟨∞⟩   THE CONCEPT OF CULTURAL TRANSLATION IN BRITISH SOCIAL ANTHROPOLOGY

All anthropologists are familiar with E. B. Tylor's famous definition of culture: "Culture or Civilization, taken in its wide ethnographic sense, is that complex whole which includes knowledge, belief, art, morals, law, custom, and any other capabilities and habits acquired by man as a member of society." It would be interesting to trace how and when this notion of culture, with its enumeration of "capabilities and habits" and its emphasis on what Linton called *social heredity* (focusing on the process of learning) was transformed into the notion of a text—that is, into something resembling an inscribed discourse. One obvious clue to this change is to be found in the way that a notion of language as the precondition of historical continuity and social learning ("cultivation") came to dominate the perspective of social anthropologists.

In a general way, of course, such an interest in language predates Tylor, but in the nineteenth and early twentieth centuries it tended to be central to varieties of nationalist literary theory and education (cf. Eagleton 1983, chap. 2) rather than to the other human sciences. When and in what ways did it become crucial for British social anthropology? I do not intend to attempt such a history here, but merely to remind ourselves that the phrase "the translation of cultures," which increasingly since the 1950s has become an almost banal description of the distinctive task of social anthropology, was not always so much in evidence. I want to stress that this apparent shift is not identical with the old pre-functionalism/functionalism periodization. Nor is it simply a matter of a direct interest in language and meaning that was previously lacking (Crick 1976). Bronislaw Malinowski, one of the founders of the so-called functionalist school, wrote much on "primitive language" and collected enormous quantities of linguistic material (proverbs, kinship terminology, magical spells, and so on) for anthropological analysis. But he never thought of his work in terms of the translation of cultures.

Godfrey Lienhardt's paper "Modes of Thought" (1954) is possibly one of the earliest—certainly one of the most subtle—examples of the use of this notion of translation explicitly to describe a central task of social anthropology. "The problem of describing to others how members of a remote tribe think then begins to appear largely as one of translation, of making the coherence primitive thought has in the languages it really lives in, as clear as possible in our own" (97). This statement is quoted and criticized in the article by Ernest Gellner that I analyze in the next section, and I shall return to it in the context of Gellner's argument. Here I draw attention briefly to Lienhardt's use of the word *translation* to refer not to linguistic matter per se but to "modes of thought" that are embodied in such matter. It may not be without significance, incidentally, that Lienhardt has a background in English literature, that he was a pupil of F. R. Leavis's at Cambridge before he became a pupil and collaborator of E. E. Evans-Pritchard's at Oxford.

Oxford is, of course, famous as the anthropological center in Britain most self-conscious about its concern with the translation of cultures. The best-known introductory textbook to emerge from that center, John Beattie's *Other Cultures* (1964), emphasized the centrality of the problem of translation for social anthropology and distinguished (but did not separate) "culture" from "language" in a way that was becoming familiar to anthropologists—though not necessarily therefore entirely clear (see 89–90).

It is interesting to find Edmund Leach, who has never been associated with Oxford, employing the same notion in his conclusion to a historical sketch of social anthropology a decade later:

We started by emphasizing how different are "the others"—and made them not only different but remote and inferior. Sentimentally we then took the opposite track and argued that all human beings are alike; we can understand Trobrianders or the Barotse because their motivations are just the same as our own; but that didn't work either, "the others" remained obstinately other. But now we have come to see that the essential problem is one of translation. The linguists have shown us that all translation is difficult, and that perfect translation is usually impossible. And yet we know that for practical purposes a tolerably satisfactory translation is always possible even when the original "text" is highly abstruse. Languages are different but not so different as all that. Looked at in this way social anthropologists are engaged in establishing a methodology for the translation of cultural language. (1973, 772)

Even Max Gluckman (1973, 905), responding shortly afterward to Leach, accepts the centrality of cultural translation, while proposing a very different genealogy for that anthropological practice.

Yet despite the general agreement with which this notion has been accepted as part of the self-definition of British social anthropology, it has received little systematic examination from within the profession. One partial exception is Rodney Needham's *Belief, Language, and Experience* (1972). This is a complex, scholarly work that deserves extended treatment. Here, however, I wish to concentrate on a shorter text, Ernest Gellner's "Concepts and Society," which appears to be fairly widely used in undergraduate courses at British universities and is still available in several popular collections. I propose, therefore, to devote the next section to a detailed examination of that essay and then to take up some points that emerge from my discussion in the sections that follow.

A Theoretical Text

Gellner's "Concepts and Society" is concerned with the way in which functionalist anthropologists deal with problems of interpreting and translating the discourse of alien societies. His basic argument is that (a) contemporary anthropologists insist on interpreting exotic concepts and beliefs within a social context, but that (b) in doing so they ensure that apparently absurd or incoherent assertions are always given an acceptable meaning, and that (c) while the contextual method of interpretation is in principle valid, the "excessive charity" that usually goes with it is not. The paper contains several diagrams intended to fix and clarify the relevant cultural processes visually.

Gellner introduces the problem of interpretation by reference to Kurt Samuelsson's *Religion and Economic Action* (1961), which is an economic historian's attack on the Weberian Protestant Ethic thesis. Samuelsson takes issue with the fact that Weber and his supporters have reinterpreted religious texts in a way that enables them to extract meanings that confirm the thesis. Gellner presents this example merely to bring out more sharply the contrasting position of the functionalist anthropologist:

> I am not concerned, nor competent, to argue whether Samuelsson's employment, in this particular case, of his tacit principle that one must not reinterpret the assertions one actually finds, is valid. What is relevant here is that if such a principle is made explicit and generalized, it would make nonsense of most sociological studies of the relationship of belief and conduct. We shall find anthropologists driven to employ the very opposite principle, the insistence rather than refusal of contextual re-interpretation. (20)

But this modest disclaimer of competence allows too many interesting questions to drift by. To begin with, it should be noted that Samuelsson does not hold to the principle that one must *never* reinterpret. Nor does he insist that there is *never* a significant connection between a religious text and its social context, but only that the conclusion the Weber thesis seeks to make cannot be established (see, e.g., Samuelsson 1961, 69). There is, furthermore, a real contrast that Gellner might have picked up between the Samuelsson example and the typical anthropologist's predicament. For economic historians and sociologists involved in the Weber debate, historical texts are a primary datum in relation to which the social contexts must be reconstructed. The anthropological fieldworker begins with a social situation within which something is said, and it is the cultural significance of these enunciations that must be reconstructed. This is not to say, of course, that the historian can ever approach his archival material without some conception of its historical context, or that the fieldworker can define the social situation independently of what was said within it. The contrast, such as it is, is one of orientation, which follows from the fact that the historian is *given* a text and the ethnographer has *to construct one.*

Instead of investigating this important contrast (and how it actually works in practice), Gellner rushes along to define and commend what he calls "moderate Functionalism" as a method, which consists of the insistence on the fact that concepts and beliefs do not exist in isolation, in texts or in individual minds, but in the life of men and societies. The activities and institutions, in the context of which a word or phrase or set of phrases is used, must be known before that word or those phrases can be understood, before we can really speak of a *concept* or a belief. (22)

This is certainly well put. At this point, the reader might expect a discussion of the different ways in which language is encountered by the ethnographers in the field, how utterances are produced, verbal meanings organized, rhetorical effects attained, and culturally appropriate responses elicited. After all, Wittgenstein had already sensitized British philosophers to the complexity of language-in-use, and J. L. Austin had set up distinctions between the different levels of speech production and reception in a way that foreshadowed what anthropologists would later call *the ethnography of speaking*. But Gellner had previously rejected the suggestion that this philosophical movement had anything of value to teach (see his polemic in *Words and Things,* 1959), and like other critics, he always insisted that its concern with understanding everyday language was merely a disguise for defending established ways of speaking about the world, for denying that it was possible for such speechways to be illogical or absurd. Gellner has always been determined to maintain the distinction between defending and explaining "concepts and beliefs" and to warn against the kind of anthropological translation that rules out a priori the critical distance necessary for explaining how concepts actually function, for "to understand the *working* of the concepts of society," he writes, "is to understand its institutions" (18; see also note 1 on the same page).

This is why Gellner's brief statement about moderate functionalism quoted above leads him immediately to a discussion of Durkheim's *Elementary Forms of the Religious Life,* which, besides being "one of the fountainheads of Functionalism in general" (22), is concerned to explain rather than to defend concepts—to explain, more precisely, "the compulsive nature of our categorial concepts" (223) in terms of certain collective processes. Thus:

> Our contemporary invocations of the functional, social-context approach to the study and interpretation of concepts is in various ways very different from Durkheim's. Durkheim was not so much con-

cerned to defend the concepts of primitive societies: in their setting, they did not need a defence, and in the setting of modern and changing societies, he was not anxious to defend what was archaic, nor loath to suggest that some intellectual luggage might well be archaic. He was really concerned to explain the compulsiveness of what in practice did not seem to need any defence (and in so doing, he claimed he was solving the problem of knowledge whose solution had in his view evaded Kant and others, and to be solving it without falling into either empiricism or apriorism). Whether he was successful I do not propose to discuss: for a variety of reasons it seems to me that he was not. (23)

It is clear that Gellner has recognized the basic project of *Elementary Forms*—namely, its attempt to explain the compulsive nature of socially defined concepts—but he moves too hastily from a consideration of what might be involved in such a problem to a dismissal of Durkheim's attempt at explanation. The possibility that a priori *denunciation* may not further the purposes of explanation any better than *defense* does not seem to be envisaged in "Concepts and Society." Instead, the reader is reminded, by way of quotation from Lienhardt, that the contemporary anthropologist typically "appears to make it a condition of a good translation that it conveys the coherence which he assumes is there to be found in primitive thought" (26). So we have here what I think is a misleading contrast—Durkheim's attempt to explain versus the contemporary anthropologist's attempt to defend. I shall return to this point later, but here I want to insist that to argue for a form of coherence by which a discourse is held together is not ipso facto to justify or defend that discourse; it is merely to take an essential step in the problem of explaining its *compulsiveness*. Anyone familiar with psychoanalysis would take this point quite easily. We might put it another way; the criterion of abstract "coherence" or "logicality" (Gellner tends to use these and other terms interchangeably) is not always, and in every case, decisive for accepting or rejecting discourse. This is because, as Gellner himself correctly observes, "Language functions in a variety of ways other than 'referring to objects' " (25). Not every utterance is an assertion. There are many things that language-in-use does, *and is intended to do,* which explains why we may respond positively to discourse that may seem inadequate from a narrow, "logical" point of view. The functions of a particular language, the intentions of a particular discourse, are of course part of what every competent ethnographer tries to grasp before he can attempt an adequate translation into his own language. In this sense, an assumption of coherence is indispensable to any translation.

Gellner does occasionally come near this point, but quickly brushes it aside in his eagerness to display the "excessive charity" of functionalist anthropologists.

> The situation, facing a social anthropologist who wishes to interpret a concept, assertion or doctrine in an alien culture, is basically simple. He is, say, faced with an assertion S in the local language. He has at his disposal the large or infinite set of possible sentences in his own language. . . .
>
> He may not be wholly happy about this situation, but he cannot avoid it. There is no third language which could mediate between the native language and his own, in which equivalences could be stated and which would avoid the pitfalls arising from the fact that his own language has its own ways of handling the world, which may not be those of the native language studied, and which consequently are liable to distort that which is being translated.
>
> Naively, people sometimes think that *reality* itself could be this kind of mediator and "third language." . . . For a variety of powerful reasons, this is of course no good. (24-25)

Again, this sensible statement might seem to some readers to support the demand that the ethnographer must try to reconstruct the various ways in which the native language handles the world, conveys information, and constitutes experience, before translating an alien discourse into the language of his ethnographic text. But Gellner's account proceeds in a different, and very dubious, direction.

Having located an equivalent English sentence, he continues, the anthropologist notices that it inevitably carries a value connotation—that it is, in other words, either Good or Bad. "I do not say 'true' or 'false,' for this only arises with regard to some types of assertion. With regard to others, other dichotomies, such as 'meaningful' and 'absurd' or 'sensible' or 'silly' might apply. I deliberately use the 'Good' and 'Bad' so as to cover all such possible polar alternatives, whichever might best apply to the equivalent of S" (27).

Have we not got here some very curious assumptions, which no practiced translator would ever make? The first is that evaluative discrimination is always a matter of choosing between polar alternatives; second, that evaluative distinctions are finally reducible to "Good" and "Bad." Clearly, neither of these assumptions is acceptable when stated as a general rule. And then there is the suggestion that the translator's task necessarily involves matching sentence for sentence. But if the skilled translator looks first for any principle of coherence in the discourse to be translated, then tries to reproduce that coherence as nearly as he can in his own language, there cannot be a general rule as to what units the translator will employ—sentences, paragraphs, or even larger units of discourse. To turn my point around: *The appropriateness of the unit employed itself depends on the principle of coherence.*

But Gellner's parable of the anthropologist-translator requires the assumption that it is sentences that the latter matches, because that makes it easier to display how the sin of excessive charity occurs. Having made an initial equivalence between a sentence in the local language and one in his own, the anthropologist notices that the English sentence carries a "Bad" impression. This worries the anthropologist because, so runs Gellner's parable, an ethnographic account giving such an impression might be thought to disparage the natives he has studied, and to disparage other cultures is a sign of ethnocentrism, and ethnocentrism in turn is a symptom of poor anthropology, according to the doctrines of functionalist anthropology. Functionalist method requires that sentences always be evaluated in terms of their own social context. So the worried anthropologist reinterprets the original sentence, with a more flexible and careful use of the contextual method, in order to produce a "Good" translation.

The sin of excessive charity, and the contextual method itself, are together linked, Gellner writes, to the relativistic-functionalist view of thought that goes back to the Enlightenment:

> The (unresolved) dilemma, which the thought of the Enlightenment faced, was between a relativistic-functionalist view of thought, and the absolutist claims of enlightened Reason. Viewing man as part of nature, as enlightened Reason requires, it wishes to see his cognitive and evaluative activities as parts of nature too, and hence as varying, legitimately, from organism to organism and context to context. (This is the relativistic-functionalist view.) But at the same time in recommending life according to Reason and Nature, it wished at the very

least to exempt this view itself (and, in practice, some others) from such a relativism. (31)

Typically, Gellner's philosophical formulation presents this "unresolved dilemma" as an abstract opposition between two concepts—"a relativistic-functionalist view of thought, and the absolutist claims of enlightened Reason." But how do these two concepts work as "correlates of . . . the institutions of [Western] society"? (cf. Gellner, 18). It would not be difficult to argue that the claims of "enlightened Reason" are materially more successful in third world countries than many relativistic views, that they have exerted greater authority than the latter in the development of industrial economies and the formation of nation-states. I shall have occasion to discuss this further when examining translation as a process of power. The point is that "the absolutist claims of enlightened Reason" are in effect an institutionalized force,[1] and that as such it is by definition committed to advancing into and appropriating alien territory, and that its opponents (whether explicitly relativistic or not) are by definition defensive. Thus, when Gellner continues on the same page to characterize this abstract dilemma in the attitudes of anthropologists, he fails to consider what cultural translation might involve when it is considered as institutionalized practice, given the wider relationship of unequal societies. For it is not the abstract logic of what individual Western anthropologists say in their ethnographies, but the concrete logic of what their countries (and perhaps they themselves) do in their relations with the third world that should form the starting point for this particular discussion. The dilemmas of relativism appear differently depending on whether we think of abstracted understanding or of historically situated practices.

However, Gellner says he is not in principle against anthropological relativism. "My main point about tolerance-engendering contextual interpretation," he writes, "is that it calls for caution" (32). But why such caution is reserved for "tolerance-engendering" as opposed to *in*tolerance-engendering contextual interpretations is not explained.

---

1. "The eighteenth century witnessed the unfolding of bourgeois society, which saw itself as the new world, laying intellectual claim to the whole world and simultaneously denying the old. It grew out of the territories of the European states and, in dissolving this link, developed a progressive philosophy in line with the process. The subject of that philosophy was all mankind, to be unified from its European centre and led peacefully towards a better future" (Koselleck 1988, 5–6).

After all, Gellner insisted earlier that all translated sentences are bound to be received either as "Good" or as "Bad." Why should we be suspicious only of those that appear "Good"? If "it is the *prior* determination that S, the indigenous affirmation, be interpreted favourably, which determines just how much context will be taken into consideration" (33), can we perhaps escape this vicious circularity by adopting an *unsympathetic* attitude? Gellner does not address himself directly to this possibility here, but one must assume that it cannot be a solution, especially in view of the claim that "there is nothing in the nature of things or societies to dictate visibly just how much context is relevant to any given utterance, or how the context should be described" (33).

Surely this last remark cannot be meant seriously. "Nothing"? How, then, is communication even between individuals in the same society ever possible? Why does one ever say to foreigners that they have misunderstood something they heard or saw? Does social learning produce no skills in the discrimination of relevant contexts? The answers to these questions should be obvious, and they are connected with the fact that the anthropologist's translation is not merely a matter of matching sentences in the abstract, but of *learning to live another form of life* and to speak another kind of language. Which contexts are relevant in different discursive events is something one learns in the course of living, and even though it is often very difficult to verbalize that knowledge, it is still knowledge about something "in the nature of society," about some aspect of living, that indicates (although it does not "dictate") just how much context is relevant to any given utterance. The point, of course, is not that ethnographers cannot know what context is appropriate for giving sense to typical statements, or that they are induced to be more charitable than they should be in translating them, but that their attempts at translation may meet with problems rooted in the linguistic materials they work with *and* the social conditions they work in—both in the field and in their own society. More on this later.

The latter half of Gellner's essay is devoted to examples from ethnographic studies in order to display, first, excessive charity in translation, and then, the explanatory advantages of taking a critical look at the logic of alien religious discourse.

The first set of examples comes from Evans-Pritchard's *Nuer Religion* (1956), in which odd-sounding initial translations of Nuer religious discourse, such as the notorious statement that "a twin is a bird," are reinterpreted. "This kind of statement," Gellner observes, "appears to be in conflict with the principle of identity or non-contradiction, or with common sense, or with manifest observable fact: human twins are *not* birds, and vice versa" (34). According to Gellner, Evans-Pritchard's reinterpretation absolves Nuer thought from the charge of "pre-logical mentality" by an arbitrary use of the contextual method. The apparent absurdity is reinterpreted to deny that Nuer beliefs conflict with manifest fact by relating the meaning of the "absurd" statement to "logical" behavior. Gellner indicates how this is done by quoting (with the omission of one significant sentence) from Evans-Pritchard:

> No contradiction is involved in the statement which, on the contrary, appears quite sensible and even true, to one who presents the idea to himself in the Nuer language and within their system of religious thought. [He does not then take their statements about twins any more literally than they make and understand them themselves.] *They are not saying that a twin has a beak, feathers, and so forth. Nor in their everyday relations as twins do Nuers speak of them as birds or act towards them as though they were birds.* (35: Sentence in brackets omitted by Gellner; emphasis supplied by Gellner)

At this point Gellner breaks off the quotation and interjects in mock despair: "But what, then, *would* count as pre-logical thought? Only, presumably, the behaviour of a totally demented person, suffering from permanent hallucinations, who *would* treat something which is perceptibly a human being as though it had all the attributes of a bird" (35). So eager is Gellner to nail utterances that must count as expressions of "pre-logical thought" that he does not pause to consider what Evans-Pritchard is trying to do. In fact, Evans-Pritchard devotes several pages to explaining this strange sentence. It is plain that he is concerned to explain (in terms of Nuer social life), not to justify (in terms of Western common sense or Western values). The aim of this kind of exegesis is certainly not to persuade Western readers to adopt Nuer religious tradition. Nor does it rule out the possibility that individual speakers make mistakes or utter absurdities in their religious discourse when employing their traditional ways of thinking. It is not clear, therefore, why Gellner should point to this example from *Nuer Religion* to substantiate his charge of excessive charity on the part of functionalist anthropologists. Evans-Pritchard is trying to explain the coherence that gives Nuer religious discourse its sense, not to defend that sense as having a universal legitimacy—after all, Evans-Pritchard himself was a convert to Catholicism, not to Nuer religion at the time his monograph was written.

Whether Evans-Pritchard succeeds in explaining the basic coherence of Nuer religious discourse is, of course, another question. Several British anthropologists—for example, Raymond Firth (1966)—(though not, to my knowledge, any Nuer themselves) have disputed aspects of Evans-Pritchard's interpretation. But such disagreements are still about different ways of making sense of Nuer religious discourse, not about too much or too little "charity" in translation. In fact, contrary to Gellner's allegations, Evans-Pritchard's exegesis *does* make quite explicit apparent "contradictions," or at least ambiguities, in Nuer concepts—for example, between the notion of a "supreme and omnipresent being" and that of "lesser spirits," both of which are categorized as *kwoth*. And it is precisely because Evans-Pritchard insists on keeping the different senses of *kwoth* together as parts of one concept and does not treat them as homonyms (as Malinowski might have done by relating the word to different contexts of use) that the Nuer concept of spirit might be said to be contradictory. But whether the identification of ambiguities and contradictions in the basic conceptual repertoire of a religious language provides obvious evidence of "pre-logical thought" is, of course, a different issue. I would suggest that it is not, because as an analytical construct, pre-logical thought conflates the common-sense idea of logical mistakes in everyday life with an Enlightenment story of science as the culmination of reason purified at last from magic and religion.

Unfortunately, Gellner's discourse typically evades the issues it seems to be raising, in a style that seeks to hurry the reader along over a series of disclaimers:

> I do not wish to be misunderstood: I am *not* arguing that Evans-Pritchard's account of Nuer concepts is a bad one. (Nor am I anxious to revive a doctrine of pre-logical mentality *à la* Levy-Bruhl.) On the contrary, I have the greatest admiration for it. What I am anxious to argue is that contextual interpretation, which offers an account of what assertions "really mean" in opposition to what they seem to mean in isolation, does not by itself clinch matters. (38)

Now, who would have claimed it did? Certainly Evans-Pritchard does not. In any case, the opposition between a contextual interpretation and one that is not contextual is entirely spurious. Nothing has meaning in isolation. The problem is always, what kind of context?

But that is something Gellner never discusses, except by suggesting that the answer must involve a vicious circularity—or by uttering repeated warnings against excessive charity. (When is charity not excessive?) He appears unaware that for the translator the problem of determining the relevant kind of context in each case is solved by skill in the use of the languages concerned, not by an a priori attitude of intolerance or tolerance. And skill is something that is learned—and therefore something that is necessarily circular, but not viciously so. We are dealing not with an abstract matching of two sets of sentences but with a social practice rooted in modes of life. A translator may make mistakes, or she may knowingly misrepresent something—much as people make mistakes or lie in everyday life. But we cannot produce a general principle for identifying such things, particularly not through warnings to be careful of "the contextual method of interpretation."

And so to another of Gellner's disclaimers: "To say all this is not to argue for a scepticism or agnosticism concerning what members of alien languages mean, still less to argue for an abstention from the contextual method of interpretation. (On the contrary, I shall argue for a fuller use of it, fuller in the sense of allowing for the possibility that what people mean is sometimes absurd.)" (39).

But before that is done, we are given further examples of the tolerance-engendering contextual method at work in Leach's *Political Systems of Highland Burma*. Thus, according to Leach, Kachin statements about the supernatural world are "in the last analysis, nothing more than ways of describing the formal relationships that exist between real persons and real groups in ordinary Kachin society" (quoted on p. 40). At this point, Gellner intervenes: "It is possible to discern what has happened. Leach's exegetic procedures have also saved the Kachins from being credited with what they *appear* to be saying" and thus make it possible "to attribute meaning to assertions which might otherwise be found to lack it" (41). Gellner goes on to insist that he is not concerned to dispute Leach's interpretations, but merely "to show how the range of context, and the manner in which the context is seen, necessarily affect the interpretation" (41). This is a significant remark, because it is indeed not Leach's reductionism to which Gellner objects (we shall find him insisting on it himself later in connection with Berber religious ideology) but to the fact that this example of reductionism, which Gellner misleadingly calls "contextualism"—seems to defend, rather than to criticize, the discourse concerned.

Gellner's demonstration of how "the *uncharitable* may be 'contextualist' in the second, deeper and better sense" (42) begins by presenting a fictitious word in a fictitious society—the word *boble,* used in a way remarkably like the English word *noble.* Thus, we are told that it can be applied to people who actually display certain habitual forms of conduct, as well as to people who occupy a particular social status irrespective of their behavior. "But the point is: the society in question does not distinguish *two concepts,* boble (a) and boble (b). It only uses the word boble tout court" (42). The logic of bobility is then analyzed further to show how

> bobility is a conceptual device by which the privileged class of the society in question acquires some of the prestige of certain virtues respected in that society, without the inconvenience of needing to practice it, thanks to the fact that the same word is applied either to practitioners of those virtues or to occupiers of favoured positions. It is, at the same time, a manner of reinforcing the appeal of those virtues, by associating them, through the use of the same appellation, with prestige and power. But all this needs to be said, and to say it is to bring out the internal logical incoherence of the concept—an incoherence which, indeed, is socially functional. (42)

In fact, the concept of "bobility" is not shown to be incoherent, even if it be accepted that the ambiguity of the *word* allows it to be used in political discourse to consolidate the legitimacy of a ruling class (and therefore, in principle, also to undermine that legitimacy). Gellner's conclusion to his fictional example is surely far too hasty: "What this shows, however, is that the over-charitable interpreter, determined to defend the concepts he is investigating from the charge of logical incoherence, is bound to misdescribe the social situation. *To make sense of the concept is to make nonsense of the society*" (42; emphasis added). Clearly, the word "bobility" makes sense to its users in particular statements (or they would not use it), and it makes sense also, although of a different kind, to Gellner, who states that by deceiving its users it somehow upholds a social structure. Sense or nonsense, like truth or falsehood, applies to *statements* and not to abstract concepts. There seems to me no evidence here of a nonsensical concept, because there is no analysis of socially situated statements in which that concept is deployed.

But there is also a more important failure evident in this example: the lack of any attempt to explore its *coherence*—that which makes its social effect such a powerful possibility. Of course, political discourse employs lies, half-truths, logical trickery, and so on. Yet that is not what gives it its compulsive character—any more than the use of true or clear statements does—and compulsiveness is precisely what is involved in Gellner's example. It is not the abstract logical status of concepts that is relevant here, but the way in which a specific political (or religious) discourse that employs them seems to mobilize or direct the behavior of people within given situations. The compulsiveness of "bobility" as a political concept is a feature not of gullible minds but of coherent discourses and practices. That is why it is essential for a translator of powerful political or religious ideologies to attempt to convey something of this coherence. To make nonsense of the concept is to make nonsense of the society.

Gellner's final example comes from his own fieldwork among the central Moroccan Berbers, and is intended to clinch the argument that an uncharitable contextualist makes better sense of the society he describes by emphasizing the incoherence of its concepts. "Two concepts are relevant," he writes, *"baraka* and *agurram* (pl. *igurramen*). Baraka is a word which can mean simply 'enough,' but it also means plenitude, and above all blessedness manifested amongst other things in prosperity and the power to cause prosperity in others by supernatural means. An *agurram* is a possessor of *baraka"* (43).

Igurramen—translated as "saints" in Gellner's later writings (e.g., 1969)—are a fairly privileged and influential minority in the tribal society of central Moroccan Berbers who act as foci of religious values and also as mediators and arbitrators amongst the tribal population with whom they live. "The local belief is that they are selected by God. Moreover, God makes his choice manifest by endowing those whom he has selected with certain characteristics, including magical powers, and great generosity, prosperity, a consider-the-lilies attitude, pacifism, and so forth" (43).

This is Gellner's translation. But his too-fluent use of a religious vocabulary with strong, and perhaps irrelevant, Christian overtones must prompt doubts and questions at this point. What, precisely, are the behaviors and discourses translated here as "a consider-the-lilies attitude," "makes his choice manifest," and "endowing," for instance? Do the Berbers believe that God *endows* their "saints" with dispositional characteristics such as "great generosity" and "pacifism," or do they take it, rather, that these characteristics are *conditions* of saintliness, of the closeness of *igurramen* to God? Do the Berbers really behave as though religious and moral virtues were manifestations of divine choice? What do they say and how do they behave when people fail to display the virtues they *ought* to have? By whom is an *agurram's* behavior conceptualized as a consider-the-lilies attitude, given that he has both family and property, and that this fact is taken by the Berbers to be perfectly in order? Gellner does not give the reader the relevant evidence for answering these important questions, whose significance for his translation will emerge in a moment.

> The reality of the situation is, however, that the *igurramen* are in fact selected by the surrounding ordinary tribesmen who use their services, by being called to perform those services and being preferred to the rival candidates for their performance. What appears to be *vox Dei* is in reality *vox populi*. Moreover, the matter of the blessed characteristics, the stigmata [*sic*] of *agurram*-hood is more complicated. It is essential that successful candidates to *agurram* status be *credited* with these characteristics, but it is equally essential at any rate with regard to some of them, that they should not really possess them. For instance, an *agurram* who was extremely generous in a consider-the-lilies spirit would soon be impoverished and, as such, fail by another crucial test, that of prosperity.
>
> There is here a crucial divergence between concept and reality, a divergence which moreover is quite essential for the working of the social system. (43-44)

It is not at all clear from the account given by Gellner what is meant by the statement, "The local belief is that they are selected by God"—selected for what, exactly? For being arbitrators? But arbitration must be initiated by one or another member of the tribal society, and that fact can hardly be unknown to the tribesmen. For being pacific? But pacifism is a virtue, not a reward. For worldly success and prosperity? But that cannot be a local definition of saintliness, or the French colonial rulers would have been regarded as more saintly than any *agurram*.

It is really no great explanatory achievement for a European anthropologist to inform his agnostic and/or modern European readers that the Berbers believe in a particular kind of direct intervention of the deity in their affairs; that they are, of course, mistaken in this belief; and that this mistaken belief can have social consequences. In this kind of exercise, modern readers do not learn what the Berber tribesmen believe, only that what they believe is wrong: thus, the Berbers believe that God "selects" *igurramen;* we know God does not exist (or if some of us still believe he does, we know he does not intervene directly in secular history); ergo, the selector must be another agent whom the tribesmen do not know as the agent—in fact, the surrounding tribesmen themselves. The *igurramen* are selected (for a particular social role? for a moral virtue? for a religious destiny?) by the people. The selection appears to be *vox Dei* and is in reality *vox populi.* Or is it?

In reality, the social process described by the anthropologist as "selection" is the locus of a *vox* only if it is pretended that that process constitutes a cultural text. For a text must have an author—the one who makes his voice heard through it. And if that voice cannot be God's, it must be someone else's—the people's. Thus, Gellner insists on answering a theological question: Who is it that speaks through history, through society, through culture? In this particular case, the answer depends on the text containing at once the "real," unconscious meaning and its appropriate translation. This fusion of signifier and signified is especially evident in the way in which the Islamic concept of *baraka* is made to sound remarkably like the Christian concept of grace as portrayed by an eighteenth-century skeptic, so that the conditions defining the *agurram's baraka* are referred to with a knowing Gibbonian smile as "stigmata"—and by that deft sign, a portion of the Berber cultural text is at once constructed (made up) and designated (shown up) within Gellner's text, as exquisite a union of word and thing as any to be found in all his writings.

But society is not a text that communicates itself to the skilled reader. It is people who speak. And the ultimate meaning of what they say does not reside in society—society is the historical condition in which speakers act and are acted upon, speak, hear, and overhear. The privileged position that the anthropologist accords himself for decoding the *real* meaning of what the Berbers say (regardless of what they think they say) can be maintained only by someone who supposes that translating other cultures is essentially a matter of matching written sentences in two languages, such that the second set of sentences becomes the "real meaning" of the first—an operation he alone controls, from field notebook to printed ethnography. In other words, it is the privileged position of someone who does not, and can afford not to, engage in a genuine dialogue with those he or she once lived with and now writes about (cf. Asad 1973, 17).

In the middle of his article, when discussing anthropological relativism, Gellner complains that "anthropologists were relativistic, tolerant, contextually-comprehending vis-à-vis the savages who are after all some distance away, but absolutistic, intolerant vis-à-vis their immediate neighbours or predecessors, the members of our own society who do not share their comprehending outlook and are themselves 'ethnocentric' " (31).

Why have I tried to insist that anyone concerned with translating from other cultures must look for coherence in discourses, and yet devoted so many pages to showing that Gellner's text is largely incoherent? The reason is quite simple: Gellner and I speak the same language, belong to the same academic profession, live in the same society. In taking up a critical stance toward his text I am contesting what he says, not translating it, and the radical difference between these two activities is precisely what I insist on. Still, the purpose of my argument is not to express an attitude of intolerance toward an immediate neighbor but to try to identify incoherencies in his text that call for remedy, because the anthropological task of translation deserves to be made more coherent. The purpose of this criticism, therefore, is to further a collective endeavor. Criticizing "savages who are after all some distance away," in an ethnographic monograph they cannot read, does not seem to me to have the same kind of purpose. In order for criticism to be responsible, it must always be addressed to someone who can contest it.[2]

2. Does my condition for responsible criticism make it impossible to criticize one's historical ancestors, since they are, after all, in no position to answer back? I do not think so. Criticism of past authors is, in an important sense, criticism of present authorities. Arguments about our intellectual, moral, and political heritage are really carried on with contemporaries, not with deceased ancestors. Disagreement with traditional discourses and practices is not really an engagement with past figures, but only with their authoritative reception in the present.

The Inequality of Languages

A careful reading of Gellner's paper shows that although he raises a number of important questions, he not only fails to answer them but misses some of the most crucial aspects of the problem with which the ethnographer is engaged. The most interesting of these, it seems to me, is the problem of what one might call "unequal languages"—and it is this I want now to discuss in some detail.

All good translation seeks to reproduce the structure of an alien discourse within the translator's own language. How that structure (or "coherence") is reproduced will, of course, depend on the genre concerned (poetry, scientific analysis, narrative, etc.)and on the resources of the translator's language, as well as on the interests of the translator and/or her readership. All successful translation is premised on the fact that it is addressed within a specific language, and therefore also to a specific set of practices, a specific form of life. The further that form of life is from the original, the less mechanical is the reproduction. As Walter Benjamin wrote: "The language of a translation can—in fact must—let itself go, so that it gives voice to the *intentio* of the original not as reproduction but as harmony, as a supplement to the language in which it expresses itself, as its own kind of *intentio*" (1969, 79). It is, incidentally, for the reader to evaluate that *intentio,* not for the translator to preempt the evaluation. A good translation should always precede a critique. And we can turn this around by saying that a good critique is always an internal critique—that is, one based on some shared understanding, on a joint life, which it aims to enlarge and make more coherent. Such a critique—no less than the object of criticism—is a point of view, a (contra) *version,* having only provisional and limited authority.

What happens when the languages concerned are so disparate that it is very difficult to rewrite a harmonious *intentio?* Rudolf Pannwitz, quoted in the Benjamin essay on which I have just drawn, makes the following observation:

> Our translations, even the best ones, proceed from a wrong premise. They want to turn Hindi, Greek, English into German instead of turning German into Hindi, Greek, English. Our translators have a far greater reverence for the usage of their own language than for the spirit of the foreign works. The basic error of the translator is that he

preserves the state in which his own language happens to be instead of allowing his language to be powerfully affected by the foreign tongue. Particularly when translating from a language very remote from his own he must go back to the primal elements of language itself and penetrate to the point where work, image and tone converge. He must expand and deepen his language by means of the foreign language. (1969, 80–81)

This call to transform a language, in order to translate the coherence of the original, poses an interesting challenge to the person satisfied with an absurd-sounding translation on the assumption that the original must have been equally absurd: the good translator does not immediately assume that unusual difficulty in conveying the sense of an alien discourse denotes a fault in the latter, but instead critically examines the normal state of his or her own language. The relevant question therefore is not how tolerant an attitude the translator ought to display toward the original author (an abstract ethical dilemma) but how she can test the tolerance of her own language for assuming unaccustomed forms.

But this pushing beyond the limits of one's habitual usages, this breaking down and reshaping of one's own language through the process of translation, is never an easy business, in part because it depends on the willingness of the translator's language to subject itself to this transforming power. I attribute, somewhat fictitiously, volition to the language because I want to emphasize that the matter is largely something the translator cannot determine by individual activity (any more than the individual speaker can affect the evolution of his or her language)—that it is governed by institutionally defined power relations between the languages and modes of life concerned. To put it crudely, because the languages of third world societies—including, of course, the societies that social anthropologists have traditionally studied—are seen as weaker in relation to Western languages (and today, especially to English), they are more likely to submit to forcible transformation in the translation process than the other way around. The reason for this is, first, that in their political-economic relations with third world countries, Western nations have the greater ability to manipulate the latter. And, second, Western languages produce and deploy desired knowledge more readily than third world languages do. (The knowledge that third world languages deploy more easily is not sought by Western societies in quite the same way, or for the same reason.)

Take modern Arabic as an example. Since the early nineteenth century, there has been a growing volume of material translated from European languages—especially French and English—into Arabic. This includes scientific texts as well as social science, history, philosophy, and literature. And from the nineteenth century, Arabic as a language has begun as a result to undergo a transformation (lexical, grammatical, semantic) that is far more radical than anything to be identified in European languages—a transformation that has pushed it to approximate to the latter more closely than in the past.[3] Such transformations signal inequalities in the power (i.e., in the capacities) of the respective languages in relation to the dominant forms of discourse that have been and are still being translated. There are varieties of knowledge to be learnt, but also a host of models to be imitated and reproduced. In some cases, knowledge of these models is a precondition for the production of more knowledge; in others, it is an end in itself, a mimetic gesture of power, an expression of desire for transformation. A recognition of this well-known fact reminds us that industrial capitalism transforms not only modes of production but also kinds of knowledge and styles of life in the third world (and with them, forms of language). The result of half-transformed styles of life will make for ambi-

---

3. "These changes in modern written Arabic include important innovations acquired from modern European languages—ranging from the use of punctuation, paragraphing, sub-headings, to new sentence structures, semantic elements, and literary styles. These changes have not yet been thoroughly studied, and such studies as there are concentrate entirely on lexical and stylistic developments. For example there is a well-known study (Stetkevych 1970) which classifies and exemplifies the following types of change: (1) stylistic borrowings affecting syntactic structure, (2) literal translations from Western languages with eventual disregard of existing Arabic equivalents, (3) stylistic borrowings made possible through semantic extension and abstraction, (4) assimilation of proverbial and idiomatic expressions. But so far as we are aware nothing has been done on the conceptual implications of having adopted European typographical conventions.

"We want to make it clear that we do not regard linguistic borrowings—like those . . . in the literary Arabic just referred to—as something to be deplored. On the contrary, some kind of accommodation is often essential to the well-being of the populations concerned. We wish simply to underline the obvious but very important fact that such changes tend to take place in a determinate direction, and that this clearly has to do with the political and economic inequalities between societies. There is, for example, no list of modifications in English or in French deriving from their reception of translations from the Arabic, comparable to the one we have mentioned for the latter language" (Asad and Dixon 1985, 172).

guities,[4] which an unskillful Western translator may simplify in the direction of his own supposedly strong language.

What does this argument imply for the anthropologist engaged in translation? It contains a warning that perhaps there is a greater stiffness in ethnographic linguistic conventions, a greater intrinsic resistance than can be overcome by individual experiments in modes of ethnographic representation.

In his perceptive essay "Modes of Thought," which Gellner criticizes for making overcharitable assumptions about the coherence of so-called primitive thought, Lienhardt says:

> When we live with savages and speak their languages, learning to represent their experience to ourselves in their way, we come as near to thinking like them as we can without ceasing to be ourselves. Eventually, we try to represent their conceptions systematically in the logical constructs we have been brought up to use; and we hope, at best, thus to reconcile what can be expressed in their languages, with what can be expressed in ours. We mediate between their habits of thought, which we have acquired with them, and those of our own society; in doing so, it is not finally some mysterious "primitive philosophy" that we are exploring, but the further potentialities of our thought and language. (1954, 96–97)

In the field, as Lienhardt rightly suggests, the process of translation takes place at the very moment the ethnographer engages with a specific mode of life—just as a child does in learning to grow up within a specific culture. He learns to find his way in a new environment and a new language. And, like a child (or a convert), he needs to verbalize explicitly what the proper way of doing things is, because that is how learning proceeds (cf. A. R. Luria on "synpraxic speech," in Luria and Yudovich 1971, 50). When the child (or the anthropologist) becomes adept at adult ways, what he has learnt becomes implicit, as assumptions informing a shared mode of life that aspires to coherence but always contains areas of unclarity.

But learning to live a new mode of life is not the same as learning

---

4. I use the teleological term *half-transformed* in order to stress that modernizing states (as well as modern Western states and international agencies) actively encourage—when they do not try to impose—a specific project of change in the third world: a particular kind of economy, politics, law, etc.

about another mode of life. When anthropologists return to their countries, they must write up "their people," and they must do so in the conventions of representation already circumscribed (already written around, bounded) by their discipline, institutional life, and wider society. Cultural translation must accommodate itself to a different language, not only in the sense of English as opposed to Dinka, or English as opposed to Kabbashi Arabic, but also in the sense of a British, middle-class, academic game as opposed to the modes of life of the nomadic, tribal Sudan. The stiffness of a powerful, established structure of life, with its own discursive games, its own strong languages, is what among other things finally determines the effectiveness of the translations. The translation is addressed to a very specific audience, which is waiting to read about another mode of life and to manipulate the text it reads according to established rules, not to learn to live a new way of life.

If Benjamin was right in proposing that translation may require not a mechanical reproduction of the original but a harmonization with its *intentio,* it follows that there is no reason why this should be done only in the same mode. Indeed, it could be argued that translating an alien form of life, another culture, is not always best done through the representational discourse of ethnography—that under certain conditions a dramatic performance, the execution of a dance, or the playing of a piece of music might be more apt. These would all be productions of the original and not mere interpretations: transformed instances of the original, not authoritative textual representations of it (cf. Hollander 1959). As such, they could become part of our living heritage and not merely of our social science. But would they be thought of by most social anthropologists as valid exercises in the translation of culture? I think not, because they all raise an entirely different dimension of the relationship between the anthropological work and its audience, the question of different uses (practices), as opposed merely to different writings and readings (meanings) of that work. And, as social anthropologists, we are trained to translate other discourses as cultural texts, not to introduce or enlarge cultural capacities, learnt from other ways of living, into our own. It seems to me very likely that the notion of culture as text has reinforced this view of our task, because it facilitates the assumption that translation is essentially a matter of verbal representation in the domain of social science.

Reading Other Cultures

This inequality in the power of languages, together with the fact that the anthropologist typically writes about an illiterate (or at any rate not an English-speaking) population for a largely academic, English-speaking audience, encourages a tendency I would now like to discuss: the tendency to read the implicit in alien cultures.

According to many social anthropologists, the object of ethnographic translation is not the historically situated speech (that is the task of the folklorist or the linguist) but "culture," and to translate culture the anthropologist must first read and then reinscribe the implicit meanings that lie beneath/within/beyond situated speech. Mary Douglas puts this nicely:

> The anthropologist who draws out the whole scheme of the cosmos which is implied in [the observed] practices does the primitive culture great violence if he seems to present the cosmology as a systematic philosophy subscribed to consciously by individuals. . . . So the primitive world view which I have defined above is rarely itself an object of contemplation and speculation in the primitive culture. It has evolved as the appanage of other social institutions. To this extent it is produced indirectly, and to this extent the primitive culture must be taken to be unaware of itself, unconscious of its own conditions. (1966, 91)

One difference between the anthropologist and the linguist in the matter of translation is perhaps this: that whereas the latter is immediately faced with a specific piece of discourse produced within the society studied, a discourse that is then textualized, the former must construct the discourse as a cultural text in terms of meanings implicit in a range of practices. The construction of "cultural discourse" and its translation thus seem to be facets of a single act. This point is brought out in Douglas's comments on her own translations of the meanings of the pangolin cult among the Lele:

> There are no Lele books of theology or philosophy to state the meaning of the cult. The metaphysical implications have not been expressed to me in so many words by Lele, nor did I even eavesdrop a conversation between diviners covering this ground. . . .
> What kind of evidence for the meaning of this cult, or of any cult, can be sensibly demanded? It can have many different levels and kinds

of meaning. But the one on which I ground my arguments is the meaning which emerges out of a pattern in which the parts can incontestably be shown to be regularly related. No one member of the society is necessarily aware of the whole pattern, any more than speakers are able to be explicit about the linguistic patterns they employ. (1966, 173–74)

I have suggested elsewhere that the attribution of implicit meanings to an alien practice regardless of whether they are acknowledged by its agents is a characteristic form of theological exercise, with an ancient history. Here I want to note that reference to the linguistic patterns produced by speakers does not make a good analogy for unconscious cultural meanings because linguistic patterns are not meanings to be translated, they are rules to be systematically described and analyzed. A native speaker is aware of how such patterns should be produced, even when he cannot explicitly verbalize that knowledge in the form of rules. The apparent lack of ability to verbalize such social knowledge does not necessarily constitute evidence of unconscious meanings (cf. Dummett 1981). The concept of unconscious meaning belongs to a theory of the repressive unconscious, such as Freud's, in which a person may be said to know something unconsciously.

The business of identifying unconscious meanings in the task of cultural translation is therefore perhaps better compared to the activity of the psychoanalyst than to that of the linguist. Indeed, British anthropologists have sometimes presented their work in precisely these terms. Thus, David Pocock, a pupil of Evans-Pritchard's, writes:

In short, the work of the social anthropologist may be regarded as a highly complex act of translation in which author and translator collaborate. A more precise analogy is that of the relation between the psychoanalyst and his subject. The analyst enters the private world of his subject in order to learn the grammar of his private language. If the analysis goes no further it is no different in kind from the understanding which may exist between any two people who know each other well. It becomes scientific to the extent that the private language of intimate understanding is translated into a public language, however specialized from the layman's point of view, which in this case is the language of psychologists. But the particular act of translation does not distort the private experience of the subject and ideally it is, at least potentially, acceptable to him as a scientific representation of it. Similarly, the model of Nuer political life which emerges in Professor Evans-Pritchard's work is a scientific model meaningful to his fellow sociologists as sociologists, and it is effective because it is *potentially acceptable to the Nuer in some ideal situation in which they could be supposed to be interested in themselves as men living in society.* The collaboration of natural scientists may from this point of view be seen as developing language enabling certain people to communicate with increasing subtlety about a distinct area of natural phenomena which is defined by the name of the particular science. Their science is, in the literal meaning of the term, their common sense, their common meaning. To move from this common sense to the "common sense" of the wider public involves again an act of translation. The situation of social anthropology, or sociology in general, is not at this level so very different. The difference lies in the fact that sociological phenomena are objectively studied only to the extent that their subjective meaning is taken into account and that the people studied are potentially capable of sharing the sociological consciousness that the sociologist has of them. (1961, 88–89; emphasis added)

I have quoted this remarkable passage in full because it states very lucidly a position that is, I think, broadly acceptable to many anthropologists who would otherwise consider themselves to be engaged in very different kinds of enterprise. I have quoted it also because the nature of the collaboration between "author and translator" is neatly brought out in the subsequent reference to the psychoanalyst as scientist: if the anthropological translator, like the analyst, has final authority in determining the subject's meanings, it is then the former who becomes *the real author* of the latter. In this view, cultural translation is a matter of determining implicit meanings—not the meanings the native speaker actually acknowledges in his speech, not even the meanings the native listener necessarily accepts, but those he is "potentially capable of sharing" with scientific authority "in some ideal situation": it is when he can say, for example, with Gellner, that *vox Dei* is in reality *vox populi,* that he utters the true meaning of his traditional discourse, an essential meaning of his culture. The fact that in that "ideal situation" he would no longer be a Muslim Berber tribesman, but someone coming to resemble Professor Gellner, does not appear to worry such cultural translators.

This power to create meanings for a subject through the notion of the implicit or of the unconscious, to authorize them, has of course been discussed for the analyst-analysand relationship (e.g., in Malcolm 1982). It has not, to my knowledge, been considered with regard to what the cultural translator does. There are, of course, important differences in the case of the anthropologist. Because the latter does not impose his translation on the members of the society whose cultural discourse he unravels, his ethnography is not authoritative in the way the analyst's case study is. The analysand comes to the analyst, or is referred to the latter by those with authority over him, as a patient in need of help. The anthropologist, by contrast, comes to the society he wants to read; he sees himself as a learner, not as a guide, and he withdraws from the society when he has adequate information to inscribe its culture. He does not consider the society, and neither do its members consider themselves to be, sick: the society is never subject to the anthropologist's authority.

But this argument is not quite as conclusive as it may seem at first sight. It remains the case that (a) the ethnographer's translation/representation of a particular culture is inevitably a textual construct, that (b) as representation it cannot normally be contested by the people to whom it is attributed, and that (c) as a "scientific text" it eventually becomes a privileged element in the potential store of historical memory for the nonliterate society concerned. In modern and modernizing societies, inscribed records have a greater power to shape, to reform, selves and institutions than folk memories do. They even construct folk memories. The anthropologist's monograph may return, retranslated, into a "weaker" third world language. In the long run, therefore, it is not the personal authority of the ethnographer but the social authority of his ethnography that matters. And that authority is inscribed in the institutionalized forces of industrial capitalist society, which are constantly tending to push the meanings of various third world societies in a single direction. This is not to say that there is no resistance to this tendency. But resistance in itself indicates the presence of a dominant force.

I must stress that I am not arguing that ethnography plays any great role in the reformation of other cultures. In this respect, the effects of ethnography cannot be compared with some other forms of representing societies—for example, television films produced in the West that are sold to third world countries. (That anthropologists recognize the power of television is reflected, incidentally, in the increasing number of anthropological films being made for the medium in Britain.) Still less can the effects of ethnography compare with the political, economic, and military constraints of the world system. My point is only that the process of cultural translation is inevitably enmeshed in conditions of power—professional, national, international. And among these conditions is the authority of ethnographers (a) to present the coherence of culturally distinctive discourses as the integration of self-contained social systems, and (b) to uncover the implicit meanings of subordinated cultural discourses. Given that that is so, the interesting question is not whether, and if so to what extent, anthropologists should be relativists or rationalists, critical or charitable, toward other cultures, but how power enters into the process of cultural translation, seen both as a discursive and as a nondiscursive practice.

Conclusion

For some years I have been exercised by this puzzle. How is it that the approach exemplified by Gellner's paper remains attractive to so many academics in spite of its being demonstrably faulty? Is it perhaps because they are intimidated by a style? We know, of course, that anthropologists, like other academics, learn not merely to use a scholarly language but to fear it, to admire it, to be captivated by it. Yet this does not quite answer the question because it does not tell us why such a scholarly style should capture so many intelligent people. I now put forward this tentative solution. What we have here is a style easy to teach, to learn, and to reproduce (in examination answers, assessment essays, and dissertations). It is a style that facilitates the textualization of other cultures, that encourages the construction of diagrammatic answers to complex social and historical questions, and that is well suited to arranging foreign concepts in clearly marked heaps of sense or nonsense. Apart from being easy to teach and to imitate, this style promises visible results that can readily be graded. Such a style must surely be at a premium in an established university discipline that aspires to standards of scientific objectivity. Is not the popularity of this style, then, a reflection of the kind of pedagogic institution we inhabit?

Although it is now many years since Gellner's paper was first published, it represents a doctrinal position that is still popular. I have in mind the sociologism according to which religious ideologies are said to get their real meaning from the political or economic structure, and the self-confirming methodology according to which this reductive semantic principle is evident to the (authoritative) anthropologist and not to the people being written about. This position therefore assumes that it is not only possible but necessary for the anthropologist to act as translator and critic at one and the same time. I regard this position as untenable, and think that it is relations and practices of power that give it a measure of viability. (For a critical discussion of this position as it relates to Islamic history, see Asad 1980.)

The positive point I have tried to make in the course of my interrogation of Gellner's text has to do with what I have called the inequality of languages. The inequality of languages is a feature of the global patterns of power created by modern imperialism and capitalism. I have proposed that the anthropological enterprise of translation may be vitiated by the fact that there are asymmetrical tendencies and pressures in the languages of dominated and dominant societies. And I have suggested that anthropologists need to explore these processes in order to determine how far they go in defining the possibilities and the limits of effective translation. My argument is directed against the assumption that translation requires the adjustment of "foreign" discourses to their new site. In my view, they should retain what may be a discomforting—even scandalous—presence within the receiving language.

6 ❧ THE LIMITS OF RELIGIOUS CRITICISM IN THE MIDDLE EAST

Notes on Islamic Public Argument

Critical Reason, the State, and Religion in the Enlightenment

Non-Westerners who seek to understand their local histories must also inquire into Europe's past, because it is through the latter that universal history has been constructed. That history defines the former as merely "local"—that is, as histories with limits. The contemporary history of political Islam has been defined in just this way.

The European Enlightenment constitutes the historical site from which Westerners typically approach non-Western traditions. That approach has tended to evaluate and measure traditions according to their distance from Enlightenment and liberal models. Thus, Islamic states are typically regarded as absolutist, and the practice of public criticism is seen as alien to them. But how did Europeans in that era of early modernity connect public critical discourse with religion while living under an absolute ruler?

My position is that anthropologists who seek to describe rather than to moralize will consider each tradition in its own terms—even as it has come to be reconstituted by modern forces—in order to compare and contrast it with others. More precisely, they will try to understand ways of reasoning characteristic of given traditions. Such anthropologists will also need to suppress their personal distaste for particular traditions if they are to understand them. Beyond that, they should learn to treat some of their own Enlightenment assumptions as belonging to specific kinds of reasoning—albeit kinds of reasoning that have largely shaped our modern world—and not as the ground from which all understanding of non-Enlightenment traditions must begin.

In this section I look at some aspects of Enlightenment reasoning briefly and mainly as they appear in Kant's famous essay "An Answer to the Question: 'What Is Enlightenment?' " This involves determining the limits imposed on religion by the early modern state. In the next section I begin my extended account of public criticism that takes place in a contemporary religious state: Saudi Arabia. Before concluding, I raise a few general questions regarding critical practices in the political relations between Western and Westernizing societies.

Although I have chosen Kant for initial attention, I do not take him to be representative of the Enlightenment as a whole,[1] any more than I take as representative of all Islam the Saudi theologians whom I discuss later. But in saying this I merely concede that no one text or authorially defined set of texts—or, for that matter, no single generation of authors—can adequately represent a complex, developing tradition of discussion and argument.[2] Particular texts draw on or resist, reformulate and quarrel with, others that constitute the tradition (see MacIntyre 1988). Thus, the temporal situatedness of all texts (their sequential as well as coexistential links) renders all abstractions partial, provisional, and limited to particular purposes. As an anthropologist or a historian, one approaches the tradition from particular directions and tries to describe the positions taken up by proponents, as far as possible in their own terms. One chooses to describe what is judged to have been historically decisive for the tradition, or to be especially relevant today, or both.

Allowing for this qualification, Kant's text may nevertheless be taken as marking a formative moment in the theorization of a central feature of "civil society," the feature concerning the possibilities of

---

1. It could scarcely be otherwise, for as Peter Gay (1973, xii) writes in the preface to his monumental study of the Enlightenment: "The men of the Enlightenment were divided by doctrine, temperament, environment, and generations. And in fact the spectrum of their ideas, their sometimes acrimonious disputes, have tempted many historians to abandon the search for a single Enlightenment." And yet, "while the Enlightenment was a family of philosophes, it was something more as well: it was a cultural climate, a world in which the philosophes acted, from which they noisily rebelled and quietly drew many of their ideas, and on which they attempted to impose their program."

2. One is reminded here of Vološinov's strictures against the methods of classical philology, made over sixty years ago: "Any utterance—the finished, written utterance not excepted—makes response to something and is calculated to be responded to in turn. It is but one link in a continuous chain of speech performances. Each monument carries on the work of its predecessors, polemicizing with them, expecting active, responsive understanding, and anticipating such understanding in return" (1973, 72).

open, rational criticism.[3] Thus, when Habermas reviewed this and other texts by Kant in his historical account of "the public sphere," he stressed their importance for later liberal theory. In Kant, he writes, "The public of 'human beings' engaged in rational-critical debate was constituted into one of 'citizens' wherever there was communication concerning the affairs of the 'commonwealth.' Under the 'republican constitution' this public sphere in the public realm became the organizational principle of the liberal constitutional state" (Habermas 1989, 106–7). So Kant's ideas of public, publicity, and critical reason have become part of a Habermasian story of the progressively liberating aspects of secular, bourgeois society.[4]

Equally, but from a different perspective, Foucault (1984) has used Kant's text on the Enlightenment to initiate some reflections on the concept of modernity. It is Kant's idea of "maturity" (i.e., of relying on one's own reason instead of on another's authority) that Foucault regards as central to that concept, and that he then goes on to link with Baudelaire's aesthetic of "self-elaboration."[5] This idea of intellectual and moral autonomy is certainly fundamental to Kant's critical philosophy, although in his case it is based on a metaphysics of reason that is absent in Foucault.

Intellectual and moral maturity, Kant tells us, consists in the ability "to use one's own understanding without the guidance of another" (54). This individualistic conception of understanding presupposes a space of freedom in which the mature individual can make use of his *own* reason in opposition to that of others. Using reason publicly, Kant goes on, is equivalent to addressing an argument, *in writing,* to a scholarly audience.[6] So for Kant, the arena in which this process takes

3. I have used the translation by Reiss in Kant 1991.
4. In the same tradition is M. Jacob's (1991) study of freemasonry in eighteenth-century Britain, France, and Holland. In this work the author proposes, with a wealth of fascinating detail, that Masonic ceremonies and practices were of major importance in the emergence of libertarian and secular ideals. Her account is deliberately set against the conventional view of the Enlightenment as an intellectual movement, arguing that it should be seen primarily as a social and political movement that provided the basic elements of a new Western identity.
5. Foucault's notion of the autonomous individual can also be traced to Jacob Burckhardt's presentation of the emerging modern self as a "work of art" in his *Civilization of the Renaissance in Italy* (1860).
6. "The public [Kant] is thinking of," observes Arendt (1982, 60), "is, of course, the reading public, and it is the weight of their opinion he is appealing to, not the weight of their votes. In the Prussia of the last decades of the eighteenth century—that is, a coun-

place is inhabited by self-determined individuals (an extremely small proportion of the citizenry) who are exercising a freedom described as "the most innocuous form of all" because it does not necessarily result in any specific action. Indeed, as Kant puts it: "A ruler who is himself enlightened and has no fear of phantoms, yet who likewise has at hand a well-disciplined and numerous army to guarantee public security, may say what no republic would dare to say: *Argue as much as you like and about whatever you like, but obey!*" (59; emphasis added). He was not alone in this view. Jeremy Bentham, writing at about the same time in what was decidedly *not* an absolutist state, declared: "Under a government of Laws, what is the motto of a good citizen? *To obey punctually; to censure freely.*"[7]

Public argument, then, is connected with obedience to the law and the rules that the sovereign (as the source of law) authorizes. In particular, the performance of a function with which a person is socially entrusted, according to Kant, requires that he or she act in accordance with the rules that define it. In this context, Kant speaks of the private use of reason, for here reason is rooted not in the open process of critical exchange but in the limited workings of an authorized social role. For example:

A clergyman is bound to instruct *his pupils and his congregation* in accordance with the doctrines of the church he serves, for he is employed by it on that condition. But as a scholar, he is completely free as well as obliged to impart to *the public* all his carefully considered, well-intentioned thoughts on the mistaken aspects of those doctrines, and to offer suggestions for a better arrangement of religious and ecclesiastical affairs. And there is nothing in this which need trouble his conscience. For what he teaches in pursuit of his duties as an active servant of the church is presented by him as something which he is not empowered to teach at his own discretion, but which he is employed to expound in a prescribed manner and in someone else's name. (56; emphases added)

---

try under the rule of an absolute monarch, advised by a rather enlightened bureaucracy of civil servants, who, like the monarch, were completely separated from 'the subjects'—there could be no truly public realm other than this reading public. What was secret and unapproachable by definition was precisely the realm of government and administration."

7. *A Fragment on Government*, 1776 (in Gay 1973, 142; emphasis in original).

Kant's distinction between the public use of reason and its private use in effect reflects a primary distinction between the principle according to which one should judge and the principle according to which one should act (Arendt 1982, 48ff.). It is concerned, therefore, not just with political freedom but also with the rational limits of individual thought, as well as with its social limits.

To sum up so far: A crucial part of the liberal tradition to which Kant contributed is the distinction between two quite separate conceptual realms: one in which unquestioned obedience to authority prevails (the juridical definitions upheld by the state); the other consisting of rational argument and exchange, in which authority has no place (the omnicompetence of criticism). Kant therefore proposes both a *sociological* limit (the literate, scholarly minority to whom the privilege of public criticism belongs) and a *political* one (the conditions in which one must refrain from open criticism).

I do not want to be taken as saying here that all liberals have the same view as Kant on this matter. They do not. What the liberal tradition shares is precisely a continuing argument over the proper boundary between the authority of the law, on the one hand, and the freedom to speak and criticize publicly, on the other, as well as about who, among those qualified to engage in the criticism, deserves special attention. Kant's was merely an early and famous statement of that problem.

The rationality of criticism, according to Kant, consists in the fact that the statuses and passions of those involved have nothing to do with judging the truth of an argument. The validity of any judgment requires that one abstract oneself from all empirical interests. Yet, significantly, the idea that arrival at the truth depends on public argument, on free and open examination that is independent of social conditions, does not always appear to prevail with the Enlightenment thinker. In an unpublished justification of his promise to the king not to write again on religious matters, Kant noted: "Repudiation and denial of one's inner conviction are evil, but silence in a case like the present one is the duty of a subject; and while all that one says must be true, this does not mean that it is one's duty to speak out the whole truth in public" (cited in Reiss 1991, 2). In this case, it seems, (religious) truth stands independently of public argument because it has been translated as *belief* (which, unlike *knowledge*, is based on personal experience), and public expressions of personal belief (although not the belief itself) must always defer to that public authority which is known as the state. For belief in the final analysis is not "objective knowledge" (science), it is merely "opinion." Thus, no damage is done to truth if opinion is denied free play in public.

This position was in keeping with Kant's Pietist upbringing, which, according to Cassirer, gave its adherents "that calm, that cheerfulness, that inner peace that is disturbed by no passion" (cited in Gay 1973, 328). "As a consequence [writes a historian of the Enlightenment] even Kant—who repudiated all but the most abstract religion, who condemned enthusiasm and refused to engage in any religious observance —even Kant himself paid Pietism the unconscious tribute of incorporating some of its teachings into his work: . . . its conviction that religion depends not on dogma or ritual or prayer but on experience" (Gay 1973, 28–29). Of course, Pietism was not the major form of Protestant religion, either then or in succeeding centuries. But the apolitical, noninstitutional character of early German Pietism was not exceptional in the development of eighteenth-century European religiosity.[8]

Historians of seventeenth- and eighteenth-century Europe have begun to recount how the constitution of the modern state required the forcible redefinition of religion as belief, and of religious belief, sentiment, and identity as personal matters that belong to the newly emerging space of private (as opposed to public) life. In the eyes of those who wanted a strong, centralized state, the disorders of the Reformation proved that religious belief was the source of uncontrollable passions within the individual and of dangerous strife within the commonwealth. It could not, for this reason, provide an institutional basis for a common morality—still less a public language of rational criticism. More aggressively, Hobbes contended that institutionalized religion—but not the prince—was a vested interest, and that consequently it had to be subordinated to the monarch.[9] In

8. I say early Pietism because some historians have shown that Pietism in the nineteenth century contributed significant intellectual and emotional elements to the development of German nationalism. See Pinson 1968.

9. "For who is there that does not see, to whose benefit it conduceth, to have it believed, that a King hath not his Authority from Christ, unlesse a Bishop crown him? That a King, if he be a Priest, cannot Marry? That whether a Prince be born in lawfull Marriage, or not, must be judged by Authority from *Rome*? . . . That the Clergy, and Regulars, in what Country soever, shall be exempt from the Jurisdiction of their King, in cases criminall? Or who does not see, to whose profit redound the Fees of private

this way, Hobbes postulated the unity and sovereignty of the modern state.

Scholars are now more aware that religious toleration was a political means to the formation of strong state power that emerged from the sectarian wars of the sixteenth and seventeenth centuries rather than the gift of a benign intention to defend pluralism. As contemporaries recognized, the locus of intolerance had shifted. "L'heresie n'est plus auiourd'huy en la Religion," insisted a French jurist of the period, "elle est en l'Estat" (cited in Koselleck 1985, 8).

According to Lipsius (Oestreich 1982), the influential religious skeptic writing at the end of the sixteenth century, the prince should follow any policy that would secure civil peace regardless of moral or legal scruples. If religious diversity could be *forcibly* eliminated, so much the better, Lipsius urged; if that was impossible, then religious toleration should be *enforced* by the state.[10] Locke's famous argument for religious toleration a century later was similarly motivated by a concern for the integrity and power of the state: it was because he considered the beliefs of Catholics and atheists dangerous to civil peace that he thought they should not be tolerated by the state (Mendus 1989, 22–43).

Not only were religious beliefs now constitutionally subordinated to the state, but the principles of morality were henceforth to be theorized separately from the domain of politics.[11] In practice, of course, things were always more complicated. Some historians have even argued that the Enlightenment broke precisely on this point with absolutism and initiated a new tradition. Thus, according to Koselleck (1988), the philosophes (including Kant) helped to push the demands of a transcendent secular moralism into the domain of political practice.[12]

Masses, and Vales of Purgatory; with other signes of private interest, enough to mortifie the most lively Faith, if (as I sayd) the civill Magistrate, and Custome did not more sustain it, than any opinion they have of the Sanctity, Wisdome, or Probity of their Teachers? So that I may attribute all the changes of Religion in the world, to one and the same cause; and that is, unpleasing Priests; and those not onely amongst Catholiques, but even in that Church that hath presumed most of Reformation" (Hobbes 1943, 62).

10. See Tuck 1988. Tuck's thesis is that in early modern Europe religious skeptics were no more inclined toward tolerance than religious believers were. They drew the force of their intolerance, he suggests, from their distrust of all passion. See also in this connection Levi 1964, especially the chapter on Montaigne and Lipsius.

11. This liberal tradition is reflected in Weber's famous opposition between "an ethic of responsibility" and "an ethic of ultimate ends" (1948).

12. J. S. Mill's moralized utilitarianism is central to this liberal tradition. For a dev-

By the time we get to Kant, one can see how a private religion of sentimental sociability was beginning to take the place of a public religion of passionate conviction. It has become a commonplace among historians of modern Europe to say that religion was gradually compelled to concede the domain of public power to the constitutional state, and of public truth to natural science.[13] But perhaps it is also possible to suggest that in this movement we have the construction of religion as a new historical object: anchored in personal experience, expressible as belief-statements, dependent on private institutions, and practiced in one's spare time.[14] This construction of religion ensures that it is part of what is *inessential* to our common politics, economy, science, and morality. More strongly put: religion is what actually or potentially divides us, and if followed with passionate conviction, may set us intolerantly against one another.

Of course, the concepts and practices of religion and state have not remained unchanged since Kant. But liberals continue to invoke his principle of the public use of reason as the arbiter of true knowledge (even when they do not accept all his philosophical doctrines) and remain alert to the disruptive possibilities of religion as defined—for Christian as well as non-Christian traditions—by the Enlightenment.

The formation of strong state power in the contemporary Middle East has a very different genealogy. In most cases, strong states have inherited colonial forms; a few owe their formation to Islamic movements. In such polities, there is no public use of reason in Kant's sense, nor are religious truth and religious criticism typically regarded by their public spokesmen as matters properly confined to the personal domain. This is not to say that non-Enlightenment societies do not know what reasoned criticism is, or that nonliberal governments

---

astating critique of Mill's concept of a secular "religion of humanity," see Cowling 1990.

13. It is sometimes forgotten, however, that in the world outside Europe, evangelical Christianity often played a central political role in the nineteenth and early twentieth centuries (see, e.g., Stokes 1959; Comaroff and Comaroff 1991). Missions were also extremely important in the modernization of secondary and higher education in the Middle East. Local Christian minorities, educated and sometimes converted by European missionaries, not only played a notable part in popularizing Western ideas of history, archaeology, politics, and so on, but their role in adapting Western nationalist ideologies to local conditions was also outstanding (see, e.g., Hourani 1962; Farag 1969).

14. For a discussion of the idea of "spare time" as a category of industrial capitalist society, see Dumazedier 1968.

can never permit the public expression of political dissent. On the contrary: institutionalized forms of criticism, made accessible to anonymous readers and listeners, are integral to many non-Enlightenment states. Among them is contemporary Saudi Arabia.

Islamic Religious Orthodoxy: An Irrational Opposition to Change?

The kingdom of Saudi Arabia was built on a historical alliance between two families, the House of ash-Shaikh (descendants of the eighteenth-century Najdi religious reformer Muhammad bin 'Abdul-Wahhāb) and the House of Sa'ud (now the royal clan, descendants of a Najdi tribal chief). This origin appears to correspond to a neat complementarity between two ruling principles: (religious) reason and (political) power. In reality, things are less tidy.

Although the religious establishment is no longer primarily recruited from the House of ash-Shaikh, it remains basic to the structure of the contemporary Saudi kingdom. The kingdom was formally set up in 1932 with the incorporation of the Hijaz (a province that belonged to the Ottoman Empire until its collapse in World War I) by the Najdi chief 'Abdul-'Azīz. The enormous flow of oil wealth during the last few decades has led to many social changes in Saudi Arabia—including the formation of a substantial middle class—but apparently not to any diminished reliance on Islamic authority by the state. The continuing prominence of Islamic legal and educational practices, as well as of Islamic rhetoric used by the government, has encouraged numerous Western writers to see Saudi Arabia as a fundamentalist state[15]—a state whose elites reaffirm "traditional modes of understanding and behaviour" in a modernizing environment (Humphreys 1979, 3).

This official commitment to upholding "traditional Islam" in a

15. For example: (a) "Among the major Arab states . . . Saudi Arabia is the only one which closely approximates the Fundamentalist criteria" (Humphreys 1979, 8); (b) "The Hanbali School of Law constitutes the foundation of Wahhabi fundamentalism—the ideology of the Saudi Kingdom" (Dekmejian 1985, 15); (c) "Saudi Arabia is often viewed in the West as the epitome of 'fundamentalist' Islam, and in many ways it is. The government is explicitly based on Islamic law, and infractions of this law are, in principle, severely punished" (Munson 1988, 74). I hold that the notion of a fundamentalist Islam is a product of lazy thinking, and one that also happens to be convenient to many policy makers (and would-be policy advisers) in Western governments.

society undergoing rapid modernization is regarded by Western observers as the source of serious tensions. The seizure of the Haram
(Sanctuary) in Mecca in 1979 by mahdist (i.e., millenarian) insurgents,
and their social and religious condemnation of the regime, was identified as dramatic evidence of those tensions. One Western writer put it
as follows: "Suddenly *a tightly controlled country, where the free expression
of dissent was nearly impossible,* was shown to have a significant opposition, one willing to die for its religious position" (Ochsenwald 1981,
284; emphasis added).

"A tightly controlled country" sounds very much like the kind of
place Kant lived in, where one was obliged to obey the king's command not to write on religious matters. And yet although as an expression of dissent this violent incident is without parallel in Saudi Arabia,
there has, of course, been criticism of the government both before and
since. The story of how the *'ulamā* (divines) unsuccessfully opposed
the introduction of radio and television into the country has often
been told. Typically, a Western historian observes: "These episodes
may serve to illustrate the traditional opposition of the ulama to modernization in the kingdom. Besides the question of harming religious
values, the innovations could contribute to the creation of a new class
of leaders, not of religious origin, and thus give rise to a direct threat to
the ulama" (Bligh 1985, 42). What is interesting about such explanatory accounts is precisely the manner in which particular *episodes* of
dissent are presented as *illustrations* of a self-evident general thesis; the
Saudi *'ulamā* (sing., *'ālim*), being traditional, reject any change in the
status quo, because refusal to change is the essence of tradition. The
implication is that this was not *reasoned* criticism but simply irrational
rejection of everything "modern."[16]

16. The rejection by militant Muslims of changes that we who live (or aspire to live)
in the modern world find reasonable and attractive is often characterized in Western
accounts as irrational and distasteful. For example: "Everything from the inflow of
ever-larger quantities of Western consumer goods to changes in feminine dress and
behaviour, often resented by traditionalist men, to Western films and TV is seen as part
of a veritable plot to undermine local ways and products and to make of third world
men and women consumers of the least useful and most degrading of Western imports
and customs" (Keddie 1982, 276). The trouble with the use of impressionistic terms such
as "resentment" or the facile imputation of paranoia ("seen as part of a veritable plot")
to account for complex social phenomena is that it tells us more about the writer's
notions of psychological and political normalcy than about the actual motives of those
involved or the persuasive power of their discourses.

Actually, innumerable foreign techniques *were* absorbed into Saudi society even before the oil boom in the seventies with little or no objection from the *'ulamā:* new forms of transport including paved roads, new modes of building and printing, electricity, new medicines and types of medical treatment, and so forth. Clearly, something more complicated is involved here than "a traditional opposition" to modernization by the *'ulamā.*[17] As a start I would propose that what the *'ulamā* are doing is to attempt a definition of orthodoxy—a (re)ordering of knowledge that governs the "correct" form of Islamic practices. In effect, what we have today is essentially part of the same process by which *long-established indigenous practices* (such as the veneration of saints' tombs) were judged to be un-Islamic by the Wahhabi reformers of Arabia (see 'Abdul-Wahhāb A.H. 1376, 124–35) and then forcibly eliminated. That is, like all practical criticism, orthodox criticism seeks to construct a relation of discursive dominance.

I argue that the critical discourses of Saudi *'ulamā* (like those of Muhammad 'Abdul-Wahhāb before them) presuppose the concept of an orthodox Islam. Muslims in Saudi Arabia (as elsewhere) disagree profoundly over what orthodox Islam is, but *as Muslims* their differences are fought out on the ground of that concept. It is too often forgotten that the process of determining orthodoxy in conditions of change and contest includes attempts at achieving discursive coherence, at representing the present within an authoritative narrative that includes positive evaluations of past events and persons. Because such authority is a collaborative achievement between narrator and audience, the former cannot speak in total freedom: there are conceptual and institutional conditions that must be attended to if discourses are to be persuasive. That is why attempts by social scientists at rendering such discourses as instances of local leaders manipulating religious symbols to legitimize their social power should be viewed skeptically. This is not simply because "manipulation" carries a strong sense of

---

17. Of course, writers who speak of modernization in this context are invoking an old model of social development, which specifies more than the adoption of modern technology. But the model of an integrated society, in which industrial production goes hand in hand with particular political and legal institutions, as well as particular forms of sociability and styles of consumption, has long been criticized for confounding a normative model with a descriptive one. This fact does not appear to discourage those who continue to draw on the oversimplified notion of modernization in writing about the Middle East today.

cynical motivation, even in cases where evidence for such an imputation is not forthcoming, but more broadly because it introduces the
notion of a deliberative, rationalistic stance into descriptions of relationships where that notion is not appropriate. For the same reason,
the metaphor of "negotiation"—with its overtones of calculation—
seems to me equally suspect. Although these familiar metaphors are
central to market transactions everywhere and to politics in liberal
societies, this fact does not make them suited to explicating every kind
of practice in all societies.[18]

"Orthodoxy" is not easy to secure in conditions of radical change.
This is not because orthodox discourse is necessarily against any change
but because it aspires to be authoritative. In fact, the redefinition of
sharī'a rules (religious laws) has been amply documented in the history of Islam, even prior to direct European intervention in the Middle East.[19] What is involved in such changes is not a simple ad hoc
acceptance of new arrangements but the attempt to redescribe norms
and concepts with the aid of tradition-guided reasoning. The authority of that redescription, among those familiar with and committed to
that tradition, has depended historically on how successful the underlying reasoning was judged to be. This is not to say that the *implemen-
tation* of those changes has depended entirely on that authority.

The aspiration to authority among those who would speak for
Islamic orthodoxy cannot be a simple matter of anathematizing foreign behavior and objects of consumption. In fact, Islamic legal-moral

18. I refer below to a very different metaphor (the figure of the Muslim as God's
slave) that is employed in Islamic discourse, which liberal readers may well find repugnant. But not to address such metaphors directly—as so many liberals do today—is, in
my view, to mistranslate them. The anthropologist engaged in translation should retain
figures that bring together conceptual elements in unfamiliar—even uncomfortable—
ways. Whether this results in her readers simply confirming their inherited prejudices
(as it did for many Europeans writing or reading about Islam) cannot, of course, be
predicted. In any case, prejudice is certainly reinforced if we translate potentially disturbing concepts from other cultures into terms palatable to the liberal world-view.

19. Coulson (1964, chap. 10) recounts some of these changes in the area of civil transactions. More recently, Johansen (1988) has argued that a network of concepts in Hanafi
law relating to property, rent, and taxation of cultivated land underwent thorough-
going changes in the Ottoman Empire. The Western province of what is now Saudi
Arabia, which contains the sacred mosques in Mecca and Medina, was part of the Ottoman Empire until World War I; the dominant legal school of that empire (the Hanafi) is
still recognized there.

tradition contains a graded scheme for classifying behavior—*wājib* (mandatory), *mandūb* (recommended), *mubāh* (permitted), *makrūh* (disapproved), *harām* (forbidden). This classification forces specific questions onto people who belong to that tradition: Into which category does a given new behavior fall? Is it really new, or is it an analogue of something whose classification is not in dispute? The application of these categories to behavior engaged in by one's fellow Muslims often involves an elaborate work of reconceptualizing the context itself in ways that aim to be plausible to a Muslim audience. To take an extreme example: Should someone who continuously sins by committing what Islam forbids and omitting what it prescribes be considered a Muslim—albeit a sinful one *('āsī)*—or an infidel *(kāfir)*? Is an entire society of such people (like Egypt, say) nevertheless a Muslim society, or is it (as Sayyid Qutb and his followers in Egypt have argued)[20] a modern society of heathens, a *jāhiliyya*? And if it is the latter, then how can a real Muslim maintain his "religion" *(dīn)* within it? By withdrawal from society or by the violent seizure of political power? Within Egypt, these are real questions today.[21]

In Saudi Arabia, however, the *'ulamā* who criticize their government reject these extreme options, although they too seek to be authoritative in the concepts of their tradition. They say that it is precisely because they regard their government as legitimate *(hukūma shar'iyya)* and their society as Islamic that they make the criticisms they do in the way they do. But there is an interesting double sense to the adjective *shar'iyya* here. For while it connotes the general modern sense of "legitimate," it derives from the specific Islamic concept of "the divinely sanctioned law-and-morality" *(ash-sharī'a)*, which does not simply legitimize the ruler but binds him. The Saudi government explicitly claims to be based on the *sharī'a*. Thus, what the critics offer is "advice" *(nasīha)*, something called for by the *sharī'a* as a precondition of moral rectitude *(istiqāma)*, not "criticism" *(naqd)*, with its adversarial overtones.[22]

20. See Qutb 1991, especially chapter 3, "The Formation of Muslim Society and Its Characteristics."
21. The struggle for and over the interpretation of authoritative texts has been intrinsic to the Islamic tradition since its beginning. I discuss this in Asad 1980.
22. I elaborate on the concept of *nasīha* below, but it may be worth noting here that in classical Arabic the verbal form *nasaha* always indicates a direct person-to-person relationship. The verbal form *naqada* (or *intaqada*), by contrast, often signifies a direct

An Islamic Tradition of Public Criticism

Even in a nonliberal (illiberal) state such as Saudi Arabia, then, there is a tradition of social criticism that is open and institutionalized. The most important form in which this tradition finds expression is the Friday sermon *(khutba)* delivered in the larger mosques, but it is also practiced in the form of theological lectures in the Islamic universities.

After the Haram incident in 1979 the Ministry of Endowments *(wazārat ul-awqāf)* took over direct control of all the mosques and even tried to specify the topics dealt with each Friday in the sermons. In the mid-eighties, the government's grip was relaxed, especially as the sermons consisted largely of pious exhortations. At about the same time, the practice of tape recording the more famous *khutabā* (sing., *khatīb*), or orators—even when they lectured at universities—and selling the cassettes to the general public became established. The adoption of this modern technology enabled an indefinite extension of the audience and the possibility of repeated listenings.

When the gulf crisis exploded in the summer of 1990, starting with the Iraqi invasion of Kuwait and culminating in the massive buildup of U.S. troops in the eastern province of Saudi Arabia, moral exhortation in the sermons was inevitably directed at the common peril facing all Saudis. As always, emphasis on the importance of strengthening one's faith in God was combined with a call for greater vigilance in ensuring proper Islamic practice throughout Saudi society. In the past, the latter formula had been understood as a criticism of the administration's laxity in preventing "un-Islamic" literature from entering the country. Now it was inevitably concerned with the greater danger of an un-Islamic army stationed in Arabia. Through an unusually wide distribution of cassettes, the substance of the sermons and lectures reached large audiences, including Western-educated Saudis, many of whom would not have normally been interested in them.

The bolder *khutabā* went one step further and addressed the theologically alarming situation in which a Muslim aggressor was being confronted with the aid of a force of unbelievers. Most of these men, incidentally, were in their thirties, graduates of the new Islamic universities in Saudi Arabia. One of the most eloquent and outspoken,

---

person-to-object relation—as in *intaqada ash-shi'ra 'ala qā'ilihi,* "he picked out the faults of the poetry and urged them against its author" (see Lane 1863-93).

Safar al-Hawāli, condemned the Baathist regime in Iraq not only for its aggression but for its atheism and its Arab nationalist ideology. He also strongly criticized the Saudi government's reliance on the military help of unbelievers to defend Muslims. This criticism was politically unspecific: while it condemned the resort to military help from non-Muslims and urged greater reliance on God, it did not offer any political alternatives. But that feature made the criticism more difficult to counter, since the argument of the sermons could be represented as moral exhortation and therefore not "political" in the modern sense. The government was not explicitly attacked for its policy *(siyāsa)*. The Saudi people as a whole were simply being advised about the danger that they now faced as Muslims. On this theme, many of the sermons cited medieval histories and legal texts warning against trusting non-Muslims as military allies.[23]

The criticism directed at both the government and the people for their laxity was offered by way of *nasīha,* a concept of central importance in Islamic moral theology. *Nasīha* signifies advice that is given for someone's good, honestly and faithfully. It also has the meaning of sincerity, integrity, and doing justice to a situation. *Nasīha,* then, is much more than an expression of good intention on the part of the advice giver *(nāsih)*: since in this context it carries the sense of offering moral advice to an erring fellow Muslim *(mansūh)*, it is at once an obligation to be fulfilled and a virtue to be cultivated by all Muslims. Thus, in the context of the sermons and religious lectures under discussion here, *nasīha* refers specifically to morally corrective criticism.

A Theological Text: *Nasīha* as Moral-Political Criticism

The preconditions and modalities of this kind of practical criticism are expounded in an oration by a well-known *khatīb* and lecturer, Āl Za'ayr, which takes as its central text the famous *hadīth* entitled, "Religion is integrity *(ad-dīnu an-nasīhatu)*."[24] The entire *hadīth* may be rendered thus: "Religion is integrity. We said: To whom? [The

23. Especially al-Hawāli's lecture entitled *ahkām ahl idh-dhimma* ("Regulations pertaining to the Non-Muslim Subjects of a Muslim Prince"). Safar al-Hawāli often speaks at a large mosque in Jiddah, and he teaches at the Islamic University in Mecca.

24. This is available on a two-sided tape recording under the same title: *Ad-dīnu an-nasīhatu.* The recording is widely distributed and easily accessible in Saudi Arabia as well as among Saudi students in Western Europe and North America.

Prophet] said: To God, and to His Book, and to His Prophet, and to the leaders of the Muslims and to their common folk."[25]

What is notable about Za'ayr's lecture is that although it is delivered as a formal exposition of a theological concept, it is at the same time an exhortation urging upon Muslims the *duty* of criticizing political authority. This stands in sharp contrast to the Enlightenment view of criticism as a *right*, whose exercise is therefore optional.[26]

Za'ayr explains the linkage between *dīn* (religion) and *nasīha* (moral advice) in the form of three axioms:

> First: The rightness of everything that people do, in all their affairs, is attainable only through subjection to God's authority—and that is what religion *(dīn)* is. Second: God's authority extends over each and every aspect of life. Third: Non-subjection to God's authority in any aspect of life must result in its being faulty and deranged. These three truths derive from the principle that the soundness of a people's affairs is bound up, all of it, with religion. If people's religion is soundly based, their affairs will be soundly based; if their religion is faulty, their entire life will be faulty too. Thus we say that religion is the proper condition of the people, and that *nasīha* is the foundation of religion.

Nasīha is therefore a benefit to the recipient—or, as Za'ayr puts it, "*nasīha* is a comprehensive word signifying the acquisition of that which is good for the person advised *(mansūh)*."

A major theme of the oration is the duty of *every* Muslim, ruler and subject alike, to undertake *nasīha*. Thus, Za'ayr cites the famous thirteenth-century jurist ibn Taymiyya to the effect that it is the ruler's

---

25. The perfect verb *nasaha*, and its derived forms, occur in several places in the Qur'ān (see Kassis 1983, 857).

26. Kant bases his argument for this right at least partly on utilitarian grounds: "The citizen must, *with the approval of the ruler,* be entitled to make public his opinion on whatever of the ruler's measures seem to him to constitute an injustice against the commonwealth. For to assume that the head of state can neither make mistakes nor be ignorant of anything would be to imply that he receives divine inspiration and is more than a human being. . . . To try to deny the citizen this freedom does not only mean, as Hobbes maintains, that the subject can claim no rights against the supreme ruler. It also means withholding from the ruler all knowledge of those matters which, if he knew about them, he would himself rectify, so that he is thereby put into a self-stultifying position" ("On the Common Saying: 'This May Be True in Theory, But It Does Not Apply in Practice,'" in Kant 1991, 84–85; emphasis added).

duty to establish institutions in accordance with God's authority, to ensure that his subjects do not flout that authority, and to defend them against oppression and injustice. To that extent, the ruler has special responsibilities, including the establishment of a supervisory organization whose members devote their energies "to commanding what is good and forbidding what is evil *(al-amr bi-l-ma'ruf wa-nnahy 'an al-munkar)*." In Saudi Arabia this organization is known as the *mutāwi'a,* which foreigners call "the purity police."

In this latter form, *nasiha* was often used in the past to bolster the authority of Muslim rulers.[27] But in the contemporary Saudi context, Za'ayr insists that *nasiha* cannot be left only to the ruler or his agents to carry out.

> Each individual must be watchful first over himself in order to estab-
> lish God's authority in his very being. No single group can supervise
> every individual to do this for him. Therefore each individual must be
> watchful first of all over himself, and then over other individuals in
> society, to help them establish God's authority. That is the only possi-
> ble way the community of believers *(umma)* can prosper.

As a practice that is everyone's responsibility,[28] *nasiha* is thus indepen-
dent of the ruler's authority. Furthermore, the critical role of ordinary Muslims does not create the duty to report transgressions to the political authorities; it merely requires a direct engagement with the trans-
gressor. True, that engagement may eventually result in resorting to the coercive power of the authorities, but only when the full comple-

---

27. Thus, in a recent history of the Ottoman state in the early modern period, Abou-El-Haj (1992, 51–52) draws attention to an interesting set of decrees "issued to rectify widespread acts described only euphemistically, and whose redress was alluded to by the expression 'proper faith is good advice' *(ad-din ul-nasiha)*. . . . From the official point of view, laxity in adherence to the tenets of the faith was tantamount to immoral acts *(mekruh)*. But apparently, the decrees meant to condemn something much more specific, namely, indulgence in magical acts and superstitious or pagan practices. The un-
derlying meaning of the decrees, however, is inferred from the historical context. The decrees were issued as rebellions were breaking out in the Balkan and Crimean prov-
inces. . . . In the eyes of the state . . . resistance . . . was portrayed in the decrees as failure in proper indoctrination and acculturation. Therefore the admonition, ad-din ul-nasiha, which literally translates as 'proper faith is in being properly guided (by accepting advice),' is therefore meant to enjoin absolute obedience to those in authority."

28. This is categorized in the *shari'a* as *fard 'ayn,* as opposed to a duty that is fulfilled on behalf of the community by a minimum number of people (for example performing the collective Friday prayer) technically called *fard kifāya.*

tion of *nasīha* calls for it, not because the political authorities have a superior right to intervene. More important, neither the ruler nor his officials are exempt from criticism by the upright Muslim. For if the ruler's role includes the duty of defending his subjects against injustice, the Muslim subject has not simply the right but the obligation to criticize the unjust ruler.[29] This conclusion has far-reaching implications in the context of contemporary Saudi Arabia.

Nevertheless, Za'ayr does not push the idea of criticizing the ruler to the point where it incites disobedience. On the contrary, he explicitly repudiates such an inference.

> Now it is said of some preachers that they are revolutionaries *(thuw-wār)*, that they are rebels *(khawārij)*,[30] and that they are against the state. Why *is* this said? It is claimed that in their lectures these preachers call for change in the status quo which they consider to be sinful *(harām)*, and if the state doesn't respond favourably to their demands they will seek to change things by violence. Who says this? What are these suppositions? What are these delusions? . . . This is not the first time that you will have heard this kind of talk hostile to the preachers, this kind of accusation. There are people who have a vested interest in it. . . . They have an interest in likening our preachers to certain Islamic groups in other countries, knowing that there is no similarity between the two. Our preachers do not regard our government as unbelieving as the latter do, but as legitimate because our government rules according to the *sharī'a*, cooperates with the *'ulamā*, and so forth. Yet just because our preachers call for the correction of some mistakes, they are called "revolutionaries!"

Za'ayr's manner of disclaiming rebellious intent is double-edged. For by rooting the government's right to rule in its avowed commitment to the *sharī'a*, its actual performance can be criticized for failing to meet *sharī'a* standards.

29. Such an obligation is qualified by a recognition of political circumstance, as in the well-known *hadīth:* "Whosoever of you sees an evil action, let him change it with his hand; and if he is unable to do so, then with his tongue; and if he is not able to do so, then with his heart—and that is the weakest part of faith *(ad'afu-l-īmān)*."

30. Although the text typically contains "contemporary-secular" terms (e.g., *thuw-wār*) and "classical-theological" ones (e.g., *khawārij*) in the same sentence, this should not be seen as a simple mixture of the traditional and the modern. It is not the diverse origins of the vocabulary but its differential resonances that are relevant to understanding the tradition of Islamic political discourse.

Za'ayr enumerates a number of conditions and requirements for achieving *nasīha* that together define a measure of personal responsibility for its success. Here again, the duty of *nasīha* differs from the right to criticize publicly in Kant's enlightened polity.

There are two general requirements, Za'ayr reminds his listeners, for successfully undertaking *nasīha:* (1) knowledge of the rules and models of virtuous living, and of the most effective way of conveying these to others; (2) kindness and gentleness in performing the act of *nasīha.*[31] Knowledge for action and an appropriate mode of engagement are both essential, not least when undertaking *nasīha.* With regard to the former, although such knowledge may have to be obtained from those more qualified (e.g., the *'ulamā*), the responsibility for initiating *nasīha* and trying to ensure its completion rests with the actor. As for the manner of engagement, it is violence *('unf)* and not emotion that is disapproved.[32]

It should be noted here that legally confirmed transgressions ultimately carry the threat of legal punishment but that Za'ayr makes no mention of this fact anywhere.[33] One explanation of this omission is that Za'ayr's main objective is to justify criticism directed at those in authority, and here force is not normally an available option. Another is that since the use of force is contingent, it is not the essence of *nasīha,* whereas persuasion *is* part of its essence and consequently is emphasized in Za'ayr's exposition.

From the two general principles for undertaking *nasīha*—relevant knowledge and appropriate method—Za'ayr develops several maxims:

> How should one act when confronted with something that goes against God's command? . . . (1) Determine carefully whether it is really against God's command. Be sceptical of your own judgement. If necessary, consult those who know better than you. (2) If it is a transgression, consider carefully whether it affects the individual or a small

---

31. Here Za'ayr cites the well-known *hadīth:* "If something is done with kindness and gentleness it is thereby beautified, and if it is done with force and violence it is thereby rendered ugly."

32. The contemporary Arabic for "emotion"—'*ātifa*—comes from the classical word that carries the sense of "cause of inclining toward" someone. Taken in this sense and in this context, emotion and sound judgment are not necessarily mutually exclusive as they are in much Enlightenment thought.

33. The legitimate use of force as a last resort in the performance of *nasīha* is discussed in the medieval classics: for example, by Imām Ghazāli in *Ihyā 'ulūm-id-dīn,* and by ibn Taymiyya in *Siyāsa shar'iyya.*

group, or the *umma* as a whole. In the latter case, be very careful.
Consult with others, with the *'ulamā*, etc., even if this takes time.
(3) Think carefully of the best way to deliver your *nasīha* and to rectify
the error. If it relates to the *umma* as a whole, intensify your consulta-
tions with *'ulamā*, and don't hurry. Turn to God for help and enlightenment, pray to Him, especially at night. (4) After proper consulta-
tion, after you have chosen the best way, put your trust in God and
proceed. Be fully conscious of your responsibility, for you are wor-
shipping God. You are not free to do as you like, you are God's worshipper, bound to follow the Prophet. So persevere with your *nasīha*,
and reiterate it, and use your wisdom in doing so. (5) Avoid all provo-
cation, violence, rashness, and haste. (6) Don't measure the success
of your effort and your call by the immediate result. A positive result
[i.e., rectification of conduct] may be delayed for reasons beyond
your control, or that of the person advised. Do not say: I have tried
giving people *nasīha*, but it's never any use. So long as you carry out
your responsibility with integrity, to its utmost, you have done what
you can. (7) If the recipient of your *nasīha* does respond positively,
don't cease your connections with him. Urge him to take on the
responsibility of *ad-da'wa* [the call] towards others, because that is
your message and his, and that of all believers.

Za'ayr concludes by reminding his audience that *da'wa*, as the extension of *nasīha*, goes beyond the criticism of transgressions to call for
the cultivation of three central virtues: *itqān us-salāt* (the bodily mastery and spiritual perfection of prayer), *as-sabr* (self-command, for-
titude, and perseverance), and *al-yaqīn* (certainty, true knowledge,
right judgment). As virtues, *salāt, sabr,* and *yaqīn* articulate a range of
disciplined passions, each of which presupposes continuous exercise
based on discursive models. The virtuous Muslim is thus seen not as
an autonomous individual who assents to a set of universalizable maxims but as an individual inhabiting the moral space shared by all who
are together bound to God (the *umma*). Thus, *dīn* (invariably translated as religion) relates more to how one lives than to what one believes. For Muslims such as Za'ayr, it is virtues—mastery of the body,
the ability to be patient, and the capacity to judge soundly—that matter, not states of mind.

Evidently, then, *nasīha* and *da'wa* together stand in a conceptual
world quite unlike that of the Enlightenment. For unlike the former,

the latter world is inhabited by individuals aspiring to self-determination and dispassionate judgment, whose moral foundation is universal reason, not disciplined virtues.[34] In each world, the individual articulates a different motivational structure in which reasoning has a distinctive place. Thus, in the world assumed by Za'ayr, particular personal virtues must already be in place before practical reasoning can be properly carried out; in the Enlightenment world, practical reasoning yields an ethical maxim only when it is universalizable as a general law.

It is possible, I suppose, to take Za'ayr's disquisition on *nasīha* as an appeal to habitual behavior as against reason, to tradition as against modernity. But if tradition is thought of as the rejection of any idea of reasoned change, then such an understanding would be mistaken. For in fact various changes are welcomed by Za'ayr so long as they are in accord with the foundations of *dīn*. Thus, he reasons that while one may welcome the benefits of new social institutions such as schools, hospitals, banks, and television networks, one must not be blind to their "mistakes and errors," things done contrary to God's commands. It is only the latter that Za'ayr regards as the proper targets of criticism. Nevertheless, it is true that there is no place in his disquisition for the post-Enlightenment idea of moral and political progress, and if that is essential to a conception of modernity, then Za'ayr is clearly opposed to it. Indeed, he is openly contemptuous of the kind of development discourse that speaks of "catching up" with the West. That way of talking, he declares, assumes that other civilizations be taken as the Muslim model. But: "If one doesn't secure one's own independent thinking the *umma* is made into an appendage of others. And if that happens, the *umma*'s essence *(huwiyya)* and its independence disappear together."

Za'ayr's language on this matter is similar to that of nationalist

34. In Kant's words: "Moral culture must be based upon maxims, not upon discipline. Discipline prevents defects; moral culture shapes the manner of thinking. One must see to it that the child accustom himself to act according to maxims and not according to certain impulses. Discipline leaves habits only, which fade away with years. The child should learn to act according to maxims whose justice he himself perceives. . . . Morality is something so holy and sublime that it must not be degraded thus and placed in the same rank with discipline. The first endeavour in moral education is to establish a character. Character consists in the readiness to act according to maxims. At first these are the maxims of the school and later they are those of humanity. In the beginning the child obeys laws. Maxims also are laws, but subjective; they spring out of the human reason itself" (1904, 185–87).

ideologues who call for cultural authenticity, and it is evident from his
defensive remarks in response to his Westernized opponents that he is
not unfamiliar with nationalist discourse. However, his argument is
differently grounded. His overriding preoccupation is with the idea of
obedience to God's command and the exemplary practice *(sunna)* of
the Prophet. The position he takes up has nothing to do with advocat-
ing an "authentic culture" or with proposing an "independent road
to modernity." He wishes to affirm the absolute authority of God—or,
as he puts it, "The first foundation of independence for the *umma* is to
know that it is indissolubly bound *(muta'abbid)* to God, and to reject
dependence on any alternative idea." (Note, incidentally, that Za'ayr
does not regard particular commands as having authority because they
issue from God; he recognizes the commands as divine because a bond
of absolute authority is already taken for granted.)

The concept of the Muslim as indissolubly bound to God is expressed repeatedly in this lecture through the classical words 'abd and
muta'abbid. The latter derives from the former (whose sense includes
both "slave" and "worshipper") and means something like "forcibly
secured for devotion to God." Although nearly all English translations of the Qur'ān render the word 'abd as "servant" (Pickthall being
an exception), I would translate it as "slave." For liberals, a slave is
primarily someone who occupies the most despised status of all, and
therefore the institution of slavery is utterly immoral (conversely, to
be considered fully human, creatures must own themselves). Yet by
employing the metaphor of slavery to describe the human relation to
God, the Islamic rhetorical tradition stands in powerful contrast both
to the figure of kinship (God as Father) and the figure of contract (the
Covenant with God), which are part of Judeo-Christian discourse.[35]
As God's slaves, humans do not share any essence with their owner,
who is also their creator,[36] nor can they ever invoke an original agree-

35. The idea of a covenant with God—'ahd allah—is mentioned in the Qur'ān several
times, but arguably never when Muslims are addressed directly. In both the Judeo-
Christian tradition and Islam there are, of course, several metaphors for describing the
relationship of humans to God. Some of these are shared. But my purpose here is to
stress the contrastive as well as the intrinsic qualities of the idea of the Muslim as God's
slave, especially as articulated in Za'ayr's discourse. The mystical traditions of Islam
employ very different figures to convey the notion of attainable states in which human
beings can merge with God (see Baldick 1989). Such notions are anathema to the tradition to which Za'ayr belongs.

36. The absolute difference between human beings and God is enunciated in a fa-

ment with him. The relationship requires unconditional obedience. However, this is not an abstract bond between an individual believer and a transcendent power; it is embodied in an existing community with its founding texts and authorized practices (the *umma*). The community always needs correcting, under threat of divine punishment "in this world and the next *(fi-ddunyā wa-l-ākhira)*." Za'ayr warns his listeners that if Muslims fail to obey God, He will destroy their community *(umma)* as surely as he has destroyed those early communities *(umam)* whose fate is related in the Qur'ān. The members of the *umma* can be continually criticized and reformed, but they cannot become self-owning individuals, each with the right to choose his or her own ends.[37]

Finally: One should not think that what Za'ayr refers to when he speaks of the *umma* is a sociologically defined community—traditionally unified, but now subject to modern disintegration. It is not. Nowhere in his lecture does he bewail the collapse of a sense of communal sociality;[38] he simply takes it for granted that the *umma* exists, and he

mous sura *(al-ikhlās)* of the Qur'ān: "Say: 'He is the One God: God the Eternal, the Uncaused Cause of All Being. He begets not, and neither is He begotten; and there is nothing that could be compared with Him'" (Muhammad Asad's translation). *'Ibāda* (a word having the same root as *'abd* and usually translated into English as "worship") defines the relationship one properly has with God, and with God only. Hence, those who want to condemn ritual supplication at saints' tombs—which would certainly include the Wahhabi Za'ayr—will describe it as *'ibāda*. To defend such a practice—as Wahhabis themselves do in the context of prayers offered at the Prophet's tomb—one must reject that appellation and insist instead that it is *ziyāra* ("visitation"). This is more than a matter of words, of course: it marks an argument over the structure of virtues, including both inward attitude and outward behavior.

37. This stands in sharp contrast to the sentiments of liberalism as articulated by Isaiah Berlin in his celebrated essay on the essence of individual freedom: "The 'positive' sense of the word 'liberty' derives from the wish on the part of the individual to be his own master. I wish my life and my decisions to depend on myself, not on external forces of whatever kind. I wish to be the instrument of my own, not other men's, acts of will. I wish to be a subject, not an object; to be moved by reasons, by conscious purposes, which are my own, not by causes which affect me, as it were, from outside (1958, 16). Of course, this is not a simple statement of egoism but of a *universal right*. According to C. B. Macpherson, that idea has seventeenth-century foundations, whose assumptions include the following: "(i) What makes a man human is freedom from dependence on the wills of others. (ii) Freedom from dependence on others means freedom from any relations with others except those relations which the individual enters voluntarily with a view to his own interest. (iii) The individual is essentially the proprietor of his own person and capacities, for which he owes nothing to society" or to any other external force (1962, 263).

38. Which is not to deny that many people do often make just that complaint in Saudi Arabia as elsewhere in the third world.

develops his arguments about moral action on the basis of that assumption. The *umma* is the concept of a religious-political space— divinely sanctioned and eternally valid—within which rational discussion, debate, and criticism can be conducted. It is also a space of power and of punishment.

An Argument about "Proper" Islamic Public Criticism

Sermons and lectures like these helped to prepare the way for a critical event of great moment shortly after the Gulf War came to a formal end. In May 1991, an open letter, addressed to King Fahd and signed by several hundred Saudi *'ulamā*, was published in the form of a leaflet and distributed throughout the kingdom, although it received no mention in the Saudi press (whether private or state-owned) or on Saudi radio or TV.[39]

The tone of the letter is polite but firm.[40] Its formal opening addresses Fahd not as "the King" but simply as "The servant of the two noble Sanctuaries [of Mecca and Medina], may God prosper him," a title which Fahd had assumed some years earlier.[41] After reminding the reader that the Saudi state was officially based on the *sharī'a*, it declares rather pointedly that "the *'ulamā* and counsellors *(ahl un-nasīha)* continue to fulfill the obligation, imposed on them by God, of giving *nasīha* to their leaders." It then puts forward several demands that bring together longstanding criticisms made of the regime by various groups within the country. The demands include "the establishment of a consultative assembly to adjudicate on domestic and foreign affairs . . . with complete independence *(inshā' majlis ash-shūra lil-bat fi-sh-shu'ūn id-dākhiliyya wa-l-khārijiyya . . . ma'a al-istiqlāl at-tām),*" "a just distribution of public wealth *(iqāmat ul-'adl fi tawzī' il-māl il-'ām),*" "guarantee of the rights of the individual and of society *(kafā-*

<hr/>

39. It was published in Arabic newspapers abroad, however. For example, the full text, together with a photostat of the signatures, appeared in the Egyptian paper *ash-Sha'b* of 21 May 1991.

40. A little later, another letter was addressed to the king by a number of well-known Western-educated Saudis, also asking for various reforms—political, educational, and social. In contrast to the letter by the *'ulamā*, the tone of this letter is very deferential, and central stress is placed on modernization *(tahdīth)*.

41. In contrast, the "liberal" letter is addressed to "The Servant of the two noble Sanctuaries, King Fahd bin 'Abdul 'Azīz, may God support him." Unlike the other letter, it thus names the addressee as king and as the son of the Founder of the Kingdom.

lat huqūq al-fard wa-l-mujtami'), " and the removal of all infringements on the wishes and rights of people, including human dignity (al-karāma al-insāniyya), in accordance with legitimate (shar'iyya) and recognized moral rules (dawābit)—as well as a complete and thorough review of all political, administrative, and economic organizations in the kingdom to ensure that they are run in accordance with the Islamic sharī'a.

The King did not respond directly to this letter, but apparently asked the Council of Senior 'Ulamā to do so. The council published a reply through the main media, deploring the manner in which the self-proclaimed nasīha was publicized.[42] While it was right to assert that Muslims were under an obligation to give corrective advice to their fellows ("their leaders and their common folk"), there were—the council insisted—proper forms and conditions that governed nasīha. It required not only sincerity but also good intention toward the recipient, "desiring for him what one desires for oneself." For this reason it should be given personally and in private, so as not to hurt or embarrass him.

It is said that some of the King's supporters who commented on the original letter by word of mouth claimed that the manner in which it was delivered rendered this so-called nasīha (morally corrective discourse) into something close to ghība—that is, speaking of someone's faults in his or her absence (and by extension also calumniating or slandering someone). Ghība is strongly condemned in Islamic moral theology,[43] so it is not surprising that the letter writers dismissed this analogy as absurd. But the point of likening moral criticism addressed publicly to the king to the sin of backbiting in private was, of course, to suggest malicious intent, a feature that irretrievably damages the integrity of nasīha.

It is thus precisely the description of this act of criticism as nasīha that is disputed by those siding with the recipient of advice (mansūh). For the authority of the younger 'ulamā to criticize the king (and also his inordinately rich and often blatantly corrupt relatives) derives from their claim that what they are doing is giving nasīha. They appear to have thought through all the proper conditions for carrying out nasīha mentioned in the Za'ayr sermon and to have anticipated the objections

---

42. See the Saudi daily ash-Sharq al-Awsat of 4 June 1991.
43. A commonly used textbook on this topic in Saudi Arabia is 'Uwaysha n.d.

of the king's supporters. At any rate, I heard two arguments produced in defense of the publication of the *nasīha,* one moral and one tactical.

Thus, it was maintained that since the *nasīha* dealt with matters affecting the proper regulation of the *umma,* not with the personal behavior of the prince, it had to be announced publicly. The common folk needed to be reminded—no less than the prince did (albeit for different reasons)—of how the affairs of the *umma* should be conducted. There were many precedents for this in the history of Islam, examples of *'ulamā* reproving the prince in public for not doing what he ought, even if this led to their imprisonment. Perhaps the most notable of these, and the one frequently cited by Saudi *'ulamā,* was the medieval jurist ibn Taymiyya. The first justification therefore appears to have invoked publicity not as a transcendental principle but as a moral option that is appropriate in *this* situation rather than some other.

The second (and tactical) argument was that the king had often in the past been urged privately to undertake the necessary reforms but had chosen to ignore that discreet advice. The wide distribution of the printed letter was thus a second step, intended to exert greater pressure on a morally passive prince to respond—either by openly challenging the *nasīha* or by initiating authentic Islamic reform. The publicity given to the *nasīha* created a public space in which the prince was required to confront others—and himself—as a moral person. It was assumed that as a moral person he would be ashamed to be told publicly that he had failed to act as a Muslim prince ought, in his capacity as ruler, to act.

If the Saudi royal clan and its supporters are to subvert the authority of these critical younger *'ulamā* (as opposed to silencing them by force), it seems that they will have to enter the dangerous terrain of open theological argument.[44] The greatest danger in this lies not in the possibility that the king may lose the argument but precisely in his conceding a domain of public argument *in which he becomes accountable.*

This kind of publicized argument is relatively new in the sense that it is articulated by graduates of the new Islamic universities, and that the things dealt with in their discourse are often new to traditional Islamic discourse (although not external to that tradition). But

44. Another step in the argument was a book-length polemic directed formally at one of the best-known establishment *'ulamā,* Shaikh 'Abdul-'Azīz bin Bāz by Hawālī (n.d.).

if the scope of social criticism now appears more comprehensive, this is not because untraditional Islamic spokesmen have begun to extend their criticism into areas previously ignored. It is, rather, because modern institutions (administrative, economic, ideological) and modern classes (especially those who have received a Western education) have come into existence, creating a new social space that is the object of critical discourse and practice. The religious discourses and practices presuppose the new social space—the latter partly constitutes and is constituted by the former. In this important sense, they are a *part* of modernity and not a *reaction* to it, as is often said: unless, of course, it be insisted that modernity is articulated by a fixed teleology.

Those who speak for the modernizing state have begun to treat Saudi society *(al-mujtami' as-sa'ūdi)* not only as a totality but also as a totality that is undergoing a critical transformation. There now exists a theoretically all-encompassing administrative framework, a defined territory (with some ill-defined boundaries generating international disputes), national passports, budgets, development plans, foreign workers, foreign policies, a graded educational system (schools, technical institutes, universities, overseas scholarships), a centralized network of information collection (statistics, archives) and of information distribution (radio, TV). In these different elements, practice is not always congruent with official representation, nor are the elements fully integrated with one another. But that is precisely one of the things that renders all of them together a totality-in-crisis.

This general situation invites members of the Western-educated middle classes to produce critical discourses directed at mobilizing publics and to intervene thereby in the uneven movement of that totality toward its appointed goal.[45] For the Islamic graduates, on the other hand, the situation demands judgment and criticism based on knowledge of the principles by which religion regulates life—that is, *fiqh,* usually translated as jurisprudence. It should therefore not be surprising that in the new Islamic critical discourse, normative classi-

45. The more subdued criticism offered by members of the growing, Western-educated middle class is formulated in moral-political vocabularies drawn from post-Enlightenment Europe. For the most part, this takes place in private discussion groups and makes its opinions felt through personal contact with some of the princes. Many of these liberal critics have begun to exchange ideas, on matters of substance as well as tactics, with the more outspoken Islamic critics. But they do not characterize their criticisms in terms of the Islamic concept of *nasīha.*

cal concepts such as the *umma* (the moral space in which all Muslims are placed) come to be applied to a contemporary moral-political order relevant to Saudi Arabia. Or that—together with Western-educated Saudi liberals but with a very different intent—they should speak of their country as a society in crisis *(azmat ul-mujtami ')*. For the new, teleological sense of "crisis" carried by this concept is reflected in its distance from the older meaning of the word *azma:* Whereas *azma* classically signified a time of drought and dearth, in modern parlance it is employed to denote not simply a term of hardship but a sickness of the body politic that has reached a dangerous point and that consequently awaits a radical diagnosis and resolution before things can move toward a better future.[46]

Shifts in the Idea of "Critical Reason" from the Eighteenth Century to the Twentieth

The *'ulamā* I have discussed in this chapter could not conceivably assert, as Kant did two centuries ago:

> Our age is, in especial degree, the age of criticism, and to criticism everything must submit. Religion . . . and legislation . . . may seek to exempt themselves from it. But they then awaken just suspicion, and cannot claim the sincere respect which reason accords only to that which has been able to sustain the test of free and open examination.[47]

For Kant (in contrast to the *'ulamā*), criticism is intended as an alternative to religious authority, not as a means of reinforcing it. But this difference is attributable, at least in part, to the fact that in Enlightenment Europe, religious authority was already in retreat. Political authority, of course, was not.

However, Kant insisted that the freedom to criticize everything should not interfere with the duty to obey political authority. Although some subsequent commentators have described this separation as amounting to support for political authoritarianism, others have seen in it a principled statement of the *Rechtsstaat* (see Reiss

46. In the introduction to his very interesting book on the human rights debate in the Middle East, Dwyer (1991) notes the general sense of crisis among Arab intellectuals today. However, the discourse of crisis in the region is not merely contemporary; it goes back at least a quarter century—and in some cases much longer.

47. *Critique of Pure Reason* (cited in Arendt 1982, 32).

1991, 11). At the very least, these contradictory responses indicate how ambiguous Kant's doctrine is.

Foucault has suggested—in the article I cited at the beginning of the chapter—that because Kant was living in an absolutist state, it is not surprising that he should have sought to reassure the king about his authority: "Kant . . . proposes to Frederick II, in scarcely veiled terms, a sort of contract—what might be called the contract of rational despotism with free reason: the public and free use of autonomous reason will be the best guarantee of obedience, on condition, however, that the political principle that must be obeyed itself be in conformity with universal reason" (Foucault 1984, 37).

This is certainly a neat liberal solution to the paradoxes generated by Kant's separation of critical reason from political obedience.[48] But what, we may ask, are the implications for non-European histories when Enlightenment "free reason" contracts with imperial "rational despotism"? One answer, as it relates to the Muslim world, has recently been provided by the well-known Middle East scholar Leonard Binder:

> From the time of the Napoleonic invasion, from the time of the massacre of the Janissaries, from the time of the Sepoy mutiny, at least, the West has been trying to tell Islam what must be the price of progress in the coin of the tradition which is to be surrendered. And from those times, despite the increasing numbers of responsive Muslims, there remains a substantial number that steadfastly argue that it is possible to progress without paying such a heavy cultural price. (1988, 293)

Binder may be right here (indeed, I believe he is right). But it is surely no incidental detail that each of the "tellings" cited by him—when traditional authority was successfully attacked in the name of rationality and progress—was at the same time an act of violence.[49] In each of

---

48. Foucault's suggestion that Kant makes the subjects' duty of obedience conditional on the ruler's respect for universal reason would not, I think, have been acceptable to Kant himself. For Kant (1991, 126) rejects "rebellion [as] a rightful means for a people to use in order to overthrow the oppressive power of a so-called tyrant." In this respect, Kant's position is close to what today is called *constitutionalism*.

49. Some anthropologists of the Middle East regard Napoleon's invasion of Egypt as having initiated "scientific fieldwork" in the region—a nice example of the fusion of rational knowledge and military power (see Eickelman 1989).

them, Western political, economic, and ideological power increased its hold over non-European peoples.[50] That power, unleashed in Enlightenment Europe, continues to restructure the lives of non-European peoples, often through the agency of non-Europeans themselves. And if "Islamic fundamentalism" is a response to that power, then certainly so, even more thoroughly, are the intellectual currents called "modernist Islam" (which is concerned to adapt theology to the models of Christian modernism)[51] and "Muslim secularism" (which is preoccupied less with theology than with separating religion from politics in national life). And so, too, are the progressivist movements in literature and the arts, in politics and law, that have arisen in Muslim societies.

The translation of modern Western categories into the administrative and legal discourses of the non-Western world is a familiar story. It was through such discursive powers that people undergoing Westernization were compelled to abandon old practices and turn to new ones. The massive redefinition and regularization of property rights is probably the best known example of this process. But there are others.

The historiography of modernization in the Middle East recounts the measures taken in various countries to re-form the *sharī'a* in conformity with the presuppositions of Western social practice. At first, in the areas of commercial, penal, and procedural law, and later, more

50. Of course, the use of force to impose one's political will on another people was not, and is not, peculiar to the modern West. The point is that it raises distinctive moral problems for modern liberal thought, because liberalism celebrates freedom from external coercion as an absolute end, and it is also committed to extending its social arrangements across the world by coercive means. In the nineteenth century, J. S. Mill attempted, famously, to reconcile this contradiction by reference to the creative role of rational (i.e., European) despotism in relation to "unprogressive," non-European peoples. (See Mill 1975, chap. 18.)

51. Unsuccessfully, according to the verdict of Western scholars like Binder. For earlier criticisms, see Gibb 1947; Kerr 1966; and Kedourie 1966. Kedourie ends his book with a striking image of Muslims as animals, wild and domesticated: "And a year later, more sweepingly and more trenchantly [Blunt wrote]: 'The Muslims of today who believe are mere wild beasts like the men of Siwah, the rest have lost their faith.' Since his day, of course, a large proportion of the wild beasts, thanks no doubt to the modernists, has been civilised and domesticated. The few survivors are firmly confined to their reservations" (65). Beneath the offensiveness of the metaphor (which, incidentally, Western scholarly reviewers did not comment on) lies the more interesting thought that Muslims are animals of two kinds: domesticated (trained or otherwise subjected to the designs of humans) and wild (free and therefore both dangerous and useless).

hesitantly, in that part of the *sharī'a* which Western and Westernized historians call "family law" (marriage, divorce, inheritance, etc.), Western principles replaced or restricted Islamic rules and practices.[52] Reviewing these changes in the Ottoman Empire and its successor states, a historian of modern Islamic law observes:

> It might well be asked why it was that the Shari'a was thus progressively set on one side in favour of codes derived largely from the West. Initially, it seems clear, this was far less the result of any popular demand for reform . . . than imposed upon the people from above, partly in the interest of administrative efficiency and national progress, and partly in order to satisfy foreign opinion. But as time went on, the conservative opposition to these reforms was challenged by a variety of arguments put forward by the more progressive elements in the countries concerned. (Anderson 1959, 22–23)

Arguments may well have "challenged" conservatives, as progressivist historians claim, but the fact remains that the translation of Western legal categories depended less on persuasive argument than on constraints put into effect by persons acting in the name of the Westernizing state. What mattered was not that the Muslim population thought well of the legal reforms, but that once the reforms had been "imposed upon the people from above," the Westernizing state could create and maintain new conditions to which everyday practices had perforce to be related. In this context, it is not the probability that conservative opinion was persuaded that counts, but the frequency with which people responded appropriately whatever their motives.

Yes, of course, these reforms did not simply reproduce Western institutions ("local cultures make a difference"). And yes, of course, many people resisted them in a variety of ways ("people aren't puppets"). But henceforth the cultural differences were constructed under new conditions, and the acts of resistance took place in new spaces. On the one hand, there were new political languages, new social groupings, new modes of producing and consuming, new desires and fears, new disciplines of time and space; on the other, there was the critical

---

52. This process is not a simple shrinking of the scope of the *sharī'a*, for in some geographical regions the *sharī'a* has come to be applied to Muslim populations who had until recently followed varieties of custom. The crucial new feature everywhere has been the prominent role of the state in redefining the structure and application of the *sharī'a* according to Western principles.

fact that contest and conflict were increasingly relatable to *legal* demands (even when governing powers sought to deny their legality) within the framework of a modernizing state. When these new conditions had taken root, the idea of "crisis" as a historical stage in the life of Muslim society made its appearance. The modern discourse of crisis, here as elsewhere in the third world, depends on a particular form of diagnosis (radical social criticism) and proposes a particular kind of cure (emancipation from the sickness-producing past).

There can be little doubt that in this increasingly modernized world the kind of religious criticism I have described for Saudi Arabia becomes less viable. My question, however, is this: is that nonviability to be attributed to the liberating powers of transcendental reason or simply to the secular powers that destroy and reconstruct?

Apparently even an intelligent modern liberal like Binder does not find it easy to decide. On the one hand, Western critical reason is definitely held to have its own redeeming power. "By engaging in rational discourse with those whose consciousness has been shaped by Islamic culture," Binder maintains, "it is possible to enhance the prospects for political liberalism in that region and others where it is not indigenous" (2). But, on the other hand, the power to extend liberalism seems to depend critically on something else:

> So long as the West was convinced that its moral superiority rested upon the confluence of rational discourse and its own political practice, the practical example of the liberal West encouraged the liberal interpretation of Islam. But when the West began to doubt its own moral superiority, then the norm of Western liberal rationality no longer served as a plausible explanation of political experience in the world. As a consequence, it is no longer imperative that certain traditional Islamic practices be explained away, or even simply explained. (5)

In this account, it is the West's alleged loss of its sense of moral superiority over Muslim countries, and hence its inability to overawe them, that reveals, negatively, where the power of modern "Western liberal rationality" lies.

This latter account is different from the one that Kant gave of critical reason. For, according to Kant, rationality is universal because it is rooted in the abstract idea of the transcendental subject; modern liberals like Binder seem—at least some of the time—to consider rationality to be universal because it is identified with the globalizing moral and political power of the modern West.

Nineteenth-century evolutionary theorists, including those we today call anthropologists, insisted on a single distinction between rationality (which they identified essentially with European civilization) and irrationality (which they ascribed to varieties of primitivism, psychological or social). These theorists were not always fully aware that their concept of a single substantive rationality was one of the faces of power. On the contrary, they tended to believe that power was a means for instituting rationality throughout the less civilized world for that world's benefit. In the twentieth century, this belief took a more explicit political form: translating the liberal conception and practice of "the good society" into every corner of the non-Western world.[53]

Conclusion

The religious criticism described in this chapter is undeniably a vigorous expression of political opposition to the Saudi ruling elite. That criticism is not merely a one-sided assault, it invites argumentative exchange. Yet the invitation appears to increasing numbers of Westernized Saudis—who have their own complaints against their government—to be not only limited but limiting. And that is indeed what it really is. (But so, in its own way, was Kant's concept of political criticism.) It is limiting in that there are certain choices it will not allow; it is limited in that there are certain things it will not criticize. Nevertheless, I have aimed to provide an account that suggests the limitations are due not to a permanent incapacity to contemplate change, still less to an intrinsic contradiction between religion and reason.[54] The limitations are part of the way a particular discursive tradition, and its associated disciplines, are articulated at a particular point in time.

Since the objective of *nasīha* is the person who has transgressed

---

53. Thus, Lipset (1963, 439): "Democracy is not only or even primarily a means through which different groups can attain their ends or seek the good society; *it is the good society itself in operation*" (emphasis added). In other words, democracy is not simply the practice whereby a people freely chooses its government by an electoral majority; it is a style of life and a set of values.

54. This alleged contradiction is the burden of a famous critique of religion by a politically courageous (but intellectually old-fashioned) secularist, Al-'Azm (1969).

God's eternal commands, its normative reason can be regarded as a repressive technique for securing social conformity to divinely ordained norms, which many people today are unwilling to tolerate silently. But there is also another way of understanding *nasīha*. It reflects the principle that a well-regulated polity depends on its members being virtuous individuals who are partly responsible for one another's moral condition—and therefore in part on continuous moral criticism.

Modern liberalism rejects this principle. The well-regulated modern polity—so it argues—depends on the provision of optimum amounts of social welfare and individual liberty, not on moral criticism. The primary critical task, according to political liberalism, is not the moral disciplining of individuals but the rational administration and care of entire populations. Morality, together with religious belief, has become essentially a personal matter for the self-determining individual—or so the liberal likes to claim. Hence, some say, rational politics has replaced ideological politics (Bell 1960) in fully developed modern societies.

Conversely, the existence of ideological politics within a given society indicates that it is not yet fully modern. This thought is appealing to many anthropologists who write on "development." Thus, in a well-known essay on Muslim Indonesia, Geertz (1973) argued that ideology—which moralizes the domain of politics—is typical of societies that have begun to move from tradition to modernity,[55] and that its function is to cope creatively with crises of transition.[56] Ideologies are

---

55. "It is a loss of orientation that most directly gives rise to ideological activity, an inability, for lack of usable models, to comprehend the universe of civic rights and responsibilities in which one finds oneself located. The development of a differentiated polity (or of greater internal differentiation within such a polity) may and commonly does bring with it severe social dislocation and psychological tension. But it also brings with it conceptual confusion, as the established images of political order fade into irrelevance or are driven into disrepute" (Geertz 1973, 219).

56. "That Indonesia (or, I should imagine, any new nation) can find her way through this forest of problems without any ideological guidance at all seems impossible. The motivation to seek (and, even more important, to *use*) technical skill and knowledge, the emotional resilience to support the necessary patience and resolution, and the moral strength to sustain self-sacrifice and incorruptibility must come from somewhere, from some vision of public purpose anchored in a compelling image of social reality. That all these qualities may not be present; that the present drift to revivalistic irrationalism and unbridled fantasy may continue; that the next ideological phase may be even further from the ideals for which the revolution was ostensibly fought than is the present one; that Indonesia may continue to be, as Bagehot called France, the scene of political experiments from which others profit much but she herself very little, or that the ulti-

therefore to be seen in their double form as "maps of problematic social reality and matrices for the creation of collective conscience." Geertz's argument, which belongs to the end-of-ideology school, is that eventually, when "adolescent nations" have reached maturity, when serious social crises have been overcome, a realm of rational politics becomes possible.

However, the assumption is surely mistaken that modern liberal politics precludes any direct commitment to particular moral norms, or any space for ideologically based criticism. To the extent that modern politics employs the language of rights (individual or collective), ideological principles are central to it. Civil rights and human rights (including civil liberties and material entitlements) are not merely neutral legal facts, they are profoundly moralistic values constantly invoked to guide and criticize modern politics—in the domestic setting of the nation-state and beyond it in international relations. The individual citizen is not required by the political community to be virtuous, but is required to be the bearer of rights that define his or her moral capacity. Furthermore, this moral-political ideology of rights has a specific *religious* (Christian) history (see Friedrich 1964).

But even if they have a religious *origin,* human rights are no longer based on religious *reason.* That alone, so it may be said, gives them a more rational foundation. Yet when people make such claims, it is not always clear what concept of rationality or religion they are employing. Nor do they always seem to recognize that the provision of epistemological foundations is itself a problematic enterprise (and one that, ironically, connects "reason" to "origin"). Thus, Kantian philosophers have one concept of rationality, modern political liberals who stress pragmatic criteria have another, and psychiatrists yet a third.[57] Philosophers and anthropologists have long been fascinated by the question of explaining apparently irrational beliefs in nonmodern cultures and premodern epochs. There is a vast literature on the subject.[58]

---

mate outcome may be viciously totalitarian and wildly zealotic is all very true" (Geertz 1973, 229).

57. For a discussion of some historical shifts since the seventeenth century in the concept of reason in epistemology, see Blanché 1968. A longer history of the major Western traditions that have successively redefined rationality in the domain of ethics is MacIntyre's impressive *Whose Justice? Which Rationality?* (1988).

58. A recent collection on rationality (Hollis and Lukes 1982) brought together anthropologists and philosophers to debate this question. All the anthropologists (Gellner, Horton, Sperber) took the view that what appear as irrational beliefs in non-Western

Three features characterize this literature. First, natural science is usually invoked as the model for what counts as rational. But even this apparent agreement is deceptive. In fact, the debaters urge mutually incompatible concepts of rationality upon each other, partly because what is critical to the long-term success of the different natural sciences is itself the subject of continuing philosophical and historical dispute.

Second, rationality is held to be the essence of an entire secular culture, and consequently the success of modern medicine and technology is considered the guarantee of a truth shared by the culture as a whole. (This foundational claim is not to be confused with the sociological observation that science and technology are variously bound up with a range of social, economic, and political institutions.) The idea of an integrated cultural totality founded on the Truth of Science makes it difficult to understand how people come to have serious disagreements over the possibility or the desirability of particular changes in a modern polity.

Third, great importance is attached to being able to assert that "modern culture" is superior to "nonmodern cultures," as though the consequence of not being able to do so forcefully enough would lead to large-scale defections from the former to the latter. Implicit in the well-advertised fear of "relativism"[59] is the extraordinary thought that the cultural life of human beings is the product of conscious criticism and objective choice. It is extraordinary because, although arguments are clearly important in different social situations, the reasons for a person's attachment to a given way of life, or conversion to another, cannot be reduced to an idealized model of scientific theory building.

Perhaps the feeling that secular arguments are rationally superior to religious ones is based on the belief that religious convictions are the

---

cultures are in fact failed attempts at theoretical explanations of the world. (Sperber complicates the argument by distinguishing between propositional and semi-propositional beliefs, maintaining that the latter are not, strictly speaking, "irrational beliefs" but "representations that enable us to store and process as much as we understand" [Sperber 1982, 170].)

59. Hollis and Lukes open their lucid introduction to *Rationality and Relativism* with the statement, "The temptations of relativism are perennial and pervasive. In many fields of thought they are openly embraced. Within social anthropology, they have been ever-present, though partially, if firmly, resisted." One might be reading here about some socially dangerous sexual perversion, and not—as it happens—about a philosophical position.

more rigid. But there is no decisive evidence for thinking this. Religious traditions have undergone the most radical transformations over time. Divine texts may be unalterable, but the ingenuities of human interpretation are endless—quite apart from the fact that some of the conditions of human doubt and certainty are notoriously inaccessible to conscious argument. Fanatics come in all shapes and sizes among skeptics and believers alike—as do individuals of a tolerant disposition. As for the claim that among the religious, coercion replaces persuasive argument, it should not be forgotten that we owe the most terrible examples of coercion in modern times to secular totalitarian regimes—Nazism and Stalinism. The point that matters in the end, surely, is not the justification that is used (whether it be supernatural or worldly) but the behavior that is justified. On this point, it must be said that the ruthlessness of secular practice yields nothing to the ferocity of religious.

Finally: it is necessary to stress that I am not concerned with the truth or otherwise of Saudi religious beliefs but with the kind of critical reasoning involved in *nasīha*. I have tried to show that the Islamic tradition is the ground on which that reasoning takes place.[60] And that is no more than may be said about political and moral reasoning within the modern liberal tradition—except that modern liberalism deploys powers that are immeasurably greater, including the flexible power to construct a "universal, progressive history," which the other tradition does not possess. That today is the main condition that limits religious criticism in the contemporary Middle East.

---

60. There are, it is true, several Islamic traditions (which is why the clumsy anthropological claim that there are several "Islams" appears to some to be plausible—see Asad 1986a for a critique). But the several Islamic traditions are related to one another formally, through common founding texts, and temporally, through diverging authoritative interpreters.

Polemics

❦❦❦

7 ∞ MULTICULTURALISM

AND BRITISH IDENTITY

IN THE WAKE OF THE

RUSHDIE AFFAIR

It is common knowledge that the Rushdie affair precipitated a sense of political crisis in Britain. Large numbers of Muslims publicly expressed their anger and distress at the publication of *The Satanic Verses*, demonstrated in London, petitioned Penguin Books to withdraw the book, and then the government to ban it. The government rejected the call for banning and warned Muslims not to isolate themselves from their host society. Newspapers and television almost unanimously condemned the "fundamentalism" of Britain's Muslims. On February 14, 1989, Ayatollah Khomeini issued his shocking death sentence on Rushdie. This greatly aggravated the sense of crisis in Britain, although most prominent Muslims there publicly dissociated themselves from it (*Guardian* news item, 1989). Ten days later, the home secretary, Douglas Hurd, made a speech at a gathering of Muslims, emphasizing the importance of proper integration for ethnic minorities, the need to learn about British culture without abandoning one's own faith, and the necessity of refraining from violence. At the beginning of July, his deputy, John Patten, wrote an open letter along similar lines, to "a number of leading British Muslims" (1989a). Two weeks later, he produced another document, entitled "On Being British," which was circulated to the news media (1989b).

I shall discuss this text in some detail below, but first I want to pose a question. Why did the British government feel the need to make such statements at this juncture? Why were these statements widely applauded by the liberal middle classes, whose pronouncements both before and after the government's intervention repeatedly denounced "Muslim violence"? This was not because there was an un-

239

manageable threat to law and order in the country. In fact, no arrests or injuries had occurred as a result of the demonstrations against the book, although it is true that emotional threats had been made by individuals against the author and his publishers (Poulter 1990, 6).

However, it is important to bear in mind that there had been innumerable angry demonstrations through the streets of London before: by antiracists and fascists, by feminists and gays, by abortion rights activists, trade unionists, students. Scuffles had broken out between demonstrators and police—involving accusations and counter-accusations of violence, including death threats—in which injuries were sustained and arrests made. More significantly, Britain had witnessed a number of major urban riots (in Nottingham, Notting Hill Gate, Brixton, Bristol, Birmingham, Liverpool, etc.) in which pitched battles were fought between police and nonwhite immigrants, cars and buildings burned, blood spilt—though, incidentally, South Asians were rarely if ever involved in any of these violent confrontations.[1] There has also been a steady stream of racist murders of nonwhite (mostly South Asian) immigrants, and a much longer one in which they have been subjected to "attempted killing, death narrowly avoided, arson, physical assault, spitting and verbal abuse, incidents estimated to number some 70,000 each year, most of them unreported to the police or other public authority" (Gordon 1989). And, of course, supporters of the Irish Republican Army have planted bombs in London that led to death and injury. The British government had never publicly warned the white majority against individual and collective violence, nor had it lectured Irish Catholics (or more recent immigrants) in England about the essential character of Britishness.

So what is it that led government spokespersons to make such unprecedented public pronouncements in the Rushdie affair? Certainly the government isn't alone in feeling that a situation of unusual seriousness has developed in the country requiring firm handling. In a leader entitled "Dangers of the Muslim campaign" (July 20, 1989), the influential British daily newspaper *Independent* began: "The present Government does not often forcefully represent the views of left-of-centre intellectuals. . . . But the recent observations of John Patten, Minister of State at the Home Office responsible for race relations, on

1. There were one or two minor exceptions such as Southall and Bradford, where South Asian youth formed vigilante groups in self-defense.

the need for the Muslim community to integrate with British society, have broadly echoed the views of liberal opinion." And it ended, somewhat threateningly: "If Britain's more extreme Muslims ignore John Patten's advice and continue to adopt hardline positions, they are likely to turn educated, as well as popular sentiments against them."

What exactly was the danger sensed by the Tory government and "liberal opinion" in Britain? It was a perceived threat to a particular ideological structure, to a cultural hierarchy organized around an essential *Englishness,* which defines *British* identity.[2] There were already worrying developments that threaten that identity—integration into the European Community (dominated by its defeated enemy, Germany), the demands of Welsh and Scottish nationalists, and the unresolvable civil war in Northern Ireland between two collective religious identities. It was too much to be confronted in addition by immigrants from the ex-colonies (a vanished empire) trying to politicize their alien traditions in England itself. Thus, the Rushdie affair in Britain should be seen primarily as yet another symptom of postimperial British identity in crisis, not—as most commentators have represented it—as an unhappy instance of some immigrants with difficulties in adjusting to a new and more civilized world.

The Idea of a Common National Culture

John Patten, home minister responsible for race relations, intervened publicly in the Rushdie affair first by writing an open letter (published in the *Times* daily newspaper) addressed to "leaders and representatives" of Britain's Muslim community. Perhaps its most striking feature is its firm, paternal style. Referring to *The Satanic Verses,* he opens: "The Government understands how much hurt and anxiety that book has caused, and we also understand that insults, particularly to a deeply held faith, are not easily forgotten or forgiven." Here, surely, is the atavistic voice of an English colonial governor responding kindly to the injured sensibilities of his native subjects.

---

2. Contrary to what is so often asserted, Britain was not an ancient, homogeneous society into which an alien presence had suddenly been introduced. The structure of British identity is a relatively new creation. In "Englishness and the National Culture," Philip Dodd has recently summarized the evidence for the thesis that "the diverse cultural histories and contemporary cultural life of these islands were organised and stabilised as a national culture" during the period 1880–1920. See Colls and Dodd 1986, 21.

Patten does not present himself as the spokesman of a democratically elected government rejecting the political demand of a particular body of citizens that another citizen's legal right to free speech be curtailed. He does not find it sufficient to say that there is no law which would permit the banning of *The Satanic Verses*, and that the government will not extend any existing law to do so. Patten, who echoes the views of British liberal opinion, presents himself as the voice of a fatherly government addressing "the leaders and representatives" of an alien population, which now lives under its protection.

The migration of people from the ex-colonies to Britain since World War II, Patten assures the Muslims, has "added to Britain's wealth of culture and tradition." It would seem that this rich culture-and-tradition (both in the singular) is already in place, an essence that can be added to by foreigners precisely to the extent that there is an affinity between what they bring and what is essentially there. That is why Patten immediately goes on to compliment them by describing them as potential Tories: "Many have come with values that can only be admired such as firm faith; a commitment to family life; a belief in hard work and enterprise; respect for the law and a will to succeed. To their credit, they have kept those values at the core of their life in Britain, too." Of course, he goes on, he quite understands that there are inevitable stresses and strains, given the adjustments immigrants have had to make in their new environment. "No one would expect or indeed want British Muslims to lay aside their faith, traditions or heritage," he assures them (although this is precisely what many white Britishers do want, at least in the measure to which they—the latter—decide is essential). But there are various things immigrant children really *must* learn, "if they are to make the most of their lives and opportunities as British citizens." These essentials include, according to Patten, "a fluent command of English," and also "a clear understanding of British democratic processes, of its laws, the system of Government and the history that lies behind them." The remarkable thing about these demands is that they are for skills and knowledge that very few white Britishers can confidently claim to possess.

Stressing briefly the promise of a British society in which "equality of opportunity for all" will one day prevail, Patten then proceeds to praise those Muslims who have themselves kept within the law and have publicly apologized for the bad behavior of some of their fellows. It is only after this extraordinary statement at the end of the letter that

Patten explains clearly and briefly that *The Satanic Verses* cannot be banned (Patten 1989a).

But this statement provoked by the Rushdie affair was clearly felt to be insufficient, because two weeks later John Patten produced another in the form of a mimeographed news release from the Home Office (dated July 18, 1989), "On Being British." This second pronouncement is not very long—a mere four and a half pages of double-spaced typescript. It seems at first reading to contain nothing but bland platitudes and points already made in the earlier *Times* article. Yet it was summarized and cited admiringly by the serious newspapers.[3]

The phrase "On Being British" implies that Britishness is more than a matter of paying taxes, voting, using state welfare services, and in general being subject to the laws of the country: as we shall see, it is a matter of essential sentiments and loyalties. The government feels itself obliged to explain what this essence is to immigrants (including "immigrants" who were born and schooled in Britain). Patten's disquisition doesn't contain any *information,* not even a clue as to where one might go to read up one's legal rights and duties as a British citizen. Curiously, the word *state* does not appear in his text (though it is part of the author's official designation: "Home Office Minister of State"); and *government* is used only once, en passant, right at the end with reference to "its considerable support for English-teaching programmes." "On Being British" urges "cultural minority communities" to aspire to a norm. The document is an implicit description of

---

3. For example, Michael Jones, political editor of the *Sunday Times,* in his article "Ground Rules for the British Way of Life," enthused:

Patten's special contribution is to explain the government's position in the context of our rights and obligations as citizens, regardless of race or creed. He lays down two guiding principles for our role in society: freedom of speech, thought and expression, and the notion of the rule of law. It follows that if Mr Rushdie offends Muslims by his writings, it is sad but too bad.

Mr Patten made a second, even more emphatic, attempt to explain the ground rules for being British last week. Stressing the importance of what we have in common—our democracy, our laws, our history and the English language—he declared: "We are obliged to live together and work together . . . one cannot decide to accept those rights in a democracy which one likes and reject the less convenient obligations that go with them." In other words, nobody is trying to force ethnic minorities to assimilate with the rest of us. But they must actively participate in our society and that means recognising and supporting those loyalties which bind this country together.

the white cultural majority community, which supposedly sets the norm, and so of what that cultural essence is.[4]

On the very first page, Patten makes the point that "being British" has to do with "those things which . . . we have in common. Our democracy and our laws, the English language, and the history that has shaped modern Britain." At the center of this history is the idea of "freedom"—"freedom to choose one's faith, to choose one's political allegiance, to speak and write freely, to meet, argue and demonstrate, and to play a part in shaping events." The word *freedom* occurs with remarkable frequency in this short text, evoking as it does so the central theme of innumerable Whig histories of England.[5] And Englishness, as every white English native knows, lies at the core of being British.

The idea of freedom appears to consist of two interconnected ideas, tolerance and obligation, which are also repeated again and again in Patten's discourse. "Tolerance" requires acceptance of diversity ("There is, as I have said, plenty of room for diversity, precisely because our traditions are those of tolerance"), a diversity based on the individual's right to believe, act, and speak as he or she chooses. But rights create "obligations," above all the obligation to respect the rights of others— "respect for the safety of their property," no less than for their right to speak and write "freely."

Rights, of course, have to be created before the obligation to respect them can arise. And it is inevitable that some rights will conflict with others. But Patten does not point out that respect for property rights (as opposed to the right to choose and follow one's faith) takes precedence in the British way of life over the right to speak and write freely. Thus, the laws on patents, copyright (on music, images, texts), contracts in restraint of trade, protection of trade secrets, and intellectual property all involve restrictions on free expression in Britain. Unlike other restrictions, such as those relating to blasphemy or incite-

4. Fifteen years earlier, Sir William Rees-Mogg, then editor of the *Times,* had identified Britishness with civilization itself: "There are people about who hate civilization because it exists, the enemies of the inner spiritual essence of our national life" (quoted in Nairn 1988, 56). The occasion was an attempt by a man (later judged to be mentally ill) to kidnap Princess Anne from her car in the middle of London.

5. "Nineteenth-century Liberalism represented English freedom as an ideal force, deep within the national character, and capable of universal dissemination as England's special gift to the world" (Colls, "Englishness and the Political Culture," in Colls and Dodd 1986, 30).

ment to hatred, which arise because of undesirable *consequences* that public communication is assumed to have, these are property rights that consist precisely in limiting free expression. Patten does not tell us that the structure of British life is unthinkable without these legal limitations on free speech, in a sense that is not true for the laws forbidding blasphemy or incitement to hatred.

What is also not immediately clear from Patten's statements is whether "diversity" is an intrinsic feature of the British way of life or something allowed only when divergences do not contradict an essential—and therefore unchangeable—Britishness. When immigrants bring new practices, beliefs, and discourses with them to Britain, do they extend the scope of British life or are they conditionally tolerated by the British state (which is essentially the state of the cultural majority)?

Everyone, according to Patten's exposition of the British idea of freedom, has a "right to make a contribution" and a right to enter the mainstream. Apparently this is always an individual choice: "Our democratic system and processes not only recognise the value of the individual's right to make a contribution or to hold distinct personal views. Our system also protects and safeguards these rights." Only the individual, so the reader is given to understand, can be the object of tolerance and the subject of rights. And so, too, participation in "British life" is open only to individuals: "participation includes playing one's part in the economy, playing one's part as a neighbour, making a contribution which goes beyond one's own family or indeed community." According to Patten, an agreed cultural script defining the roles that British individuals may play is already in place.

Since family and community are the only groups mentioned in the document, the implication seems to be that groups have no place in the public sphere. But as this is patently false (the public sphere is occupied by a complex array of business institutions, professional bodies, trade unions, social movements, and opinion groups representing each of these), Patten's formulation must be read as intending to discourage cultural minorities from establishing themselves as corporate political actors. As far as cultural minority members are concerned, they must participate in Britishness (the quality that makes them part of the essential culture) as individuals.

This participation, Patten insists, does not mean assimilation, "forgetting one's cultural roots." But that is only because and to the extent that the "being British" to which he refers presupposes a hierarchy of cultural spaces that he does not mention. Thus, neither the English working classes nor the Scots, Welsh, and Northern Irish can be absorbed as collectivities into elite, metropolitan, English culture, for these separate cultural spaces are necessary to Englishness as the expression of a governing norm.[6] *Individual* assimilation across these spaces has always been possible and indeed encouraged. The concept of tolerance relates specifically to this ideological arrangement and to the cultural script authorized by it.

What being British involves, says Patten again at the end of his disquisition, is what "we have in common": a framework of laws, the English language, and a history. But anyone in Britain who reads Patten knows that in practice such abstractions acquire their definition from a particular elite: *(a)* those who interpret and administer what counts as *English* law (the very different framework of Roman law is basic to Scotland), *(b)* those who speak "the Queen's English" and who maintain "English literature" (a category that includes Beowulf, as well as contemporary Scots authors, but not African novelists), and *(c)* those who write and authorize the histories of England taught in schools and universities (thus excluding Indian historians of the British Empire).

The life of the English governing classes—its values, codes, and sensibilities—is the core of British culture. It is therefore only others who need to be warned against the treacherous lure of dual loyalties: "One cannot be British on one's own exclusive terms or on a selective basis, nor is there room for dual loyalties where those loyalties openly contradict one another." That is, participation in British life *does,* after all, require "forgetting one's cultural roots" if they cannot in some way be accommodated by Britishness. Diversity is to be tolerated only if it does not conflict with British identity, to which it is necessarily external.

In nationalist vocabularies, the term *loyalty* has the useful quality of fusing two meanings: legal subjection and moral attachment. Patten employs the term in this double sense here. Thus, the straightforward statement that as a British subject one is exclusively bound to the British Crown, when in Britain,[7] is linked to the moralistic judgment

---

6. As T. S. Eliot pointed out (1962, chap. 3).

7. This qualification is necessary because the United Kingdom, unlike many countries, accepts the principle of dual nationality.

that it is reprehensible to be attached to divergent identities (people, traditions) that are defined as contradictory. It is clearly felt to be insufficient to say that "speech and behaviour contrary to the law of the land will be penalised" because it is rightly assumed that breaking the law (however seriously) does not render one non-British. Indeed, crimes such as treason can be committed only by someone who *is* British.

Conceived as a medium of communication, the English language is, of course, a necessary part of "what we have in common," but it is not clear how in that sense it can be said to be the object of "loyalties," nor is it obvious that language conceived as a discursive formation (i.e., as expressions of distinctive ways of acting and thinking) can be said to be something all classes and traditions found in Britain "have in common." The loyalty demanded must therefore be loyalty to a historiography that articulates a secular unity for all of Britain: "Whether our background is Pakistani, Polish, Vietnamese, or whatever, we all need to know our particular background and to cherish our own history and special traditions," says Patten. "Alongside that, however, a sound and detailed knowledge of British history and of Britain's part in world history, a feeling for what has shaped our institutions, is vital to living in and understanding the complexities of Britain today. It is essential to 'being British.'" It is evident that Patten assumes there is no significant contradiction between "our own history and special traditions" and an account of "Britain's part in world history" accepted by most British teachers, textbook writers, and examiners—or if there is, then our "loyalties" must be given to the latter. Not surprisingly, the teaching of history in schools has become a matter of primary concern for the present government and the opposition (Kettle 1990). An authorized history, so it is hoped, will express "British culture" and help develop in all children a sense of loyalty toward it. But as the educational system is not designed to make all children equally familiar with that history, the nationalist hope must be that loyalty will be given to those who speak in its name, those who draw on it to make the framework of laws which "we have in common."

A contested history might, however, raise some questions regarding Patten's easy assumption that "being British" essentially presupposes tolerance. For let us not forget that British imperial history (through which British identity was recently constructed) initiated the forcible transformation of innumerable conquered societies in the direction of "British culture."

Patten's document is not to be described as an expression of Thatcherite neoliberalism. On the contrary, it draws on a much broader liberal tradition, including elements from the older, collectivist liberalism of J. S. Mill and T. H. Green (Hobhouse 1964 [1911]). What Patten seeks to articulate and defend (with the approval of a wide range of opinion outside the Conservative Party) is the notion of a culture, *a common way of life,* that defines at once the substantive values of a secular British identity and the formal basis of a diversified and rationally justifiable society.

"Culture" as a Project of the Modernizing State/Empire

To recapitulate my main argument briefly: The political mobilization of Muslim immigrants in Britain to get *The Satanic Verses* banned produced an emotional reaction on the part of the liberal elite which was out of all proportion to what actually happened. It also produced an unprecedented statement from a government minister about British identity that was directed at the Muslim minority, a statement that was warmly welcomed as representative of liberal elite opinion. I argue that these extraordinary facts require explaining, and suggest that an explanation should be sought by looking for what the British liberal elite felt was being threatened. My view is that the perceived danger is a matter neither of law and order nor of freedom of speech; it is a matter, rather, of the politicization of a religious tradition that has no place within the cultural hegemony that has defined British identity over the last century—especially as that tradition has come from a recent colonial society.

Before I proceed with a discussion of the contemporary British scene, a note on the concept of culture may be useful.

Raymond Williams reminded us in *Key Words* that the complex semantic structure of the word *culture* is of comparatively recent origin. He identified three interconnected senses of the noun: First, the processes of intellectual, spiritual and aesthetic development, a usage dating from the eighteenth century; second, an inherited way of life, whether of a particular people (as in Herder) or of humanity in general (as in Klemm and Tylor); finally, in its most familiar form, the activities and creations of literary and artistic endeavor (Williams 1983, 90; Kroeber and Kluckhohn 1952).

In *Culture and Society,* Williams had traced the evolution of that structure in the arguments of English social critics of the nineteenth and early twentieth century. The distinctively modern sense of culture, he argued, emerges with the formation of industrial liberal society. Where once culture meant the training that provided mind and soul with their intellectual and moral accomplishments, it now also means an entire way of life—the common way of life of a whole people.

> The idea of culture is a general reaction to a general and major change in the conditions of our common life. *Its basic element is its effort at total qualitative assessment.* The change in *the whole form of our common life* produced, as a necessary reaction, an emphasis on attention to this whole form. Particular change will modify an habitual discipline, shift an habitual action. General change, when it has worked itself clear, drives us back on *our general designs,* which we have to learn to look at again, and as a whole. *The working-out of the idea of culture is a slow reach again for control.* (Williams 1961, 285; emphases added)

This totalizing project expressed itself in the inclusion of the entire adult population in the electoral processes of parliamentary democracy, as well as in the growing articulation (interconnection, expression, and construction) of civil society. An inevitable consequence of this development was the fact that all aspects of life (in its social as well as biological senses) were now to be politicized.

The last quarter of the nineteenth century and the first half of the twentieth witnessed the development of integrating, improving institutions: industrial and welfare legislation, public-sector education, the arts (museums, libraries, etc.), local (i.e., municipal) government, national insurance, public hygiene and health care, trade unions, etc. These institutions were the outcome of initiatives by members of the upper classes, as well as of pressure from militant dissenters and working-class organizations, but they should not be thought of as expressing a single, essential social logic. They involved diverse motives and practices, and they certainly did not create a "common life" (in the sense of work and leisure, of worship and sensibility, of commitments and aspirations) for all classes in Britain. Nevertheless, the dominant political ideology of new liberalism enabled these developments to be conceptualized in relation to a normalizing project, thus making it plausible to think of culture in the way Williams has traced.

Although Williams does not describe these conditions in *Culture and Society* (which is largely concerned with the opinions of literary men and not with administrative practices), it is important to stress that they defined the political relevance of the modern sense of culture in Britain. For in these conditions was constructed an increasingly differentiated domain on which the "common life" of a whole people (the British nation) could be conceived in order to be rationally re-created. Never without tensions and conflicts, and certainly not every-where successful, the work of constructing an integrated British soci-ety (with its core culture) reveals one aspect of the modern faith in liberal reason.

But there is another aspect to the career of the modern concept of culture in Britain that Williams does not mention: the British Empire.

"Empire," wrote the eminent Cambridge historian Sir Ernest Barker, "is not only a form of government. It is also a mission of culture—and of something higher than culture" (Barker 1941, 20). In the period between the two world wars, the British Empire consisted of the dominions (white settler-dominated countries like Canada, Aus-tralia, and South Africa), the dependent colonies (including Africa and the West Indies), and India (both princely states and British India). "The problem of culture," as it was formulated in the reflections of the British elite, applied only to the nonwhite populations and had to do with the practices of controlled reconstruction. Barker (1941, 31) describes it initially as emerging from the clash of unequal cultures:

> The cultural problem emerges from, and it has its analogies with, the biological and the economic problems. It is a problem which begins in the conflict of different social habits, different forms of political order, different worlds . . . of knowledge and of art: it is a problem which proceeds from conflict to contact, and, in so proceeding, rises to the level of a problem of intermixture, or at any rate co-ordination.

When the culture of "a dominant stock" (who, it is assumed, must have common social habits) comes into contact with a "native cul-ture," Barker observes, the question of contact becomes critical for the latter. It can be enriched, or it may disintegrate, with the introduc-tion of new (i.e., Western) elements: everything depends on a proper coordination (conceptual and political) of the process.

The fact of imperial rule thus renders "the problem of culture" into the British obligation to identify, study, and normalize the cul-ture of its subject peoples (whence the importance of "the rise of sociology and anthropology" (Barker 1941, 32), and also to help integrate them into modern (i.e., Western) civilization by way of "amalgamation" and "persuasion." This obligation applies equally to India[8] and to the colonies,[9] although the native peoples in each case belong to different levels of progress. What is interesting here is that this imperial talk of "amalgam" (like the contemporary radical talk of "hybridity") presupposes the idea of original ("pure") cultures coming into contact to create a new, emergent, and more progressive historical identity.

For their part, British functionalist anthropologists of the interwar period conceptualized the problem of culture in a way that directly addressed the problem of reconstruction. "We meet this tri-partite division—old Africa, imported Europe, and the New Composite Culture—all along the route of 'plane, railway, and motor road," observed Malinowski (1938, viii). What mattered for dealing rationally with this emergent cultural identity was what actually survived of a native culture together with the new European elements absorbed by it: the totality that could be controlled, improved, protected, and developed was the way of life that actually existed now, not the "reconstituted past"—as Malinowski put it—of life before European contact. "What, therefore, is relevant from the practical point of view?" Malinowski writes. "Obviously, the still surviving quota of culture and tradition observable in present-day field-work. It seems unnecessary to emphasize that only what still lives [within the new composite identity] can

8. "A century ago, when English became the language of education (after Lord William Bentinck had stated, in 1835, that 'the great object of the British Government ought to be the promotion of European literature and science among the natives of India'), trade and government, the two previous links, began to pass into a contact of culture which made a firmer and far subtler link. In this new but now century-old process of culture contact, the old culture of India has drawn on the culture of the West: it has absorbed Western ideas of nationalism and constitutionalism: it has begun to fuse into a new amalgam with Western culture—an amalgam which has still to settle the nature of its own further development and (more important still) the nature of the contribution it can make to the general progress of man. A great responsibility is laid upon Great Britain, the partner with India in the making of this amalgam—as great, and even greater, is laid upon India herself—for the settling of that future and the making of that contribution" (Barker 1941, 113–14).

9. "[The British] have sought, with a growing sense of the trust imposed upon them, to introduce among the native peoples of their colonial empire a culture which is without compulsion, and a faith which acts by persuasion. . . . When the British Government declares that 'it is the mission of Great Britain to work continuously for the training and education of the African towards a higher intellectual, moral and economic level,' it is not using idle words" (Barker 1941, 161–62).

give any guidance to those who have to control a living native society. Only forces of tradition actively influencing the sentiments of living men and women matter for those who have to deal with their destiny" (Malinowski 1938, xxxi). Although the expression is not used, this might be described as an attempt to conceptualize the problem of "multiculturalism" in colonial settings. The new, syncretic society in Africa requires the proper theoretical and practical coordination of dominant (European) and subordinate (native) cultures: equal respect for all cultures, but the realities of political power require the subordinate (less progressive) to adjust to the dominant (more progressive). "There are cultural elements which are not allowed to continue," Malinowski (1938, xxviii) points out, "because they are repugnant to Whites." And so eventually, in the new composite culture, they become repugnant also to Blacks.

Incidentally, I do not regard Malinowski's views as representative of all British anthropologists (nor should my comments be taken as an attempt at a moral criticism of Malinowski's views). Thus, unlike Malinowski, Radcliffe-Brown and his pupils considered the concept of culture theoretically uninteresting.[10] My concern is to identify culture as part of a language of total colonial reconstruction (which should not, in any case, be confused with the *practices* of colonial rule—still less with the practices and discourses of the colonized). My point is that a striking feature of this language was its exclusive focus on a presently existing, directly observable, and therefore normalizable totality of elements having a heterogeneous origin—and in this respect Malinowski's writings are no different from Radcliffe-Brown's.

What emerges from the observations by Barker and Malinowski is that the concept of culture, in the distinctively modern sense of a common life, and representable as such, had become, by the thirties and forties, part of a language of controlled reconstruction—in the terrain of empire as in Britain itself—according to the dictates of liberal reason. It would be wrong to represent this language simply as a cyni-

---

10. For Radcliffe-Brown the central theoretical concept was social structure, which he believed was directly observable: "We do not observe a 'culture,' since that word denotes, not any concrete reality, but an abstraction, and as it is commonly used a vague abstraction. But direct observation does reveal to us that . . . human beings are connected by a complex network of social relations. I use the term 'social structure' to denote this network of actually existing relations" (1952, 192). The above quotation comes from an essay first published in 1940.

cal device of imperial rule,[11] because a similar logic was at work both in Britain and in the empire—namely, the aim of transforming (and enabling) subjects and not merely of repressing them. This is not to suggest, of course, that political domination in the empire was the same as in Britain. My argument is only that in both contexts the concept of culture was part of that totalizing project which Williams identified with the emergence of industrial, liberal society. The unclarity of the notion of multiculturalism lies precisely in the question of its compatibility with that project after the arrival of nonwhite immigrants from what was once the empire into a self-proclaimed liberal society.

"Other Races," "Other Religions": Ex-colonial Labor Comes to Britain

In the immediate postwar period, the labor shortage in Britain was met by workers imported from Poland and Italy, and then, from the end of the 1950s to the end of the 1960s, from ex-colonial countries, mostly the Caribbean, India, Pakistan, and Bangladesh. At first, they were mainly recruited by the British to work in the London transport system, the nationalized health service, and the privately owned textile mills in the north of England. Subsequently, others joined them on an individual or family basis. During this period, large numbers of Irish immigrants also entered the country—as, indeed, they had done throughout the preceding hundred years.

In contemporary Britain, the word *immigrant* has come to be identified by public opinion with non-European settlers—largely people from the Caribbean and South Asia. This is significant because the term is applied to the offspring of these immigrants, even though they have been born in Britain, but it does not apply to white immigrants, who are, according to the 1981 census, a more numerous category than nonwhite immigrants. According to that census, out of a total population of nearly 53 million, nonwhite immigrants (including those born in Britain) were a little more than two million, and of these Muslims accounted for less than half. We are dealing here with comparatively small numbers.[12]

---

11. See G. Viswanathan's illuminating monograph on literary study and British rule in India (1989).

12. Compare this with Europe, where the overwhelming majority of nonwhite im-

These immigrants from ex-colonial countries are not simply importers of "cultural differences" which they are free to synthesize and develop as they please in their new social environment. They have been inserted into very specific economic, political, and ideological conditions. Most of them live in relatively deprived inner-city areas, have poorly paid jobs, are overrepresented in manufacturing industries compared with the total population, and suffer from very much higher rates of unemployment—especially among the young who have been born in Britain. The everyday practices of immigrants are constrained in different ways by preexisting British institutions: Parliament, city administrations, employers, trade unions, the police, the English system of law, state schools, the welfare system, and so forth.

In his comparative study of race in the United States and Britain, Katznelson has given an account of how, in the early years of immigration, the British liberal elite sought to exclude the issue of race from politics (Katznelson 1973, 125). After an initial brief period when the existence of *any* problem was denied—which ended with the first race riots in Nottingham and London at the end of the fifties—a new, bipartisan consensus was arrived at in the form of the 1965 Race Relations Bill. "The structural arrangements announced by the political consensus White Paper," Katznelson notes, "did not integrate the Third World immigrants into the politics of institutionalized class conflict that characterize the liberal collectivist age, but rather set up alternative political structures to deflect the politics of race from Westminster to the National Committee for Commonwealth Immigrants, and from local political arenas to voluntary liaison committees" (150). This was, he suggests, an adaptation of colonial principles of indirect rule to the special conditions created in Britain itself. Such an arrangement, he points out, did not mean that the immigrants were now reconciled to their predicament, only that the problem of racial discrimination and resentment was cast in a form that proved virtually intractable.

However, according to more recent studies, this political exclusion does not appear to have been as effective at the time as Katznelson suggests. For example Anwar (1986) describes, in detail, the increasingly organized involvement of nonwhites in British party politics im-

---

migrants are Muslims. Here, too, anti-Muslim sentiments have recently become disturbingly prominent—as in *l'affaire des foulardes Islamiques* in France.

mediately after the 1966 general elections. Because they were on the whole settled in large urban concentrations and thus able to generate higher levels of turnout at elections, they were able to influence electoral results in a number of marginal seats. Most nonwhite voters conformed to their socioeconomic category by voting Labour, but other parties were also able to attract them. One of the most remarkable indications of this was the formation of an Anglo–West Indian Conservative Society and the more vigorous Anglo-Asian Conservative Society. The latter, especially, was given high priority by the Conservative Central Office; Thatcher is now its president, and other leading Tories are among its vice-presidents. All major political parties have begun to adopt nonwhite candidates and to canvass for them. A small number of nonwhites have succeeded in being elected to Parliament, and much larger numbers have emerged at the level of local (city) government. Indeed, in 1985 the first Asian lord mayor in Britain (Labour Councillor Mohammed Ajeeb) was elected in Bradford, the city that has since gained worldwide publicity as the place where *The Satanic Verses* was publicly burned.

Katznelson's argument regarding the nonintegration of the politics of race in Britain into an "institutionalized class conflict framework" (1973, 185) needs to be revised. Nonwhites (especially South Asians) have begun, however marginally, to make the political parties respond to their electoral power—the level at which institutionalized class conflict finds expression in Britain. But there is another, even more important point. Precisely because the prevalent mode of dealing with nonwhite immigrants (whether through institutions like the Commission for Racial Equality or through the party system) has been in terms of race, the liberal political system has been preoccupied, as in the case of class politics, with the problem of distributive justice. Immigrants are represented as citizens who suffer relative deprivation, analogous to (and sometimes, as in the recently popularized notion of the underclass, congruent with) that of class. The political problem, for race as for class, is how to eradicate discrimination (unequal treatment) in civil society. The question of traditions and identities—that is, of maintaining and elaborating one's own difference—is assumed to be either already settled or something to be settled outside the sphere of national politics, for that sphere is where something called "core values" and "what we have in common" are said to be located.

In fact, of course, traditions and identities are neither finally settled nor relegatable beyond the sphere of the political. The very concept of "being British," as presented by Patten and reaffirmed by liberal opinion in post-Rushdie Britain, is political. But so, too, are the categories that are used to describe and deal with the immigrants who are urged to identify themselves with "British culture."

Political Vocabularies for Talking about Difference

The terms *colored* or *New Commonwealth immigrants, blacks, ethnic,* or *cultural minorities,* as used in Britain, belong to slightly different historical phases and political contexts, but all of them serve to make a primary separation between the so-called host society, or white majority, and the immigrants, blacks, or cultural minorities.

In fact, nonwhites relate to British society in a variety of ways. Thus, although they all suffer from institutionalized racial discrimination, West Indians are in some ways more akin to the indigenous English than are most South Asians. They are Christians (although most belong to their own churches), and at home they speak English. Their younger generation has taken a leading part in the formation of British pop culture and has excelled in British sport. When the first postwar West Indian immigrants arrived in Britain (and before they had absorbed the full brunt of British racism), they often spoke of coming to "the mother country."[13] In these respects, South Asians were and still remain culturally quite unlike other black immigrants, as this statement from a study of British racism and black culture underlines: "Some inner-city whites, particularly the young, may find much in 'West Indian' culture which they can evaluate positively. If black culture appears in syncretized Afro-Caribbean forms which are relatively desirable and attractive [to whites] when contrasted to the more obviously 'alien' Asian varieties, the white racist may be faced with considerable problems."[14]

13. This was often echoed in government rhetoric of the time. For example, in 1954, Henry Hopkinson, Tory minister of state for the colonies, observed, "in a world in which restriction on personal movement and immigration have increased we can still take pride in the fact that a man can say *civis Britannicus sum* whatever his colour may be, and we take pride in the fact that he wants to and can come to the mother country" (*Hansard,* 5 November 1954, col. 827).

14. Gilroy 1987, 231. This argument seems careless: there is surely no inconsistency in racists finding the arts (even the bodies) of those they consider "racially inferior" to be attractive.

The term *black,* signifying all nonwhite immigrants and their off-spring (West Indian as well as South Asian), is used equally by the left and the right in Britain. While for the right it implies a racial or cultural unassimilability, for the left it underlines the experience of racial discrimination and the determination to organize politically against it through a radically reconstructed cultural identity. But South Asians have begun to argue that in using it in this way, both right and left share the assumption that South Asian traditions and identities cannot become part of modern Britain. "The drawback with 'black' used as a descriptive term," one South Asian writer observed recently, "is that it defines people not in terms of their own identity but by the treatment [of them] by others; the aspirational use [of black], on the other hand, overcomes this deficiency but at the price of making British Asians have to define themselves in a framework historically and internationally developed by people in search of African roots" (Madood 1988). This viewpoint does not reject the call for alliances in the face of British racism, but only the assumption that Asians must elaborate their identities in Britain along the same lines as do immigrants from the West Indies.

The expressions *cultural* (or *ethnic*) *minorities* have also become current over the last two decades. But terms like *majority* and *minority* (which today belong to the vocabulary of electoral and parliamentary politics), when used together with the word *culture,* raise an interesting ambiguity. For whereas "majority" and "minority" relate to the principle by which public policies are made and unmade, "culture" is virtually coterminous with the social life of particular populations, including habits and beliefs conveyed across generations. One is always born into a culture, and even if one alters one's way of life later, one always belongs to traditions by reference to which one's difference is constructed and elaborated. Belonging to an electoral majority or minority is a matter of being enumerated ex post facto. To the extent that the mutually dependent concepts of majority and minority belong to the liberal political system, they presuppose a constitutional device for *resolving* differences. To speak of cultural majorities and minorities is therefore to posit ideological hybrids. It is also to make the implicit claim that members of some cultures truly belong to a particular politically defined place, but those of others (minority cultures) do not—either because of recency (immigrants) or of archaicness (aborigines).

The expressions *cultural minorities* and *ethnic groups* (the former, incidentally, is never applied to the English upper classes; the latter never to the English, Scots, Welsh, or Irish) are more than part of public political discourse. They have recently acquired the status of law. The definition of ethnic group as a legal category was established in the leading case *Mandla v. Dowell Lee* (1983), which went up to the House of Lords. In the words of Lord Fraser:

> For a group to constitute an ethnic group in the 1976 [Race Relations] Act, it must . . . regard itself and be regarded by others, as a distinct community by virtue of certain characteristics. Some of these characteristics are essential; others are not essential but one or more of them will commonly be found and will help to distinguish the group from the surrounding community. The conditions which appear to me to be essential are these: (1) a long shared history, of which the group is conscious as distinguishing it from other groups, and the memory of which keeps it alive; (2) a cultural tradition of its own, including family and social customs and manners, often but not necessarily associated with religious observance. In addition to those two essential characteristics the following characteristics are . . . relevant: (3) either a common geographical origin, or descent from a small number of common ancestors; (4) a common language, not necessarily peculiar to the group; (5) a common literature peculiar to the group; (6) a common religion different from that of neighbouring groups or from the general community surrounding it; (7) being a minority or being an oppressed or a dominant group within a larger community, for example a conquered people . . . and their conquerors might both be ethnic groups.[15]

Although relevant criteria logically apply to the Scots, the Welsh, and the Protestants and Catholics in Northern Ireland, the term "ethnic group" is not applied to any of them. The legal category "ethnic group" is in effect a device enabling English courts to normalize "ethnic customs" as exemptions from the rule[16]—without, however, giving the

15. Quoted in Poulter 1986, 185–86. The particular concern of *Mandla v. Dowell Lee* was to determine whether Sikhs were an ethnic group and protected as such against discrimination under the provisions of the 1976 Race Relations Act.

16. For example: "Marriage ceremonies must generally be conducted in the presence of either an officiating clergyman of the Church of England or a registrar or an 'authorised person' (usually a minister of the religious group concerned). In most instances it is a criminal offence knowingly and wilfully to celebrate a marriage outside

populations concerned corporate status. There is by now a fair body of case law in this domain, but precisely because it is by definiti>n concerned with *exceptions,* it has tended to give legal ballast to the idea of cultural *minorities.* It should be stressed, however, that the courts are concerned to ensure a single legal authority for "ethnic communities" and "the general community surrounding" them, not to promote or bring about an inclusive common life. True, the customs of ethnic communities must be consistent with certain existing laws (for example, children may not marry, and they must receive what is defined as a proper education, regardless of so-called ethnic customs). But consistency of ethnic customs with existing laws does not make for a unitary British culture, in spite of the imperializing morality of the English liberal middle class.

Perhaps the crucial point about a politically established cultural minority is that constitutionally it cannot authorize new cultural arrangements but only request them. Furthermore, the majority may bind itself to tolerate the permanent difference represented by a minority, and even to respect it as an exception, but by definition the minority cannot be accorded equality. This has been the source of a disturbing political dilemma for those who advocate multiculturalism as a general policy for dealing with the immigrant population. Does equal respect for cultural diversity mean the exclusion of cultural minorities from equal power?

All attempts to resolve this dilemma by insisting on some version of the distinction between public (equal access) and private (exclusive and heterogeneous) domains have failed.[17] And this is because—as

---

the hours of 8 am to 6 pm though a marriage solemnised outside these hours will nevertheless remain valid. Marriages in a register office or registered building must be solemnised with open doors, i.e. the public must not be excluded if they wish to attend, and the bride and groom must attend in person and exchange their vows using a standard form of words. . . . From all these regulations concerning solemnisation two select groups are exempt. These are Quakers and 'persons professing the Jewish religion.' . . . Their ceremonies may take place at any hour of the day or night, need not be in any particular building (and may even be celebrated in a private home or garden) and do not require the presence of any state official. They are merely required to follow the usages of the Society of Friends or the usages of the Jews, as the case may be" (Poulter 1986, 34).

17. For example, John Rex (1987), a prominent British sociologist specializing in race relations, argues, like many others in Britain today, that the construction of a *democratic* multicultural society requires a distinction between a "public domain," equally accessible to all citizens, and "private domains" in which religious and familial distinctions can be cultivated.

decades of studies dealing with the social workings of the modern British state have made clear—the so-called private domain is continuously structured and restructured by political, economic, and legal practices that supposedly belong to the public domain.

Multiculturalism: For and Against

Over the last two decades, multiculturalism has become a widely accepted goal for British society (Swann 1985). The main reason for this lies not in an ideological commitment to cultural diversity but in the attempt to deal with practical problems encountered in education and the social services—two major institutions of Britain's welfare state. It is here that we observe the construction of diversity as an *effect* of modern government.

It was "the problem of underachievement" by immigrant children that first led to increased attention being paid to institutionalized racism, including the negative attitudes of teachers toward the ethnic background of their immigrant pupils. This resulted in a small number of schools being established outside the state sector by worried immigrant parents.[18] But many Local Education Authorities, responding to a variety of political pressures, encouraged schools to use teaching materials from the cultural and historical backgrounds of those pupils—and in some cases even to develop Black Studies—in order to give them a positive self-image.[19] Multicultural education has subsequently attracted nonwhite critics who see in it a compensatory model based on the conception of immigrants as inherently limited and thus as a special problem for white society. Some radical critics have even argued that multiculturalism is simply a means of "containing the black problem," and they insist (in words that Malinowski would have approved of) that "teachers should represent the present strengths rather than the past history of the black population."[20] These critics see multiculturalism as a kind of false consciousness and not as a mode

18. In the case of Muslims, there were also religious motives for setting up such separate schools.

19. In an analysis of recent examination results from London schools, Parekh (1989b, 35) concludes that "racism cannot account for the differences and we need to look at their economic and cultural backgrounds."

20. Carr-Hill and Chadha-Boreham 1988, 153. For a more extended criticism of multicultural education from a Marxist perspective, see Sarup 1986.

of normalization within the modern state. In this respect, they are basically in agreement with those who propose multiculturalism as the proper form of education for *all* British children (Halstead 1988), because both assume that learning about different ways of life at school is a way of respecting (or perpetuating) those differences outside school.

In the provision of social services, the notion of multiculturalism (cultural diversity) has had a trajectory comparable to that in education. It has emerged out of a concern to engage effectively (and equally) with a variety of immigrant communities. But social workers wanting to take the cultural diversity of their clients seriously have been criticized for being ineffective and worse:

> The primary objection to cultural diversity as an organising principle is that it ignores the material and political realities of contemporary Britain. The difficulties faced by the black population are the result not only of migration and differences in culture and language but also of living in a society which is hostile to black people, denies them equal life chances and can expose them to enormous material and psychological pressure. The clients of social services [are] present[ed] with not only linguistic and cultural complexities, but also with the profound effects of racism. In order to offer effective help social services institutions must therefore be sensitive not only to language and culture but also the processes of racism. (Roys 1988, 221)

The main argument against multiculturalism from the radical left has been that it ignores the power of racism. This complaint is justified, though not always in the sense in which it is intended—namely, that entrenched racist prejudices (individual and institutional) prevent the full realization of ethnic equality. For, in education as in the social services, the discourse and practice of multiculturalism have been integral to the process of administrative normalization within the framework of the British state. Because fundamentally *different* traditions are described as in themselves *contradictory* (and therefore in need of regulation), state power extends itself by treating them as norms to be incorporated and coordinated.

In insisting that the fundamental issues to be contested by immigrants can all be reduced to the problem of racism, radical critics have made it difficult to theorize from the left about difference—apart, that is, from the liberal principle of the *individual's* right to believe, act, and express herself differently. For while difference is certainly a crucial issue at the level of the law's treatment of individual citizens (the bearers of rights and duties), it is also relevant to the individual's desire to have and to maintain a collective identity. This desire is certainly not properly addressed through the vague notion of multiculturalism, according to which pupils learn about each other's cultural beliefs and customs at school and so develop an equal respect for these differences in the world outside. The crux of the matter lies not in the criticism that multiculturalism freezes cultural differences between entire communities or that it sanctions oppressive customs. It lies in the problematic connection between learning *about* difference and learning *to become* different; and, as in all learning, that connection is fraught with questions of power and authority.

Recently, some radical authors and cultural critics (Gilroy, of West Indian origin, and Bhabha, born in India) have argued, by drawing on a variety of postmodern ideas, against multiculturalism and in favor of what they claim is a dynamic concept of British culture and identity. Thus, Gilroy insists that

> culture is not a fixed and impermeable feature of social relations. Its forms change, develop, combine and are dispersed in historical processes. The syncretic cultures of black Britain exemplify this. They have been able to detach cultural practices from their origins and use them to found and extend the new patterns of metacommunication which give their community substance and collective identity. (1987, 217; see also 219)

That is, a fluid, syncretic black culture defines the possibility of a continuously reconstructed British identity for everyone.

Bhabha takes up a similar position. *The Satanic Verses,* he thinks, has changed the vocabulary of our cultural debate:

> It has achieved this by suggesting that there is no such whole as the nation, the culture, or even the self. Such holism is a version of reality that is most often used to assert cultural or political supremacy and seeks to obliterate the relations of difference that constitute the languages of history and culture. . . . Salman Rushdie sees the emergence of doubt, questioning and even confusion as being part of that cultural "excess" that facilitates the formation of new social identities that do not appeal to a pure and settled past, or to a unicultural present, in order to authenticate themselves. Their authority [?] lies

in the attempt to articulate emergent, hybrid forms of cultural identity. (1989b)

In other words, social identities *do* need to be authenticated, but Rushdie has taught us—so Bhabha claims—that their authentication derives from our ability continuously to reinvent ourselves out of our confused cultural conditions.[21]

One can appreciate that such writers are trying to say something significant about modern Britain, but they do so in ways that do not help to clarify thought. It is, of course, a truism to say that everything can be shown to be ultimately connected with everything else (though surely not in the same way), or that everything changes (but certainly not at the same time or at the same rate), or that everything can be conceptually subdivided (not, however, thereby losing its conceptual unity). Yet it is also a truism that cultural unities can be defined, attacked, defended, subverted, and governed. To acknowledge that cultural unities are ideological is not therefore to dismiss them as unreal. To demonstrate that elements making up a given cultural unit have diverse origins (that it is syncretic) is no proof that a unity does not exist; an account of origins tells us nothing about whether the unity is coherent—or how it may be authenticated. To argue that a culture must be seen as a process does not exclude the possibility that it is a coherent process. A coherent cultural process is not necessarily one without contradictions; rather, relations of contradiction between cultural elements themselves presuppose an embracing unity, however temporary. In short, an ostensible cultural unity may indeed not be a coherent whole—but that is something to be demonstrated, not made into a truth about every cultural unit by definition.

Let us be clear: to speak of cultural syncretism or cultural hybrids presupposes a conceptual distinction between preexisting ("pure") cultures. Of course, all apparent cultural unities are the outcomes of diverse origins, and it is misleading to think of an identifiable cultural unity as having neutrally traceable boundaries. But the term *hybridity* (like *amalgam* or *composite*) does not seem to me very useful in thinking

21. It is not clear from Bhabha's statement as to whether he thinks (a) that it is not worth appealing to the past as a way of authenticating social identities because the act of articulating emergent identities authenticates itself. Or he thinks (b) that the past, although unsettled, is not worth contesting because it is merely an aesthetic resource for inventing new narratives of the self.

about this problem. If we conceive of social life as always presupposing inherited narratives by which the unity of a life, of interconnected lives, is defined and redefined, then the matter appears in a different light. We are back again at the concept of "the whole form of our common life," which Williams historicized, but this time via MacIntyre's idea of tradition (1981, 1988). For the discursive devices of inclusion and exclusion, and the ways in which their effects come to be socially instituted through various traditions, are always integral to the concept of the whole form of our common life. In the sense of being the political *effect* of discursive traditions, "culture" does after all have boundaries, even though they are not eternally fixed. Talk about "British identity," whether by Patten or by Gilroy, presupposes an identification with something that is not French, Egyptian, Japanese, and so on.

Contrary to Bhabha's claim that "political supremacy . . . seeks to obliterate . . . difference," I have argued that it works effectively through institutionalized differences. It is a notorious tactic of political power to deny a distinct unity to populations it seeks to govern, to treat them as contingent and indeterminate. The strategy of disaggregating subject populations in order better to administer them does not require a "pure and settled past"—all it requires is a manipulable, re-creatable present. It is precisely the viewpoint of interventionist power that insists on the permeability of social groups, the unboundedness of cultural unities, and the instability of individual selves. Since speech is the first and continuous condition of political dispute, it is in the interest of interventionist power to ensure that the effectively dissolved subject cannot speak even for herself, let alone for a group. Her fragmented, indeterminate, incomplete identity can, however, be temporally "completed," "cured," "authenticated," by universal reason— or, more precisely, by its guardians.

To put the matter in concrete terms: How can South Asian immigrants in Britain defend, develop, and elaborate their *collective and historical* difference if neither their traditions nor their selves can ever be identified as *aspirations to integrity?* How can their religious traditions be criticized (whether by insiders or outsiders) if they cannot even be identified, if everything is up for grabs?

(And let us be clear, incidentally, on this matter of criticism: *no regular life*—let alone coherent "translation" or articulation of "new social identities"—can be practiced if it is continually subjected to "doubt, questioning, and even confusion.")

One may want to insist that the immigrant traditions should not be maintained in British schools—or, more strongly, that Muslims should not be allowed to have religious schools,[22] although Roman Catholics and Jews have them—but that is quite a different matter from saying that there cannot be any form of continuous tradition for immigrants in Britain because of the drastic (and supposedly welcome) change to which they are being subjected.[23] It is merely an Enlightenment prejudice that counterposes "tradition" to "change" and "reason."

The demand of British Muslims to reproduce their traditions in their own schools and, more generally, their politicization of religious beliefs and practices is a paradoxical consequence of the liberal principle of the "freedom to choose one's faith, [which is equal to the freedom] to choose one's political allegiance" (Patten). And it is a demand that seems to threaten the assumptions on which British secular identity is constructed. Neither the invention of an expressive youth culture (music, dance, street fashions, etc.), as Gilroy seems to think, nor the making of hybrid cultural forms, as Bhabha supposes, holds any anxieties for defenders of the status quo. On the contrary, such devel-

22. The British school system consists of a "maintained sector" (state schools) and an "independent sector" (private schools). All private schools must be registered and inspected for suitability of buildings and educational provisions in order to operate. If independent schools fulfill certain requirements, they may obtain voluntary maintained status; that is, they will be largely financed by the state although retaining an independent character. At present there are large numbers of voluntary aided religious schools: Roman Catholic (by far the largest single group), Church of England, Jewish, and Methodist; there are no Muslim schools in this category (see Coussins 1989). Muslim attempts to acquire voluntary aided status for their schools have been meeting with strong resistance (see Caute 1989).

23. In February 1989, a group of prominent Westernized Asians in London (academics, authors, journalists, and actors) met to issue a statement in support of Rushdie. It was entitled "Beyond Fundamentalism and Liberalism," written up by Bhabha, and published in *New Statesman and Society*, 3 March 1989. It is not clear why they felt themselves called upon to comment *as Asians* (not as Muslims, for there were non-Muslims among them, nor as immigrants, for there were no West Indians among them), but anyway they were quite persuaded that "where once we could believe in the comforts and continuities of Tradition, today we must face the responsibilities of cultural Translation," and they evidently expected that Britain's immigrant Muslims would take due note and reorder their lives accordingly.

opments are comfortably accommodated by urban consumer capitalism and by the liberal celebration of what Patten has called "the rich and diverse heritage which has added to Britain's wealth of culture and tradition." Perhaps there is no overriding moral or political reason why these developments should *not* be so accommodated. My point is simply that the claim to their having revolutionary potential is absurd.

I am not arguing against multiculturalism or syncretism in the abstract. Instead, I have tried to indicate that the specific way in which they have been practiced in contemporary Britain has meant the reinforcement of centralized state power and the aestheticization of moral identities, and that therefore neither has been seen as a potential threat to British identity. The politicization of religious traditions by Muslim immigrants is, however, quite a different matter: such a development serves to question the inevitability of the absolute nation-state—of its demands to exclusive loyalty and its totalizing cultural projects. It is a banal fact of contemporary existence that economic forces, communication systems, military interventions, and ecological disasters continually transcend nation-state boundaries, yet state authorities remain deeply suspicious of all international movements, loyalties, and relationships that they cannot regulate. It is especially in this context that the discourse of essential cultural loyalties becomes salient.

The Rushdie affair has helped to promote a new political discourse on Britishness. There have been renewed calls for assimilation, and in the general chorus about the need to teach South Asians how to be properly British, even Roy Hattersley's statement at the height of the Rushdie affair of the liberal principle of multiculturalism[24] was widely denounced by excited writers and journalists[25] as a craven appeasement of dangerous forces.

24. Thus, Roy Hattersley (1989): "The principle is clear enough. Salman Rushdie's rights as an author are absolute and ought to be inalienable. A free society does not ban books. Nor does it allow writers and publishers to be blackmailed and intimidated. The death threats are intolerable whether they are seriously meant or the rhetoric of hysteria. . . . Every group within our society must obey the law. But support for that principle is not the same as insisting that 'they' must behave like 'us.' The doctrine of assimilation is arrogant and patronising. . . . In a free society the Muslim community must be allowed to do what it likes to do as long as the choice it makes is not damaging to the community as a whole."

25. For example, the liberal journalist Edward Pearce (1989): "The Hattersley faction of the Labour party has taken up a position at once illiberal, repressive and abjectly deferential to a bunch of Islamic clergy firmly planted in the 15th century. . . . The problem of Mr Hattersley and certain allies is that they sit for bits of Birmingham,

Why this determination to remold South Asian immigrants in accordance with unitary principles? The assumption is that the presence of unassimilated immigrants constitutes a threat to social cohesion.[26] But exactly what kind of threat is it that is feared in this context, and why does it lead to invocations of a "core of common values"?[27] As I argued at the beginning of this chapter, this threat cannot be the one that is signaled when there are riots and other forms of collective violence. These explosions can be managed by new policing strategies that aim to anticipate, contain, and minimize physical damage. Whether the violence occurs at the bidding of a "foreign power" or not, the resources available to the British state are felt to be more than adequate to deal with the threat—as the measured liberal reactions to the repeated Irish bombings in London have demonstrated. In my view, the fear aroused in the Rushdie affair (and the often unrestrained language it has generated among normally staid persons) has to do with a perceived threat to authority, not to power: more precisely, the fear is generated by the fact that people who do not accept the secular liberal values of the governing classes are nevertheless able to use the liberal language of equal rights in rational argument against the secular British elite, and to avail themselves of liberal law for instituting their own strongly held religious traditions. In that context, what is crucial for government is not homogeneity versus difference as such but its authority to define crucial homogeneities *and* differences. The frighten-

---

Bradford and Leicester where the imams can cut up nasty at election time. Low politics is low politics, contemptible but understandable. In Mr Hattersley's case matters go further. Behind sanctimoniousness lies power worship. Part sycophant, part bully, he seeks fearfully to accommodate the imams and respect their power. . . . Mr Hattersley, who does his cringing with panache, says that deference to the imams should extend to curtailing publication." This vituperative language is highly unusual for a "serious" liberal newspaper talking about a right-of-center Labour politician. Even Enoch Powell did not provoke such emotional outbursts from the same source for his racist speeches. What, one is led to wonder, is the cause of this intemperateness on the part of what is, and knows itself to be, the majority opinion?

26. Thus, the final seminar in a series organized by the Commission for Racial Equality in London in the wake of the Rushdie affair was devoted to "the kind of society Britain needs to evolve into if it is to reconcile the demands of social cohesion and national integration with proper respect for cultural diversity and autonomy" (Parekh 1990).

27. As one anxious liberal writer put it: "A random and balkanised series of religious perspectives on society and its cultural diversity does not and cannot provide that core of common values which can hold society together" (Lynch 1990, 33). Durkheim, it may be recalled, maintained that a common collective consciousness was the principle of solidarity in primitive—as opposed to modern—societies.

ing thing about the Rushdie affair for the British liberal elite is the existence of political activity by a small population that seeks authority for its difference in its own religious traditions that appear to disrupt—spatially and temporally—the ideological unity of the nation-state.[28] (There was a time, not so long ago, when Jews, too, were suspected of harboring dual loyalties.) And it does so in a discourse and through institutions that the liberal elite has itself consecrated.

28. The Muslims in Britain are not homogeneous in terms of class, language, or sect—nor do they have a single body to represent them, like the Jewish Board of Guardians. Apart from important doctrinal disagreements concerning clerical authority between Sunnis (the great majority in Britain) and Shi'is (not all of whom belong to the Ithna 'Ashari sect, which prevails in Iran), the de facto authority of religious leaders among British Muslims is very variable. But none of this affects my main argument, which has to do with liberal constructions and anxieties.

8 ✂ ETHNOGRAPHY, LITERATURE, AND POLITICS

*Some Readings and Uses of
Salman Rushdie's* Satanic Verses

It is commonly accepted within anthropology that the discipline emerged as part of the Enlightenment project of writing a so-called universal history, yet not all anthropologists would agree that that inscription presupposes a Western perspective on non-European peoples. Such disagreement draws its force, I would suggest, from an understanding of the project as essentially representational. However, the Enlightenment project consists not simply of looking and recording but of recording and remaking, and as such its discourses have sought to inscribe on the world a unity in its own image.

Ethnographies and proto-ethnographies have, of course, often pitched themselves against that powerful current, producing a valuable understanding of singular worlds (but inevitably with only minor social effect). We know that ethnographic modes of representation evolved as an integral part of the great imperial expansion of Europe (and especially of England), as part of the desire to understand—and manage—the peoples subordinated to it. The implications of that fact seem to me inadequately worked out in contemporary discussions about ethnography. I do not mean to say that ethnography can be reduced to the politics of imperial domination, that anthropology has contributed to the political rule of non-Europe by Europe and is therefore, in some unforgivable way, morally tainted. I mean that it is, in various ways, inserted into (as well as being outside) imperializing projects, but that we do not fully understand what these projects are and how they work themselves out.

Yet having said this, it is necessary to add that imperial power has made itself felt in and through many kinds of writing, not least the kind we call fiction. I want to consider one such work, Salman Rushdie's *The Satanic Verses,* for several reasons. First, because it is a textual representation of some of the things anthropologists study (religion, migration, gender and cultural identity) and I wish to bring a critical anthropological understanding to bear on this representation. Second, because it is itself a political act, having political implications far beyond any that ethnography has ever had, implications that all anthropologists ought to consider. And third, because it is generated by the encounter between Western modernity—in which anthropology is situated—and a non-Western Other, which anthropologists typically seek to understand, to analyze, to translate, to represent, but which in this case is also *in* the West.

In all the recent concern with writing ethnographies, we have tended to pay insufficient attention to the problem of reading and using them, to the motives we bring to bear in our readings, and to the seductions of text and context we all experience. In reading imaginative texts, we inevitably reproduce aspects of ourselves, although this is not simply a matter of arbitrary preference or prejudice. We are all already-constituted subjects, placed in networks of power, and in reproducing ourselves it is also the latter we reproduce. To do otherwise is to risk confronting the powers that give us the sense of who we are, and to embark on the dangerous task of reconstructing ourselves along unfamiliar lines. It is, understandably, easier to use our readings to confirm those powers.

In what follows I want to distinguish between a number of readings of the book, and to relate them briefly to a complex political field in contemporary Europe. That is, of course, my own strategy for reading it, because I am persuaded that this text is generated by and is a reflection upon one very specific political-cultural encounter—and that it is so read and used in postcolonial Britain. I shall then try to reconstruct some authorial intentions and to place them within the political field, and to follow that with a political reading of some parts of the novel. This will involve a consideration of the modern category of "literature" as it operates within the text of the novel as well as outside it.

I make no claim to have captured the total meaning of *The Satanic Verses* (whatever that may be), still less to describe the Rushdie affair in all its international ramifications. My aim is to intervene in the political debate surrounding the publication of the book by raising some questions about the ambiguous heritage of liberalism as it affects non-Western immigrants in the modern European state, particularly in Britain.

A Political Setting

In December 1989, the prominent British parliamentarian Enoch Powell referred to his notorious 1968 "rivers of blood" speech, in which he had warned against the presence of non-European immigrants in Britain: "I am talking," he declared, "about violence on a scale which can only be described as civil war. I cannot see there can be any other outcome" (quoted in Roberts 1989). Twenty years before, Powell had advocated a two-pronged policy: a complete stop to any further immigration of nonwhites and government-assisted repatriation of those in Britain. The first of these has been officially accepted by both major parties, the second has not. But for Powell and others who think like him the situation is impossible to resolve peacefully, the alien presence is too large and too entrenched, and too many of them are British-born.

A year before the publication of *The Satanic Verses,* former Belgian interior minister Joseph Michel said that in Europe, "We run the risk of becoming like the Roman people, invaded by barbarian peoples such as Arabs, Moroccans, Yugoslavs and Turks, people who come from far afield and have nothing in common with our civilization" (quoted in Palmer 1988). Such sentiments are neither very rare nor confined to right-wing parties in Western Europe. There is generalized hostility toward immigrants of Asian and African origin, which finds expression in a variety of forms ranging from racial murder (see Gordon 1989) to discriminatory legislation (Moore and Wallace 1976; Dummett 1978). But particular developments in recent years have made that hostility especially sharp toward Muslims (see Gerholm and Lithman 1988; Kepel 1988).

To begin with, the overwhelming majority of non-European immigrants in Continental countries are Muslims, proletarians of rural origin imported to meet the needs of postwar industrial expansion. In Britain they form a majority of those who have come from the Indian subcontinent—that is, that part of the immigrant population that is seen and referred to as being most alien. The salience of the Muslim presence in Europe is due not merely to numbers but also to political conditions, both foreign and domestic.

The emergence of radical Islamic movements in the Middle East—and, most notably, the Islamic Republic of Iran—which openly declare the West as their enemy, has fueled longstanding European antipathies. But the domestic circumstances are, in my view, more interesting. Increasingly, Muslim immigrants have begun to organize themselves into mosque institutions and to assert themselves, not as victims, but as the heirs of an equal civilization who now live permanently in the West. They do not simply ask to be included in the wider political society, they make detailed demands of the state to enable them to live out their lives in a culturally distinctive manner. They want to bury their dead in their own way, to have special times and places set aside for worship, to slaughter animals according to proper ritual rules, to educate their children in their own schools—or at least in prescribed conditions (see Poulter 1990). Although Muslim groups in Western Europe are far from united (differences of language, sect, and local origin contribute to their organizational disunity), their demands increasingly evoke a unified response. What the European majority finds so provocative is the immigrants' expectation that institutional changes will be made by the state to accommodate them in their religious specificity.

The European sense that these demands constitute a kind of perverse behavior is largely a reflection of two things: the ideological structure of modern European nation-states and the altered site of the European encounter with its Other.

The liberal nation-state consists of an aggregate of citizens, each with the same legal personality, equal members of and equally entitled to represent the body politic. Religious communities belong, strictly speaking, to civil and not to political society—that is, to the private domain, where difference is permitted. In Britain, of course, an exception is made for the Church of England, which, since the seventeenth century, has had a central institutional and ideological position within the state. The notion (common certainly in Britain) that the population of a modern nation-state must be committed to "core values," an essential culture that must be shared by all if society is to hold together, belongs to a discourse about the limits of political society. It is easier to deploy in discourses that exclude particular differences than in those that describe what the core values of British culture are. The core values of nonwhite immigrants are *not*—so the hegemonic discourse goes—part of British culture, and therefore to live permanently in Britain they must—as political minorities—assimilate into that culture.

However, minorities have not always had to make this kind of adjustment. When Europeans went to Asia, Africa, and the Americas, as settlers, administrators, missionaries, they did not need to adopt the core values of the majority populations among whom they lived. On the contrary, they sought with great success to change them. But that immigrants from those populations should now presume to act as though they had a right to something that power did not accord them— that is quite another story. In *that* story it is their presumptuous behavior that needs explaining and correcting, not the postures adopted by the British.

I do not want to be taken as saying that there is a single deep divide in Britain today that separates Muslims and non-Muslims in some simple way. Of course, there are protagonists among both who are intent on creating a single divide, although that divide is not conceived in the same way by both. It is evident, however, that for some years now a new dimension of politics has been emerging that is resented in Europe. Nothing that is published there about Muslim beliefs and practices can therefore be without political significance, not even in a work of fiction. As Salman Rushdie insisted in 1984, in a critical essay on recent English television serials about India: "Works of art, even works of entertainment, do not come into being in a social and political vacuum; and . . . the way they operate in a society cannot be separated from politics, from history. For every text, a context." "What I am saying is that politics and literature, like sport and politics, do mix, are inextricably mixed, and *that that mixture has consequences*" (130 and 137; emphasis added).

Unlike Rushdie, I do not hold that all literature is essentially political, but only that any piece of literary writing can become politicized. But there can be no doubt that *The Satanic Verses* is a political book. It is political not merely because it claims to speak of political matters but also because it intervenes in political confrontations already in place, and is consequently bound to be fought over in an asymmetrically structured political terrain.

Some British Readings of a Postcolonial Novel

Salman Rushdie is not only the author of *The Satanic Verses,* he has also volunteered its authoritative reading. Thus, in his open letter to the prime minister of India, published shortly after his book was banned in that country, he wrote:

> The section of the book in question (and let's remember that the book in question isn't actually *about* Islam, but about migration, metamorphosis, divided selves, love, death, London and Bombay) deals with a prophet—who is not called Mohammed—living in a highly fantastical city made of sand (it dissolves when water falls upon it). He is surrounded by fictional followers, one of whom happens to bear my own first name. Moreover, this entire sequence happens in a dream, the fictional dream of a fictional character, an Indian movie star, and one who is losing his mind, at that. *How much further from history could one get?* (Rushdie 1988b; emphasis added)

This gloss is not without its difficulties, but it is unequivocal: history (or ethnography) produces a kind of writing whose rhetorical status is distinct from that produced in a novel. Six months later, Rushdie supplied another reading:

> Nowadays, a powerful tribe of clerics has taken over Islam. These are the contemporary Thought Police. They have turned Muhammad into a perfect being, his life into a perfect life, his revelation into the unambiguous, clear event it originally was not.[1] Powerful taboos have been erected. One may not discuss Muhammad as if he were human, with human virtues and weaknesses. *One may not discuss the growth of Islam as a historical phenomenon, as an ideology born out of its time.* These are the taboos against which *The Satanic Verses* has transgressed. . . . It is for this breach of taboo that the novel is being

---

1. Would it be unjust to describe this reference to a monolithic "Islam" directed by a "powerful tribe" as an opportunistic bid for support in the West? Rushdie himself might have described it so before the publication of *The Satanic Verses:* "it needs to be said repeatedly in the West that Islam is no more monolithically cruel, no more an 'evil empire' than Christianity, capitalism or communism" (1988a). It is incorrect and irresponsible to imply that there is a unity of doctrine among even so-called fundamentalist regimes and movements in the Muslim world today. It is absurd to suggest that belief in Muhammad's uniqueness and in the unambiguity of the Qur'ān as revelation is the product of a recent clerical coup; both principles have been cardinal to Islamic popular faith and theological discourse.

anathematized, fulminated against, and set alight. (Rushdie 1989a; emphasis added)

Why these apparently contradictory readings? Instead of trying to establish the right reading, let's ask, "What is it that motivates the shift?" and seek the answer not in speculations about the author's mind but in the wording of the texts in altered contexts. Thus, the latter piece concludes:

> Inside my novel, its characters seek to become fully human by facing up to the great facts of love, death, and (with or without God) the life of the soul. Outside it, the forces of inhumanity are on the march. "Battle lines are being drawn in India today," one of my characters remarks. "Secular versus religious, the light versus the dark. Better you choose which side you are on. Now that the battle has spread to Britain, I only hope it will not be lost by default. *It is time for us to choose.*" (Emphasis added)

We can see that the shift is motivated by a sense of the overriding political crisis now being faced: an apocalyptic war between good and evil has spilt over into Britain because *The Satanic Verses* has dared to challenge taboos set up by the forces of inhumanity.[2] Thus, Rushdie's latter reading insists that a central message of the book is not doubt but conviction, not argument but war. True, I am here citing Rushdie's views on his book and not the book itself. I shall discuss parts of the book in some detail below, but I want to insist that what Rushdie has said about his book is not less relevant than the pronouncements of other critics on it, although I do not necessarily take any of them at their face value. For instance, when Bhabha (1989b) comments that "the book is written in a spirit of questioning, doubt, interrogation and puzzlement which articulates the dilemma of the migrant, the émigré, the minority," he offers a judgment (shared by other critics) which is itself an echo of what Rushdie has said. Yet what is really interesting in this claim is the way *representations* of questioning, doubt, and so on, *in* the text are read backward into an authorial intention (the "spirit" of the writing) that *produced* the text.

2. Consistency is not exactly Rushdie's strong point. "Most of our problems begin," he observed in a prepublication interview, "when people try to define the world in terms of a stark opposition between good and evil." (Originally published in the autumn/winter 1988 *Waterston's Selection Catalogue*, a shorter version was reprinted in Rushdie 1989b.) But perhaps inconsistency is the privilege of an "interesting" writer.

In fact, all these utterances (writings), and others about the context, are intertexts that readers bring to bear on the novel. When critics quote from the novel in order to reflect on the political world at large (and when Rushdie quotes from it to clarify his own position as a secular author), a charge is set up between text and context which can not be channeled only one way. The question of the author's intention cannot therefore be fenced off as being irrelevant to the novel, as so many critics have claimed. I therefore cite Rushdie again and again on his book, not because I believe that he is the best authority on his work, but because glosses by Rushdie the embattled author are a crucial part of the book's context and therefore of its meaning. However, in this section I want to refer briefly to the views of a variety of readers who are (with the exception of the first of them) not writers of fiction.

Thus, Rushdie's friend Fay Weldon, the distinguished English feminist writer, has responded to his second reading with a vigorous attack on the Qur'ān, the central sacred text of Islam, in a pamphlet entitled *Sacred Cows,* which has rapidly acquired a certain fame in its own right. She reads *The Satanic Verses* as bringing new certainty, a renewed sense of the divine. Not doubt, but an uncompromising insistence on liberal truth is what she feels Rushdie's work calls for: we must reject the call for radical cultural differences in our British society. Somewhat quaintly she writes: "The uni-culturalist policy of the United States *worked,* welding its new peoples, from every race, every nation, every belief, into a whole: let the child do what it wants at home; here in the school the one flag is saluted, *the one God worshipped,* the one nation acknowledged" (Weldon 1989, 32; emphasis added). This reference to a fictional America is, of course, a condemnation of that immigrant difference which seems to threaten the assumed stability of "genuine" British culture. The emphasis on schooling as a political function, essential to the transformation of difference into unity, invokes a basic liberal principle: Individuals have the inalienable right to choose, but they must first be authoritatively constituted as persons who will make the right moral and political choices.

Weldon is quite explicit that Islam must be debarred from this great work of personal and national construction, though not Christianity, for "The Bible, in its entirety, is at least food for thought. The Koran is food for no-thought. It is not a poem on which a society can be safely or sensibly based" (6).[3] Like so many Britons who have leapt to Rushdie's side, Fay Weldon may be aware that Christian rhetoric can be harnessed in the cause of a secular crusade.[4] But it is certainly true to say that the play of familiar imagery from the Bible considered as literature is something most of her readership will respond to.

"Salman Rushdie," she writes,

> ex-colleague of mine in an advertising agency, is too humane, too modern, too witty, too intelligent, to lay down rules of conduct[5] for the human race, let alone issue threats if they are not obeyed, but as a piece of revelatory writing *The Satanic Verses* reads pretty much to me like the works of St John the Divine at the end of our own [*sic*] Bible, left in, not without argument, by our own church elders, likewise made pretty doubtful by the contents. St Salman the Divine. Too far? Probably. But if into the weevily meal and the brackish water of our awful, awful society, this good yeast is dropped, and allowed to fizz and fizzle, froth and foam to good purpose, all may yet be well and our brave new God of individual conscience may yet arise. (42)

Saints are privileged by their direct access to God, and by the certainty of their visions. The saint invoked here by Fay Weldon is certainly the author of haunting religious imagery, although the claim that he shares an essential quality with someone described as "humane," "modern," "witty," and "intelligent" must seem a little puzzling to anyone familiar with "The Revelation of Jesus Christ"—for

---

3. This judgment, incidentally, has a long lineage in the Christian West. Thus, Carlyle (1897, 64–65): "I must say, it is as toilsome reading as I ever undertook. A wearisome confused jumble, crude, incondite; endless iterations, long-windedness, entanglement; insupportable stupidity, in short! Nothing but a sense of duty could carry any European through the Koran. We read in it, as we might in the State-Paper Office, unreadable masses of lumber, that we may perhaps get glimpses of a remarkable man." There is a characteristic imperial assumption here that a cultivated European has no need to learn to read the texts of non-European cultures.

4. After all, it was only as recently as 1988 that Parliament legislated that obligatory collective worship in schools had to be of "a broadly *Christian* character" (see Education Reform Act 1988, secs. 6, 7; emphasis mine). Any parent who objects to Christian indoctrination must make a specific application to have his or her child exempted from that activity (ibid., sec. 9 [3]).

5. The imperious demand that all good men and true must now come forward to join the crusade ("Secular versus religious, the light versus the dark. . . . It is time for us to choose.") is surely based on an implicit rule of conduct.

the dominant theme in that apocalyptic prose is God's fearful revenge on those "without His seal upon their forehead." And who are they— one may ask uneasily—who do not bear the Lord's seal upon their forehead in Britain today?

Perhaps they are people like Zaheera, a young Muslim teacher who has left her authoritarian family in Bradford to make her own life. She has reason to be critical of aspects of Muslim life—and indeed she speaks scathingly of the recent legal restrictions imposed on women in many parts of the Muslim world.

> I do not want to see Salman die, that is immoral and wrong, and anyway not what the majority Muslim population here would want. I don't even think the book should be banned. But right from the beginning, I have felt that everyone was treating the Muslim protest as if it was completely crazy. This freedom of expression—why do we have pornography and libel laws, and a law of blasphemy which only applies to Christianity? How can that be fair? How can they say this is a multi-racial country when there is one law for Christians and one for Muslims? And what hurts so much is that one of our own, someone I really used to admire, someone who stood up on television and told the White British how racist they were, has let us down so badly. (Quoted in Alibhai 1989)

Significantly, Zaheera employs liberal arguments, grounded in appeals to fairness and equality before the law, against the unfriendly reactions of the British majority—such as those expressed in Fay Weldon's pamphlet. Her sense of unfairness does not connect with any demand for extending the law of blasphemy; it points to an old and unresolved anxiety about minority vulnerabilities in the modern state. If the freedom of public criticism is in fact restricted by laws that protect the sensibilities only of the rich, the famous, and the majority, what happens to the rest, those who are always Others in liberal society?

It would be misleading to suggest that all Muslims in Britain hold a negative view of the book. There are some—including some of the most Westernized—who have supported it unreservedly as a celebration of a more progressive cultural identity.

> One of the strengths of *The Satanic Verses* [observes Yasmin Ali], what gives it its authenticity as a cultural product of cosmopolitan Britain, is that it reflects with love and sympathy, and an acute comic eye, the

joyful diversity of our subcontinental origins and experiences. The moral and political uniformity that some of our brothers and sisters today would have us accept as the norm, is a denial of our experiences. (Ali 1989)

For Yasmin Ali, the book's authenticity is confirmed by the seeming correspondence between its images and the individual reader's experience. The possessive pronoun in "our experiences" claims to speak representatively for a collectivity, but which collectivity? The beliefs, practices, and attachments of the many immigrant Muslims who were hurt by the novel are clearly not included in "our" experiences. But the joyful resonance that the book has evoked among its mostly Western readers is a pointer to the conditions in which "our experiences" are *normatively* defined. Zaheera's experience does not qualify because it does not conform to a secular liberal literary reading of the book.[6]

A Hindu professor of political theory in England, Bhikhu Parekh, related to me in the summer of 1989 how he first read the book with unreserved admiration. He was delighted with it, he said, for two main reasons: first, because it showed that a fellow Indian could handle the English language more brilliantly than most English writers, and second, because its treatment of religion seemed to advertise the loyalty of a secular Muslim to a nonsectarian, progressive India. But then he reread the text with the help—as he put it—of two Muslim friends, and found himself making very different sense of it, which he has now set out in a thoughtful review. *The Satanic Verses*, in his opinion, is

> an immensely daring and persistently probing exploration of the human condition, which only a rootless immigrant can undertake, [but it] lies ill at ease with timid obeisance to the latest literary and political fashions; profound seriousness lapses suddenly and without warning into pointless playfulness. The sacred is interlaced with flippancy,

6. The difficulty of constructing a coherent politics in the modern state on the basis of experience alone has long been recognized on the left: see, for example, Williams 1979, 168–72. While Williams's primary concern here is to rehabilitate the notion of experience in the face of Althusserian assaults, he emphasizes its limitations for political understanding in modern societies. Nevertheless, he does not supply the necessary distinction between experience and its expression. For since there is often a hiatus between experiences that cannot be adequately expressed and what can be expressed but is not quite adequate to experience, there is always a danger in making hasty equations (as Yasmin Ali does) between "cultural products" and "authentic experiences."

the holy with the profane. Intensely delicate explorations of human relationships and emotions are overshadowed by an almost childlike urge to shock, hurt and offend. (1989, 31)

Like Zaheera, Parekh stresses the liberal value of fairness, as well as compassion and humanity, in the need to understand Muslim immigrant protest. But when he speaks, as others have done, of "the first generation of Muslims who turned to religion to give some meaning and hope to their empty lives" (31), one is made uncomfortably aware that in a modern state, such understanding and tolerance is often based on the medicalization of its "problem" subjects—that is, on the categorization of religiously based identity as a condition of individual or collective pathology requiring curative treatment. Why else would the notion of "empty lives" be applied to immigrants who have brought their non-Christian religion with them? Which authority defines the proper content of *full* lives? There are, of course, well-intentioned as well as sinister versions of this categorization.[7] But in either case, the strategy of medicalizing religious opposition, together with the centralized control of compulsory schooling, leads to the following paradox: on the one hand, liberal political theory insists on the sanctity of individual experience; on the other, it requires the state to construct and cure it.

Another, more angry shift than the one undertaken by Parekh, is signaled in this letter by the Hindu Marxist immigrant Gautam Sen (1989, 6):

When the crisis over *The Satanic Verses* first broke, my reflex response, like that of many black radicals and anti-racists, was one of anger. I found myself cursing the bigots and signing a newspaper advertisement in Rushdie's support, though I felt very disturbed at the price paid subsequently with lives in India and Pakistan. But the events of the past months have drawn me inexorably closer to the protesters against *The Satanic Verses*. All sorts of racists are crawling out of the woodwork to clarify a more important prior division between white society and blacks, transcending any disagreements within white so-

---

7. The sinister versions include those used in Russian political psychiatry. But they also appear in such statements as the following by the eminent liberal journalist Conor Cruise O'Brien (1989), which in effect recommend specific political and administrative measures: "Arab and Muslim society is sick and has been sick for a long time."

ciety itself. The astonishing flight from elementary logic in the face of satanic, black, masculine forces by the heavyweight feminist intelligentsia [including Fay Weldon] has been pointed out by Homi Bhabha ("Down among the Writers," *New Statesman and Society,* 28 July). I was not born a Muslim, but I have to say that we blacks are all Muslims now. I feel a real sense of emotional oneness with the "smelly, dark aliens" who made the utterly assimilated Asian woman novelist Bharati Mukherji "feel physically and emotionally harassed" by their mere arrival in Canada. (*Guardian,* 19 July)

For Gautam Sen, the revised reading was occasioned by developments in the British political context that appeared more threatening to all immigrants, Muslims and non-Muslims alike. What obviously alarmed him most was the combination of paternalist and assimilationist attitudes displayed in all their self-righteous arrogance by the British middle class.

Enforced assimilation is also a major concern of Shabbir Akhtar, an articulate young Bradford Muslim, who has written a passionately argued book on the Rushdie affair. Akhtar finds *The Satanic Verses* inferior as a work of fiction, and the chapters recounting the story of Mahound deliberately insulting to Muslims. The Prophet Muhammad, he points out, represents for believers the paradigm of virtue; an attack on him is therefore seen by Muslims as an attack on their highest moral and religious ideals. Rushdie has the right, he says, to disbelieve in any of the sacred teachings of Islam, and even to criticize Muslims for their erroneous beliefs, but not to do so in a provocative manner. He wants the book banned and supports the protests to that end. He is bitter at what he, like Zaheera, calls the double standard of Western public opinion. Nevertheless, he is not entirely pessimistic.

> I believe that the Rushdie controversy is not intractable. To show that it is incapable of rational resolution would be effectively fatal to the Muslim case. It is clearly in the interests of the liberal and non-Muslim constituency to pretend that Islamic demands concerning Rushdie's book are unacceptably foreign to the spirit of Western democracy. But are these demands, properly assessed, incapable of being met? (1989b, 123)

Akhtar's answer to this rhetorical question is that they can be met if only British politicians and commentators were to recognize their "prejudice and unfair attitudes" (124). What he wants is not an extension of the blasphemy law as such but an agreement that the basic identity of Muslim immigrants—like that of all British citizens—should be legally protected against wanton attacks.

While it is perhaps true that such demands are not "unacceptably foreign to the spirit of Western democracy," it is arguable that the assumption by which they are propelled is regarded as outmoded by bourgeois civil society. Insult to religious identity is, like insult to individual or group honor, a concept that modern law finds hard to deal with. This is not merely because religious belief is regarded as a private matter but rather because of its peculiar notion of injury. Thus, the law of libel, to which reference has so often been made in this matter, revolves around the question of whether material damage can be proved—which is why the legal penalty, if applicable, takes the form of financial compensation to the injured party. Free speech can be restrained when it is shown that the plaintiff suffers materially as a consequence. Modern law cannot cope with the idea of malicious statements leading to moral or spiritual injury because it cannot locate and quantify the damage in monetary terms. All this should be quite understandable in a capitalist society.

The real problem with the Muslim minority's demands, however, may not be the formal legalistic incompatibilities (Akhtar is surely right in insisting that where there is a political will, the legal means can be found). Nor is the problem simply one of prejudice against Muslims (which certainly exists). The real difficulty consists in the British *style* of liberal politics; for in Britain, the politics of rule requires its immigrant subjects to struggle with "the baffling idioms and codes of the white chameleon, which is cunningly Christian yet secular, Conservative yet liberal, repressive yet permissive" (Caute 1989).[8]

Postcolonial Literature and the Western Subject's Self-recognition

Many commentators have insisted that most protesting Muslims have not read the book. Clearly, most of them have not. However, as pastiche *The Satanic Verses* draws on a wide variety of literary texts, reproduces words and phrases from half a dozen languages, and al-

8. In this article, Caute provides a useful account of dissatisfactions within the Bradford immigrant community with the political record of the Labour party.

ludes to as many national and religious settings. In what sense, precisely, can Western readers who have little familiarity with these multiple references be said to have read the book? One might legitimately respond that reading need not conform to an a priori set of norms and knowledges in order to qualify as reading. At any rate, most people who have used it to commend or oppose particular political positions in Britain have not read it in any conventional literary sense, either. But, then, the way this text has fed into very different kinds of politics is itself, I would argue, part of the reading. *The Satanic Verses* is without doubt a deliberately provocative rhetorical performance in an already charged political field; *that* context has inevitably become integral to the text. Since the context is uncontrolled, the attempt to include more or less of it in the reading has become part of the political struggle.

Oddly enough, the "fundamentalist" position—according to which the text is self-sufficient for arriving at its meaning—is being taken here not by religious fanatics but by liberal critics. For example, the novelist Penelope Lively refers to a recent essay of Rushdie's: "I think, sadly, it points up the basic confrontation: here is a novelist trying to explain his purpose to fundamentalists who cannot, or will not, understand what fiction is or does" (quoted in Hinds and O'Sullivan 1990). In that essay, Rushdie had explained the classic literary doctrine that fiction (unlike fact) was essentially self-contained, and that if a novel's meaning had any external authority, it could only be the imaginative intention of its author, not the imaginative reception of its politically situated readers. "[The writer of] fiction uses facts as a starting-place and then spirals away to explore its own concerns, which are only tangentially historical. Not to see this, to treat fiction as if it were fact, is to make a serious mistake of categories. The case of *The Satanic Verses* may be one of the biggest category mistakes in literary history" (Rushdie 1990a). But Rushdie's argument here, shared by innumerable authors and literary critics who have commented on the affair, is less decisive than it appears. For once the principle of the total self-sufficiency of the text is breached by reference to the imaginative intention of the author, the claim that there are here clearly separable orders of events is subverted. That is why, in the real political world, the modern law of libel insists on making that "category mistake."[9]

9. As indeed do Salman Rushdie and his legal advisers. Thus, when the English playwright Brian Clark wrote a play alluding to Rushdie's tragic predicament, he was

Quite apart from the question of relevant context, the technique of literary pastiche makes it possible for a wide range of readers to recognize and seize upon parts of an entire text almost as they please. Those who have been offended by *The Satanic Verses* are thus responding to the fragmentary nature of the text. But by evoking recognition of characters, actions, events, atmosphere, the text also produces a sense of delighted confirmation,[10] as in this confession by an anglicized woman of Bangladeshi parents: "With each character I squealed with recognition, as a face from my past or present gazed at me from within the pages of the book" (Ali 1989).

Recognition in itself tends to be a conservative act, reproducing the images one possesses in memory. I do not imply by this that recognition can occur only in a conservative project. Nor do I believe that there is something inherently wrong with conservative projects as such. My argument is that in this book self-recognition works to confirm the self-satisfied reader in her/his established predispositions and prejudices instead of inviting her to think herself into a new world. This may seem a gross accusation against a work that many have described as an exploration into the possibilities of new identities in the migrant's world. But that is precisely my argument. The book deploys

---

confronted with a veiled threat of legal action: "Mr Rushdie responded by leaving a message on my answer-phone saying he was appalled that I would think the play which postulated his death could in any way be acceptable to him, that he would resist its being performed. As Mr Rushdie is nowhere portrayed or even named in the play it was easy to change the title to *Who Killed the Writer?* (though it would be disingenuous to pretend the play was not predicated on his position). But I was shocked to be in receipt of a letter from Mr Rushdie's agent saying that if we intended production we should send him a formal note so that he could 'establish Salman's legal rights.' The irony of Mr Rushdie wishing to suppress a play because it offended him was so obvious that it became clear to me he could not be thinking well" (1990, 21). A greater irony was Rushdie's insistence that "the writer" in Clark's text *referred to something outside that text.* "So what?" Rushdie's admirers might interject, "Rushdie's judgments are not always faultless—whose are?" But my point is that this is not a case of a lapse on his part—on the contrary. It is a case of someone interpreting from a specific, interested position: a beleaguered man concerned about a work of art apparently reflecting on his unhappy predicament. And in these matters everyone interprets from a specific, interested position.

10. The recognitions are highly seductive, for through them the reader delivers his/her assent. Thus, Peter Fuller in his review (1989) of George Steiner's *Real Presences:* "I was drawn on through page after page by the sheer joy of corroboration, the excitement of having these things affirmed so robustly." In such a reading there can scarcely be any room for the joy of discovering new things—let alone undergoing the uncomfortable process of questioning one's complacency.

categories that are available and sanctioned in the liberal (especially literary) world, and even in its playfulness, its satire, and its ambiguities, it evokes responses (whether of anger or delight) that work on recognition.

The English journalist Malise Ruthven is undoubtedly correct in observing that "the rage with which this . . . novel has been greeted by a number of Muslim organisations proves that Rushdie has touched upon some extremely raw nerves" (1989, 22–23). But can it not, in the same way, be argued that its aggressively enthusiastic reception by Western readers proves that among *them* some very different nerves have been touched by this book? That among them images are joyfully recognized because they are already formed in the layered discourses of a commonly inhabited historical world?

It is partly to this phenomenon that the Urdu Marxist poet and literary critic Aijaz Ahmed referred some years ago when he observed that

> the few writers who happen to write in English are valorized beyond measure. Witness, for example, the characterization of Salman Rushdie's *Midnight's Children* in the *New York Times* as "a Continent finding its voice"—as if one has no voice if one does not speak in English.[11] . . . The retribution visited upon the head of an Asian, an African, an Arab intellectual who is of any consequence and who writes in English is that he/she is immediately elevated to the lonely splendour of a "representative"—of a race, a continent, a civilization, even the "third world." (Ahmed 1986, 5)

Or even, one might add, of those figures of modernity, "the homeless migrant," "the heroic inhabiter of a godless universe," "the self-fashioning author."

I refer to these familiar figures in order to suggest that the representative status of which Ahmed speaks is not simply accorded to a foreign writer seeking admission; the writer's text is constructed from the start within a field of modern reading and writing that extends

11. It now appears that Salman Rushdie agrees with the *New York Times:* his life's work is "to create a literary language and literary forms in which the experience of formerly-colonized, still-disadvantaged peoples might find full expression" (Rushdie 1990a). Until Rushdie, the Creator, fashions and gifts an appropriate (English *literary*) language, an entire world of formerly colonized peoples remains unable to express fully their manifold experiences.

beyond the activities of literary figures to include the scope of modern politics; the text acquires its representative authority by tapping the network of images and powers made available in *that* field and not another. Among these, of course, are the self-fashioning narratives of militantly atheist readers who remember a repressive religious upbringing in Catholic or Low-Church families.[12] And there are also the textualized memories—the metanarratives—of a post-Enlightenment struggle against the institutional and moral hegemony of the Church in Europe and the very recent acquisition there of secular liberties.[13] Thus, my argument is not that European readers applaud *The Satanic Verses* because they are all filled with an irrational hatred of Islam, but because it brings into play metanarratives of Western modernity that conflict with Islamic textualities by which Muslim immigrants in Britain try to define themselves. Embarrassingly opposed to Western stories of progress there stands the Qur'ān, confounding the Western reader's expectations of progressive narrative—an expectation that has become (for all familiar with the Bible) the indisputable measure of a religious text's sense.

Aspects of the Bourgeois Rhetoric of Literature

"Dr Aadam Aziz," writes Rushdie (1989a) in one of his many glosses, "the patriarch in my novel *Midnight's Children,* loses his faith and is left with 'a hole inside him, a vacancy in a vital inner chamber.' I, too, possess the same God-shaped hole. Unable to accept the unarguable absolutes of religion, I have tried to fill up the hole with literature." Rushdie's narrative interlacing of characters from novel and

---

12. Since Freud, we have learnt to ask whether modern autobiographical narratives preserve a pure truth or present the truth of interested subjects (see Spence 1982). To what extent are such memories (as opposed to the experiences they recount) the consequence of direct religious repression—and to what extent the integrative principle of antireligious subjects? This question does not presuppose that the memories must be false, but that in translating a remembered childhood experience of repressive-parents-using-religious-rules into "religious repression," the adult subject has entered a discourse that already has high value in liberal secular culture.

13. This metanarrative often takes the history of post-Revolutionary anticlericalism in France as paradigmatic, thereby suppressing the much more complicated role played by religion in England. The religious struggle of Nonconformists against the established church was an extremely important source of social and political rights in that country.

autobiography should alert us to the fictional ways the self is so often constructed in a literature-producing and -consuming world.[14] For the politically engaged reader, this deliberate merging invites the reconstitution of authorial intention within the novel, even when it disavows itself.

Clearly, the word *literature* in Rushdie's confession does not denote just any writing that addresses the world. Rushdie does not mean that he turned to books on political economy, philosophy, or theology, but that he read and wrote fiction, literary criticism, and poetry for spiritual sustenance. And not just any fiction, of course—not the innumerable paperbacks sold by the million in supermarkets, airports, and railway stations by authors that cultivated readers have never heard of. When Rushdie says "literature," he means a very specific body of writing. His statement, and others like it, obviously belong to modern bourgeois culture—not because unbelief is either modern or bourgeois but because of something else: the assumption that the discourse called literature can fill the role previously performed by religious textuality.[15] The idea that literature is the quintessential space for producing reflections on the profoundest experiences of moderns has become quite familiar to us,[16] although the genealogy of that idea, which includes higher biblical criticism and Lutheran fundamentalism, is less widely appreciated than it should be. For that genealogy reveals a profound shift from a hermeneutic method that was essentially parasitic on a pregiven sacred text to one that *produced* literature out of an infinite variety of published texts. The emergence of literature as a modern category of edifying writing has made it possible for a new discourse to simulate the normative function of religious texts in an increasingly secular society.

The remarkable value given to self-fashioning through a particular kind of individualized reading and writing is entirely recognizable to Western middle-class readers of literary novels but not to most Mus-

14. For an interesting analysis of this modern phenomenon, see Gutman 1988.

15. In the Islamic tradition, the Qur'ān is not regarded as literature *(adab)* in the critical modern sense of the term. Although some recent specialists in Arabic literature have tried to approach it as a literary text (see, for example, Abdurrahmān 1969, 13–19), the purpose of the exercise has been to enrich its status as a divine—and therefore miraculous—discourse.

16. It is nicely reproduced in Foucault's (1984) well-known presentation of Baudelaire as the paradigmatic figure of modernity (a *literary* man, you will note—not a bureaucrat, not an entrepreneur, not an engineer, not even a journalist).

lims in Britain or the Indian subcontinent. And since *The Satanic Verses* as a whole reproduces that post-Enlightenment approach to textuality, its seductiveness is likely to work on the former and not the latter.

Thus, it is not mere personal prejudice against Islam that leads Rushdie to represent it as psychosis (Gibreel's experiences),[17] superstition (the events in Titlipoor), and chicanery (the story of Mahound).[18] What is more interestingly at work here is the familiar post-Enlightenment conception of literature as the legitimate source of spirituality. There is good reason for presenting Alleluia Cone's mystical experience on the snow-topped Himalayas with sympathy (see 108–9). Her overpowering sense of the sublime comes upon her at first in the form of a temporary hallucination of communion with God. The truth emerges when her experience is narrativized in her account to the schoolchildren. It is thus the possibility of transmuting religion into literature that makes Alleluia's narrative about her mountain experience an acceptable form of substitute religiosity for the author— as well as a recognizable one for many Western and Westernized readers.

The strongly sympathetic characterization of Sufyan—"ex-schoolteacher, self-taught in the classical texts of many cultures" (243)—belongs to the same authorial reason. For when we read that "secularist Sufyan swallowed the multiple cultures of the subcontinent" (246), that he could "quote effortlessly from Rig-Veda as well as Quran-Sharif, from the military accounts of Julius Caesar as well as the Revelations of St John the Divine" (245), it is the devotion of this life to literature that we are asked to admire. Not life itself, but the Great Books of Civilization (by Tagore, Shakespeare, Lucretius, Virgil, Ovid,

17. The idea that the Prophet's religious experience was due to mental disturbance is a theme in more than one nineteenth-century discussion of Muhammad. But then rationalist accounts of Christian religiosity took a similar view. Freud's account of religion as akin to neurosis in his essay "Obsessive Actions and Religious Practices" belongs to this nineteenth-century rationalist tradition.

18. Note the author's identification with the fictional poet Baal: " 'Whores and writers, Mahound. We are the people you can't forgive.' Mahound replied, 'Writers and whores. I see no difference here' " (392). Or rather, one should say: note Baal's identification *of* the author—a finger pointing from the text to its originator. The suggestion that the Prophet was hostile to all poets is, incidentally, historically inaccurate: there were poets among his followers, notably Hassan bin Thābit. (But who cares? This is not history, it is a work of literary invention.) More surprising, however, is the romantic idea presented here that writers are necessarily subversive of authority.

and many others), have fashioned the gentle, unworldly Sufyan and taught him the wisdom of life's sorrows.[19] So, too, spoken language (his believing wife's bitter complaints about his religious laxity) teaches him the evil that issues from actual ritual practice (his one-time pilgrimage to Mecca): "whereas for most Muslims a journey to Mecca was the great blessing, in his case it had turned out to be the beginning of a curse" (290). The practice of religion is transmuted into malign utterance, the truth of language stands against the antilife of ritual.

The doctrine that literature is the truth of life is repeated in a lecture by Rushdie (1990b): "Literature is the one place in any society where, within the secrecy of our own heads, we can hear *voices talking about everything in every possible way.* The reason for ensuring that that privileged arena is preserved is not that writers want the absolute freedom to say and do whatever they please. It is that we, all of us, readers and writers and citizens and generals and godmen, need that little, unimportant-looking room."[20]

This doctrine has gained such ideological ascendancy that the anthropological concept of culture is now beginning to be thought of once again in the mode of literature. For example, James Clifford writes: "Twentieth-century identities no longer presuppose continuous cultures and traditions. Everywhere individuals and groups improvise local performances from (re)collected pasts, drawing on foreign media, symbols and languages" (Clifford 1988, 14).[21] But everyday life is not so easily invented, abandoned, reinhabited, as this notion of culture, modeled on the postmodern idea of an imaginative work of art, suggests. Nor does everyone in the modern world have an equal power to

19. "*Sunt lacrimae rerum,* as the ex-teacher Sufyan would have said" (404). It is a curious feature of Sufyan's catholic taste in literature that he seems always to quote from Great Books of the West (including Virgil's *Aeneid*) and never from Islamic texts, except (if we are to credit the narrator's report—but should we?) from the Qur'ān.

20. Rushdie's claim that literature is the privileged stage for every possible representation—in itself incorrect because that claims too much and too little *for literature as literature*—is still a claim about representing life, not about living it.

21. Rushdie's own conceit of literature as life has recently acquired an astonishing formulation: "I want to say to the great mass of ordinary, decent, fair-minded Muslims, of the sort I have known all my life, and who have provided much of the inspiration for my work: *to be rejected and reviled by, so to speak, one's own characters is a shocking and painful experience for any writer*" (1990a, 53; emphasis added). Thus, Muslims in the world are not what his novel is about, they *are* his novel—characters turning ungratefully against their creator. Can it be that this author does not understand his own characters?

invent or to resist the imposition of someone else's invention. To say this is not merely to remind ourselves of the enormous injustices of class, race, and gender that still exist. It is certainly not to argue *for* tradition *as against* individual talent (in any case, the two are not mutually exclusive). My concern is to argue against the idea that social life can be usefully likened to a work of art, because social life as a whole is not constructed out of preexisting matter as works of art are. Life is essentially itself. Only the part of it that can be narrativized may be said to be "made up" like a story by an artist.

More concretely, I contend that although the strictly privatized role of religion in the modern Western state makes it easy for English believers and nonbelievers to assimilate it to the category of literature, most Muslim immigrants in Britain find it difficult to assimilate their practical religious traditions to this category.

The bourgeois doctrine that literature is, more than merely life itself, the very truth of life, has had a close connection with imperial culture. One may recall here the recommendation of Lord Macaulay, architect of British education in India, on the benefits of propagating "that literature before the light of which impious and cruel superstitions are fast taking flight on the banks of the Ganges. . . . And, wherever British literature spreads, may it be attended by British virtue and British freedom!" (quoted in Baldick 1983, 197). How successful this project was historically is not the point here; what needs to be underlined is the fact that British literature was always an integral part of the British mission in India—the mission to modernize an "unprogressive" population. Is it also an integral part of Salman Rushdie's mission? An outrageous question, some might suppose, to raise in connection with an anti-imperialist who celebrates hybridity and rejects the certainties of an orderly world. Yet the book assumes the categories of an imperialized world: it presents the possibility of salvation through literature, it urges upon (Muslim/immigrant) Indians a more progressive morality, it seeks to subvert their traditions in the hope that they will translate themselves into identities appropriate to the modern (i.e., *civilized*) world. In all these ways, if not in others, Rushdie stands beside Macaulay.[22] The most important difference seems to be the fact

22. It should perhaps be added that Macaulay the utilitarian and liberal would not have been opposed to Rushdie's stand against racial discrimination in Britain. At any rate, when European residents in India agitated against an act that subjected them to

that the latter wrote as a legal administrator to improve institutions and that the former wrote as a privileged author to improve ideologies.

The Politics of a Partial Text

I indicated earlier when I quoted from Rushdie's comments on his novel that the rhetorical status of the sections dealing with Islam was not entirely clear. Is it "historical exploration" or not? I want now to address myself briefly to authorial intention, to see whether this helps us understand how form and content in *The Satanic Verses* articulate with the political terrain in postcolonial Britain. I must stress that it is not Rushdie's original motive in writing the novel that interests me here but the authorial motive as constructed in the literary text and its political context.

If the book is, after all, about the growth of Islam as a historical phenomenon, one might wonder whether this object is best pursued via the fictional dream of a fictional character, an Indian movie star, and one who is losing his mind, at that. On the other hand, if the book's primary aim is to lampoon the sacred beliefs and practices of Muslim immigrants in Britain, then the literary devices employed in *The Satanic Verses* are entirely apt. Since these beliefs and practices are part of Muslim immigrants' contemporary social existence, their subversion requires a text that is a weapon. And as the weapon is to be wielded in the presence of a post-Christian audience—indeed, with the seduction of that audience as a primary condition—it draws astutely on the long tradition of Christian anti-Muslim polemics, central to which is the Christian fascination with sex in the Prophet's life. As Norman Daniel (1960, 102) noted, "It seemed very obvious to mediaeval Christians that Muhammad's behaviour with women alone made it quite impossible that he should have been a prophet."

Several commentators have suggested that the sexual episodes in the novel's account of the Prophet serve to humanize him. This may indeed be so. But the assumptions constituting that humanity are themselves the product of a particular history. Thus, in the Christian tradition, to sexualize a figure was to cut him off from divine truth, to pronounce him *merely* (sinfully) human; in the post-Christian tradi-

---

the authority of Indian judges, Macaulay attacked them fiercely (and successfully) for their attachment to "the spirit of an exclusive caste" (Stokes 1959, 215).

tion of modernity, to "humanize" a figure is to insist on his sexual desire, to disclose in it, by a discursive stripping of its successive disguises, his essential human truth.[23] Like any imperializing orthodoxy, this doctrine demands of us a universal way of "being human"—which is really a singular way of articulating desire, discourse, and gesture in the body's economy. (Although in this sense the hagiographical representation of Muhammad is "humanized" in Rushdie's novel, the very real contemporary Khomeini—"the Imam"—is heavily mythicized. These two diametrically opposed rhetorical strategies come together in the same polemical aim, however.)

But the elements in Rushdie's armory are not solely Christian. They come also from that modern tendency which regards the establishment of rules as self-evidently restrictive of liberty. Thus:

> Amid the palm-trees of the oasis Gibreel appeared to the Prophet and found himself spouting rules, rules, rules, until the faithful could scarcely bear the prospect of any more revelation, . . . rules about every damn thing, if a man farts let him turn his face to the wind, a rule about which hand to use for the purpose of cleaning one's behind. *It was as if no aspect of human existence was to be left unregulated, free.* The revelation—the *recitation*—told the faithful how much to eat, how deeply they should sleep, and which sexual position had received divine sanction, so that they learned that sodomy and the missionary position were approved of by the archangel, whereas the forbidden postures included all those in which the female was on top. Gibreel further listed the permitted and forbidden subjects of conversation, and earmarked the parts of the body which could not be scratched no matter how unbearably they might itch. He vetoed the consumption of prawns, those bizarre other-worldly creatures which no member of the faithful had ever seen, and required animals to be killed slowly, by bleeding, so that by experiencing their deaths to the full they might arrive at an understanding of the meaning of their lives, for it is only at the moment of death that living creatures understand that life has been real, and not a sort of dream. And Gibreel the archangel spec-

23. Rodinson 1971 contains a "humanist" portrait of the Prophet, with its mixture of strengths and weaknesses, remarkably similar to the one presented in Rushdie's novel—and the role of sex in establishing his human (and therefore morally flawed) status is comparable.

ified the manner in which a man should be buried, and how his property should be divided. (363–64; emphasis added)

This passage is, of course, playful in style, and that fact is part of its *literary* intention and achievement. But if that is so, surely the consideration of exactly what is being played with, and how, is relevant to that literary judgment. I do not simply complain that the passage plays with people's sacred beliefs; I refer to the need for a more discriminating understanding of playfulness. And a subtler consideration of playfulness (vivacity? unseriousness? cheerfulness? gamelike form? deceptiveness?) cannot be adequately carried out without knowledge that most Western readers do not normally have.

Most Islamic rules are contained not in the Qur'ān ("the recitation"), which Muslims believe to have been revealed by God via Gabriel, but in collections called *hadīth,* which contain the exemplary sayings and doings of Muhammad and his companions. Since Muslims do not consider *ahādīth* to be divinely revealed, Gabriel has nothing to do with them. Of all the rules given in the passage I have quoted, only the rules relating to inheritance are to be found in the Qur'ān.

For Muslims, *ahādīth* record the founding principles of a virtuous life; conversely, every principle of virtuous Muslim practice has a *hadīth* authorizing it. Over the centuries, there have been many attempts at putting together authoritative collections and classifying *ahādīth,* and there are many important differences in the *ahādīth* accepted by the various sects as authentic. Thus, no Sunni collection contains a *hadīth* prohibiting the consumption of prawns, a prohibition followed only by Shi'is. Nor does any Sunni canonical work contain the rules about sexual intercourse that are cited in *The Satanic Verses.* The question that an informed reader may want to ask is why the rules of *hadīth* are presented as having been revealed by Gabriel, and further, why sectarian rules are presented as though they were accepted by all Muslims. The answer to that would, no doubt, be, "Because the dreams of demented Indian actors aren't scholarly treatises, they are satire." But this response will not do.

When we call a piece of writing satire we are, of course, claiming a respectable status for it. A satire is supposed to deal with prevailing vices, but the vices must be recognized as such by those against whom the satire is directed. In that sense, the satirist's project is a conservative one. The satirist need not himself be a believer, but he must have a firm understanding of the moral structure of the people he is satirizing—that is, of the difference between their professed high ideals and their actual interested behavior. Otherwise, the writing may degenerate into a sneer. Simply to represent another people's beliefs and customs as vices is not in itself satire (which is not to say that it is therefore without effect). Indeed, derogatory representations have been, throughout Europe's nineteenth century, an integral part of imperial propaganda and an essential justification of its "civilizing mission" among the audience at home. But unlike satire, which is a mode of moral engagement,[24] such expressions of contempt for the beliefs and practices of natives (Macaulay's "cruel superstitions") depend for their force on persuasive bullying.

The item that is surely the most startling in Gibreel's dream about Islamic rules is the repulsive explanation offered for the way Muslims butcher animals for food to make the meat *halal* (kosher). That the explanation is contained neither in the Qur'ān nor in any canonical *hadith* is of no concern to would-be satirists, of course. More important, however, is the fact that most British readers will immediately associate this item with the notorious media campaign a few years ago against what was described as "that cruel and barbarous" Islamic practice. The pressure of public opinion resulted in a government commission that recommended that "ritual slaughter" be rendered illegal; but fortunately for the Muslims, the Jewish religious authorities prevailed upon the government not to follow this recommendation. This seems to confirm the suspicion that Rushdie's sneer is directed particularly at Muslim immigrants in Britain, a small and politically vulnerable community that is already in some difficulty for its attachment to religious traditions. In a crusade, there can be no scholarly scruples, only the determination that light shall triumph against darkness.[25]

24. Walzer has written well on the ancient theme of internal criticism with reference to Jewish tradition in his *Interpretation and Social Criticism* (1987), and one wonders why he avoids any mention of that theme when dealing with Islamic tradition in "The Sins of Salman" (1989). The questions addressed in the latter (concerning blasphemy and free speech) are discussed in a predictable manner—and therefore are, no doubt, predictably welcomed by most sensible readers. What it does not address is how that novel's critical posture relates to the idea of internal criticism.

25. In one of the more successful chapters of *Purity and Danger* (1966), Douglas offers a fascinating explanation of the dietary rules in Leviticus, which persuades the reader that they are coherent; but then her aim, contrary to Salman Rushdie's, is not mockery.

Of course, Rushdie is under no obligation to engage seriously with beliefs and practices that he rejects, or for that matter to refrain from making fun of them. But in choosing to laugh at them he situates himself very clearly on the ground of quite another tradition that is already powerfully in place—that of the liberal middle classes in a post-colonial Western state. The reader of *The Satanic Verses* should not allow herself to be misled by the accusations of British racism it contains into supposing that the novel is fundamentally at odds with liberal tradition: such accusations are entirely consonant with a liberal distress at racist prejudice in contemporary Britain.[26]

More significant, I think, is this: In deriding the very idea of rules of conduct ("rules about every damn thing. . . . It was as if no aspect of human existence was to be left unregulated, free"), Rushdie invokes liberal individualism, which reached its apogee in Mrs. Thatcher's Britain. Yet neither in politics nor in morality is it an uncontested truth to say that being unregulated is being really free.[27]

I repeat: I do not say that Rushdie's position outside the Islamic tradition means that his criticism is *therefore* invalid. I argue that the *force* of that criticism depends on the fact that he is situated in a Western liberal tradition and is perceived to be addressing an audience that shares it. I also maintain that while vilification of people's cherished beliefs and practices *may* lead to their deciding to abandon them, such a change is effected by superior power (creating feelings of shame, fear, etc.) and not by moral argument. I find it ironic that Western liberalism (by which I intend to include more than strictly political liber-

26. Besides, according to a comment made by Rushdie to his English interviewer in London, such things are much worse in India: "It isn't a question of making a sociological example of London. If you go to India these days, you see things happening which are 10 times worse than any of the things happening here, and there it's Indians doing it to Indians, and often for racial reasons" (1989b, 1155). This comment is consistent with my argument about the book's critical site. From a liberal point of view, things are indeed always ten times worse in India than in the West.

27. Taylor (1979, 177) points out that in contrast to liberal theories of negative freedom—where freedom consists of the absence of obstacles—doctrines of positive freedom are concerned with "a view of freedom which involves essentially the exercising of control over one's life. On this view one is free only to the extent that one has effectively determined oneself and the shape of one's life. The concept of freedom here is an exercise-concept." Rules of behavior, I would suggest, are typically integral to what Taylor has called freedom as an "exercise-concept." From the viewpoint of freedom as an "opportunity-concept" (negative freedom), rules define what may not be done and are therefore no more than obstacles.

alism), a tradition that prides itself in being uniquely based on the use of reasoned argument and the avoidance of cruelty, should nevertheless applaud a novel that is so given to intimidating rhetoric.

Political Traces on a Postcolonial Life

I do not want to give the impression that I think *The Satanic Verses* is to be read entirely—or even mainly—in terms of the author's conscious intentions. The text of this novel is not in control of itself. The tensions and contradictions it reveals are far more interesting than anything that takes place on the surface of the narrative. And they allow us to make a political reading of fragments of the novel, as opposed to its politics, which was the topic of my previous section.

For example: In the course of a hymn to the glories of Shakespeare, Rushdie's Chamcha makes a striking remark: "Pamela, of course, made incessant efforts to betray her race and her class" (398). Yet what is apparent to any reflective reader is that Pamela betrays *not* her race and her class but her Indian husband—by going slumming among immigrants instead of helping to complete and confirm his transformation into the authentic Englishman. Indeed, Pamela is aware of Chamcha's desperate desire for the very thing she rejects (180).

But why is her attitude toward her class represented as betrayal? Anyone educated, as Rushdie's Chamcha is, at an English public school must know that upper middle-class parents would not regard a daughter's radical politics as betrayal (mere "youthful idealism" is how they would view it) but would so view her marriage to an Indian. It is inconceivable that Rushdie's Chamcha should be innocent of this knowledge. Indeed, he does know it but cannot admit it to himself, so it must be suppressed and displaced.

Chamcha resents Pamela's unwillingness to confirm him as a real English gentleman, and he knows that this unwillingness is related directly to her rebellious politics. He cringes as she repeatedly subverts his attempts at being English and despises her for her left-wing politics. However, this does not quite explain his resort to the bitter accusation of treachery, an accusation never leveled at Zeeny, the radical Indian who mocks him for aping English attitudes. Nor does it explain why he feels it is her *race* and her class that are betrayed, not himself. Coming from Rushdie's Chamcha, this accusation is entirely apt, but only because it covers a complex play between desires for self-transformation and ideas of genetic purity that is not fully dissected in the novel.

To be a self-consciously "authentic" English gentleman is to enact a racist ideology—to engage in a discourse on "generative essence," one in which Indians have a different place. As concept and practice, that ideology acquired its most elaborate development in British India. In his desire to metamorphose himself into that kind of Englishman, Rushdie's Chamcha struggles with an impossible ideological dilemma: to become English, he must reject his Indianness; marriage to an Englishwoman must surely bring the fulfillment of his desire nearer; yet Pamela marries him *because* he is Indian, thereby adulterating the authentic Englishness he desires through her (her adultery with Chamcha's Indian friend Joshi is merely a playing out of her marriage as racial adultery), and she seeks to reproduce a half-English child. It is thus Pamela's sexual history, not her politics, that constitutes real betrayal of Chamcha *precisely because it is a betrayal of an essential (i.e., racially pure) Englishness*. Yet in the final analysis, her betrayal is simply the motivated figure of his own impossible attempts to become that different species, an authentic English gentleman. There is a double displacement at work here, for Chamcha is at once the object of betrayal and the ultimate betrayer—the self-hating colonial.[28]

The final resolution is that Chamcha returns to India, his essential place, and to Zeeny, his essential kind:

> Childhood was over, and the view from this window was no more than an old and sentimental echo. To the devil with it! Let the bulldozers come. *If the old refused to die, the new could not be born.* "Come along," Zeenat Vakil's voice said at his shoulder. It seemed that in spite of all his wrong-doing, weakness, guilt—in spite of his *humanity*—he was getting another chance. There was no accounting for one's good fortune, that was plain. There it simply was, taking his elbow in its hand. "My place," Zeeny offered. "Let's get the hell out of here." "I'm coming," he answered her, and turned away from the view.[29] (547; emphasis added)

28. The Canadian writer Mukherji comes close to making this point (in "Prophet and Loss," 1989) but does not notice the class character of this sense of betrayal, which is what gives it its complexity and destructive power. In this context, one cannot usefully speak of a generalized "colonial subject," as she and other critics do—or, for that matter, of a universalized "immigrant."

29. As Spivak (1989) has pointed out, *The Satanic Verses* ends with a sexual offer to the male hero Saladin. There is, in fact, a disturbing incongruity between the book's

But this optimistic resolution is only possible after his father's death brings him a comfortable inheritance in India—an inheritance acquired, ironically, in accordance with rules from the Divine Recitation.[30] It also helps that his English wife, the incarnation of his self-betrayal, has been conveniently disposed of—burned to death, an unnamed corpse with her half-Indian child unborn, whose death is recounted in the form of a casual police report (464–65).

If the old refused to die, the new could not be born. As an empirical generalization, this is, of course, foolish. But as a justification for destroying the old in the continuous pursuit of novelty, it is the classic morality of consumer capitalism. Rushdie's Chamcha destroys his own past—his mother,[31] his father, his wife, his friends, his alter ego Gibreel, recognizable parts of London, even his affection for England[32]—*and then forgives himself for that destruction.* In such a morality, there is no reason to suppose there can ever be an end to the cycle of destruction, self-forgiveness, and the creation of new identities. When there are no obligations to the past, every destruction is only a new beginning, and new beginnings are all one can ever have.

Chamcha's solution to the problem of conflicting identities, a return to his real place, is scarcely open to many immigrants, although the idea of deporting colored immigrants to their country of origin is

---

overtly feminist gestures (what Spivak describes as "his anxiety to write woman into the narrative of history") and its frequently brutal or dismissive treatment of women (which is not, however, what Spivak complains of). Perhaps one of Rushdie's most startling inscriptions of women occurs in the name given to a female character in *Shame,* "Virgin Iron-Pants," which, surprisingly, none of his feminist admirers has objected to. Even Spivak, perceptive critic that she is, observes only that "in *Shame,* the women seem powerful only as monsters, of one sort or another." It is not his inability to portray women as impressively as he does men that I am worried by (as Spivak is when she claims that "Ayesha, the female prophet, lacks the existential depth of 'the businessman prophet' "). What makes me uneasy is the text's curious ambivalence, which links progressive views about women's oppression with repeated narrative violence toward them. I am led to wonder why prominent feminist critics have remained silent about this. More broadly: why are readers sometimes prepared to overlook in one author what they would find intolerable in another?

30. In India and Pakistan, personal law is administered in accordance with religious affiliation.

31. His mother's end, oddly enough, is not at all like his father's—it verges on the comic. A woman who chokes to death on a fishbone while her affluent party guests dive under the dining table in fear of a Pakistani air raid is not likely to provide the male hero with a dignified model for a secular death. What—one is prompted to wonder—are the gendered determinants of dying?

32. "Chamcha, who loved England in the form of his lost English wife" (425).

one that right-wingers in Britain, including Enoch Powell, have always favored. It is the social, economic, and cultural consequences of British rule in India, not the mythicized origins of Islam in seventh-century Arabia, that constitute the source of political problems for Indian and Pakistani immigrants in contemporary Britain. Indeed, the book's articulation of time is self-consciously mythical—an admiring reviewer identified it as "cyclically Hindu and dualistically Muslim" (Mukherji 1989, 9),[33] while its central dilemma and resolution are deeply rooted in historically specific class situations.

It may be argued that Chamcha's return to India is not the only solution in the novel to the immigrant's difficulties. After all, there is Mishal, daughter of the Bangladeshi café owner Sufyan, who stays on to struggle for a nonracist England. But Mishal, born and bred in England, is already in a crucial sense English—in her manner of speaking, her attitude toward her mother, her sexual behavior, her dress, and her radical politics—even though it must be understood that in a racist society she will not be seen as English by racists in England. (Her petty-bourgeois Englishness is, of course, to be distinguished from the gentleman's Englishness Chamcha aspires to.) Nevertheless, it is Mishal who lives, while her immigrant parents—symptomatically—are burned to death. The stirring speech allegedly made in court by Sylvester Roberts, alias Dr. Uhuru Simba, reads oddly: "we are here to change things. . . . We have been made again: but I say that we shall also be the ones to remake this society, to shape it from the bottom to the top. We shall be the hewers of the dead wood and the gardeners of the new. It is our turn now" (414). In the light of an almost systematic destruction of immigrant difference in the book (apart from skin color and a taste for curry), this passage assumes a self-mocking quality.

The remarkable thing about *The Satanic Verses,* considering what has been said about it, is that it is not about the predicament of most immigrants at all. Nor is it, as some reviewers have claimed, a profound statement about the immigrant as universal representative of our epoch. Indeed, apart from the Sufyan family, the out-of-work radical Joshi, and Chamcha himself, there are virtually no immigrants in the book. True, there is the Cone family, middle-class Jewish refu-

---

33. Cyclical or dualistic is not quite the kind of temporality that modern historians work with. That is why in the novel it is the imam figure (Khomeini) who is condemned for wanting to stop the *linear* march of secular history (210).

gees from Poland: old Otto, the father, commits suicide after his comical attempts at assimilation; his widow, Alicia, becomes religious and emigrates to California, where she settles down with a nice man; and the two daughters, Alleluia and Elena, each meets with an unpleasantly violent death. End of the Cone family of immigrants. Is there a pattern here?

Most Muslim immigrants in Britain are proletarians, large numbers of whom have settled in communities in the mill towns of northern England. Neither do they retire to where they came from, nor do they appear to wish to assimilate entirely to "the core values" of British culture. The book's stories do not connect with the political-economic and cultural experiences of this population. What they do powerfully connect with are the highly ambivalent emotions generated by an anglicized Indian's gaze at the ruling class of imperial Britain. Rushdie's Chamcha has been excluded from entry into that class, not merely because of racism, but because (as he gradually discovers) good old England, the *authentic gentleman's* England, is no longer in place. Responding to Valence's loud-mouthed praise for Thatcher's class revolution, Chamcha comes to this unhappy conclusion: "It hadn't been Chamcha's way; not his, nor that of the England he had idolized and come to conquer" (270). Yet only a colonialized bourgeois could have worshiped a gentleman's England that never was. The decent England that Rushdie's Chamcha had idolized and wanted to inhabit was also the country whose ruling class conducted a continuous war against its organized working classes, against the Irish peasantry, and against the diverse populations absorbed into its vast empire. Significantly, his awakening begins, not with a recognition that his yearning for the gentleman's England was based on illusion, but with a nostalgia for the England no longer here to receive him. Most Muslim immigrants, having very different class origins and religious traditions from those of Rushdie's Chamcha, propelled by quite other aspirations to migrate, and living now in straitened conditions—these had not and could not have entertained the illusions that he had had about England.

Finally: even if all I have said about the novel is persuasive, I concede that it does not settle the question of its ultimate merit as a work of art. That question I am obliged to leave to critics who are the guardians of our literary canon. My concern has been with trying to describe the imaginative spaces of power it expresses and inhabits.

Some British Uses of a Postcolonial Novel

I have said something about the readings but almost nothing about the uses of Salman Rushdie's *The Satanic Verses* in the context of British politics. In a sense, the most startling use of this book has been, of course, its public burning in Bradford. This was done deliberately by the Muslims in that city to attract media attention—and that they got with a vengeance. Commentators of various political persuasions denounced the act with horror, comparing it with the notorious Nazi book burnings of the thirties. That reaction should interest anthropologists, among others. When characters in a novel are burned to death (or vilified), we are reminded that it is, after all, "only a story." And yet a literalist response does not seem equally convincing to us when we are told that the book burned is, after all, "only paper and ink." The liberal expressions of outrage at *this* symbolic act—no less than the anger of South Asian Muslims at the publication of the book— deserve to be explored more fully than they have been (or than I can do here) so that we can understand the sacred geography of modern secular culture better than we now do.

It is one thing for liberal opinion to reject the call for banning a publication, quite another to react with horror at the symbolic act of burning it on this occasion. Why was there no liberal outrage at the public burning of copies of immigration laws by dissenting members of Parliament some years ago? More relevant, perhaps, is the case of Rabbi Mordecai Kaplan, who redefined classical Judaism in accordance with modern ideas not as a religious faith but as a civilization that included language and custom: "When Rabbi Kaplan published a prayer book in 1945 embodying these ideas, it was publicly burned before an assembly of the Union of Orthodox Rabbis of the United States and Canada" (Goldman 1989). Why was there no secular outrage at this symbolic book burning? My point is not that all this shows up double standards but that we are missing something.

Perhaps the crucial difference in the case of the Bradford event (apart from the fact that it was perpetrated by Muslims, who must expect a generally unfavorable press in the West) is that it was the burning of a novel by a famous literary author. It was "literature" that was being burned, not just any printed communication.[34] And it was burned by people who did not understand the sacred role performed by literature in modern culture.

Whatever a full symbolic analysis of the book burning may come to look like, it needs to be stressed that the two expressions of outrage are not equivalent, in that Muslim immigrants (like all South Asian immigrants) do not possess anything like the resources of power and violence available to the British state. True, this double outrage has also become entangled with the issue of Khomeini's shocking death threat against a British citizen. But it is also true that prominent British Muslims have publicly disassociated themselves from the Iranian pronouncement, and that they are trying to restrain the intemperate declarations of some of their co-religionists.[35] Salman Rushdie's tragic predicament—his having to be guarded by the British police against the possibility of murder—is certainly part of the story. So, too, is this fact: the steady stream over the years of murders of black British citizens by white racists has never provoked a denunciation, by the government or by liberal opinion, of the white British population. Nor do ordinary black British citizens, who are constantly threatened by white racists, always obtain the police protection they need. *Their* security evidently cannot receive the same practical and ideological attention that liberal society gives to an internationally famous author.[36] It is quite understandable, therefore, that when ordinary British citizens are threatened with death by white racists, and murdered, there should be no liberal outcry that the foundations of Western civilization are

34. That this event has become a key symbol of the entire Rushdie affair is evident in the way iconic reproductions of the burning are used—as, for example, on the cover of Appignanesi and Maitland 1989 and of Ruthven 1990, not to mention innumerable articles in newspapers and periodicals commenting in general terms on the affair.

35. Pallister, Morris, and Dunn 1989. And John Patten (1989a), home office minister for race relations, stated: "I am glad to be able to say that the particular concerns raised by *The Satanic Verses,* have been, for the most part, handled in a responsible way by the great majority of the Muslims in this country. . . . I am grateful, too, that Muslim leaders have made public their regret for the behaviour of a very small minority who use the peaceful demonstrations as an excuse for violent disorder."

36. This observation applies equally to the condition of the wretched hostages in Lebanon: innocent persons held by ruthless men in appalling conditions and under daily threat of murder. How often have we seen paid newspaper advertisements in which long lists of distinguished writers take a principled stand against the inhuman predicament of these victims?

being attacked—but merely liberal expressions of dismay at the violent intolerance of their lower classes.[37] I should stress that I am indicating here not an instance of inadequate white sympathy for the plight of black immigrants but an aspect of the liberal concept of violence: for violence becomes a serious object of liberal concern only when something that they really value seems to be threatened.

As a consequence of the inequality in power between immigrants and the governing classes, the book is now being used as a stick with which to beat the immigrants in a variety of political arenas—in education, local government, and parliamentary constituencies. The hitherto confused notion of multiculturalism is now vigorously attacked in the name of core cultural values right across the political spectrum.

For Labourite Sean French, the Bradford book burning and the Muslim fury at Rushdie have brought about a change of heart regarding the virtues of multiculturalism: "There has been little time in Britain for the melting-pot attitudes to immigrants—especially on the left. Multi-cultural, mother-tongue teaching has been considered almost self-evidently good. It would produce the riches of a many-cultured society. Well we now have it" (1989). French, like many others on the left and the right,[38] regards multiculturalism as a disruptive principle. But so too, surely, is the melting-pot policy. The unhappy history of race relations between English-speaking, Christian immigrants from the Caribbean (who were ready from the first to be assimilated) and the dominant white society is evidence enough of that. The clue, it seems to me, lies in the anxiety on the part of most liberal

37. This is nicely brought out in a recent piece by the liberal columnist Ian Aitken. Referring to the 1958 Notting Hill Gate Riot, in which a gang of white youths terrorized blacks and were eventually sentenced to four years each, he writes: "But the event caused particular anguish to liberal-minded, leftish sort of people, and not just because of what had happened. The trouble was that the 'riot' and its aftermath brought two cherished liberal attitudes—opposition to racial harassment and the belief that underprivileged young offenders [in this case white racists] should be treated with compassion—into direct and embarrassing collision." *Nowhere in this article does Aitken speak of the terror of black immigrants hunted by murderous whites in a white society, but only of the embarrassment felt by liberals at the conflict between two "attitudes."* As for the Rushdie affair: "What needs to be demonstrated, and quickly, is that our secular Western democracies are not going to yield to militant Islam the very liberties our ancestors wrenched so recently from Christian theocrats" (1990).

38. See the enthusiastic discussion in an article by the political editor of the *Sunday Times* (Jones 1989) of the document titled "On Being British," written by John Patten, the Tory government's home office minister for race relations.

British about who and what is to be disrupted: if anybody is to be radically transformed, it must not be the British themselves.

Thus, Hugo Young, the well-known British liberal columnist, writes:

> One claim for which *they can be allotted no scintilla of sympathy* is the claim some Muslim leaders now make to destroy British freedoms, or escape the restraints of English and Scottish law. The law protects us all, including them. *They do not seem to understand that, nor yet had comprehension thrust upon them.* For that, and that alone, one is entitled to suggest to anyone who does not like it that he might find another country which meets his demands. If not Gravesend, why not Tehran? (Young 1989; emphasis added)

The intimidating tone of this piece, delivered in imperial cadences (marred by the odd instance of faulty syntax), is typical of much media coverage of the Rushdie affair in Britain. Peaceful attempts by immigrant leaders to petition for legal action banning the novel are not merely rejected but represented in hysterical terms as a bid "to destroy British freedoms." An Asian minority's wish to change the law, and its resort to means that have always been lawful in modern democracies (parliamentary petitions, public demonstrations—including the shouting of angry slogans[39]—and passionate argument in the media) are virtually criminalized. But in fact such statements are not directed at illegality in any strict sense, especially as it was common knowledge that no arrests for breach of the law had actually occurred at the time. Their function is to convey a clear message to immigrants: if you don't like an arrangement that is a part of core British values, don't dare to try and change it—just leave our country.

This seems eminently reasonable—democratic, even. But it is worth examining critically what the assumption amounts to. British core values appear to mean the historical values of the British majority. However, they can easily be translated as *hegemonic interests,* so that the demand that immigrant minorities concede without question existing core values if they are to be accepted as full members of the political

---

39. In a famous demonstration, an effigy of Nicholas Ridley, the environment secretary, was publicly burnt by irate middle-class residents of an attractive rural area scheduled by the government for housing development. And, of course, these protesters won.

community becomes revealed as a famous bourgeois ruse. If that principle were ever to be conceded, neither race nor gender could become legitimate politics in modern states.

It is a well-known but often conveniently suppressed fact that not only have ways of life in Britain changed radically over the last two centuries, the concept of culture itself has emerged as the political product of a profound historical struggle. There was a time when the values and aspirations of the English working classes—as well as the beliefs and practices of Nonconformist Christians—were not included in the secular, humanist concept of culture.[40] The singularity of Britain was not defined in terms of an all-encompassing culture. It was only with such recent developments as universal adult male suffrage, a legalized trade union movement, popular education, and a reformed system of city government that "British culture"—originally "English culture"—began to acquire the inclusive sense and the legitimacy that it now possesses. This continuous work of historical contestation and reconstruction needs to be kept in mind when reading British liberal commentaries about the Rushdie affair. I want to stress that this point has nothing to do with whether British culture, like all cultures, is "mixed" or "pure"; it has to do with what gets included and what excluded (how and by whom) in the construction of a domain within which a legitimate politics can be practiced—a politics to defend, develop, modify, or redefine given traditions and identities.

Conclusion

I began by addressing the question of ethnography, which has recently become the focus of much anthropological interest, and I want to return to it now.

My discussion of Rushdie's novel is motivated by the assumption that the crucial issue for anthropological practice is not whether ethnographies are fiction or fact—or how far realist forms of cultural representation can be replaced by others. What matters more are the kinds of political project in which cultural inscriptions are embedded. Not experiments in ethnographic representation for their own sake, but

---

40. See Williams 1961. Still an indispensable text for thinking about this question, it is, we can now see, marked by a surprising absence: it contains no discussion of imperialism.

modalities of political intervention should be our primary object of concern. More precisely, a major question for anthropologists concerned with the West's Other *in* the West is this: How do discursive interventions by anthropologists articulate the politics of difference in the spaces defined by the modern state?

In many quarters of the contemporary world there is now an increasing awareness of the ambiguous legacy of the Enlightenment. Two decades ago, Arthur Hertzberg assembled a powerful case to argue that the modern roots of anti-Semitism lay in the homogenizing thrust of post-Enlightenment "emancipation." Complete assimilation[41] or the status of despised difference—not to mention other, more terrible, alternatives[42]—appear to be the only options that the modern nation-state has been able to provide for its minorities.[43] Must our critical ethnographies of other traditions in modern nation-states adopt the categories offered by liberal theory? Or can they contribute to the formulation of very different political futures in which other traditions can thrive?

In the West today, intolerance of Europe's Others has again become more strident. Collective cruelty is, of course, neither new nor confined to the West. Muslims, Jews, Hindus, Buddhists, and Christians continue in our day to perpetrate acts of violence and cruelty. But it is the secular modern state's awesome potential for cruelty and destruction (see Bauman 1989) that deserves our sustained attention—as citizens and as anthropologists of modernity.

41. Of the completely assimilated Jews during the nineteenth and twentieth centuries, Hertzberg (1968, 365–66) writes: "A certain discomfort was inherent in their situation; it caused pain in the souls of many. This 'new Jew' had been born into a society which asked him to keep proving that he was worthy of belonging to it. Unfortunately, this 'new Jew' was never quite told exactly what he had to prove and before which tribunal."

42. Which explains Akhtar's (1989a) fearful remark, made at the height of the Rushdie crisis in Britain: "The next time there are gas chambers in Europe, there is no doubt concerning who'll be inside them."

43. The renewed use of gas chambers (to which Akhtar referred) is not yet with us, but the practice of "ethnic cleansing" directed at Muslims in Europe appears to be accepted as reasonable by many liberals. Thus, writing on the recent Bosnian crisis, the well-known British journalist Edward Pearce (1993) expresses a view that is not at all unusual. From the confusing premise, "Despite the horrible expression 'ethnic cleansing' there are no ethnic divisions among the Slavs of Yugoslavia. The Croats, the Bosnian Muslims, and the Serbs are the same people," there eventually emerges the impeccably logical (but sinister) conclusion: "An enlarged Serbia is a perfectly rational thing, so is a Muslim-free city of Sarajevo, drawn generously."

'Abdul-Wahhāb, M. A.H. 1376. *masā'il ul-jāhiliyya.* Cairo: al-Matba'atu-salafiyya.

'Abdurrahmān, 'A. 1969. *at-tafsīr al-bayāni lil-qur'ān al-karīm.* Vol. 1. Cairo: Dar al-Ma'arif.

Abou-El-Haj, R. A. 1992. *Formation of the Modern State: The Ottoman Empire, Sixteenth to Eighteenth Centuries.* Albany: State Univ. of New York Press.

Ahmed, A. 1986. "Jameson's Rhetoric of Otherness and the 'National Allegory.'" *Social Text,* no. 15.

Aitken, I. 1990. "Rushdie and the Notting Hill Syndrome." *Guardian* (London Daily), 5 February.

Akhtar, S. 1989a. "Whose Light? Whose Darkness?" *Guardian* (London Daily), 27 February.

———. 1989b. *Be Careful with Muhammad!* London: Bellew.

Ali, Y. 1989. "Why I'm Outraged." *New Statesman and Society,* 17 March.

Alibhai, Y. 1989. "Satanic Betrayals." *New Statesman and Society,* 24 February.

Anderson, J.N.D. 1959. *Islamic Law in the Modern World.* London: Stevens.

Anscombe, G.E.M. 1957. *Intention.* Oxford: Basil Blackwell.

Anwar, M. 1986. *Race and Politics.* London: Tavistock.

Appignanesi, L., and S. Maitland, eds. 1989. *The Rushdie File.* London: Fourth Estate.

Arendt, H. 1975. *The Origins of Totalitarianism.* New York: Harcourt Brace Jovanovich.

———. 1982. *Lectures on Kant's Political Philosophy.* Chicago: Univ. of Chicago Press.

Asad, T. 1970. *The Kababish Arabs.* London: Hurst.

———. 1972. "Market Model, Class Structure, and Consent: A Reconsideration of Swat Political Organisation." *Man* 7, no. 2.

———, ed. 1973. *Anthropology and the Colonial Encounter.* London: Ithaca Press.

———. 1980. "Ideology, Class, and the Origin of the Islamic State." *Economy and Society* 9, no. 4.

————. 1986a. *The Idea of an Anthropology of Islam*. Occasional Papers Series. Washington, D.C.: Georgetown Univ. Center for Contemporary Arab Studies.

————. 1986b. "Medieval Heresy: An Anthropological View." *Social History* 11, no. 3.

————. 1987. "Are There Histories of Peoples without Europe?" *Comparative Studies in Society and History* 29, no. 3.

Asad, T., and J. Dixon. 1985. "Translating Europe's Others." In *Europe and Its Others*, vol. 1, edited by F. Barker et al. Colchester: Essex Univ. Press.

Auerbach, E. 1953. *Mimesis*. Princeton: Princeton Univ. Press.

Austin, J. L. 1962. *How to Do Things with Words*. Oxford: Clarendon.

Autiero, A. 1987. "The Interpretation of Pain: The Point of View of Catholic Theology." In *Pain: A Medical and Anthropological Challenge*, edited by J. Brihaye et al. New York: Springer-Verlag.

Aylwin, S. 1985. *Structure in Thought and Feeling*. London: Methuen.

'Azm, S. al-. 1969. *naqd ul-fikr id-dīni*. Beirut: Dar ut-tali'a.

Bacon, F. 1937 [1597]. *Essays*. London: Oxford Univ. Press.

————. 1973 [1605]. *The Advancement of Learning*. Edited by G. W. Kitchen. London: Dent.

Baker, D. 1972. *"Vir Dei:* A Secular Sanctity in The Early Tenth Century." In *Popular Belief and Practice*, edited by C. J. Cuming and D. Baker. Cambridge: Cambridge Univ. Press.

Baldick, C. 1983. *The Social Mission of English Criticism: 1848-1932*. Oxford: Oxford Univ. Press.

Baldick, J. 1989. *Mystical Islam*. London: Tauris.

Baldwin, J. W. 1961. "The Intellectual Preparation for the Canon of 1215 against Ordeals." *Speculum* 36.

————. 1970. *Masters, Princes and Merchants: The Social Views of Peter the Chanter and His Circle*. Princeton: Princeton Univ. Press.

Barker, Sir Ernest. 1941. *Ideas and Ideals of the British Empire*. Cambridge: Cambridge Univ. Press.

Barthes, R. 1977. "From Work to Text." In R. Barthes, *Music-Image-Text*, edited and translated by S. Heath. Glasgow: Fontana.

Bauman, Z. 1989. *Modernity and the Holocaust*. Ithaca: Cornell Univ. Press.

Beattie, J. 1964. *Other Cultures*. London: Cohen and West.

Beidelman, T. O. 1966. "Swazi Royal Ritual." *Africa* 36.

Bell, D. 1960. *The End of Ideology: On the Exhaustion of Political Ideas in the Fifties*. Glencoe, Ill.: Free Press.

Benjamin, W. 1969. *Illuminations*. New York: Schocken.

Benveniste, E. 1973. *Indo-European Language and Society*. London: Faber and Faber.

Berger, J. 1972. *Selected Essays and Articles*. Harmondsworth, Middlesex: Penguin.

Berlin, I. 1958. *Two Concepts of Liberty*. Oxford: Clarendon.

Bettenson, H., ed. 1956. *The Early Christian Fathers*. London: Oxford Univ. Press.

Bevan, E. 1921. *Hellenism and Christianity.* London: Allen and Unwin.

Bhabha, H. 1989a. "Beyond Fundamentalism and Liberalism." *New Statesman and Society,* 3 March.

————. 1989b. "Down among the Women." *New Statesman and Society,* 28 July.

Bieler, L., ed. 1963. *The Irish Penitentials.* Dublin: Instit. for Advanced Studies.

Binder, L. 1988. *Islamic Liberalism.* Chicago: Univ. of Chicago Press.

Blacking, J., ed. 1977. *The Anthropology of the Body.* London: Academic Press.

Blanché, R. 1968. *Contemporary Science and Rationalism.* Edinburgh: Oliver and Boyd.

Bligh, A. 1985. "The Saudi Religious Elite (Ulama) as Participant in the Political System of the Kingdom." *International Journal of Middle East Studies* 17.

Bloch, M. 1974. "Symbols, Song, Dance, and Features of Articulation: Is Religion an Extreme Form of Traditional Authority?" *European Journal of Sociology* 15.

————, ed. 1975. *Political Language and Oratory in Traditional Society.* London: Academic Press.

Bloomfield, M. W. 1952. *The Seven Deadly Sins.* East Lansing, Mich.: Michigan State Univ. Press.

Blum, O. J. 1947. *St. Peter Damian.* Washington, D.C.: Catholic Univ. of America Press.

Bourdieu, P. 1977. *Outline of a Theory of Practice.* Cambridge: Cambridge Univ. Press.

Bowler, P. J. 1989. *The Invention of Progress.* Oxford: Basil Blackwell.

Brihaye, J., F. Loew, and H. W. Pia, eds. 1987. *Pain: A Medical and Anthropological Challenge.* New York: Springer-Verlag.

Brooke, C.N.L. 1985. "Monk and Canon: Some Patterns in the Religious Life of the Twelfth Century." In *Monks, Hermits, and the Ascetic Tradition,* edited by W. J. Shields. Oxford: Oxford Univ. Press.

Brown, P. 1967. *Augustine of Hippo.* London: Faber and Faber.

————. 1981. *The Cult of the Saints: Its Rise and Function in Latin Christianity.* London: SCM.

Burckhardt, J. 1950 [1860]. *The Civilization of the Renaissance in Italy.* London: Phaidon.

Burling, R. 1977. Review of *Political Language and Oratory in Traditional Society,* by Maurice Bloch. *American Anthropologist* 79.

Burns, E. 1990. *Character: Acting and Being on the Pre-Modern Stage.* New York: St. Martin's.

Butler, C. 1924. *Benedictine Monachism.* Cambridge: Cambridge Univ. Press.

Butterfield, H. 1931. *The Whig Interpretation of History.* London: Bell.

Bynum, C. W. 1980. "Did the Twelfth Century Discover the Individual?" *Journal of Ecclesiastical History* 31, no. 1.

Caenegem, R. C. van. 1965. "La preuve dans le droit du moyen âge occidental." *La Preuve,* Recueils de la société Jean Bodin pour l'histoire comparative des institutions, vol. 17. Brussels.

Carlyle, T. 1897 [1840]. *On Heroes and Hero-Worship and the Heroic in History.*
London: N.p.

Carr-Hill, R., and H. Chadha-Boreham. 1988. "Education." In *Britain's Black
Population,* edited by A. Bhat, R. Carr-Hill, and S. Ohri. Aldershot:
Gower.

Caute, D. 1989. "Labour's Satanic Verses." *New Statesman and Society,* 5 May.

Chadwick, H. 1967. *The Early Church.* Harmondsworth, Middlesex: Penguin.

Chadwick, O. 1964. *The Reformation.* Harmondsworth, Middlesex: Penguin.

Chenu, M-D. 1968. *Nature, Man, and Society in the Twelfth Century: Essays on
Theological Perspectives in the Latin West.* Chicago: Univ. of Chicago Press.

Christian, W. A. 1982. "Provoked Religious Weeping in Early Modern Spain."
In *Religious Organisation and Religious Experience,* edited by J. Davis. London: Academic Press. (A.S.A. Monographs, no. 21.)

Chydenius, J. 1960. "The Theory of Medieval Symbolism." *Societas Scien-
tiarum Fennica: Commentationes Humanarum Litterarum* 27.

Clark, B. 1990. Letter. *Independent on Sunday,* 11 February.

Clausewitz, C. von. 1968. *On War.* Harmondsworth, Middlesex: Penguin.

Clifford, J. 1988. *The Predicament of Culture.* Cambridge, Mass.: Harvard
Univ. Press.

Colish, M. L. 1968. *The Mirror of Language: A Study in the Medieval Theory of
Knowledge.* New Haven, Conn.: Yale Univ. Press.

Collingwood, R. G. 1938. *The Principles of Art.* London: Oxford Univ. Press.

Colls, R., and P. Dodd, eds. 1986. *Englishness: Politics and Culture, 1880-1920.*
London: Croom Helm.

Comaroff, J., and J. Comaroff. 1991. *Of Revelation and Revolution.* Chicago:
Univ. of Chicago Press.

Cooper, H. 1984. "Location and Meaning in Masque, Morality, and Royal
Entertainment." In *The Court Masque,* edited by D. Lindley. Manchester:
Manchester Univ. Press.

Cotta, S. 1985. *Why Violence? A Philosophical Interpretation.* Gainesville: Univ.
of Florida Press.

Coulanges, Fustel de. 1873. *The Ancient City: A Study on the Religion, Laws,
and Institutions of Greece and Rome.* Boston: Lothrop, Lee and Shepherd.

Coulson, N. J. 1964. *A History of Islamic Law.* Edinburgh: Edinburgh Univ.
Press.

Coussins, J. 1989. "Voluntary Maintained Religious Schools: A Draft Policy
Paper." Commission for Racial Equality. London: C.R.E. July.

Cowling, M. 1990. *Mill and Liberalism.* 2d ed. Cambridge: Cambridge Univ.
Press.

Crick, M. 1976. *Explorations in Language and Meaning.* London: Malaby.

Cromer, Lord. 1913. *Political and Literary Essays, 1908-1913.* London: Macmillan.

Cross, F. L., ed. 1974. *The Oxford Dictionary of the Christian Church.* 2d ed.
London: Oxford Univ. Press.

Daniel, N. 1960. *Islam and the West.* Edinburgh: Edinburgh Univ. Press.

Dekmejian, R. H. 1985. *Islam in Revolution: Fundamentalism in the Arab
World.* Syracuse: Syracuse Univ. Press.

De Man, P. 1983. *Blindness and Insight: Essays in the Rhetoric of Contemporary Criticism*. 2d ed., rev. Minneapolis: Univ. of Minnesota Press.

Denny, F. M. 1985. "Islamic Ritual: Perspectives and Theories." In *Approaches to Islam in Religious Studies*, edited by R. C. Martin. Tucson: Univ. of Arizona Press.

Dijk, C. van. 1964. "L'instruction et la culture des frères convers dans les premiers siècles de l'Ordre de Cîteaux." *Collectanea Ordinis Cisterciensium Reformatorum* 24.

Dimier, A. 1972. "Violences, rixes, et homicides chez les Cisterciens." *Revue de Sciences Religieuses* 46.

Dörries, H. 1962. "The Place of Confession in Ancient Monasticism." In *Studia Patristica: Papers Presented to the Third International Conference on Patristic Studies Held at Christ Church, Oxford, 1959*. Vol. 5, edited by F. L. Cross. Berlin: Akademie Verlag.

Douglas, M. 1966. *Purity and Danger*. London: Routledge and Kegan Paul.

———. 1970. *Natural Symbols*. London: Barrie and Rockliff.

———. 1975. *Implicit Meanings*. London: Routledge and Kegan Paul.

———. 1978. *Cultural Bias*. London: Royal Anthropological Instit. of Great Britain and Ireland.

Duby, G. 1980. *The Three Orders: Feudal Society Imagined*. Chicago: Univ. of Chicago Press.

Dumazedier, J. 1968. "Leisure." *Encyclopedia of the Social Sciences*. New York: Macmillan.

Dummett, A. 1978. *A New Immigration Policy*. London: Runnymede Trust.

Dummett, M. 1981. "Objections to Chomsky." *London Review of Books*, September.

Dumont, L. 1971. "Religion, Politics, and Society in the Individualistic Universe." *Proceedings of the Royal Anthropological Institute for 1970*.

Durkheim, E. 1915. *Elementary Forms of the Religious Life*. London: Allen and Unwin.

———. 1960 [1914]. "The Dualism of Human Nature and Its Social Conditions." In *Emile Durkheim, 1858–1917*, edited by K. Wolff. Columbus: Ohio State Univ. Press.

Dwyer, K. 1991. *Arab Voices*. Berkeley: Univ. of California Press.

Eagleton, T. 1983. *Literary Theory*. Oxford: Oxford Univ. Press.

Eickelman, D. 1989. *The Middle East*. Englewood Cliffs, N.J.: Prentice Hall.

Eliot, T. S. 1962. *Notes towards the Definition of Culture*. London: Faber and Faber.

Esmein, A. 1914. *A History of Continental Criminal Procedure*. London: John Murray.

Evans, G. R. 1983. *The Mind of St. Bernard*. Oxford: Clarendon.

Evans, J. 1931. *Monastic Life at Cluny: 910–1157*. London: Oxford Univ. Press.

Evans-Pritchard, E. E. 1937. *Witchcraft, Oracles, and Magic among the Azande*. Oxford: Clarendon.

———. 1940. *The Nuer*. Oxford: Oxford Univ. Press.

———. 1951. *Social Anthropology*. London: Cohen and West.

————. 1956. *Nuer Religion*. Oxford: Clarendon.

————. 1965. *Theories of Primitive Religion*. Oxford: Clarendon.

Farag, N. 1969. "Victorian Influences on Arab Thought: A Moment of Emulation, 1876–1900." Ph.D. diss., Oxford Univ.

Fielding, H. 1967. *The Works of Henry Fielding: Miscellaneous Writings*. Vol. 1, edited by W. E. Henley. New York: Barnes and Noble.

Finucane, R. C. 1977. *Miracles and Pilgrims: Popular Beliefs in Medieval England*. London: Dent.

Firth, R. 1966. "Twins, Birds, and Vegetables." *Man* 1, no. 1.

Foucault, M. 1979. *Discipline and Punish*. New York: Vintage.

————. 1982. "Le combat de la chasteté." *Communications*, no. 35.

————. 1984. "What Is Enlightenment?" In *The Foucault Reader*, edited by P. Rabinow. New York: Pantheon.

————. 1988. *Technologies of the Self: A Seminar with Michel Foucault*. Amherst: Univ. of Massachusetts Press.

Frantzen, A. J. 1983. *The Literature of Penance in Anglo-Saxon England*. New Brunswick, N.J.: Rutgers Univ. Press.

French, S. 1989. "Diary." *New Statesman and Society*, 24 February.

Freud, S. 1907. "Obsessive Actions and Religious Practices." In *The Complete Works*, edited by J. Strachey. Vol. 9. London: Hogarth.

Friedrich, C. J. 1964. *Transcendent Justice: The Religious Dimension of Constitutionalism*. Durham, N.C.: Duke Univ. Press.

Fry, T. 1981. "The Disciplinary Measures of the Rule of Benedict." Appendix 4 to *The Rule of St. Benedict*, edited by T. Fry. Collegeville, Minn.: Liturgical Press.

Fuller, P. 1989. Review of *Real Presences*, by George Steiner. *Guardian* (London Daily), 19 May.

Gaudemet, J. 1965. "Les ordalies au moyen âge: Doctrine, législation et pratique canoniques." *La Preuve*, Recueils de la société Jean Bodin pour l'histoire comparative des institutions, vol. 17. Brussels.

Gay, P. 1973. *The Enlightenment: An Interpretation*. 2 vols. London: Wildwood House.

Geertz, C. 1973. *The Interpretation of Cultures*. New York: Basic Books.

————. 1980. *Negara: The Theatre State in Nineteenth-Century Bali*. Princeton: Princeton Univ. Press.

————. 1983. *Local Knowledge: Further Essays in Interpretive Anthropology*. New York: Basic Books.

Gell, A. 1975. *Metamorphosis of the Cassowaries: Umeda Society and Ritual*. London: Athlone.

Gellner, E. 1959. *Words and Things*. London: Gollancz.

————. 1969. *Saints of the Atlas*. London: Weidenfeld and Nicolson.

————. 1970. "Concepts and Society." In *Rationality*, edited by B. R. Wilson. Oxford: Basil Blackwell.

Gerholm, T., and Y. G. Lithman, eds. 1988. *The New Islamic Presence in Western Europe*. London: Mansell.

Gibb, H.A.R. 1947. *Modern Trends in Islam*. Chicago: Univ. of Chicago Press.

Gilroy, P. 1987. *There Ain't No Black in the Union Jack*. London: Hutchinson.

Gilson, E. 1955. *History of Christian Philosophy in the Middle Ages*. London: Sheed and Ward.

Gluckman, M. 1954. *Rituals of Rebellion*. Manchester: Manchester Univ. Press.

——. 1955. *The Judicial Process among the Barotse of Northern Rhodesia*. Manchester: Manchester Univ. Press.

——. 1958. *Analysis of a Social Situation in Modern Zululand*. Manchester: Manchester Univ. Press.

——. 1973. "The State of Anthropology." *Times Literary Supplement*, 3 August.

Godding, P. 1973. *La Jurisprudence*. Typologie des sources du moyen âge occidental. Univ. of Louvain. Turnhout: Brepols.

Goffman, E. 1961. *Asylums*. Garden City, N.Y.: Anchor.

Goldman, A. 1989. "Reconstructionist Jews Turn to the Supernatural." *New York Times*, 19 February.

Gordon, P. 1989. "Just Another Asian Murder." *Guardian* (London Daily), 20 July.

Gougaud, L. 1927. *Devotional and Ascetic Practices in the Middle Ages*. London: Burns, Oates and Washbourne.

Greenblatt, S. 1980. *Renaissance Self-fashioning*. Chicago: Univ. of Chicago Press.

Grice, P. 1989. *Studies in the Way of Words*. Cambridge, Mass.: Harvard Univ. Press.

Guha, R., and G. C. Spivak, eds. 1988. *Selected Subaltern Studies*. New York: Oxford Univ. Press.

Gutman, H. 1988. "Rousseau's Confession: A Technology of the Self." In *Technologies of the Self*, edited by L. H. Martin, H. Gutman, and P. H. Hutton. Amherst: Univ. of Massachusetts Press.

Habermas, J. 1989. *The Structural Transformation of the Public Sphere*. Cambridge, Mass.: MIT Press.

Hacking, I. 1982. "Language, Truth, and Reason." In *Rationality and Relativism*, edited by M. Hollis and S. Lukes. Oxford: Basil Blackwell.

——. 1990. *The Taming of Chance*. Cambridge: Cambridge Univ. Press.

Halstead, J. M. 1988. *Education, Justice, and Cultural Diversity*. London: Falmer.

Hardison, O. B. 1965. *Christian Rite and Christian Drama in the Middle Ages*. Baltimore: Johns Hopkins Press.

Harré, R. 1981. "Psychological Variety." In *Indigenous Psychologies*, edited by P. Heelas and A. Lock. London: Academic Press.

——, ed. 1986. *The Social Construction of the Emotions*. Oxford: Basil Blackwell.

Harrison, P. 1990. *"Religion" and the Religions in the English Enlightenment*. Cambridge: Cambridge University Press.

Hattersley, R. 1989. *Independent* (London Daily), 21 July.

Hawali, S. al-. n.d. *kashf al-ghumma 'an 'ulamā al-umma*. N.p.

Heald, S. 1986. "The Ritual Use of Violence." In *The Anthropology of Violence*, edited by D. Riches. Oxford: Basil Blackwell.

Heath, J. 1981: *Torture and English Law*. London: Greenwood.

Heath, R. G. 1976. *Crux Imperatorum Philosophia: Imperial Horizons of the Cluniac Confraternitas, 964–1109.* Pittsburgh: N.p.

Henderson, J. 1978. "The Flagellant Movement and Flagellant Confraternities in Central Italy, 1260–1400." In *Religious Motivation,* edited by D. Baker. Oxford: Basil Blackwell.

Hertzberg, A. 1968. *The French Enlightenment and the Jews.* New York: Columbia Univ. Press.

Hinds, D., and J. O'Sullivan. 1990. "Writers Welcome Rushdie's Defence of 'Satanic Verses.'" *Independent* (London Daily), 4 February.

Hobbes, T. 1943. *Leviathan.* London: Dent. Everyman Edition.

Hobhouse, L. T. 1964 [1911]. *Liberalism.* New York: Oxford Univ. Press.

Hocart, A. M. 1952. "Ritual and Emotion." In A. M. Hocart, *The Life-giving Myth,* edited by Lord Raglan. London: Methuen.

Hodgen, M. T. 1964. *Early Anthropology in the Sixteenth and Seventeenth Century.* Philadelphia: Univ. of Pennsylvania Press.

Hofstadter, D. 1979. *Gödel, Escher, Bach: An Eternal Golden Braid.* New York: Basic Books.

Holdsworth, C. J. 1973. "The Blessings of Work: The Cistercian View." In *Sanctity and Secularity,* edited by D. Baker. Oxford: Basil Blackwell.

Hollander, J. 1959. "Versions, Interpretations, and Performances." In *On Translation,* edited by R. A. Brower. Cambridge, Mass.: Harvard Univ. Press.

Hollis, M., and S. Lukes. 1982. Introduction to *Rationality and Relativism.* Oxford: Basil Blackwell.

Hourani, A. 1962. *Arabic Thought in the Liberal Age, 1798–1939.* London: Oxford Univ. Press.

Hugh of St. Victor. 1951. *On the Sacraments of the Christian Faith,* edited by R. J. Defarrari. Cambridge, Mass.: Harvard Univ. Press.

Humphreys, R. S. 1979. "Islam and Political Values in Saudi Arabia, Egypt, and Syria." *Middle East Journal* 33, no. 1.

Hyams, P. R. 1981. "Trial by Ordeal: The Key to Proof in the Early Common Law." In *On the Laws and Customs of England,* edited by M. S. Arnold et al. Chapel Hill: Univ. of North Carolina Press.

Idung of Prüfening, 1977. *Cistercians and Cluniacs: The Case for Cîteaux,* edited by J. F. O'Sullivan et al. Kalamazoo, Mich.: Cistercian Publications.

Irvine, J. 1979. "Formality and Informality in Communicative Events." *American Anthropologist* 81.

Islamoglu-Inan, H., ed. 1987. *The Ottoman Empire and the World-Economy.* Cambridge: Cambridge Univ. Press.

Jackson, M. 1983. "Knowledge of the Body." *Man,* n.s. 17, no. 2.

Jacob, M. 1991. *Living the Enlightenment: Freemasonry and Politics in Eighteenth-Century Europe.* New York: Oxford Univ. Press.

Johansen, B. 1988. *The Islamic Law on Land Tax and Rent.* London: Croom Helm.

Jones, M. 1989. "Ground Rules for the British Way of Life." *Sunday Times,* 23 July.

Kant, I. 1904. *The Educational Theory of Immanuel Kant.* Edited by E. F. Buchner. Philadelphia: Lippincott.

———. 1991. *Kant: Political Writings.* Edited by H. Reiss. Cambridge: Cambridge Univ. Press.

Kapferer, B., ed. 1976. *Transaction and Meaning.* Philadelphia: Instit. for the Study of Human Issues.

Kassis, H. E. 1983. *A Concordance of the Qu'rān.* Berkeley: Univ. of California Press.

Katznelson, I. 1973. *Black Men, White Cities.* London: Oxford Univ. Press.

Keddie, N. 1982. "Islamic Revival as Third Worldism." In *Le cuisinier et le philosophe: Hommage à Maxime Rodinson,* edited by J. P. Digard. Paris: Maisonneauve et Larose.

Kedourie, E. 1966. *Afghani and 'Abduh: An Essay on Religious Unbelief and Political Activism in Modern Islam.* London: Cass.

Kepel, G. 1988. *Les Banlieues de l'Islam: Naissance d'une religion en France.* Paris: Editions du Seuil.

Kerr, M. H. 1966. *Islamic Reform: The Political and Legal Theories of Muhammad Abduh and Rashid Rida.* Berkeley: Univ. of California Press.

Kettle, M. 1990. "Thatcher Prefers Learning by Rote." *Manchester Guardian Weekly,* 15 April.

Knowles, M. D., ed. 1951. *The Monastic Constitutions of Lanfranc.* London: Nelson.

———. 1955. *Cistercians and Cluniacs: The Controversy between St. Bernard and Peter the Venerable.* London: Oxford Univ. Press.

———. 1963. *The Monastic Order in England: 940–1216.* 2d ed. Cambridge: Cambridge Univ. Press.

Koselleck, R. 1985. *Futures Past.* Cambridge, Mass.: MIT Press.

———. 1988. *Critique and Crisis: Enlightenment and the Pathogenesis of Modern Society.* Cambridge, Mass.: MIT Press.

Kroeber, A. L., and C. Kluckhohn. 1952. *Culture: A Critical Review of Concepts and Definitions.* Papers of the Peabody Museum, vol. 47, no. 1. Cambridge, Mass.: Peabody Museum.

Kuklick, H. 1991. *The Savage Within: The Social History of British Anthropology, 1885–1945.* Cambridge: Cambridge Univ. Press.

La Fontaine, J. 1985. *Initiation, Ritual Drama, and Secret Knowledge across the World.* Harmondsworth, Middlesex: Penguin.

Lamaison, P. 1986. "From Rules to Strategies: An Interview with Pierre Bourdieu." *Cultural Anthropology* 1.

Lane, E. W. 1863–93. *An Arabic-English Lexicon.* 8 vols. London: Williams and Norgate.

Langbein, J. H. 1977. *Torture and the Law of Proof.* Chicago: Univ. of Chicago Press.

Lawrence, C. H. 1984. *Medieval Monasticism.* London: Longman.

Lea, H. C. 1866. *Superstition and Force.* Philadelphia: Lea Bros.

———. 1888. *A History of the Inquisition of the Middle Ages.* Philadelphia: Lea Bros.

———. 1896. *A History of Auricular Confession and Indulgences in the Latin Church.* 3 vols. Philadelphia: Lea Bros.

Leach, E. R. 1954. *Political Systems of Highland Burma.* London: Bell.

———. 1973. "Ourselves and Others." *Times Literary Supplement,* 6 July.

Leavitt, J. 1986. "Strategies for the Interpretation of Affect." Manuscript.

Leclercq, J. 1957. "Disciplina." In *Dictionnaire de Spiritualité,* 3. Paris: Beauchesne.

———. 1966. "The Intentions of the Founders of the Cistercian Order." *Cistercian Studies* 4.

———. 1971. "Le cloître est-il une prison?" *Revue d'ascétique et de mystique* 47.

———. 1977. *The Love of Learning and the Desire for God: A Study of Monastic Culture.* 2d ed. New York: Fordham Univ. Press.

———. 1979. *Monks and Love in Twelfth-Century France.* Oxford: Oxford Univ. Press.

Leclercq, J., and G. Gärtner. 1965. "S. Bernard dans l'histoire de l'obéissance monastique." *Annuario De Estudios Médiévales* 2.

Le Goff, J. 1980. *Time, Work, and Culture in the Middle Ages.* Chicago: Univ. of Chicago Press.

Lekai, L. J. 1977. *The Cistercians: Ideals and Reality.* Kent, Ohio: Kent State Univ. Press.

Lerner, D. 1958. *The Passing of Traditional Society: Modernizing the Middle East.* New York: Free Press.

Levi, A. 1964. *French Moralists: The Theory of the Passions, 1585 to 1649.* Oxford: Clarendon.

Lévi-Strauss, C. 1981. *The Naked Man.* New York: Harper and Row.

Lienhardt, G. 1954. "Modes of Thought." In *The Institutions of Primitive Society,* edited by E. E. Evans-Pritchard et al. Oxford: Basil Blackwell.

———. 1961. *Divinity and Experience.* Oxford: Clarendon.

Lipset, S. M. 1963. *Political Man: The Social Bases of Politics.* Garden City, N.Y.: Anchor.

Luckman, T. 1967. *The Invisible Religion.* New York: Macmillan.

Luijpen, W. A. 1973. *Theology as Anthropology.* Pittsburgh: Duquesne Univ. Press.

Luria, A. R., and F. I. Yudovich. 1971. *Speech and the Development of Mental Processes in the Child.* Harmondsworth, Middlesex: Penguin.

Luscombe, D. E., ed. 1971. *Peter Abelard's Ethics.* Oxford: Clarendon.

Lynch, J. 1990. "Cultural Pluralism, Structural Pluralism, and the United Kingdom." In *Britain: A Plural Society; Report of a Seminar Organized by the Commission for Racial Equality and the Runnymede Trust.* London: C.R.E.

Lynch, J. H. 1975. "Monastic Recruitment in the Eleventh and Twelfth Centuries: Some Social and Economic Aspects." *American Benedictine Review* 26.

MacIntyre, A. 1971. *Against the Self-images of the Age.* London: Duckworth.

———. 1981. *After Virtue: A Study in Moral Theory.* London: Duckworth.

———. 1988. *Whose Justice? Which Rationality?* London: Duckworth.

McLaughlin, M. M. 1975. "Survivors and Surrogates: Children from the

Ninth to the Thirteenth Centuries." In *The History of Childhood,* edited by L. de Mause. New York: Harper and Row.

McNeill, J. T. 1933. "Folk-Paganism in the Penitentials." *Journal of Religion* 13.

McNeill, J. T., and H. M. Gamer, eds. 1938. *Medieval Handbooks of Penance.* New York: Columbia Univ. Press.

Macpherson, C. B. 1962. *The Political Theory of Possessive Individualism: Hobbes to Locke.* Oxford: Oxford Univ. Press.

Madood, T. 1988. "'Black,' Racial Equality and Asian Identity." *New Community* 14, no. 3.

Mair, L. 1962. *Primitive Government.* Harmondsworth, Middlesex: Penguin.

Malcolm, J. 1982. *Psychoanalysis: The Impossible Profession.* London: Pan.

Malinowski, B. 1938. "Introductory Essay: The Anthropology of Changing African Cultures." In *Methods of Study of Culture Contact in Africa.* International African Institute Memorandum, no. 15. London: Oxford Univ. Press.

———. 1945. *The Dynamics of Culture Change.* New Haven: Yale Univ. Press.

Mauss, M. 1972. *A General Theory of Magic.* London: Routledge and Kegan Paul.

———. 1979. "Body Techniques." In M. Mauss, *Sociology and Psychology: Essays,* edited and translated by B. Brewster. London: Routledge and Kegan Paul.

Meagher, J. C. 1962. "The Drama and the Masques of Ben Jonson." *Journal of the Warburg Institute* 25.

Meisel, J. T., and M. L. Del Mastro, eds. and trans. 1975. *The Rule of St. Benedict.* Garden City, N.Y.: Image Books.

Melzack, R., and P. Wall. 1982. *The Challenge of Pain.* Harmondsworth, Middlesex: Penguin.

Mendus, S. 1989. *Toleration and the Limits of Liberalism.* Atlantic Highlands, N.J.: Humanities.

Michaud-Quantin, P. 1949. "La classification des puissances de l'âme au XII siècle." *Revue du moyen âge latin* 5.

———. 1962. *Somme de casuistique et manuels de confession du moyen âge, XII–XVI siècles.* Montreal: Librairie Dominicaine.

Mikkers, E. 1962. "L'idéal religieux des frères convers dans l'Ordre de Cîteaux aux XII et XIII siècles." *Collectanea Ordinis Cisterciensium Reformatorum* 24.

Mill, J. S. 1975 [1861]. "Considerations on Representative Government." In *Three Essays.* Oxford: Oxford Univ. Press.

Moore, R., and T. Wallace. 1976. *Slamming the Door.* London: Martin Robertson.

Morgan, J. 1977. "Religion and Culture as Meaning Systems: A Dialogue between Geertz and Tillich." *Journal of Religion* 57.

Mukherji, B. 1989. "Prophet and Loss." *Voice Literary Supplement,* March.

Munson, H. 1988. *Islam and Revolution in the Middle East.* New Haven: Yale Univ. Press.

Murphy, J. J. 1974. *Rhetoric in the Middle Ages.* Berkeley: Univ. of California Press.

Musson, A. E., and E. Robinson. 1969. *Science and Technology in the Industrial Revolution*. Manchester: Manchester Univ. Press.

Musurillo, H. 1956. "The Problem of Ascetical Fasting in the Greek Patristic Writers." *Traditio* 22.

Nairn, T. 1988. *The Enchanted Glass: Britain and Its Monarchy*. London: Hutchinson.

Needham, R. 1972. *Belief, Language, and Experience*. Oxford: Basil Blackwell.

Norbeck, E. 1963. "African Rituals of Conflict." *American Anthropologist* 65.

Oakley, T. P. 1923. *English Penitential Discipline and Anglo-Saxon Law in Their Joint Influence*. New York: Columbia Univ. Press.

———. 1932. "The Cooperation of Medieval Penance and Secular Law." *Speculum* 7.

———. 1937. "Alleviations of Penance in the Continental Penitentials." *Speculum* 12.

O'Brien, C. C. 1989. "Sick Man of the World: Conor Cruise O'Brien Reviews a Sharp Book of Disobliging Truths about the State of Islam." *Times*, 11 May.

Ochsenwald, W. 1981. "Saudi Arabia and the Islamic Revival." *International Journal of Middle East Studies* 13, no. 3.

Oestreich, G. 1982. *Neo-Stoicism and the Early Modern State*. Cambridge: Cambridge Univ. Press.

O'Hanlon, R. 1988. "Recovering the Subject: Subaltern Studies and Histories of Resistance in Colonial South Asia." *Modern Asian Studies* 22, no. 1.

O'Hanlon, R., and D. Washbrook. 1992. "After Orientalism: Culture, Criticism, and Politics in the Third World." *Comparative Studies in Society and History* 34, no. 1.

Olphe-Galliard, M. 1957. "L'Ascèse painne." In *Dictionnaire de Spiritualité*, 1. Paris: Beauchesne.

Orgel, S. 1975. *The Illusion of Power: Political Theatre in the English Renaissance*. Berkeley: Univ. of California Press.

Orsini, N. 1946. "'Policy' or the Language of Elizabethan Machiavellianism." *Journal of the Warburg Institute* 9.

Ortner, S. 1984. "Theory in Anthropology since the Sixties." *Comparative Studies in Society and History* 26, no. 1.

Paine, R., ed. 1981. *Politically Speaking: Cross-Cultural Studies of Rhetoric*. Philadelphia: Instit. for the Study of Human Issues.

Pallister, D., M. Morris, and A. Dunn. 1989. "Muslim Leaders Shun Rushdie Death Call." *Guardian* (London Daily), 21 February.

Palmer, J. 1988. "Human Rights Groups Fear Europe Will Close Its Doors to Immigrants." *Guardian* (London Daily), 27 December.

Parekh, B. 1989a. "Between Holy Text and Moral Void." *New Statesman and Society*, 28 March.

———. 1989b. "Educational Achievement and Ethnic Minority Children." *Perspectives in Education* 5, no. 1.

———. 1990. Introduction to *Britain: A Plural Society; Report of a Seminar*

Organized by the Commission for Racial Equality and the Runnymede Trust. London: C.R.E.

Patten, J. 1989a. "The Muslim Community in Britain." *Times*, 5 July.

———. 1989b. "On Being British." Mimeograph. London, Home Office, 18 July.

Payer, P. J. 1984. *Sex and the Penitentials.* Toronto: Univ. of Toronto Press.

Pearce, E. 1989. "Wielding a Racist Stick in God-fearing Politics." *Sunday Times*, 23 July.

———. 1993. "Lessons for the War Party." *Manchester Guardian Weekly,* 23 August.

Peirce, C. S. 1986. *Writings of C. S. Peirce.* Vol. 3. Bloomington: Indiana Univ. Press.

Peters, E. 1973. Introduction to H. C. Lea, *Torture.* Philadelphia: Univ. of Pennsylvania Press.

Piltz, A. 1981. *The World of Medieval Learning.* Oxford: Basil Blackwell.

Pinson, K. S. 1968. *Pietism as a Factor in the Rise of German Nationalism.* New York: Octagon.

Pocock, D. 1961. *Social Anthropology.* London: Sheed and Ward.

Polhemus, T., ed. 1978. *Social Aspects of the Human Body.* Harmondsworth, Middlesex: Penguin.

Poschmann, B. 1964. *Penance and the Anointing of the Sick.* London: Burns and Oates.

Postan, M. M. 1975. *The Medieval Economy and Society.* Harmondsworth, Middlesex: Penguin.

Poulter, S. 1986. *English Law and Ethnic Minority Customs.* London: Butterworth.

———. 1990. "Cultural Pluralism and Its Limits—a Legal Perspective." In *Britain: A Plural Society; Report of a Seminar Organized by the Commission for Racial Equality and the Runnymede Trust.* London: C.R.E.

Prakash, G. 1990. "Writing Post-Orientalist Histories of the Third World: Perspectives from Indian Historiography." *Comparative Studies in Society and History* 32, no. 2.

———. 1992. "Can the 'Subaltern' Ride? A Reply to O'Hanlon and Washbrook." *Comparative Studies in Society and History* 34, no. 1.

Quine, W. O. 1961 [1953]. "Two Dogmas of Empiricism." In *From a Logical Point of View.* Cambridge, Mass.: Harvard Univ. Press.

Qutb, S. 1991. *maʿalim fi-ttariq.* Cairo: Dar ush-Shurūq.

Radcliffe-Brown, A. R. 1952 [1939]. "Taboo." In *Structure and Function in Primitive Society.* London: Cohen and West.

———. 1952. *Structure and Function in Primitive Society.* London: Cohen and West.

Reiss, H. 1991. Introduction to *Kant: Political Writings.* Cambridge: Cambridge Univ. Press.

Rex, J. 1987. "The Concept of a Multicultural Society." *New Community* 14, no. 1/2.

Riché, P. 1975. "L'enfant dans la société monastique au XII siècle." In *Pierre Abélard et Pierre le Vénérable.* Paris: Colloques Internationaux du Centre National de la Recherche Scientifique.

Rigby, P. 1968. "Some Gogo Rituals of 'Purification': An Essay on Social and Moral Categories." In *Dialectic in Practical Religion*, edited by E. R. Leach. Cambridge: Cambridge Univ. Press.

Roberts, P. 1989. "Fertile Ground for Fascism." *Living Marxism*, May.

Rodinson, M. 1971. *Mohammad*. London: Allen Lane.

Roehl, R. 1972. "Plan and Reality in a Medieval Monastic Economy: The Cistercians." *Studies in Medieval and Renaissance History* 9.

Rogerson, J. W. 1978. *Anthropology and the Old Testament*. Oxford: Basil Blackwell.

Rosenwein, B. 1971. "Feudal War and Monastic Peace: Cluniac Liturgy as Ritual Aggression." *Viator* 2.

Roys, P. 1988. "Social Services." In *Britain's Black Population*, edited by A. Bhat, R. Carr-Hill, and S. Ohri. Aldershot: Gower.

Rushdie, S. 1984. "Outside the Whale." *Granta* 11.

———. 1988a. "Zia Unmourned." *Nation*, 19 September.

———. 1988b. "India Bans a Book for Its Own Good." *New York Times*, 19 October.

———. 1989a. "The Book Burning." *New York Review of Books*, 2 March.

———. 1989b. "Between God and Devil." *Bookseller*, 31 March.

———. 1990a. "In Good Faith." *Independent on Sunday*, 4 February.

———. 1990b. "Is Nothing Sacred?" Extracts from Herbert Read Memorial Lecture, *Manchester Guardian Weekly*, 18 February.

Ruthven, M. 1989. Review of *The Satanic Verses*. In *The Rushdie File*. See Appignanesi and Maitland.

———. 1990. *A Satanic Affair*. London: Chatto and Windus.

Sahlins, M. 1985. *Islands of History*. Chicago: Univ. of Chicago Press.

———. 1988. "Cosmologies of Capitalism: The Trans-Pacific Sector of 'The World System.'" *Proceedings of the British Academy* 74.

Samuelsson, K. 1961. *Religion and Economic Action*. London: Heinemann.

Sarup, M. 1986. *The Politics of Multicultural Education*. London: Routledge and Kegan Paul.

Schmitt, J. C. 1978. "Le geste, la cathédrale et le roi." *L'Arc* 72.

Schneider, D. 1984. *A Critique of the Study of Kinship*. Ann Arbor: Univ. of Michigan Press.

Schroeder, H. J., ed. 1937. *Disciplinary Decrees of the General Councils*. London: Herder.

Searle, J. 1985. *Intentionality*. Cambridge: Cambridge Univ. Press.

Sen, G. 1989. Letter. *New Statesman and Society*, 4 August.

Sigler, G. J. 1967. "Ritual, Roman." In *New Catholic Encyclopaedia*, vol. 12. New York: McGraw-Hill.

Skorupski, J. 1976. *Symbol and Theory*. Cambridge: Cambridge Univ. Press.

Smalley, B. 1964. *The Study of the Bible in the Middle Ages*. Notre Dame, Ind.: Univ. of Notre Dame Press.

Smith, P. 1982. "Aspects of the Organization of Rites." In *Between Belief and Transgression*, edited by M. Izard and P. Smith. Chicago: Univ. of Chicago Press.

Smith, W. R. 1912. *Lectures of William Robertson Smith*. Edited by J. S. Black and G. Chrystal. London: A. and C. Black.

Southern, R. W. 1959. *The Making of the Middle Ages*. London: Arrow.

———. 1970. *Western Society and the Church in the Middle Ages*. Harmondsworth, Middlesex: Penguin.

Southwold, M. 1979. "Religious Belief." *Man*, n.s. 14.

Spence, D. 1982. *Narrative Truth and Historical Truth: Meaning and Interpretation in Psychoanalysis*. New York: Norton.

Sperber, D. 1975. *Rethinking Symbolism*. Cambridge: Cambridge Univ. Press.

———. 1980. "Is Symbolic Thought Prerational?" In *Symbol and Sense*, edited by M. L. Foster and S. H. Brandes. London: Academic Press.

———. 1982. "Apparently Irrational Beliefs." In *Rationality and Relativism*, edited by S. Lukes and M. Hollis. Oxford: Basil Blackwell.

Spivak, G. 1989. "Reading The Satanic Verses." *Public Culture* 2, no. 1.

Starobinski, J. 1982. "A Short History of Body Consciousness." In *Humanities in Review* 1.

Steiner, F. 1956. *Taboo*. London: Cohen and West.

Stock, B. 1975. "Experience, Praxis, Work, and Planning in Bernard of Clairvaux: Observations on the *Sermones* in Cantica." In *The Cultural Context of Medieval Learning*, edited by J. E. Murdoch and E. D. Sylla. Dordrecht: D. Reidel.

Stocking, G. W. 1987. *Victorian Anthropology*. New York: Free Press.

Stokes, E. 1959. *The English Utilitarians and India*. Oxford: Clarendon.

Struve, T. 1984. "The Importance of the Organism in the Political Theory of John of Salisbury." In *The World of John of Salisbury*, edited by M. Wilks. Oxford: Oxford Univ. Press.

Swann, Lord. 1985. *Education for All: The Report of the Committee of Enquiry into the Education of Children from the Ethnic Minority Groups* (The Swann Report). London: HMSO.

Sykes, N. 1975. "The Religion of Protestants." In *The Cambridge History of the Bible*. Vol. 3, edited by S. L. Greenslade. Cambridge: Cambridge Univ. Press.

Sylla, E. D. 1975. "Autonomous and Handmaiden Science: St. Thomas Aquinas and William of Ockham on the Physics of the Eucharist." In *The Cultural Context of Medieval Learning*, edited by J. E. Murdoch and E. D. Sylla. Dordrecht: D. Reidel.

Symons, T., ed. and trans. 1953. *Regularis Concordia*. London: Nelson.

Tambiah, S. J. 1979. "A Performative Approach to Ritual." In *Proceedings of the British Academy* 65. London.

———. 1990. *Magic, Science, Religion, and the Scope of Rationality*. Cambridge: Cambridge Univ. Press.

Taylor, C. 1979. "What's Wrong with Negative Liberty?" In *The Idea of Freedom*, edited by A. Ryan. Oxford: Oxford Univ. Press.

Tentler, T. N. 1974. "The Summa for Confessors as an Instrument of Social Control." In *The Pursuit of Holiness in Late Medieval and Renaissance Religion*, edited by C. Trinkaus and H. Oberman. Leiden: E. J. Brill.

———. 1977. *Sin and Confession on the Eve of the Reformation.* Princeton: Princeton Univ. Press.

Thiébaux, M. 1974. *The Stag of Love: the Chase in Medieval Literature.* Ithaca: Cornell Univ. Press.

Thomas, N. 1991. "Against Ethnography." *Cultural Anthropology* 6.

Tigar, M. E., and M. R. Levy. 1977. *Law and the Rise of Capitalism.* New York: Monthly Review Press.

Toren, C. 1983. "Thinking Symbols: A Critique of Sperber (1979)." *Man* 18.

Tuck, R. 1988. "Scepticism and Toleration in the Seventeenth Century." In *Justifying Toleration: Conceptual and Historical Perspectives,* edited by S. Mendus. Cambridge: Cambridge Univ. Press.

Turner, V. 1969. *The Ritual Process.* London: Routledge and Kegan Paul.

———. 1976. "Ritual, Tribal, Catholic." *Worship* 50.

Tylor, E. B. 1871. *Primitive Culture.* London: J. Murray.

———. 1893. "Inaugural Address." In *Transactions of the Ninth International Congress of Orientalists.* Vol. 2, edited by E. D. Morgan. London: Committee of the Congress.

Ullman, W. 1947. "Some Medieval Principles of Criminal Procedure." *Juridical Review* 59.

———. 1975. *Medieval Political Thought.* Harmondsworth, Middlesex: Penguin.

'Uwaysha, H. al- n.d. *al-ghība wa atharuhā as-say'u fi-l-mujtami' al-islāmi.* N.p.

Vidler, A. R. 1961. *The Church in an Age of Revolution: 1789 to the Present Day.* Harmondsworth, Middlesex: Penguin.

Vigne, M. 1928. "Les doctrines économiques et morales de Saint Bernard sur la richesse et le travail." *Revue d'histoire économique et sociale* 4.

Viller, M., and M. Olphe-Galliard. 1957. "L'Ascèse chrétienne." In *Dictionnaire de Spiritualité,* 1. Paris: Beauchesne.

Viswanathan, G. 1989. *Masks of Conquest.* New York: Columbia Univ. Press.

Vološinov, V. N. 1973. *Marxism and the Philosophy of Language.* New York: Seminar.

Vygotsky, L. S. 1962 [1934]. *Thought and Language.* Cambridge, Mass.: MIT Press.

———. 1978. *Mind in Society.* Cambridge, Mass.: Harvard Univ. Press.

Wagner, R. 1984. "Ritual as Communication." *Annual Review of Anthropology* 13.

Walzer, M. 1987. *Interpretation and Social Criticism.* Cambridge: Harvard Univ. Press.

———. 1989. "The Sins of Salman." *New Republic,* 10 April.

Watkins, O. D. 1920. *A History of Penance.* 2 vols. London: Longmans.

Weber, M. 1930. *The Protestant Ethic.* London: Allen and Unwin.

———. 1947. *The Theory of Social and Economic Organization.* Glencoe, Ill.: Free Press.

———. 1948. "Politics as a Vocation." In *From Max Weber: Essays in Sociology,* edited by H. H. Gerth and C. W. Mills. London: Routledge and Kegan Paul.

Weinstein, D., and R. M. Bell. 1982. *Saints and Society: The Two Worlds of Western Christendom, 1000–1700.* Chicago: Univ. of Chicago Press.

Weldon, F. 1989. *Sacred Cows.* London: Chatto and Windus.

Wenzel, S. 1968. "The Seven Deadly Sins: Some Problems of Research." *Speculum* 43, no. 1.

Werbner, R. 1977. "The Argument in and about Oratory." *African Studies* 36.

Willey, B. 1934. *The Seventeenth-Century Background.* London: Chatto and Windus.

Williams, R. 1961. *Culture and Society: 1780–1950.* Harmondsworth, Middlesex: Penguin.

———. 1979. *Politics and Letters.* London: New Left.

———. 1983. *Key Words: A Vocabulary of Culture and Society.* Rev. ed. Glasgow: Fontana.

Wilson, G., and M. Wilson. 1945. *The Analysis of Social Change: Based on Observations in Central Africa.* London: Cambridge Univ. Press.

Wolf, E. 1982. *Europe and the People without History.* Berkeley: Univ. of California Press.

Wolff, K., ed. 1960. *Emile Durkheim, 1858–1917.* Columbus: Ohio State Univ. Press.

Worgul, G. S. 1980. *From Magic to Metaphor: A Validation of the Christian Sacraments.* New York: Paulist.

Young, H. 1989. "Terrorising the Guardians of Liberty." *Guardian* (London Daily), 21 February.

ACKNOWLEDGMENTS

All the essays except Chapter 6 have previously been published. A shorter version of that chapter was presented at a conference entitled "Political Cultures of Criticism," held in November 1991 at the South Asian Institute of Heidelberg University. Chapter 1 is a revised version of an article that appeared in *Man* in 1983, and Chapter 2 an expanded version of my contribution to *Vernacular Christianity: Essays in the Social Anthropology of Religion Presented to Godfrey Lienhardt,* edited by W. James and D. H. Johnson, and published by JASO, Oxford, in 1988. The remaining essays have been subjected to very minor, mainly stylistic, changes. Chapters 3 and 4 originally appeared in *Economy and Society* in 1983 and 1987, respectively. Chapter 5 was part of *Writing Culture,* edited by J. Clifford and G. Marcus, and published by the University of California Press in 1986. *Politics and Society* first published Chapter 7 in 1990, and *Cultural Anthropology* published Chapter 8 in the same year. My thanks to the editors and publishers of the above for permission to reprint.

A number of people have read and criticized these essays at one stage or another, and I record my gratitude to them: Ismail Abdallah, Rifaat Aboul-Haj, Meena Alexander, Tanya Baker, José Casanova, John and Molly Dixon, Michael Herzfeld, Charles Hirschkind, U. Kalpagam, Rodney Needham, Keith Nield, Bhikhu Parekh, Rayna Rapp, David Schneider, David Scott, and Sam Wheeler III.

Genealogies of Religion

Designed by Ann Walston

Composed by Connell-Zeko
in Galliard

Printed by The Maple Press Company
on 50-lb. Glatfelter Eggshell

23606747R00203

Made in the USA
Lexington, KY
17 June 2013